IN THE SHADE OF
THE QUR'ĀN

In the Name of God, the Lord of Grace, the Ever Merciful

Sayyid Quṭb

IN THE SHADE OF
THE QUR'ĀN

Fī Ẓilāl al-Qur'ān

VOLUME XVII

SŪRAHS 62–77

Al-Jumuʿah – Al-Mursalāt

Translated and Edited by
Adil Salahi

THE ISLAMIC FOUNDATION
AND
ISLAMONLINE.NET

Published by

THE ISLAMIC FOUNDATION,

Markfield Conference Centre,
Ratby Lane, Markfield, Leicestershire
LE67 9SY, United Kingdom
E-mail: publications@islamic-foundation.com
Website: www.islamic-foundation.com

Quran House, PO Box 30611, Nairobi, Kenya

PMB 3193, Kano, Nigeria

ISLAMONLINE.NET,
PO Box 22212, Doha, Qatar
E-mail: webmaster@islam-online.net
Website: www.islamonline.net

Distributed by: Kube Publishing Ltd.
Tel: 44(01530) 249230, Fax: 44(01530) 249656
E-mail: info@kubepublishing.com

British Library Cataloguing-in-Publication Data
Qutb, Sayyid, 1903–1966
    In the shade of the Qur'an = Fi zilal al-Qur'an
    Vol. 17: Surahs 62–77 al-Jumu'ah – al-Mursalat
    1. Koran – Commentaries
    I. Title   II. Salahi, M.A.
    III. Islamic Foundation (Great Britain)
    297.1'229

ISBN: 978-0-86037-412-1 *casebound*
ISBN: 978-0-86037-417-6 *paperback*

Typeset by: N.A.Qaddoura
Cover design by: Imtiaze A. Manjra

Contents

Transliteration Table

Consonants. Arabic

initial: unexpressed medial and final:

ء	ʾ	د	d	ض	ḍ	ك	k
ب	b	ذ	dh	ط	ṭ	ل	l
ت	t	ر	r	ظ	ẓ	م	m
ث	th	ز	z	ع	ʿ	ن	n
ج	j	س	s	غ	gh	هـ	h
ح	ḥ	ش	sh	ف	f	و	w
خ	kh	ص	ṣ	ق	q	ي	y

Vowels, diphthongs, etc.

Short: ﹷ a ﹻ i ﹹ u

long: ـَا ā ﹻـي ī ﹹـو ū

diphthongs: ﹷـوْ aw

ﹷـىْ ay

x

Introduction

Sayyid Quṭb the Peaceful Advocate of Islam

With this volume we complete the long undertaking to present Sayyid Quṭb's monumental work, *In the Shade of the Qur'ān,* to English readers. It started shortly after the author's martyrdom in 1966, when a students' magazine, *The Muslim*, published every month the commentary on a short *sūrah*. That early effort culminated in the publication, in 1979, of what constitutes Volume XVIII in the present edition. The effort continued for a long while at a very slow pace, producing about two pages a week. The Islamic Foundation gave new impetus to this endeavour with the publication of Volume I in 1999. Now we see the work completed by God's help. All praise is due to Him, for without His help, no endeavour can attain to fruition.

God intended His book, the Qur'ān, to provide guidance for all mankind, in all generations, until the end of human life on earth. He, therefore, made it simple and lucid, available to all, immune to distortion or corruption. Yet there are many voluminous works interpreting the Qur'ān. Hardly any century has passed, since the beginning of the Islamic message, without a major scholar writing a commentary on the Qur'ān. Most of these run into volumes. Other works provide very concise explanations, and some concentrate on explaining single words that people may find difficult, depending on their level of education and knowledge of classical Arabic. With all this wealth of knowledge available, the question arises: do we need another new commentary, and a lengthy one at that?

By the beginning of the twentieth century, the Muslim world was at a very low ebb. Large areas of it were under foreign rule, and the level of education available was very poor. Things were not much better throughout the Ottoman Caliphate where the majority of the population were illiterate. Autocratic rule had weakened the state. Moreover, some of its regions, like Egypt, only nominally belonged to it, while in effect they were ruled by Western powers. The people were mostly Muslims, but Islam had been reduced in their perception to no more than a handful of traditions and worship rituals. The collapse of the Ottoman Caliphate, as a result of World War I, completed the subjugation of the Muslim world, with the Arab world largely yielding to foreign rule, mainly British and French, taking it further away from Islam and its values and principles.

Yet Islam is never long on the downward trend. There were several attempts in history to crush Islam and wipe it out altogether, but every time the enemies felt that this great prize was within their reach, they were surprised to see Islam making a comeback and re-establishing itself. It is the power of the Qur'ān that does this. Unless the light of the Qur'ān is completely put out and Muslim populations forget about it altogether, it will continue to revive the Islamic spirit and bring Muslims back to their faith. Victory will not then lag much behind.

In fact, the work of Islamic revival had already started by the end of World War I, and by the late 1920s, its activities moved a stage further, addressing the public at large. Until then it had confined itself to elite groups, distinguished personalities and scholarly circles. As the work of Islamic revival continued, it became apparent that what Muslims urgently needed was a proper understanding of the Qur'ān. Hence, Maulana Mawdūdī began to write his most excellent work, *Tafhīm al-Qur'ān*, in Urdu, most of which is now published in English under the title, *Towards Understanding the Qur'ān*, and Sayyid Quṭb began writing his priceless Arabic commentary, *Fī Ẓilāl al-Qur'ān*, the English version of which is now completed with the publication of the present volume.

What both works aimed at is to provide a correct understanding of the Qur'ān for the modern reader. Earlier commentaries on the Qur'ān provide a wealth of knowledge, but they may not answer what today's reader needs. Moreover, the approach in most of them is rather difficult for the average reader. Hence, a modern approach that presents contemporary readers with an understanding of the Qur'ān close to what the Prophet's Companions gathered was needed.

What is important about this work, *In the Shade of the Qur'ān*, is that it seeks to explain the Qur'ān to modern readers in their own language, steering away from controversy, so that the message of the Qur'ān is fully understood in perfect clarity. The objective Sayyid Quṭb set for himself was to present the message of the Qur'ān as it was understood by the Arabs who were the first to listen to it recited by Muḥammad (peace be upon him), God's Messenger, upon whom it was bestowed from on high. All scholars agree that the backwardness and weakness of the Arabs and the Muslims generally, over the last three centuries, has been due to the fact that the Qur'ān has gradually been relegated to a very secondary position in their lives. It was no longer the criteria by which to evaluate things, or the guidance through which they decided their actions, or the standard that gave them their values. They were lost in the midst of a sea of conflicting ideas and philosophies. To regain their character and re-establish their identity, they needed to understand the Qur'ān and to derive from it their concept of life. Hence, Sayyid Quṭb's work in this book did not concentrate on any particular aspect that made the Qur'ān unique: its literary style, imagery, music, scientific facts, legislative consistency or serious approach to life, etc. Instead, his primary focus was the holistic and clear vision of life, the universe, man and God which the Qur'ān presents. What Sayyid Quṭb wanted to tell his readers is that their whole lives will undergo a fundamental change when they understand the Qur'ān in this light. The change will be as far-reaching as that experienced by the Prophet's Companions when the Islamic message was first advocated.

Sayyid Quṭb was highly qualified for this great undertaking. By the time he started, he was a highly respected figure in literary circles. He was a fine poet and a literary critic. I also have it on authority from a famous professor of Arabic literature at the University of Cairo that Sayyid Quṭb's book *al-Naqd al-Adabī,* or *Literary Criticism,* would have been the preferred text book had it not been for the government's attitude towards the author. When Naguib Mahfouz was just starting out on his career as a novelist, Sayyid Quṭb was the first critic to praise him, saying that he was a young novelist of immense promise who could achieve a high degree of excellence. Mahfouz was to become the first Arab to win the Nobel Prize for Literature in the late 1990s. Sayyid Quṭb himself wrote one or two novels and was much involved in Egypt's literary and cultural life. However, he was also keenly involved in the country's social and political life. How could he refrain from such involvement when Egypt was only a semi-independent state, with a British military base in Suez, and the British Ambassador acting like a higher authority than the king and government put together? Yet Sayyid Quṭb was no politician. He did not join any political party and did not contest any elections. From a social point of view, he keenly felt the plight of the poor who constituted the overwhelming majority of the Egyptian people. Yet he also saw an aristocratic minority carrying on with their corrupt lifestyle, caring little for the masses. Hence, his writings in the late 1930s and 1940s expressed the hopes of his countrymen, while denouncing the system that perpetuated such a social and political imbalance.

The literary scene in Egypt during the late 1920s and 1930s witnessed highly vocal battles between prominent literary figures. These were not limited to the main figures at the forefront, but rather each battle was joined by a number of younger writers defending one or other point of view. Sayyid Quṭb participated fully in one of these, siding with the prominent literary figure 'Abbās Maḥmūd al-'Aqqād against Muṣṭafā Ṣādiq al-Rāfi'ī, who was defending the Islamic point of view. Yet it was also during this time, in 1935, that Sayyid Quṭb produced his first Islamic book, *Al-Taṣwīr al-Fannī fī al-Qur'ān*, or *Artistic Imagery in the Qur'ān*. However, this was a purely literary study of the Qur'ān in which Sayyid Quṭb explored hitherto untrodden areas in studying the Qur'ānic style.

Combined with his reinvigorated commitment to Islam at the half point of the twentieth century, these factors gave Sayyid Quṭb more than the necessary qualification to undertake the task he set for himself. What crowned it all, however, was his penetrative look into what influences people and what modifies social direction. He felt that society in Egypt as elsewhere in the Muslim world needed a complete re-orientation if it were to regain its truly Islamic character. This could be brought about only through a better understanding of the Qur'ān, in the same way as the Prophet's Companions understood it.

Yet, as he went about his task, a fundamental change in his approach was gradually taking place. Perhaps the full dimension of the necessary change was not even clear to Sayyid Quṭb himself at the start. Hence the different style and approach he adopted in the last few volumes and the re-writing of the first 13 volumes of the Arabic edition (the first 10 volumes in the English edition).

It is often asked: what so radicalized Sayyid Quṭb? Two factors are often mentioned by way of explanation: his trip to the United States and his long imprisonment in terrible conditions. We need to cast a brief look at both. He went to America on a scholarship from the Egyptian government, to study the possible ways for the future development of university education in Egypt. Unlike students who study for a degree, his was an open scholarship with no time limit. He could stay as long as he wanted. In fact, the Egyptian government decided to send him on this mission as the best way to get rid of him, because they were very unhappy with his regular three articles published weekly in three papers with different political leanings. He was interrogated after the publication of each article, but nothing could be done about him because, unlike its military successor, the Egyptian monarchy maintained a reasonable standard of the rule of law. Hence, it was felt that by giving him such a scholarship he was in essence being sent into exile, albeit in a civilized way.

Sayyid Quṭb was shocked by the decline of morality in America, particularly the widespread sexual permissiveness. He wrote *The America I have Seen*, describing all aspects of American life, but this book was never published.[1] However, he quotes from it at length in his later works, particularly *Al-Islam wa Mushkilāt al-Ḥaḍārah*, or *Islam and the Problems of Civilizations*. It is widely assumed that the whole book is devoted to issues of loose morality and sexual permissiveness. This assumption is based on quotations taken from it, but it is often forgotten that what

---

1. I am told that shortly before his first imprisonment in early 1954, Sayyid Quṭb gave this book's manuscript to a friend, as he feared arrest and thought his papers might be taken away. The friend, who was not an Egyptian, took the manuscript with him when he left Egypt, and it was neither returned nor published. Apparently, another copy remained in Egypt and was later accessible to the author, but it was incomplete.

he quoted was only what was suited to the issues he discussed in this later book, where a considerable section, about one-third of the book, is devoted to relations between the two sexes. What is certain, however, is that *The America I have Seen* is much wider in scope and aimed to provide a full picture, without concentrating on a single issue. A prolific writer with broad interests in life and society was certain to formulate a full view of America where he stayed for two years.

It is also certain that he took his decision to join the Muslim Brotherhood while he was still in the US. He wrote a letter to his brother mentioning his intention. One particular event is mentioned as being most instrumental in this decision, but I feel that this was not due to any single event. More probably, his being away from daily life in Egypt gave him a chance to reflect more fully on what Egypt needed to regain its freedom and its own character. He saw that Egypt could never become a fully Westernized country, as was advocated in certain circles, and by some intellectuals. In America, he had been able to see the positive and negative aspects of Western political and economic systems. He felt that only a return to a proper Islamic way of life could make Egypt's goals easier to achieve.

On his return to Egypt, his writings reflected his new commitment and his broader vision. He published three books during this period: *al-Salām al-'Ālamī wal-Islam*, or *Islam and World Peace*; *Ma'rakat al-Islam wal Ra'smāliyyah*, or *Islam's Battle against Capitalism*, and *al-'Adālah al-Ijtimā'iyyah fi al-Islam*, or *Social Justice in Islam*.

When people speak of Sayyid Quṭb becoming radicalized, they do not mean this period at all. They tend to think of his last few years, during his second term of lengthy imprisonment (1954–1964). They particularly mention his last book, *Ma'ālim fi al-Ṭarīq*, or *Milestones*. They certainly do not include his joining the Muslim Brotherhood or those early books as manifestations of such radicalization. They see these as signs of his new commitment to Islam, which is certainly true. However, when we look at these early Islamic writings, particularly the one on Capitalism, we find the same powerful style, the same committed arguments, the same eagerness to drive it home to his reader that only through Islam can there be any hope for Egypt, the Muslim world and mankind generally.

The other factor in this assumed radicalization is Sayyid Quṭb's long imprisonment. He spent ten years in jail, under very tough conditions. There is no doubt that long imprisonment affects a prisoner's mentality and his outlook on life. Psychologists and psychiatrists can tell us a great deal about numerous cases where imprisonment only led to the hardening of a criminal's outlook on society. It is true that if such long imprisonment is totally unfair, as was the case of the Muslim Brotherhood generally, then it is sure to be met with at least deep-seated resentment. In the conditions applied to the Muslim Brotherhood under Nasser's regime, it was only to be expected that some would move towards extremism. The group that was later to be popularly known as *al-Takfīr wal-Hijrah* was born in *al-Harbi* Prison, where the population almost entirely belonged to the Muslim Brotherhood. It was a military prison, with very poor facilities, and where torture was brutally and indiscriminately applied to all inmates. This group called itself *Jamāʿat al-Muslimīn*, or The Muslim Community, implying that anyone who did not belong to it was not a Muslim.

It is easy to assert that an intellectual like Sayyid Quṭb, who was very sensitive to what troubled Egyptian society, was committed to Islamic values, abhorred all types of corruption, and who initially welcomed the 1952 Revolution and became a friend to several of its leaders, including Nasser himself, should be acutely affected by his imprisonment. I accept that this was the case. What is totally unacceptable, however, is the assumption that such an effect could only have one direction, nurturing within the prisoner an ever-increasing grudge against those who put him in jail and a desire for revenge. Western writers who discovered Sayyid Quṭb after the horrid events of 11th September 2001, when it was suggested that his writings gave the intellectual justification for such actions, pointed to his imprisonment as the main cause of his assumed radicalization. Some of them wondered: what else could have been expected of such an intellectual finding himself unfairly imprisoned in harsh conditions with no hope of release?

Such a question is legitimate when we look at the case purely in the terms of this life and its limited duration, particularly if we adopt a Western materialistic stance. Such writers do not reckon with ideologies driving people towards noble goals and making them willing to sacrifice everything for their cause. Nobody ever suggested that Nelson Mandela was radicalized as a result of his 27 years of imprisonment when he never wavered in his opposition to apartheid and his pursuit of a fully democratic South Africa. Why cannot writers in the Western media imagine that Sayyid Quṭb's ideal of a proper Islamic reawakening helped him to accept his ordeal as part of the sacrifice necessary for such a reawakening to flourish and gather momentum?

Indeed Western writers, followed by some Arab media, have even gone so far as to try to establish a hierarchy of 'Islamic extremism', with three main figures at the helm, Ibn Taymiyyah, Sayyid Quṭb and Usamah Bin Ladin. How ill-judged! Ibn Taymiyyah was a prominent scholar who lived over 700 years ago and did much to mobilize action against the Tartars and other deviant groups. He wrote extensively on different issues, and he is still held in very high esteem by most Islamic scholars. Yet Sayyid Quṭb hardly ever quotes Ibn Taymiyyah, although he occasionally quotes his closest disciple, Ibn al-Qayyim. Although Ibn al-Qayyim occupies a top position in the rankings of Islamic scholars, no one accuses him of being 'extremist', as is sometimes alleged of Ibn Taymiyyah. Bin Ladin, on the other hand, follows a line that is fundamentally contrary to what is clear in Sayyid Quṭb's writings and actions.

So what is behind this attempt to establish such a ridiculous connection? To find the answer we need perhaps to look at certain historical events, particularly at those leading to lasting divisions. We note that often such division starts from a political base, but later acquires some religious aspect. The Church of England came into existence when King Henry VIII issued the Act of Supremacy in 1534, declaring the English monarch as Head of the Church of England. This break with the Catholic Church was the result of the Pope's refusal to annul Henry VIII's marriage to his first wife, Catharine of Aragon. After Henry's death, more Protestant reforms had to be introduced in England so that its Church could strengthen its roots away from Catholicism. In Islam, the differences that led to the Shī'ah and the Khawārij breaking away were purely of a political origin. It was later that these differences were clothed with religious aspects to ensure continuity. By nature, political trends, ideas and differences are transitory. They tend to change as one generation succeeds another. If certain political leaders want to perpetuate what they stand for, they have to give it a religious outfit.

This phenomenon also works in reverse. If old religious hostility needs to be revived, it has to be given political clothing so as to bring it into the present and to mobilize public opinion to take necessary action. Over the last 40 years or so, a distinct anti-Islamic trend has been sustained in the West, trying to label Islam as inherently terrorist. Now, whenever a terrorist attack takes place, Western media try to associate it with Islam, without even waiting for the outcome of investigations. The attacks of 11 September 2001 sealed this trend to the effect that if a terrorist attack happens anywhere in the world, it is blamed on so-called Islamic terrorism, unless there is compelling evidence to direct the blame elsewhere. Yet the second half of the twentieth century witnessed the terrorist activities of several groups such as Baadr Meinhoff, the Red Brigades, the IRA, the Japanese Red Army, etc. All these are now forgotten, and terrorism is solidly attached to Islam.

To give this idea an historical dimension, the line connecting Ibn Taymiyyah, Sayyid Qutb and Bin Ladin has been dreamt up. The first provides the historical aspect, while the second the modern intellectual background and the third the spectacular action that rallies the masses against its perpetrators. If such a connection can be shown to exist, then those who want to give Islam a bad name in the minds of the people everywhere in the world will have achieved their target. People look at terrorism with instinctive disgust, because terrorism often attacks the innocent and unsuspecting, making them the fuel of a narrow grudge or localized conflict. Obscure organizations often resort to terrorist attacks as the best way to ensure publicity for their cause. Yet the fact that the actions are often irrational and the victims are often innocent men and women makes terrorism exceedingly abhorrent. What prize for the enemies of Islam can be greater than showing it to be historically terrorist?

In our modern world, with the great rush to cover events and the competition to be the first with the news, ideas are sometimes floated and circulated without difficulty, with one media channel taking from the other, and news agencies circulating their outputs all over the world in seconds. On the other hand, a piece of research can be shown to give credence to a theory that otherwise lacks support. When the idea connecting Sayyid Quṭb with Ibn Taymiyyah and Bin Ladin was first advanced, providing publicity for it was the best means to establish it in people's minds. Thus, documentaries and other media programmes were produced to drive the point home. In this way, it gets mentioned and quoted, and soon it becomes a fact. If you say that it is untrue, the onus of proof is on you, rather than with those who dreamt it up. Who will today read the great many volumes Ibn Taymiyyah wrote in order to establish his thoughts on terrorism? Who will check the hundreds of half sentences quoted from Sayyid Quṭb to verify whether or not he would have approved of terrorist attacks? Yet, I can say categorically, that Sayyid Quṭb did not write a single sentence justifying violence, or the overthrow of any government, or the taking of power by force. Nevertheless, he is thought by many, who might not even have read anything he wrote, to be the 'philosopher of Islamic terrorism' as the *New York Times* labelled him.

Such is unfortunately the state of our world. We have thousands of universities and research centres, yet prejudice can override objective studies and evaluations, particularly when international media presents prejudiced views as facts. It does Sayyid Quṭb no harm to be linked with Ibn Taymiyyah, but it does do him great injustice to be put into the same category as Bin Ladin. Ibn Taymiyyah was a scholar of immense courage who sought to educate the people and who helped them to live up to what Islam required of them. Sayyid Quṭb wanted to achieve the same goal by presenting Islamic principles in all clarity to a public that had long forgotten what true Islamic life really meant. He felt that only through education could this goal be achieved. Hence, he shunned all other methods and tried hard to re-orientate the activities of Islamic advocacy so as to concentrate on education only. Bin Ladin's methods are too well known to need explanation. Suffice it to say that neither Sayyid Quṭb nor Ibn Taymiyyah would have approved of them. Sayyid Quṭb's method of action takes a line that is diametrically opposed to that of Bin Ladin.

Yet people may say that Sayyid Quṭb's style is hard hitting. His is certainly a powerful style, but there is a world of difference between a powerful style and the use of force and violence. A writer might do a great deal of harm advocating violence, yet his style and use of language may be of a very ordinary standard. Another writer may be very powerful in advocating a peaceful strategy. Sayyid Quṭb was concerned with presenting the Qur'ān. This is the work that represents two thirds or more of what he wrote after committing himself to Islamic revival. The Qur'ān certainly hits hard against those who try to obstruct the progress of the divine faith, showing them their erring ways and the fallacy of their beliefs. At the same time, it works tirelessly to present the faith and its main principles in a very clear, lucid and powerful way. When a gifted writer like Sayyid Quṭb undertakes to present the Qur'ānic argument in a way that can be easily understood by his contemporaries, the power of the Qur'ān will certainly enhance his own powerful style. Yet this does not make for prejudice. It simply reflects commitment to Islam and its values and principles in a clear, unequivocal way. Time after time, Sayyid Quṭb stated that people are free to choose Islam or reject it. Everyone makes up their own minds. Yet they have the right to know it so that they take their stand on the basis of full understanding. Hence, there must be no hindrance of Islamic advocacy. All that Islam requires is the freedom of expression, and that people should have the freedom to choose their beliefs. In the Qur'ān, God instructs the Prophet to make the following declaration: *"Say: The truth [has now come] from your Lord. Let him who wills, believe in it, and let him who wills, reject it."* (18: 29) This principle of freedom of choice is clearly stated in the Qur'ān: *"There shall be no compulsion in religion. The right way is henceforth distinct from error."* (2: 256)

Sayyid Quṭb was clearly committed to the Qur'ān. He cannot be described as radical unless we attach the same description to the Qur'ān itself which would be a gross mistake. All Muslims believe that the Qur'ān outlines the middle way for human life. Sayyid Quṭb did not try to twist the Qur'ānic argument so as to support any radical or uncompromising stand. There are certain issues on which the Qur'ān does not permit any thought of compromise, such as God's oneness or dominion. No Muslim who knows the basics of his faith will ever accept any compromise on these. To accept such compromise takes a person outside the fold of Islam altogether. The Qur'ān argues these principles most forcefully. So what is to be expected from a writer like Sayyid

Quṭb, known for his powerful and elegant style, when he presents such principles to a readership that has felt long trodden upon by a succession of ignorant governments, colonial rulers and native dictators?

There is no doubt that Sayyid Quṭb was totally committed to Islam, but his vision of Islam is that which respects the human mind and allows it unrestricted freedom. That is his understanding of the Qur'ānic maxim: *"There shall be no compulsion in religion. The right way is henceforth distinct from error."* (2: 256)

So, let's take a closer look at Sayyid Quṭb's method of writing this commentary on the Qur'ān. I may sum it up here by saying that for a whole month Sayyid Quṭb read only the text he wanted to present in his next volume. He might read that text once or twice, or even more, every day trying to grasp fully every point presented in the message. When he felt he had fully gathered its import, he would write his thoughts as fast as he could. Only when he had finished writing, would he refer to earlier commentaries and *aḥādīth* related to the subject matter. He checked his own understanding against that of past commentators. He might add any scientific support to his arguments, or quotations from other writers. This method could only be adopted by someone of exceptional literary merit, but also provided he was absolutely convinced of the fact that the Qur'ān is God's word.

Something anyone who is familiar with Qur'ānic commentaries is bound to note about *In the Shade of the Qur'ān* is the fact that Sayyid Quṭb makes few references to earlier books, including those he seems to highly value, such as Ibn Kathīr's commentary. This is due to three factors. The first is the method he adopted, which gave particular weight to his own understanding of the text. He did not need to refer to anyone in order to understand the meaning of any phrase, sentence or verse. So, the meaning was already clear to him. Sometimes, knowledge of the occasion on which a particular verse, passage or *sūrah* was revealed would be of much help, and he referred to works that detail such occasions. However, even this might not have held much importance, as the overall concept or ruling such a passage imparts would have general application. The second factor is that most other commentaries rely on earlier scholars, going back to the Prophet's Companions. They quote these one after the other, different as they may be. They often leave the reader at a loss as to which view carries more weight or has better foundation. Sometimes, a very early scholar such as Ibn 'Abbās, the Prophet's cousin, is quoted giving two or more views about the same verse. He would obviously have given these on different occasions, perhaps within the context of questions, but the context is rarely given.

The third factor is Sayyid Quṭb's desire to steer away from controversy. We note how he mentions different viewpoints on a particular verse and points out that they can be reconciled, or taken as probable. Where the difference of opinion is concerned with something that belongs to the realm beyond human perception, he prefers not to go into any discussion of the different opinions, as none can be proven. He would take the Qur'ānic statement at face value and stop there. This is undoubtedly a very sound approach. Since we cannot arrive at a definitive understanding of something that belongs to a different world, any attempt to do so is futile. Hence, it is better left out.

This stand is useful in strengthening faith. When we interpret something that belongs to the world beyond in terms of what is familiar to us in our world, we impose on it a particular understanding that may be altogether wrong. The right thing is to accept such statements as they are, without attaching to them any meaning beyond the one immediately apparent. This approach instils into us the proper approach to the Qur'ān, believing every word in it as true, coming from God.

The Qur'ān refers to some scientific facts, particularly in relation to man and his constitution, the earth he lives on, the natural elements affecting his life and the universe at large. Many of these facts were not known to any human being at the time of the revelation of the Qur'ān. With scientific discoveries, man is now able to establish these and prove them by his own methods and tools. Many Muslims find in this a powerful argument endorsing the Qur'ān and proving that it comes from God. How else could Muḥammad have hit on these facts when no one on earth could ever have imagined them during or before his own lifetime? A pertinent example is the development of a human embryo from the moment of its conception. This is referred to in several places in the Qur'ān, with different emphasis attached each time. An example is the verses that say: "*Indeed, We create man out of the essence of clay, then We place him, a gamete, in a safe place of rest. Then We create out of the gamete a clinging cell mass, and out of the clinging cell mass We create an embryo. Then We create within the embryo bones, then We clothe the bones with flesh. We then bring this into being as another creation. Exalted be God, the best of creators. And then, after all this, you are destined to die; and then, you shall be restored to life on the Day of Resurrection."* (23: 12–16) We can now ascertain these stages with the help of scans and other sophisticated monitoring facilities, but 1,400 years ago, when the Qur'ān was being revealed, how could Muḥammad (peace be upon him) present such accurate information unless he was informed by the Creator who ordained this process of creation?

There are numerous other references in the Qur'ān to scientific facts that could not have been known to any human being at the time of its revelation. Many have now been proven, which gives the verses speaking about them added weight. In recent years, there has been a trend pointing to 'scientific miracles' outlined in the Qur'ān. This trend cites such facts as irrefutable proofs of the truth that the Qur'ān originates from God Almighty. This trend has recently earned tremendous public appeal throughout the Muslim world. Sayyid Quṭb takes a totally different standpoint. He welcomes scientific facts that endorse Qur'ānic statements, but he does not accept that any scientific discovery should be treated as providing the total meaning of any Qur'ānic statement. He points out that science does not treat any new discovery as final or providing the ultimate truth. New discoveries are made all the time by scientists in different fields. A new discovery in one field may have a huge bearing on other fields, leading to the questioning of what used to be thought of as true. Science always disproves or amends what it used to accept as true. Hence, we cannot tie any Qur'ānic statement to any 'proven' scientific fact, because it may be disproved tomorrow. The Qur'ān addresses people across all generations, allowing each generation to understand its meaning as best they can. Scientific facts mentioned in the Qur'ān are phrased in simple language that points to what people know through their experience. What these tell a modern reader of the Qur'ān is perhaps more detailed than what they told a reader ten centuries ago, but the truth they express remains the same. Hence, Sayyid Quṭb accepts any scientific evidence that may be quoted in support of Qur'ānic statements, but he makes clear that we must not impose such evidence on the Qur'ān so that we do not tie it to our own scientific experience. Future discoveries may disprove what is today thought of as true and they would thus point Qur'ānic statements in a different direction. The Qur'ān remains true whether human knowledge at any particular period is able to confirm its truth or not.

Sayyid Quṭb makes clear that the Qur'ān is neither a book of science, nor a book of history, nor indeed a book of any particular discipline or branch of study. It is a message calling on people to believe in God. Thus, it is a book of advocacy of the divine faith. It provides historical accounts, but these are not meant to record the events of the past, as historians view their own mission.

The Qur'ān at times refers to a historical event, or series of events, several times in different *sūrahs*. However, each time it highlights different details, laying special emphasis on particular points, so that each time it brings out most clearly its relevance to the subject matter of the *sūrah* in which it occurs. Thus, the same event may be related four times in four *sūrahs*, but each time it appears perfectly new, as if it is not mentioned anywhere else. Other accounts are given only once, and in these cases the event is given in full details. In either case, the Qur'ān relates the event to the particular context in which it occurs and seeks to give a clear message that is relevant to the addressees who are, in the first instance, the Prophet's own contemporaries and subsequently all future generations.

Just like the scientific facts it relates, the Qur'ān's historical accounts are given to endorse the message it aims to deliver. They are not meant to record history, in the same way as the scientific facts the Qur'ān mentions are not meant to provide any scientific insight of how things work.

As a literary critic and a man of letters, Sayyid Quṭb could speak at length on the Qur'ān's artistic elements, recognized by all writers as being a literary masterpiece of the highest excellence. Long before he joined the Muslim Brotherhood, he had written two books dealing with such aspects, but these were purely literary endeavours. When he undertook to write the present book, it would have been expected that those literary aspects were to form an important dimension of the work. Yet we find that references to such aspects are always given minor importance. Sayyid Quṭb may speak about the style employed in each *sūrah* and how it suits its subject matter, or how it distinguishes it from other *sūrahs* dealing with the same facts and issues, but such references are short, unlike what would have been expected from the literary figure he was. When he discusses the artistic elements in the way a particular story is related, his discussion is adequate but limited to essentials. Invariably, he refers us to his special chapter on story-telling in his first book on the Qur'ān, *Al-Taṣwīr al-Fannī fī al-Qur'ān*, or *Artistic Imagery in the Qur'ān*.

Sayyid Quṭb is no doubt a critic of fine taste. He always tells us about the particular rhythm, beat and music employed in a particular *sūrah* or passage to enhance its effect. At times, he analyses the musical factor that gives a particular *sūrah* a distinctive character. An example is seen in his discussion of *Sūrah* 70, Ways of Ascent, in the present volume. This discussion, and similar ones, are by necessity abridged in translation because they do not apply to the translated text. Yet we find in these a highly interesting aspect of study which gives enjoyment and provides insight into an aspect that makes the Qur'ān easy to memorize. It is well known that in every generation thousands of people, in every Muslim country, memorize the Qur'ān in full.

In his last book, *Milestones*, however, Sayyid Quṭb decries any attempt to study the Qur'ān in purely scientific, literary, aesthetic or historical terms. The Qur'ān is none of these, yet it includes aspects of all of them. Therefore, it should be approached as it is: a message from God to mankind. When we study it in this light, we are bound to receive everything it contains, the scientific, the literary and the aesthetic, without any of these being our main preoccupation.

Such was Sayyid Quṭb's commitment to the Qur'ān. It is the commitment of a believer who has no doubt about the truth of God's message and its infallibility, and who clearly knows where a believer should stand and what role he should play. He certainly did so himself, showing his determination to stand up for his beliefs, even when he was certain that this meant his death, as it actually did. He was at pains to explain to advocates of Islam that they may be called upon to sacrifice much for their cause. They may have to fight against all sorts of adversity. No matter what pressures they have to withstand, and what sacrifices they have to make, they must not look for any prizes in this world. He even tells them to forget the best prize this life can offer, which is the triumph of Islam over its enemies. They must not look to achieving this through their own efforts. Their only prize is what they have been promised in the life to come. This is the mark of their acceptance by God. Nothing else comes into the equation. They have to sacrifice their all, looking for nothing in this world.

Yet sacrifice is an essential part of Islamic advocacy, and ever since Sayyid Quṭb committed himself to the Islamic cause, he viewed himself as an advocate. He realized that the time was certain to come when he would be called upon to make such sacrifices. The Qur'ān mentions this in several *surahs*, and Sayyid Quṭb speaks at length about it every time it is mentioned. What comes clearly to the fore in his writings is that an advocate of Islam should be ready to make any sacrifice he may be called on to make, even if this means his life, looking for absolutely no reward in this world. He emphasizes this point time after time, making it clear that advocates of Islam should not even covet the prize of the triumph of Islam at their own hands, by their own efforts, or through their own sacrifices. They are only advocates of the Islamic cause, but the cause itself belongs to God and He alone guides its march and determines its outcome. Many times we read in this book that the very fact that those working for this cause are advocating Islam is enough prize for them, no matter how much they have to suffer. If they are sincere, they will feel the value of this prize within themselves, in the contentment of their hearts, and in the blessing of feeling that they follow in the footsteps of the Prophet and his Companions, as well as the long line of advocates of the divine message from the time of the Prophet Noah.

Thus, Sayyid Quṭb was always clear in his mind that adversity is part and parcel of the line he decided to follow. A writer who forcefully puts his views across, Sayyid Quṭb accepted this and was always ready to practise what he preached. There is no good in advocating something if you are only prepared to pay lip service to it while things are comfortable, but when matters get tough you turn away. Sayyid Quṭb was no coward. He was ready for the sacrifice, and determined not to give up the ideal he believed in. Therefore, he continued to write in prison, working on the project to which he dedicated his thoughts, time and effort, i.e. the presentation of the Qur'ān in a way that promotes a correct understanding of it. He believed that once this understanding is achieved, people will make the same commitment to Islam the group of the Prophet's Companions known as the Anṣār made when they pledged their allegiance to him, promising to make whatever sacrifice was necessary for the defence of Islam. In return for honouring such commitment, they were told that they could expect no reward in this world. The only reward promised was admittance into heaven.

In this work, Sayyid Quṭb speaks repeatedly about this, making it clear that any worldly prizes should be viewed as extremely secondary by the advocates of Islam. He felt that only when the Islamic revivalist movements realize this, can they begin to lay down a sound foundation of such revival. Hence, to imagine that the imprisonment, or the tough conditions of the prison, or his ill health in prison affected his vision and moved him towards an extreme position is to be grossly mistaken.

In prison he continued to work on this book because he realized that the most important thing for the advocates of Islam is to develop a complete and correct understanding of the Qur'ān. He considered it the most important task to be undertaken. Hence, he worked on it whenever he could, regardless of the harsh conditions he had to endure. At times, he could only write sitting on the staircase at night, with nothing but a small candle to give him light. Whatever he needed for his writings was smuggled in, because he was allowed neither pen nor paper, let alone reference works. Likewise, whatever he wrote needed to be smuggled out for publication.

Yet we see throughout the book that he was in no doubt as to the eventual triumph of the message he was advocating. Enemies may be allied against it, and they may score victories and be able to press their advantage in every conceivable way, yet this will all be no more than a temporary and flimsy victory. The advocates of Islam should never be deceived by it, or entertain any doubt in the truth of the message they are advocating. They must understand that they are not after any prize in this world. Their ultimate victory is when the message of Islam is understood by people and they are free to accept it, if they so wish. They must ask for no more than such freedom of belief.

This is what we read time after time in this book, whenever the occasion arises to drive this idea home. The Qur'ān presents a message for mankind, and this message has to be fully understood. Hence, its main concepts and values are presented in a broad variety of forms and discussions, spread throughout its *sūrahs*. This gives Sayyid Quṭb the chance to frequently harp on this idea, to ensure that it is properly understood. What we see is a determined attempt by the author to drive home to his readers, particularly those of them who are committed to Islamic revival, that they must neither expect, nor work for, any prize in this life. Islamic government, which is often seen as the ultimate goal of Islamic revival, is a very secondary issue. The main issue is to present Islam to people and that they should be free to accept it if they so wish. Moreover, it is not the advocates of Islam who can decide whether they are worthy of the trust of establishing Islamic government or not. This is God's own prerogative, and they cannot question it.

In practice, Sayyid Quṭb stood by what he said. When he was released in 1964, he was contacted by the leaders of five different groups of young men who were working on reviving the Muslim Brotherhood. They wanted him to take over the leadership. He explained his views to them in extensive discussions over several meetings. He questioned them about their objectives. They told him that they first wanted revenge for the persecution suffered by the Muslim Brotherhood over the previous ten years. They also told him that they had arranged for some arms to be smuggled into the country for possible anti-government action. In response, he told them that this was all wrong. The idea of revenge should be totally removed from their minds. It would not bring about any good result. Besides, how would revenge further the cause of Islam? On the issue of arms, he wanted to stop the very idea but was told that it could not be done. He, therefore, arranged for this consignment to be sent immediately to a remote village in Upper Egypt, making it clear that it was not to be used in any way against the government. He painstakingly worked to change the outlook of these groups, so that they would come round to his idea, which insisted that the development of a clear and correct view of Islam, and advocating it among the people was the only way to bring about Islamic revival.

Thus we see that his practical policy was fully consistent with the ideas he was keen to propagate through his writings: no revenge, no armed conflict, no attempt to take power by force, no hastening of results. This may seem too idealistic to some people. If a movement interested in public affairs does not try to take over government, how can it hope to implement its programme? This is a legitimate question for any political movement or party. They are active in the political field because they have different programmes which they want to see through. Moreover, they want to be in power and when they get it, their leaders and prominent figures are given ministerial posts. Not so the Islamic message, as Sayyid Quṭb understood and advocated it. Islamic government comes into existence as a result of society turning to Islam and wishing to conduct its life affairs according to Islamic teachings. A society cannot become Islamic because a few personalities or a party committed to Islam are able to hold power through a military *coup* or parliamentary elections. To imagine that this is possible is to put the cart before the horse. Therefore, Islamic advocacy must remain at the grassroots. The only way to change people's attitude to Islam is through conviction. There must be no hastening of results.

This is totally different from the policies of many an Islamic movement or organization that demands the implementation of Islamic law in their respective countries. To Sayyid Quṭb, such demands divert the advocacy work from its proper objective and will not achieve any real progress. People will come to look at such movements and organizations as mere political parties. Islam cannot be advocated in this way. The advocacy effort should present the people with the totality of Islam, telling them that under Islam, their entire lives will be changed. This because they will be looking up to God, serving Him and doing what He bids them.

Sayyid Quṭb's commitment in all this is especially apparent in the way he sees evidence of the Qur'ān being God's book. Whether he is discussing detailed legislation pertaining to family relations, or a passage highlighting the natural forces God has made subservient to man, or speaking about God's endless creation in the vast universe, Sayyid Quṭb often points out how it is impossible for any human being to have come up with such statements unless they were granted to him by the Almighty. There are numerous verses that clearly point to God as the Qur'ān's author. Before Sayyid Quṭb, however, perhaps no one saw such a pointer as is contained in the following verse: "*With Him are the keys to what lies beyond the reach of human perception: none knows them but He. He knows all that the land and sea contain; not a leaf falls but He knows it; and neither is there a grain in the earth's deep darkness, nor anything fresh or dry but is recorded in a clear book."* (6: 59)

Sayyid Quṭb is perhaps at his best when he discusses a Qur'ānic verse which aims to establish God's unique characteristics, or touches on the direct relation between God and man, or between a believer and the Qur'ān. One of the best examples of the first type is the verse which we have just quoted. Another example relating to man's relation with God is: *"Whatever grace God opens up to man, none can withhold it; and whatever He withholds, none other than Him can release. He alone is Almighty, Wise."* (35: 2) Of the other type we may cite the verse that says: *"Mankind, there has come to you an admonition from your Lord, a cure for all that may be in your hearts, and guidance and grace for all believers."* (10: 57) When he dwells on the meaning of such verses, we see through his lines a believer against whom neither pressure nor temptation can make any headway. He is living with the Qur'ān in a totally different world. He may be physically on earth, but his spirit is in a much higher and superior world, a world where he feels God's grace and revels in it.

In his commentary, Sayyid Quṭb tries to explain his experience with the Qur'ān. You need only to read his introduction in the first volume to realize what such long association with the Qur'ān meant for him. Yet can anyone put such an experience into words? If anyone can do so, then Sayyid Quṭb, with his literary talent, certainly could. He certainly did his very best, and my rendering of his superb effort into a different language dwarfs in comparison with the original. Yet it opens up for us a way to understand the Qur'ān better and to recognize its relevance to our lives today, just as the Prophet's Companions related it to their lives when it was first revealed.

London
Muharram 1429
January 2008

Adil Salahi

In Conclusion

This long undertaking to produce an English version of one of the best commentaries on the Qur'ān has now finally been completed. It seems an age since I saw the author, in a dream, telling me that English-speaking Muslims needed his work. This was in September 1966, one week after he met his Lord, a noble martyr for the cause of Islam. Upon waking, I resolved to do my best to fulfil this task. Today, as the last of its 18 volumes is finished, I cannot praise and thank God enough for enabling me to complete this undertaking. All glory belongs to Him alone. It is only through what He has given us that we, humans, achieve what we set out to do. It is He who gives everyone their abilities, from Him all efforts stem, to Him all results are submitted and it is He who gives everyone their fair reward. I humbly pray to Him to accept my effort in rendering this explanation of His blessed and glorious words. Its many failings I acknowledge, yet it is the best my limited ability could achieve.

Thanks are due to Ashur Shamis who put in much valuable work in the early stages of this endeavour. In fact, the first few volumes were a joint effort. Unfortunately, circumstances dictated that I should continue the effort alone. This work has also benefited greatly by the expert editing of the English text by Dr Susanne Thackray, who made many valuable suggestions and improvements. I am very grateful to her as also to her assistant, Maryam Laurence. Thanks are also due to the Islamic Foundation, Leicester, for undertaking the publication of this work. There were others who provided funds to enable the work to continue, but they prefer to remain anonymous, dedicating their contributions purely to God. Their help has been most appreciated.

Special thanks are due to my wife, Hayfa, for her great help throughout the years that this project has taken to complete.

My parents were the ones who instilled in me the love of the Qur'ān from an early age. I pray to God to shower His mercy on them. To their blessed souls I dedicate this effort.

One last point to remember: Volume XVIII was the first to be published back in 1979. At the beginning we concentrated on it as it is the part of the Qur'ān read most often by Muslims throughout the world. In this series, it was published ahead of several other volumes as demand for it was pressing.

Al-Jumu 'ah
(The Congregation)

Prologue

This *sūrah* was revealed after *Sūrah* 61, The Ranks, and whilst both deal with the same theme, the current chapter nonetheless takes a different approach, using a different style and different effects. It aims to drive home to the Muslim community in Madīnah that it has been chosen to undertake responsibility for the divine faith. It wants the Muslim community to understand that to be in such a position of trust is a great favour God has bestowed on it. It also wants them to understand that by God choosing His last Messenger from among the Arabs is yet another great favour, one that merits a proper expression of gratitude to God. In this context, the *sūrah* provides certain duties that must be fulfilled by the people who responded to God's Messenger and who accepted the trust. Both the community and the trust are to continue across generations, without fail, because God has determined that the seed planted by the Prophet will continue to grow. The Muslim community has taken over the trust abandoned and neglected by the Children of Israel. They severed their relation with heaven so as to carry the Torah in the same way as an ass would carry books.

The *sūrah* drives this fundamental truth home to Muslims in general, starting in particular with the first Muslim community in Madīnah, which was responsible for implementing a practical model of the Islamic system. It also applies to all future Muslim generations, as the *sūrah* clearly indicates.

At the same time, the *sūrah* addresses certain situations relevant to that first Muslim community, during its long and elaborate transformation process in accordance with Islamic requirements. This process involved the elimination of a host of hindrances, such as a keenness to make quick material gains and other temptations relating to money. These were to be replaced by proper awareness of the great trust assigned to the Muslim community. The *sūrah* also refers to a particular incident when the Prophet was once delivering his Friday sermon. A trade caravan had arrived at the same time, and the moment people learned of this, they left the mosque to take part in the music and entertainment that traditionally accompanied a caravan's arrival. According to some reports, only 12 of the Prophet's Companions, including Abū Bakr and 'Umar, remained listening to his sermon. Whilst these reports may not be very accurate as regards the numbers they mention, nonetheless the departure of some people from the mosque was certain. Hence, it merited this mention in the Qur'ān.

This incident demonstrates the great effort exerted in the cultivation of that first Muslim community's fine manners and behaviour, this until it achieved a lofty standard, making it a unique example in the history of Islam and mankind generally. In this way, the *sūrah* teaches us to always remain patient when we try to build the Islamic character in any community.

The *sūrah* also includes an invitation to the Jews to a mutual prayer wishing death for those who advocate falsehood. This comes in reply to their claims that they were God's only friends and His chosen people and that God's Messenger must be one of them. The *sūrah* confirms their unwillingness to accept such an invitation because they felt that the Muslims' claims were unfounded. The *sūrah* comments that death, from which such people try to escape, will inevitably catch up with them. They will be returned to God who knows all, and He will tell them the truth of their doings. This statement does not, however, only apply to the Jews. Rather, the *sūrah* facilitates its appreciation by believers as well. They too must realize this fact in order to be able to discharge the duties assigned to them as advocates of God's message.

The Day of Congregation

Al-Jumu'ah
(The Congregation)

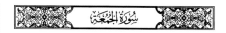

In the Name of God, the Lord of Grace, the Ever Merciful

All that is in the heavens and all that is on earth extol the limitless glory of God, the Sovereign, the Holy, the Almighty, the Wise. (1)

It is He who has sent to the unlettered people a Messenger from among themselves to declare to them His revelations, to purify them and to instruct them in the Book and in wisdom, yet before that they were indeed in manifest error, (2)

to them and to others yet to join them. He is indeed the Almighty, the Wise. (3)

Such is God's favour: He grants it to whom He will. God is One who bestows great favours. (4)

ذَٰلِكَ فَضْلُ ٱللَّهِ يُؤْتِيهِ مَن يَشَآءُ وَٱللَّهُ ذُو ٱلْفَضْلِ ٱلْعَظِيمِ ٤

Those who were entrusted with the burden of implementing the Torah but then failed to do so are like an ass that carries a load of books. Wretched is the example of those who deny God's revelations. God does not guide the wrongdoers. (5)

مَثَلُ ٱلَّذِينَ حُمِّلُوا ٱلتَّوْرَىٰةَ ثُمَّ لَمْ يَحْمِلُوهَا كَمَثَلِ ٱلْحِمَارِ يَحْمِلُ أَسْفَارًا ۚ بِئْسَ مَثَلُ ٱلْقَوْمِ ٱلَّذِينَ كَذَّبُوا بِـَٔايَٰتِ ٱللَّهِ ۚ وَٱللَّهُ لَا يَهْدِى ٱلْقَوْمَ ٱلظَّٰلِمِينَ ٥

Say: 'You who follow the Jewish faith! If you truly claim that out of all people you are God's friends, then wish for death, if your claim is true.' (6)

قُلْ يَٰٓأَيُّهَا ٱلَّذِينَ هَادُوٓا إِن زَعَمْتُمْ أَنَّكُمْ أَوْلِيَآءُ لِلَّهِ مِن دُونِ ٱلنَّاسِ فَتَمَنَّوُا ٱلْمَوْتَ إِن كُنتُمْ صَٰدِقِينَ ٦

But they will never wish for it because of what their hands have wrought in this life. God is well aware of the wrongdoers. (7)

وَلَا يَتَمَنَّوْنَهُۥٓ أَبَدًۢا بِمَا قَدَّمَتْ أَيْدِيهِمْ ۚ وَٱللَّهُ عَلِيمٌۢ بِٱلظَّٰلِمِينَ ٧

Say: 'The death from which you are trying to run away will certainly overtake you. You will then be returned to the One who knows the imperceptible and that which can be witnessed. He will then tell you all that you have done.' (8)

قُلْ إِنَّ ٱلْمَوْتَ ٱلَّذِى تَفِرُّونَ مِنْهُ فَإِنَّهُۥ مُلَٰقِيكُمْ ۖ ثُمَّ تُرَدُّونَ إِلَىٰ عَٰلِمِ ٱلْغَيْبِ وَٱلشَّهَٰدَةِ فَيُنَبِّئُكُم بِمَا كُنتُمْ تَعْمَلُونَ ٨

Believers! When the call to prayer is made on Friday, go straightaway to the prayer and leave off your trading. This is best for you, if you but knew it. (9)

يَٰٓأَيُّهَا ٱلَّذِينَ ءَامَنُوٓاْ إِذَا نُودِيَ لِلصَّلَوٰةِ مِن يَوْمِ ٱلْجُمُعَةِ فَٱسْعَوْاْ إِلَىٰ ذِكْرِ ٱللَّهِ وَذَرُواْ ٱلْبَيْعَ ذَٰلِكُمْ خَيْرٌ لَّكُمْ إِن كُنتُمْ تَعْلَمُونَ ۝

When the prayer is finished, disperse in the land and seek God's bounty. Remember God often so that you may be successful. (10)

فَإِذَا قُضِيَتِ ٱلصَّلَوٰةُ فَٱنتَشِرُواْ فِي ٱلْأَرْضِ وَٱبْتَغُواْ مِن فَضْلِ ٱللَّهِ وَٱذْكُرُواْ ٱللَّهَ كَثِيرًا لَّعَلَّكُمْ تُفْلِحُونَ ۝

Yet when people see some trade or entertainment, they head off towards it, leaving you standing there. Say: 'That which is with God is far better than any entertainment or trade. God is the best of providers.' (11)

وَإِذَا رَأَوْاْ تِجَٰرَةً أَوْ لَهْوًا ٱنفَضُّوٓاْ إِلَيْهَا وَتَرَكُوكَ قَآئِمًا قُلْ مَا عِندَ ٱللَّهِ خَيْرٌ مِّنَ ٱللَّهْوِ وَمِنَ ٱلتِّجَٰرَةِ وَٱللَّهُ خَيْرُ ٱلرَّٰزِقِينَ ۝

A Universal Glorification

All that is in the heavens and all that is on earth extol the limitless glory of God, the Sovereign, the Holy, the Almighty, the Wise. (Verse 1)

The *sūrah* starts with a statement confirming the fact that everything in the heavens and earth extols God's glory, adding a number of His attributes that have a subtle bearing on the theme of the *sūrah*. The *sūrah* is given the name *al-Jumu'ah*, meaning Friday, and it gives instructions about the special congregational prayer on that day, identifying that its time should be dedicated to remembrance of God. All distractions and business should be abandoned in pursuit of what is with God, which is better than everything else. Hence, the *sūrah* mentions God's attribute, the Sovereign, who owns everything. This is relevant to business, since

5

all trade normally seeks profit. The *sūrah* also states that God is Holy; He who is revered and glorified by all creatures in the universe. This attribute of God's contrasts with the entertainment mortals seek, distracting them from His remembrance. This opening verse also mentions that God is Almighty, which is relevant to the invitation made to the Jews for mutual prayer, and also to the death that is bound to happen to all. The last of God's attributes mentioned in this opening is His wisdom. Such divine wisdom determined the choice of the unlettered people from among whom God's last Messenger was selected to declare to them God's revelations, purify them and teach them the scriptures and wisdom.

The Messenger's Terms of Reference

Having started with this sublime glorification of God's limitless glory, the *sūrah* goes straight to its main theme:

> It is He who has sent to the unlettered people a Messenger from among themselves to declare to them His revelations, to purify them and to instruct them in the Book and in wisdom, yet before that they were indeed in manifest error, to them and to others yet to join them. He is indeed the Almighty, the Wise. (Verses 2–3)

It is said that the Arabs were called *ummiyyūn*, or 'unlettered', because the great majority of them could neither read nor write. It is reported that the Prophet once defined how many days there are in a month, joining his two hands and pointing with his ten fingers three times, and saying: "We are an unlettered community: we neither reckon figures nor write." It is also said that a person who does not write is called *ummī*, meaning he is the same as when his mother, or *umm*, gave birth to him. Writing is something that is only learnt when a child grows up.

Alternatively, the Arabs might have been called Goyim, a Hebrew form by which the Jews called all non-Jews, and meaning Gentiles. Thus the word *ummiyyūn* becomes a form of *umamiyyūn*, which means 'belonging to other communities or nations'. Thus they distinguished themselves as God's chosen people, while the rest of mankind are Gentiles. Perhaps this suggestion is closer to the theme of the *sūrah*.

6

The Jews were awaiting a final Messenger from God who would arise from among themselves, uniting them after they had been divided into divergent groups, giving them power and leading them to victory. They used to tell the Arabs that he was soon to come. In His infinite wisdom, God chose an Arab as His last Messenger, i.e. a Gentile, because He knew that the Jews no longer had the qualities necessary to provide mankind's new leadership. Indeed, they had long deviated and were deep in error, as stated in *Sūrah* 61, The Ranks. Hence, they were no longer capable of being entrusted with God's message.

Moreover, in earlier times Abraham and his son Ishmael had said a prayer as they worked on building the Ka'bah: "*Our Lord, accept this from us; You are the One that hears all and knows all. Our Lord, make us surrender ourselves to You, and make out of our offspring a community that will surrender itself to You. Show us our ways of worship and accept our repentance; You are the One who accepts repentance, the Merciful. Our Lord, send them a Messenger from among themselves who shall declare to them Your revelations, and instruct them in the Book and in wisdom, and purify them. You are Mighty and Wise.*" (2: 127–129) Addressed centuries earlier, this prayer remained with God to be answered at the appropriate time, according to God's wisdom. Only then would it fulfil its role within the overall plan God has set in place for the universe. In this plan nothing occurs earlier or later than its appropriate time.

This prayer was answered in its exact wording, which is repeated here in this *sūrah*, reminding us of Abraham's own words: "*A Messenger from among themselves to declare to them His revelations, to purify them and to instruct them in the Book and in wisdom.*" (Verse 2). Even God's attributes mentioned in Abraham's prayer are used at the end of these verses to remind the Muslim community of God's favours: "*He is indeed the Almighty, the Wise.*" (Verse 3)

When the Prophet was asked about himself, his answer was: "I am the answer to Abraham's, my father's, prayer, and the good news given by Jesus. When my mother was pregnant, she saw a light coming out of her, lighting before her the palaces of Buṣrā in Syria."

"*It is He who has sent to the unlettered people a Messenger from among themselves to declare to them His revelations, to purify them and to instruct them in the Book and in wisdom, yet before that they were indeed in manifest error.*" (Verse 2) The favour God has granted to these unlettered people is evident: He chose them to hold the trust embodied in His final message and sent them a Messenger from among themselves to elevate them to a noble position. He took them out of their state of ignorance, highlighted in their being unlettered, giving them instructions in God's book and in wisdom. Thus, their situation changed completely, clearly making them distinguished among all other people on earth.

"*To purify them.*" What the Prophet gave them was far-reaching purification. He purified their feelings and consciences, their actions and behaviour, their marital and family lives as also their social lives. Their purification meant that they rose from the depths of idolatrous beliefs to believing in God's oneness, from erroneous concepts and enigmatic legends to the true and clear faith, from disgraceful immorality to the clean moral values propounded by Islam, from the filthy gains of usury and fraud to clean and legitimate earnings. It was a total purification of the individual and the community, of inner feelings and outward life. Such purification elevates man and his concepts, his role and existence to the high horizon of maintaining his bond with God and with the community on high.

"*To instruct them in the Book and in wisdom.*" When they are thus instructed, they become the holders of a divine book. They thus learn how to evaluate matters properly. They can also make accurate judgements and define their course in life in the light of such wisdom.

"*Yet before that they were indeed in manifest error.*" (Verse 2) During their pre-Islamic days, they were certainly in manifest error. Their situation is best described by Ja'far ibn Abī Ṭālib when he was questioned about Islam by Negus, the King of Abyssinia. A number of Muslims had migrated there when the Prophet wanted to establish a new base for Islam. The Quraysh, in turn, had also sent a delegation led by 'Amr ibn al-'Āṣ to request their extradition. 'Amr tried to paint a distorted picture of the Muslim immigrants to the king, but the Negus wanted to listen to their version. In this context, Ja'far said to him:

> In our recent past we were ignorant people: we worshipped idols, ate carrion, committed all sorts of sins, attached little value to maintaining good relations with our kinsfolk and behaved badly

to our neighbours. Our overruling maxim was that might was right. This continued to be our situation until God sent us, from among ourselves, a Messenger whose good name, honesty, sincerity and integrity were well known to us. He called on us to believe in God, the one and only God, and to stop worshipping all idols which we and our forefathers used to worship alongside Him. He commanded us always to speak the truth and be honest, to be good to our relatives and neighbours, to preserve life and shed no blood, to refrain from sin, perjury, robbing the property of orphans entrusted to our care, and making false accusations against honourable women. He also commanded us to devote our worship to God alone, ascribing to Him no partners of any sort. He further commanded us to pray regularly, to give away certain purifying alms and to fast, etc.[1]

Worthy of Trust

Despite all their negative qualities during their pre-Islamic days, God knew that the Arabs were the ones to be entrusted with the new faith and that they would be true to their trust. He was also aware of their great potential once they were put on the right way. They could use all this potential for their new faith, whereas the Israelites no longer had it. The latter had endured humiliation for a long time in Egypt under Pharaonic rule. As a result they portrayed many aspects of deviation and ill feeling. Indeed, they were unable to rid themselves of these negative effects, whether during Moses' lifetime, or later. Hence, they incurred God's anger and deserved to be expelled from His grace. He, therefore, removed the trust of His faith from them for the rest of human life.

In His perfect and absolute knowledge, God knew that the Arabian Peninsula was the best cradle for His new faith. This was a faith that aimed to liberate the whole world from the erroneous ways of ignorance and rid it of the decadence that had eaten deep into the great civilizations,

---

1. Adil Salahi, *Muhammad: Man and Prophet*, The Islamic Foundation, Leicestershire, 2002, p. 129.

leaving them hollow. At that time, the state of the world was very low, as described by J.H. Denison, a European writer:

> In the fifth and sixth centuries the civilized world stood on the verge of chaos. The old emotional cultures that had made civilization possible, since they had given to men a sense of unity and of reverence for their rulers, had broken down, and nothing had been found adequate to take their place...
>
> It seemed then that the great civilization that it had taken four thousand years to construct was on the verge of disintegration, and that mankind was likely to return to that condition of barbarism where every tribe and sect was against the next, and law and order were unknown. *The old tribal sanctions had lost their power. Hence the old imperial methods would no longer operate.* The new sanctions created by Christianity were working division and destruction instead of unity and order. It was a time fraught with tragedy. Civilization, like a gigantic tree whose foliage had overreached the world and whose branches had borne the golden fruits of art and science and literature, stood tottering, its trunk no longer alive with the flowing sap of devotion and reverence, but rotted to the core...
>
> It was among these people that the man was born who was to unite the whole known world of the east and south... Mohammed...[2]

This is the view of an European author, but from the Islamic perspective, conditions looked far darker and gloomier. God chose a Bedouin nation in a largely desert peninsula to be entrusted with His faith, knowing that once put on the right course, their mentality

---

2.   Denison, J.H., *Emotion as the Basis of Civilization*, New York and London, 1928, pp. 265–269.

– This quotation runs in the Arabic text as one continuous paragraph. Apparently, the author relied on a quoted text in a book by an Indian author which was translated into Arabic. It may be that the original quotation was an abridged one, and it may be that when it was translated, some variation of emphasis occurred in places. The italicized sentence is omitted in the Arabic text, but it was felt necessary to include it here in order not to affect the flow of the author's meaning. – Editor's note.

and qualities would enable them to shoulder this great responsibility. Moreover, they had the potential to willingly deliver great sacrifices for their faith. Therefore, He raised His last Messenger among them, to recite His revelations to them, purify them and instruct them in His book and in wisdom, thus ridding them of all traces of their old, greatly erroneous ways.

"*To them and to others yet to join them.*" (Verse 3) We have several reports explaining who these others are. Al-Bukhārī relates on Abū Hurayrah's authority: "We were sitting with the Prophet when *Sūrah al-Jumuʿah*, or The Congregation, was revealed to him, including the statement, '*to them and to others yet to join them*'. People asked who were these, but the Prophet did not answer until they had repeated their question three times. Salmān the Persian was among us. The Prophet put his hand on Salmān and said: 'Were faith to be at the top of the sky, some people or a man from among his community would attain it'." This authentic *ḥadīth* makes clear that this Qurʾānic statement includes the Persians. Hence, in his commentary on this verse, Mujāhid says: "This is a reference to all non-Arabs who believe in the Prophet."

Another *ḥadīth* is reported by Sahl ibn Saʿd who quotes the Prophet as saying: "Among the seed of the seed of the seed of men and women in my community there are some who will be admitted into heaven without having to face any reckoning of their deeds. He then quoted the verse that says: '*to them and to others yet to join them*'." This means that these belong to much later generations of Muslims.

Both these interpretations are valid. The Qurʾānic statement refers to people other than the Arabs, and to ones other than the generation that witnessed the revelation of the Qurʾān. It indicates that the Muslim community transcends both geographical area and generational context. It continues to be true to its great trust, faithful to the full form of the divine faith.

"*He is indeed the Almighty, the Wise.*" (Verse 3) He is able to choose as He pleases, and in His wisdom He is fully aware of the most appropriate choices. His choice, of both the earlier and the later generations, means a great honour to those thus chosen: "*Such is God's favour: He grants it to whom He will. God is One who bestows great favours.*" (Verse 4)

11

God's choice of a community or an individual to be responsible for the great truth, to receive the light that emanates from Him, to be the link between the earth and heaven, is a favour of unparalleled proportions. It exceeds by far any sacrifices such an individual or community may give, in wealth, effort and life. It outweighs all the trouble they may undertake, the opposition they have to encounter and the hard struggle they have to endure. God thus reminds the Muslim community in Madīnah, as well as those who will come after it, of the great favour He has granted them when He chose them for this task, sending them a Messenger to purify them and instruct them in the divine book and in wisdom. God's Messenger also left a great wealth of wisdom for future generations, whereby they learn from the practical example of that first Muslim community.

One Role Ended

The *sūrah* then adds a statement that implies that the Israelites' role as trustees of God's message has ended. Their hearts are no longer alert, dedicated and active enough to enable them to live up to the trust they were once given:

> *Those who were entrusted with the burden of implementing the Torah but then failed to do so are like an ass that carries a load of books. Wretched is the example of those who deny God's revelations. God does not guide the wrongdoers.* (Verse 5)

The Israelites were entrusted with the Torah, and charged with being true to the faith and the divine law, but they *'failed to do so'*. The initial duty of this trust is to formulate a thorough and correct understanding of the divine message, and then to implement it both within one's own life and in human life at large. Yet the history of the Israelites, as it was in the true picture painted in the Qur'ān, indicates that they did not appreciate the trust given to them. They neither understood its nature nor were they true to it. As such, they were like the example given in the *sūrah*: *"Like an ass that carries a load of books"*. The ass benefits nothing by the books it carries. It only feels their heavy load. This is a miserable picture, but it represents a true situation: "*Wretched is the example of those who deny God's revelations. God does not guide the wrongdoers.*" (Verse 5)

Likewise are all those who were given the trust of divine faith but who failed to live up to it. Muslims across many generations, as well as those living today, who have Muslim names but who fail to live up to what Islam requires, and particularly those who read the Qurʾān and Islamic books but fall short of what is required of them, are indeed like the ass carrying a load of heavy books. Unfortunately, these are numerous. The question is not that of books being carried: it is a question of understanding the books and putting into practice the teachings they impart.

The Israelites used always to allege that they were God's chosen people and His beloved race, while all others are Goyim or Gentiles. They claimed that in their position they were not required to observe the laws of their own religion in their dealings with the rest of mankind: "*For they say: "We have no obligation to keep faith with Gentiles." Thus they deliberately say of God what they know to be a lie.*" (3: 75) They made many other false allegations, providing no evidence in support of them. Therefore, the *sūrah* invites them to make a mutual prayer. This invitation was also made on other occasions to Christian and pagan groups:

> *Say: 'You who follow the Jewish faith! If you truly claim that out of all people you are God's friends, then wish for death, if your claim is true.' But they will never wish for it because of what their hands have wrought in this life. God is well aware of the wrongdoers. Say: 'The death from which you are trying to run away will certainly overtake you. You will then be returned to the One who knows the imperceptible and that which can be witnessed. He will then tell you all that you have done.'* (Verses 6–8)

What this invitation entails is that the two groups stand together face to face and they all pray to God to inflict punishment on the group upholding falsehood. All groups the Prophet invited to such mutual prayer feared to do so; essentially, they refused to take up the challenge. This indicates that deep inside they realized that what the Prophet said was the truth and that his faith was true. "Ibn ʿAbbās reports that Abū

Jahl once said: 'If I see Muḥammad praying at the Ka'bah, I will go to him and put my foot on his neck.' When the Prophet heard this, he said: 'Had he tried to do so, the angels would have taken him away in broad daylight. Had the Jews wished for death, they would have died and seen their places in hell.' Also true is that had those invited to mutual prayer stood against the Prophet in such prayer, they would have returned home to find their families and properties perished." [Related by Aḥmad, al-Bukhārī, al-Nasā'ī and al-Tirmidhī.]

These verses may only represent a challenge to them, rather than an invitation to mutual prayer. Since they alleged that they were God's only friends among all mankind, why would they fear death, and reveal themselves to be so cowardly? If their claims were true, they would be in a position of favour with God after they die. So why does the prospect of death fill them with fear? This challenge is followed by a statement making it clear that their claims were untrue. They were aware that they had not done enough good deeds to ensure a good position with God or to hope for His reward. On the contrary, they often indulged in sin, and such indulgences made them fear death and what comes after it. A person who has not prepared for his journey will always be in fear of what may happen along the road: "*But they will never wish for it because of what their hands have wrought in this life. God is well aware of the wrongdoers.*" (Verse 7)

A statement follows that establishes the nature of death and what comes after it. It shows them that their attempts to escape from death are of little use. It will inevitably overtake them. After death, all will return to God where they will have their deeds reckoned and where they will face the consequences of the same: "*Say: 'The death from which you are trying to run away will certainly overtake you. You will then be returned to the One who knows the imperceptible and that which can be witnessed. He will then tell you all that you have done.'*" (Verses 8)

This Qur'ānic statement makes clear to the addressees and to everyone else the truth that people often overlook and prefer not to think about, despite facing it all the time: namely, this life is bound to end. To stay away from God during one's lifetime will not avert a person from returning to Him, for there is no refuge from God except by returning to Him. The reckoning of everyone's deeds will inevitably follow this return. There is simply no escape. The Prophet is quoted as saying: "A person who tries to run away from death is like a fox who owes a debt to the earth. He went out roaming until he was exhausted and bleeding. When he went into his hole, the earth said to him: 'Fox! Repay the debt you owe me.' He went out again wounded. He continued to bleed and his neck was cut. He then died." [Related by al-Ṭabarī.] This *ḥadīth* so delivers a highly moving and effective picture.

The Congregation on Friday

The last section of the *sūrah* provides certain teachings concerning Friday and its congregational prayer. It refers to an event that might have been repeated; given the way it is described suggests such repetition:

> *Believers! When the call to prayer is made on Friday, go straightaway to the prayer and leave off your trading. This is best for you, if you but knew it. When the prayer is finished, disperse in the land and seek God's bounty. Remember God often so that you may be successful. Yet when people see some trade or entertainment, they head off towards it, leaving you standing there. Say: 'That which is with God is far better than any entertainment or trade. God is the best of providers.'* (Verses 9–11)

Friday Prayer is a weekly prayer that must be offered in congregation. It cannot be offered by anyone on his own. Muslims meet in Friday Prayer and listen to a sermon that reminds them of their duties towards God. We can say that it is an organizational prayer, following the Islamic method of preparing for this life and the life to come together by the same measures and the same acts of worship. Friday Prayer gives a clear and specific impression of the nature of the Islamic faith and the Muslim community, which we explained in our commentary on the previous *sūrah*, The Ranks.

There are many *aḥādīth* that speak of the value, importance and special position of this prayer, encouraging its observation after preparing for it by undertaking specific cleanliness and purification rituals. Ibn 'Umar quotes the Prophet as saying: "When any of you wishes to attend Friday

15

Prayer, he should take a bath." [Related by al-Bukhārī and Muslim.] Aws ibn Aws quotes the Prophet as saying: "Whoever washes himself and takes a bath on Friday, going out early, walking to the mosque rather than riding, draws close to the imam, listens and refrains from idle talk, will be rewarded for each step the equivalent of fasting and observing night prayer for a whole year." [Related by al-Nasā'ī, Abū Dāwūd, al-Tirmidhī and Ibn Mājah.] Imām Aḥmad reports on the authority of Abū Ayyūb al-Anṣārī that he heard the Prophet saying: "Whoever takes a bath on Friday, wears a touch of perfume if he has it, puts on some of his best clothes, goes out to the mosque where he offers voluntary prayers if he so wishes, doing no harm to anyone, listens to the imam when he delivers his sermon and then joins the prayer, all his sins between that prayer and the Friday before it will be forgiven."

The first verse in this section orders Muslims to leave off all business once they hear the call to prayer: "*Believers! When the call to prayer is made on Friday, go straightaway to the prayer and leave off your trading.*" (Verse 9) It provides encouragement for so abandoning anything related to the life of this world and its concerns: "*This is best for you, if you but knew it.*" (Verse 9) This suggests that leaving off trade and business was not easy; it required such encouragement. Moreover, it provides good and repeated education. Every now and then, people need a period of time when they free themselves from their preoccupation with earning a living and the attractions of worldly life. They need such periods when they can be in close contact with their Lord, glorifying Him and experiencing the happiness resulting from dedication to His service. They need to fill their hearts and lungs with the pure, clean and refreshing air that comes with such dedication.

When they have done so, they can then return to their business, continuing to remember God: "*When the prayer is finished, disperse in the land and seek God's bounty. Remember God often so that you may be successful.*" (Verse 10) The Islamic system provides a perfect balance between the needs of life on earth, with all that it requires of work and effort, and the need to be away from all this for a short while to attend to worship. Time spent away from the preoccupations of this life is necessary to keep the heart alive. Without it, it cannot live up to the great trust God has given us and nor can it fulfil its duties. It is important to remember God while we are busy earning our living, for such remembrance transforms our work activities into acts of worship. Nevertheless, we need such short periods of complete dedication to worship, as clearly implied in the last two verses.

'Irāk ibn Mālik, a Companion of the Prophet, used to stand near the door of the mosque after Friday Prayer and say: "My Lord! I have responded to Your call, offered the prayer You made obligatory, and I am dispersing as You have commanded me. Give me of Your bounty, for You are the best of providers." [Related by Ibn Abī Ḥātim.] These words show us how such a person treated the matter seriously but also in a very simple way. The verses give orders and these orders are carried out to the letter. Such a clear, simple and yet serious understanding is perhaps the secret behind the first Muslim community's rise to the high level it achieved, despite all the distractions it had to deal with, as described in the last verse: "*Yet when people see some trade or entertainment, they head off towards it, leaving you standing there. Say: 'That which is with God is far better than any entertainment or trade. God is the best of providers.*" (Verse 11)

Jābir ibn 'Abdullāh reports: "We were attending the prayer with the Prophet when a caravan carrying food arrived. People flocked to it, and only 12 men remained with the Prophet, including Abū Bakr and 'Umar. God then revealed the verse that says: '*Yet when people see some trade or entertainment, they head off towards it, leaving you standing there*'." The verse makes clear that what is with God is better than trade and entertainment. It reminds them that all that they have is provided by God who is the best of providers.

This event shows the great effort that was needed in order to mould the community that rose to the highest level achieved by any community of believers in human history. It also encourages those who advocate God's message in all generations to remain patient. They are bound to encounter weaknesses, for human beings often yield and fall prey to temptation. Yet they must remember that man is also able to rise to sublime standards of purity and dedication. What is needed to help such a rise is patience, proper understanding, perseverance and entertaining no thoughts of quitting midway.

SŪRAH 63

Al-Munāfiqūn
(The Hypocrites)

Prologue

Although the title *al-Munāfiqūn*, or The Hypocrites, indicates this *sūrah*'s subject matter, it is nonetheless not the only one that mentions hypocrisy and that describes the hypocrites' wicked scheming. Indeed, hardly any of the *sūrahs* revealed in Madīnah is without an express or implied reference to hypocrisy. However, the present *sūrah* is dedicated, almost entirely, to speaking about the hypocrites, referring to particular events and statements they made. The *sūrah* launches a strong attack against the hypocrites: their manners, lies, intrigue and wicked plots. It exposes their true feelings of hatred towards the Muslims, as also their cowardice and evil nature.

A warning is given at the end to the believers not to allow any of the characteristics of hypocrisy to creep near them. The first element of hypocrisy is not to be totally dedicated to God's cause, and to be instead preoccupied with money, property and children. Hypocrisy also entails slackening when invited to contribute financially to God's cause until a day comes when no such donation will be of any use.

The unbelievers' hypocrisy accelerated when Islam moved to Madīnah and continued to so grow until virtually the end of the Prophet's blessed life. Although evidence of such traits was almost uninterrupted, hypocrisy nonetheless acquired different aspects and variously resorted to different tactics. Inevitably, such behaviour had a strong bearing on the events of the period, taking up much of the Muslim community's efforts, time and energy. Indeed, hypocrisy is frequently mentioned in the Qur'ān and *Ḥadīth*, thereby indicating how prevalent it had become.

In his biography of the Prophet, *Sīrat al-Rasūl: Ṣuwar Muqtabasah min al-Qur'ān al-Karīm*, Muḥammad Izzat Darwazah, devotes a fine chapter to this issue. The following paragraphs are especially revealing:

> There were obvious reasons for the phenomenon of hypocrisy to appear in Madīnah. The early Muslims in Makkah were neither strong enough nor influential enough to make a group of people fear them or try to appease them. Indeed, the people of Makkah, and its leaders and notables in particular, opposed the Prophet in a very open manner, inflicting much harm on the Muslims, and resorted to any measure within their means to check the new religion's advance In fact, they commanded much power. Because of this persecution the Muslims were subjected to some had to migrate to Abyssinia, and thereafter to Madīnah. In fact, some of them were subjected to such unbearable pressure that they had to renounce their faith: this as a result of either torture or the lure of temptation. So extreme did this become that a few even died under torture.
>
> In Madīnah, the situation was markedly different. Prior to his migration there, the Prophet was able to recruit a number of strong and influential followers from the two tribes of the Aws and the Khazraj. He migrated only after having made sure of the favourable situation there. Indeed, there was hardly an Arab house in Madīnah without its followers of Islam in the family. There were no doubt many who rejected Islam, either because they chose not to listen to its message or because they were full of hostility realizing that the Prophet's arrival in Madīnah threatened their position of leadership and influence. They realized, however, that they could not take an openly hostile attitude to the Prophet and his Muhājirīn and Anṣār followers. Moreover, tribal affiliation was an important factor preventing such open hostility. Indeed, the

broad majority of their own tribes, the Aws and the Khazraj, were now Muslim, giving sincere and devoted support to the Prophet. They were good Muslims who looked at the Prophet as their own supreme commander, and the guide they had to follow. Therefore, the ones who still entertained thoughts of idolatry and harboured rancour in their hearts, prompting them to seek to undermine Islam, felt that their only option was to pretend to be Muslim, appearing to fulfil their Islamic duties, declaring their continued loyalty to their tribes, while at the same time resorting to plots and intrigue. At times, however, their opposition did smack of hypocrisy, this usually when the Muslims faced some tough crisis, and here the 'pretenders' counselled caution, claiming that it was the only option that served Muslim interests. Needless to say, they did not acknowledge that they were in fact unbelievers. Nonetheless, their true attitude of hypocrisy did not go unnoticed by the Prophet and his Companions. Moreover, their stand at times of crises, counselling a policy of weakness, hardened them further in their hypocrisy and unbelief. Qur'ānic revelations time after time exposed and denounced their schemes, alerting the Prophet and the believers to the need to be very cautious in dealing with them.

The hypocrites' attitude and schemes had, according to the import of Qur'ānic revelations, a far-reaching effect. We feel that there was a determined struggle, reminiscent of that between the Prophet and the Makkan elders, but with a reversal in its outcome. Within a short period, the Prophet strengthened his position in Madīnah and his influence increased. Islam was spreading and consolidating its power base. The hypocrites were neither a solid group nor a clearly identified entity. As Islam was on the ascendancy, they grew weaker and thus their influence diminished.

To appreciate the threat posed by the hypocrites, particularly in the early period of Islam in Madīnah, we need to remember however that they could still call on tribal loyalties, which remained strong among the Arabs. Besides, they had not at this juncture exposed themselves. Nor had Islam as yet consolidated its influence on its new followers. Moreover, the Prophet was

21

surrounded by idolaters on all fronts. The people of Makkah continued to enjoy a position of great influence among the Arabs, and they were on the lookout for any chance to level a crushing defeat on the still fledgling Muslim State. The Jews in Madīnah were also not long in taking a hostile stance towards the Prophet and Islam. Indeed, they were quick to cement a natural alliance with the hypocrites, defining common objectives in opposition to the Muslim community. In fact, the hypocrites could not have caused so much harm to the Prophet and his followers had they not had the support of the Jews and the sort of alliance that the two groups forged. Nonetheless, their influence gradually weakened and the danger they represented subsided only after God foiled their schemes and enabled the Prophet to achieve victory over them.

Al-Munāfiqūn
(The Hypocrites)

In the Name of God, the Lord of Grace, the Ever Merciful

بِسۡمِ ٱللَّهِ ٱلرَّحۡمَٰنِ ٱلرَّحِيمِ

When the hypocrites come to you, they say, 'We bear witness that you are indeed God's Messenger.' God knows that you are truly His Messenger and He bears witness that the hypocrites are indeed liars. (1)

إِذَا جَآءَكَ ٱلۡمُنَٰفِقُونَ قَالُواْ نَشۡهَدُ إِنَّكَ لَرَسُولُ ٱللَّهِ وَٱللَّهُ يَعۡلَمُ إِنَّكَ لَرَسُولُهُۥ وَٱللَّهُ يَشۡهَدُ إِنَّ ٱلۡمُنَٰفِقِينَ لَكَٰذِبُونَ ١

They use their oaths as a cover [for their falseness], and they turn people away from the path of God. Evil indeed is what they do. (2)

ٱتَّخَذُوٓاْ أَيۡمَٰنَهُمۡ جُنَّةً فَصَدُّواْ عَن سَبِيلِ ٱللَّهِ إِنَّهُمۡ سَآءَ مَا كَانُواْ يَعۡمَلُونَ ٢

That is because they professed to believe, then they renounced faith. So, a seal has been set on their hearts and therefore they are devoid of understanding. (3)

ذَٰلِكَ بِأَنَّهُمۡ ءَامَنُواْ ثُمَّ كَفَرُواْ فَطُبِعَ عَلَىٰ قُلُوبِهِمۡ فَهُمۡ لَا يَفۡقَهُونَ ٣

When you see them, their outward appearance may please you; and when they speak, you listen to what they say. They are like propped-up timbers. They think that every shout is directed against them. They are the real enemy; so beware of them. May God destroy them! How perverse they are! (4)

وَإِذَا رَأَيۡتَهُمۡ تُعۡجِبُكَ أَجۡسَامُهُمۡ وَإِن يَقُولُواْ تَسۡمَعۡ لِقَوۡلِهِمۡ كَأَنَّهُمۡ خُشُبٌ مُّسَنَّدَةٌ يَحۡسَبُونَ كُلَّ صَيۡحَةٍ عَلَيۡهِمۡ هُمُ ٱلۡعَدُوُّ فَٱحۡذَرۡهُمۡ قَٰتَلَهُمُ ٱللَّهُ أَنَّىٰ يُؤۡفَكُونَ ٤

When they are told, 'Come, so that God's Messenger may ask forgiveness for you,' they turn their heads away. You see them drawing back in arrogance. (5)

وَإِذَا قِيلَ لَهُمْ تَعَالَوْاْ يَسْتَغْفِرْ لَكُمْ رَسُولُ ٱللَّهِ لَوَّوْاْ رُءُوسَهُمْ وَرَأَيْتَهُمْ يَصُدُّونَ وَهُم مُّسْتَكْبِرُونَ ٥

As for them, it is all the same whether you pray for their forgiveness or you do not pray. God will not forgive them; for God does not bestow His guidance on such transgressor folk. (6)

سَوَآءٌ عَلَيْهِمْ أَسْتَغْفَرْتَ لَهُمْ أَمْ لَمْ تَسْتَغْفِرْ لَهُمْ لَن يَغْفِرَ ٱللَّهُ لَهُمْ إِنَّ ٱللَّهَ لَا يَهْدِى ٱلْقَوْمَ ٱلْفَٰسِقِينَ ٦

They are the ones who say [to one another]: 'Do not give anything to those who are with God's Messenger, so that they may abandon him.' To God belong the treasures of the heavens and the earth, but the hypocrites cannot understand. (7)

هُمُ ٱلَّذِينَ يَقُولُونَ لَا تُنفِقُواْ عَلَىٰ مَنْ عِندَ رَسُولِ ٱللَّهِ حَتَّىٰ يَنفَضُّواْ وَلِلَّهِ خَزَآئِنُ ٱلسَّمَٰوَٰتِ وَٱلْأَرْضِ وَلَٰكِنَّ ٱلْمُنَٰفِقِينَ لَا يَفْقَهُونَ ٧

They say, 'When we return to Madīnah, the more honourable will surely drive out those who are contemptible.' All honour belongs to God, His Messenger and the believers, but the hypocrites do not know. (8)

يَقُولُونَ لَئِن رَّجَعْنَا إِلَى ٱلْمَدِينَةِ لَيُخْرِجَنَّ ٱلْأَعَزُّ مِنْهَا ٱلْأَذَلَّ وَلِلَّهِ ٱلْعِزَّةُ وَلِرَسُولِهِ وَلِلْمُؤْمِنِينَ وَلَٰكِنَّ ٱلْمُنَٰفِقِينَ لَا يَعْلَمُونَ ٨

Believers! Do not let your riches or your children make you oblivious of the remembrance of God. Those who do so will surely be the losers. (9)

يَٰٓأَيُّهَا ٱلَّذِينَ ءَامَنُواْ لَا تُلْهِكُمْ أَمْوَٰلُكُمْ وَلَآ أَوْلَٰدُكُمْ عَن ذِكْرِ ٱللَّهِ وَمَن يَفْعَلْ ذَٰلِكَ فَأُوْلَٰٓئِكَ هُمُ ٱلْخَٰسِرُونَ ٩

Give, then, out of what We have provided for you, before death comes to any of you, and then he says, 'My Lord, if You would grant me a delay for a short while, I would give in charity and be one of the righteous.' (10)

وَأَنفِقُواْ مِن مَّا رَزَقْنَكُم مِّن قَبْلِ أَن يَأْتِيَ أَحَدَكُمُ ٱلْمَوْتُ فَيَقُولَ رَبِّ لَوْلَآ أَخَّرْتَنِيٓ إِلَىٰٓ أَجَلٍ قَرِيبٍ فَأَصَّدَّقَ وَأَكُن مِّنَ ٱلصَّٰلِحِينَ ۝

God does not grant a delay to any soul when its term has come. God is fully aware of all that you do. (11)

وَلَن يُؤَخِّرَ ٱللَّهُ نَفْسًا إِذَا جَآءَ أَجَلُهَا وَٱللَّهُ خَبِيرٌۢ بِمَا تَعْمَلُونَ ۝

Ugly Hypocrisy

The *surah* begins with a description of the hypocrites' attempt to disguise the truth of their unbelief. They declare themselves Muslim and testify that the Prophet is God's Messenger. They swear by God so as to convince the Muslims, while they themselves know that they are lying. Their oaths are merely a shield behind which they hope to hide their true reality and deceive the Muslims:

> *When the hypocrites come to you, they say, 'We bear witness that you are indeed God's Messenger.' God knows that you are truly His Messenger and He bears witness that the hypocrites are indeed liars. They use their oaths as a cover [for their falseness], and they turn people away from the path of God. Evil indeed is what they do. (Verses 1–2)*

They would go to the Prophet and state that they bore witness that he was God's Messenger, but theirs was only a verbal testimony lacking all conviction. They were merely engaging in deception, hoping to hide their truth from the Muslim community and so protect themselves. Therefore, God states that they were lying while making clear the truth of His message to the Prophet Muḥammad: "*God knows that you are truly His Messenger and He bears witness that the hypocrites are indeed liars.*" (Verse 1)

The phraseology here is both precise and precautionary. We note how the verse begins by confirming the truth of the Prophet's message before it states that the hypocrites' oaths were false. Without taking such care in its wording, the verse could suggest that denunciation of the hypocrites as liars applies to the subject matter of their statement, namely the Prophet's message. The verse intends no such thing. What it aims to do is to state the truth, making it clear that they did not really believe that the Prophet's message was true. In other words, they are not sincere in their statement.

"*They use their oaths as a cover.*" (Verse 2) This short statement suggests that they used to swear an oath every time they feared exposure, or whenever one of their schemes was uncovered, or some of what they said about Muslims was reported. They hoped that such oaths would protect them from the consequences of their exposure. Thus they used their false faith as a shield to hide their reality and allow them a chance to go on with their plots and schemes against the Muslim community. Thus, "*they turn people away from the path of God.*" They kept themselves and others away from God's path, using their false oaths for that end. "*Evil indeed is what they do.*" (Verse 2) Could there be anything worse than lying to mislead and deceive others?

The *sūrah* explains the reasons behind their behaviour, making it clear that they knowingly reverted to disbelief after having accepted Islam: "*That is because they professed to believe, then they renounced faith. So, a seal has been set on their hearts and therefore they are devoid of understanding.*" (Verse 3) Thus, whilst they have known what it means to accept faith, they nonetheless chose to revert to disbelief. No heart that has a sound understanding or appreciation of things, or indeed has life, would experience life under faith and then choose to return to disbelief. How can anyone who understands, appreciates and experiences the concept of life that faith promotes, with its view of the universe, and also breathes the fresh air of faith and lets the light of faith shine over his world wish to revert to the miserable and suffocating darkness of unfaith? None will make such a choice except he who is filled with grudges that blind his sight and blunt his senses. Hence, such people are in the miserable condition the verse describes: "*So, a seal has been set on their hearts and therefore they are devoid of understanding.*" (Verse 3)

26

The *surah* draws a unique picture of such people inviting ridicule and describing them as aimless, leading a futile existence, and nursing grudges. It presents an image of them that serves as an object of ridicule:

> *When you see them, their outward appearance may please you; and when they speak, you listen to what they say. They are like propped-up timbers. They think that every shout is directed against them. They are the real enemy; so beware of them. May God destroy them! How perverse they are!* (Verse 4)

Thus, they are merely an outward appearance, not real human beings who respond and interact. They may look pleasant to the eye as long as they remain silent, but when they speak they show themselves to be devoid of sense and feeling. They are like timbers, but not just any kind of wood: they are propped up against a wall, unable to move. This stone-cold picture shows the reaction of their souls, that is if they have souls at all. This is then complemented with a state of constant apprehension, perpetual fear and uncertainty: "*They think that every shout is directed against them.*" (Verse 4) They know themselves to be hypocrites, covered by a thin veil of pretence, false oaths and attempts to appease. Hence, they live under the constant dread that their reality will be exposed. The *surah* shows them always turning around, dreading every move and every shout. They imagine that every cry is setting a chase after them. Thus, spiritually, they are like propped up pieces of wood, but when it is a question of fear for one's life or property, they look like a trembling reed in a storm. In both cases, they are the main enemy of the Prophet and the Muslim community: "*They are the real enemy; so beware of them.*" They are the enemy within, hiding within Muslim ranks. Hence, they represent a greater danger than the external enemy. Therefore, the Prophet is instructed to beware of them. He is not, however, instructed here to kill them. Instead, he was to pursue a different course of action, one that reflected much wisdom and confidence that their schemes would come to nothing.

"*May God destroy them! How perverse they are!*" (Verse 4) God will indeed be their enemy wherever they turn. Such a prayer by God

Almighty means a verdict that is certain to take place. It is their inevitable outcome, as history has clearly shown.

Stirring Up Trouble

The *surah* continues to describe their actions, revealing the rancour in their hearts. It shows how they schemed against the Prophet, yet were quick with their lies when exposed. These were their known qualities:

> *When they are told, 'Come, so that God's Messenger may ask forgiveness for you,' they turn their heads away. You see them drawing back in arrogance. As for them, it is all the same whether you pray for their forgiveness or you do not pray. God will not forgive them; for God does not bestow His guidance on such transgressor folk. They are the ones who say [to one another]: 'Do not give anything to those who are with God's Messenger, so that they may abandon him.' To God belong the treasures of the heavens and the earth, but the hypocrites cannot understand. They say, 'When we return to Madīnah, the more honourable will surely drive out those who are contemptible.' All honour belongs to God, His Messenger and the believers, but the hypocrites do not know. (Verses 5–8)*

Several early scholars confirm that these verses relate to an incident in which 'Abdullāh ibn Ubayy featured prominently. Ibn Isḥāq gives a detailed account of it in his report on the expedition to forestall a planned attack by the al-Muṣṭalaq tribe:

> The Muslims were still encamping at the spring which provided the stage for their battle. Servants were taking horses to the water to drink. Among them was Jahjāh, 'Umar ibn al-Khaṭṭāb's servant. Apparently, there was some scrambling at the water among the servants. Jahjāh clashed with an 'ally' of the Khazraj, named Sinān ibn Wabr. Neither man seemed to be endowed with much wisdom: punches were exchanged and each appealed to his 'group' for help. Jahjāh called on the Muhājirīn to defend him, while Sinān called on the Anṣār. 'Abdullāh ibn Ubayy felt very angry when he heard of

this. He was attended by a group of his people, including a young man called Zayd ibn Arqam. He said to them: "I have never known such humiliation as has befallen us today. They [the Muhājirīn] are now standing up to us in our own home town. They are ungrateful to us for our favours. Our case with the refugees of the Quraysh is an apt example of the proverb: 'Fatten your dog and he will eat you.' When we go back to Madīnah the honourable among the two of us will certainly chase the humble out of it. You have only yourselves to blame for all this. You have taken them into your own homes and given them your own money until they have become rich. I swear that if you stop helping them with what you have, they will leave you and go elsewhere."

Zayd ibn Arqam recounted all this to the Prophet who was attended by 'Umar ibn al-Khaṭṭāb. 'Umar suggested that the Prophet should command 'Abbād ibn Bishr to kill 'Abdullāh ibn Ubayy. The Prophet said: "How would you like it, 'Umar, if people started to say that Muḥammad is killing his Companions? Indeed, I shall not do that. However, give orders to depart now." Thus, these orders were given at a time when the Prophet never used to depart.

'Abdullāh ibn Ubayy learnt that the Prophet had been told what he had said. He therefore hastened to him and denied any knowledge of what had been attributed to him. He swore by God that he did not say anything of the sort. Those of the Prophet's Companions who were present tried to pacify matters. They were still keen that 'Abdullāh ibn Ubayy should be given his chance to accept Islam. After all, he had been well respected among his people before the advent of Islam. They suggested to the Prophet that Zayd ibn Arqam might have misquoted or misheard 'Abdullāh.

When the orders were given to march, Usayd ibn Ḥudayr, a prominent figure among the Anṣār, came to the Prophet, greeted him with the respect due to him as Messenger of God and said: "Prophet, I see that you are marching at a time of day when you used not to march." The Prophet said to him: "Have you not heard what your friend said?" When Usayd asked for details, the Prophet told him that 'Abdullāh ibn Ubayy had said that "the honourable among the two of us will chase the humble out of Madīnah." Usayd said: "Yes indeed, Messenger of God. You can turn him out of Madīnah if you like. You are the honourable and he is the humble." Usayd then pleaded clemency and told the Prophet: "God has sent you to us when his people were preparing to crown him king. He may think that you have robbed him of his kingdom."

The Prophet marched at the head of the Muslims for the rest of the day and throughout the night, and continued marching until mid-morning, when it was burning hot. He then allowed his Companions to stop. Hardly had they sat down when they all fell asleep. This the Prophet did in order that people would not be preoccupied with what 'Abdullāh ibn Ubayy had said.

Shortly afterwards, the *sūrah* entitled *al-Munāfiqūn*, or The Hypocrites, was revealed. It describes the hypocrites and their feelings towards the Muslims and it also states the very words said by 'Abdullāh ibn Ubayy and conveyed to the Prophet by Zayd ibn Arqam. There was no longer any doubt as to the accuracy of Zayd's report. The Prophet held Zayd's ear in his hand and said: "This is the one who made good use of his ear for the sake of God."

'Abdullāh ibn Ubayy had a son whose name was also 'Abdullāh. Unlike his father, 'Abdullāh was a good believer who entertained no doubt about the truthfulness of Muhammad's message. Indeed, the Prophet was so certain of 'Abdullāh's strong faith that he appointed him to deputize for him in his absence when the Prophet headed the Muslim army on their final expedition to Badr. Moreover, 'Abdullāh was a dutiful son to his father. It was a cause of distress to him that his father acted against the Prophet. He would have done anything to bring his father within the Muslim fold. When he heard that his father uttered those wicked comments against the Prophet and the Muhājirīn he realized that this crime was a capital one. He also learnt that some of the Companions of the Prophet had counselled him to get rid of 'Abdullāh ibn Ubayy. 'Abdullāh, the son, went to the Prophet and spoke to him: "Messenger of God, I have heard that you intend to kill 'Abdullāh ibn Ubayy for what was reported to you as his words. If you must kill him, then you have only to command me and I will bring you his head. The tribe of al-Khazraj [his own tribe] is fully aware that I am its most dutiful son to his father. However, I fear that if you order someone else to kill him, I may not be able to look at my father's killer walking in the street. I may be moved to kill him. If I do so, I would be killing a believer in revenge for an unbeliever. Hell would then be my doom." The Prophet smiled and calmed him down. He said to 'Abdullāh: "We will be kind to him and treat him well as long as he is with us."

'Abdullāh ibn Ubayy remained in Madīnah and he never lost an opportunity to speak ill of Islam and the Prophet. His credibility, however, was eroded. Whenever he said or did something, his own people were the first to take issue with him and remonstrate with him, trying to make him see his error. When this was apparent, the Prophet said to 'Umar ibn al-Khaṭṭāb, the first to suggest that 'Abdullāh ibn Ubayy should be killed: "Now do you see, 'Umar? Had I killed him when you suggested that to me, some people would have been very angry, while they themselves would be prepared to kill him now if I would only order them to do so." 'Umar replied: "I certainly know that God's Messenger knows better than I do and his actions are more blessed than mine."[1]

It is reported by 'Ikrimah, Ibn Zayd and others that when the people went back to Madīnah, 'Abdullāh ibn Ubayy's son stood at the entrance to Madīnah with his sword in his hand. People passed by, then his father arrived. The son said to him: 'Stand back.' He said: 'What is the matter with you?' He said: 'By God! You shall not pass this point until God's Messenger gives you permission. He is the honourable and you are the humble.' When the Prophet arrived, for he used to walk at the rear of the army to look after anyone who may be in need of help, 'Abdullāh ibn Ubayy complained to him about his son. The son said: 'By God, he will not enter until you, Messenger of God, so permit him.' The Prophet

---

1. For a fuller treatment of this event, see, Adil Salahi (2002), *Muhammad: Man and Prophet*, Leicester: The Islamic Foundation, pp. 407–411. – Editor's note.

permitted him to go in, at which juncture the son said: 'Now that God's Messenger has given you permission, you may walk in.'

Dealing with Hypocrisy

When we consider the events and look at the people involved, as also the Qur'ānic comments, we see the divine method of cultivating the first Muslim community and we marvel at how God conducts matters and events.

Thus, we see the first Muslim community infiltrated by hypocrites who live within its ranks for almost ten years, during the Prophet's lifetime, and he does not expel them. In fact, God does not make them known to him by name or person until shortly before his own death. He would know such a one only by the tone of his speech, the way he twisted words and tried to hide things. He also knew them by their reactions to things and events. God had willed this so that people were not allowed to judge others' intentions and hearts. Judgement on these is for God alone. He alone knows what people harbour in their hearts and He alone requires people to account for them. As for us, we judge people by what we see before our eyes. Thus, no one is judged on the basis of suspicion. Even when God identified for His Messenger those who remained hypocrites until shortly before his death, the Prophet did not expel them from the Muslim community when they continued to put up a show that they were Muslims and fulfilled Islamic obligations. Instead, he kept such knowledge to himself, informing only one of his Companions, Ḥudhayfah ibn al-Yamān, of their identity. Neither of them publicized the information. Indeed, 'Umar ibn al-Khaṭṭāb wanted to be sure even of himself. Hence he went to Ḥudhayfah to ask him whether the Prophet had mentioned him as being among the hypocrites. Ḥudhayfah would only reply that he was not one of them, adding no further information. The Prophet was also ordered not to pray for any of them who might have died. His Companions would thus know by his absence from the *janāzah* prayer [i.e. the prayer for a dead person] that the deceased was among the hypocrites. After the Prophet's own death, Ḥudhayfah also refrained from attending the *janāzah* prayer of any hypocrite mentioned to him by the Prophet. 'Umar too would not offer the *janāzah* prayer for a dead person until he had made sure that their faith had remained untainted. If he saw Ḥudhayfah attending the prayer, he too would offer it. If not, he would not offer it either, but also would say nothing about this.

Thus events moved, as God had willed, fulfilling their intended purposes. They served to provide lessons and to cultivate the minds, manners and morals of the Muslim community. Furthermore, the event which led to the revelation of these verses serves to point out a number of values.

We see first 'Abdullāh ibn Ubayy: a man living among the Muslim community, close to the Prophet. Events take place in succession and signs of different sorts are seen, all confirming the truth of the Islamic faith and the message preached by the Prophet. Yet 'Abdullāh ibn Ubayy's heart is not responsive to faith. Apparently, God has not granted him the blessing of accepting faith. Something stands between him and this great flow of light: it is the grudge he harbours for not being made king of the Aws and Khazraj. He had been all but proclaimed king when the people of Madīnah began to accept Islam, following the Prophet's arrival there. This was enough for him to turn away from Islam and its divine guidance, regardless of how it was confirmed by evidence and signs aplenty. Indeed, he lived in the midst of the Muslim community, witnessing the radical change Islam brings into people's lives.

We also see his son, also named 'Abdullāh, a superior example of a dedicated Muslim. He is so miserable because of his father's attitude and so ashamed of him. Yet, he feels for him the love a dutiful son has for his father. He hears that God's Messenger wants his father dead, and he experiences greatly different emotions. He faces these with all frankness and seriousness. He is committed to Islam, loves God's Messenger and is keen to fulfil his orders, even when these are against his own father. Yet he cannot condone the thought that anyone should kill his father or that such a person would walk freely after having done that. He fears that he might weaken and that he will not overcome the desire to take revenge. Therefore, he goes to his leader, the Prophet, requesting his help in how best to deal with the conflicting emotions that so troubled him. He requests that if the Prophet wants his father killed, then he should let him be the one to carry this out. He would so obey the Prophet and do as he was told. Otherwise, if someone else killed his father, he might kill that person in revenge, thus taking the life of a believer in revenge for an unbeliever. He would then face tremendous difficulties in the life to come.

What we see here is truly awesome. It is the greatness of faith deeply enshrined in a believer's heart. The man offers the Prophet the opportunity to assign to him one of the hardest ever actions a human being can face: to kill his own father. He is sincere in his offer, and his purpose is to avoid something that has worse and graver consequences: to kill a believer in revenge for an unbeliever, thus incurring a sin that could land him in hell. We are amazed at his absolute sincerity and by the way in which he faces his human weakness towards his father. He says to the Prophet: "By God, all my tribe, the Khazraj, are fully aware that they have no son who is more dutiful towards his father than I am." He does not want the Prophet to change any orders he gives concerning his father. He knows that whatever the Prophet orders must be obeyed. All he wants is that he should be the one to carry out those orders, so as not to succumb to human weakness later on.

Impressed by such feelings of a man with profound faith, the Prophet kindly and compassionately removes all difficulty from him, saying that as far as his father is concerned: "We will be kind to him and treat him well as long as he is with us." Prior to this, the Prophet had also stopped 'Umar who had advocated that 'Abdullāh ibn Ubayy be killed by one of his tribesmen, saying: "How would you like it, 'Umar, if people started to say that Muḥammad is killing his Companions?"

We also note with admiration how the Prophet reacted as a wise, inspired leader to quell the event. He ordered the Muslims' immediate departure, and continued marching with his army to the point of fatigue. His aim was to distract people from any thought of blind tribal loyalty, which the cries of the two fighting men might have stirred. He wanted to quell the sort of strife instigated by the hypocrite 'Abdullāh ibn Ubayy who aimed to destroy the feelings of love and brotherhood that existed between the Muhājirīn and the Anṣār. These feelings were of a unique type, previously unknown in human history. We similarly note the Prophet's remarks to Usayd ibn Ḥuḍayr, which sought to mobilize his Companions spiritually against discord and strife. He wanted the man who aimed to sow discord to be stopped by his own people as he still enjoyed a high position among them.

Finally, the last scene is amazing: 'Abdullāh ibn 'Abdullāh ibn Ubayy, a firm believer, holds his sword at the entrance gate to Madīnah to prevent his father's entry. He wanted his father's own words to come true. It was he who said: "When we return to Madīnah, the more honourable will surely drive out those who are contemptible." He wanted him to know that God's Messenger was the more honourable and that he himself was the contemptible one. He forced him to stand there until the Prophet arrived and gave him permission to enter, showing him in practical measures to whom true honour belonged.

It is to such a high summit that those people attained through faith. Yet they remained ordinary humans, experiencing all human feelings and frailties. This is the most beautiful characteristic of this faith when people understand it as it should be understood. They then become its practical image, in the form of humans who eat food and walk the streets.

Arrogance and Deprivation

We will now discuss the Qur'ānic verses that refer to those events: "*When they are told, 'Come, so that God's Messenger may ask forgiveness for you,' they turn their heads away. You see them drawing back in arrogance.*" (Verse 5) They perform their actions, say whatever they may say, and then if they realize that the Prophet heard of their behaviour they resort to cowardly ways. They swear an oath in an attempt to protect themselves. If, when feeling secure that they do not have to face the Prophet, someone says to them, '*Come, so that God's Messenger may ask forgiveness for you,*' they turn away in arrogance. Both characteristics of cowardice and arrogance go hand in hand among hypocrites. However, such behaviour normally belongs to those who hold position and influence among people, yet feel themselves too weak for direct confrontation. They resort to arrogant behaviour as long as they do not have to confront the truth. Yet when they are confronted with it, cowardice and false oaths are their mark.

35

Therefore, the *sūrah* addresses the Prophet, telling him what God has determined in the hypocrites' case, and since God's judgement has been passed, there is no longer any use in praying for their forgiveness: "*As for them, it is all the same whether you pray for their forgiveness or you do not pray. God will not forgive them; for God does not bestow His guidance on such transgressor folk.*" (Verse 6)

The *sūrah* goes on to relate some aspects of their transgression that were the cause of God's judgement: "*They are the ones who say [to one another]: 'Do not give anything to those who are with God's Messenger, so that they may abandon him'.*" What they say betrays their wickedness and spitefulness. Their plan to starve the Prophet's Companions is the same strategy employed by all opponents of truth and faith in all generations and communities. In their perverted view, they think that all people are like them in giving paramount importance to food and survival. This was the plan the Quraysh followed when they imposed a total boycott on the Hāshimite clan, to which the Prophet belonged, so that they would abandon him and hand him over to them. As we are told in this verse, it was also the plan upheld by the hypocrites. They hoped that it would ensure that, once hunger had bitten hard among the believers, they would abandon the Prophet. The communists did the same when they denied the religious among their people the right to their rations. They wanted them to starve to death, or at least until they abandoned their faith in God and stopped praying. Today, the same plan is adopted by other forces hostile to Islamic revival in the Muslim world. They place believers under siege, starving them and closing down all avenues of earning a living.[2]

Thus, we see the opponents of faith, old and new, resorting to this obnoxious and dreadful method, forgetting the simple truth of which the Qur'ān reminds them in the same verse: "*To God belong the treasures of the heavens and the earth, but the hypocrites cannot understand.*" (Verse 7) It is indeed from these treasures of the heavens and the earth, which all

---

2. More recent examples may be given to confirm what the author says. The latest of these is seen in the boycott imposed by Israel and its allies on the Palestinians, causing extreme hardship and starvation so as to force them to abandon their right to their land and homes. – Editor's note.

belong to God Almighty, that these enemies of the truth receive their livelihoods; yet they try to control the means of such livelihood available to believers. Yet they cannot even create their own sustenance. How stupid and dull-minded they are when they think they can stop others from receiving their sustenance!

God thus reassures the believers and strengthens their resolve to face up to such vile and odious plans. He tells them that God's treasures in the heavens and the earth are open to all. He who gives out of these treasures to His enemies will never forget the ones who believe in Him. In His grace, He does not impose mass starvation even on His enemies. He knows that if He were to deny them their provisions they would have nothing. Yet He is too merciful to abandon His servants, even the ones hostile to Him, to what is beyond their means of control. Mass starvation is a method adopted only by the most vile, obnoxious and wicked of people.

The *sūrah* also quotes the hypocrites' other words: "*They say, 'When we return to Madīnah, the more honourable will surely drive out those who are contemptible.*" (Verse 8) We have seen how 'Abdullāh ibn Ubayy's words were made to come true at the hands of his own son, ensuring that the contemptible one could only enter Madīnah by the permission of the most honourable one. "*All honour belongs to God, His Messenger and the believers, but the hypocrites do not know.*" (Verse 8) God includes with Himself His Messenger and the believers, bestowing His own honour on them. This is a gesture of honouring that only God can bestow. What is more honourable than God's hand placing the Prophet and the believers next to Himself and saying: 'Here We are, standing under the banner of honour, and this is the rank of the honourable.'

God certainly tells the truth as He intertwines honour with faith in a believer's heart. Such is the honour that derives from God's own honour. It never shrinks, gives way or abandons a believer, not even in the most difficult of times, unless his faith weakens. When faith is solidly established in a person's heart, honour and dignity remain solid within him. "*But the hypocrites do not know.*" (Verse 8) How are they to know when they do not appreciate this sort of honour and dignity and are cut off from their eternal source?

37

Time to Be Charitable

The last address in the *sūrah* is made to the believers whom God placed, together with His Messenger, in His own rank, making them share in His honour and dignity. He wants them to climb to this high summit, ridding themselves of any characteristic that is akin to those of the hypocrites. They should prefer such superior elevation to everything else, including their property and offspring. Nothing must be allowed to divert their attention from aspiring to such lofty heights:

> *Believers! Do not let your riches or your children make you oblivious of the remembrance of God. Those who do so will surely be the losers. Give, then, out of what We have provided for you, before death comes to any of you, and then he says, 'My Lord, if You would grant me a delay for a short while, I would give in charity and be one of the righteous.' God does not grant a delay to any soul when its term has come. God is fully aware of all that you do.* (Verses 9–11)

Money and children can preoccupy a person making him oblivious to everything else, that is, unless his heart alerts him to the aim of his existence, making him feel that he has a superior goal. This goal must be one that is worthy of the creature in whom God has blown of His own spirit, giving him the aspiration to achieve a few divine characteristics, albeit within his own human limitations. God has given him riches and offspring so as to fulfil his task of building human life on earth, but not so that he is so fully preoccupied with them that they distract him from remembering God and from being in contact with the source of his humanity. Those that are so distracted *"will surely be the losers."* (Verse 9) The first thing they lose is their human identity, which is dependent on maintaining the bond with the source of man's humanity. Whoever loses himself has lost everything, regardless of the size of his wealth and the number of his offspring.

With respect to charitable donations, the *sūrah* here touches their hearts in several ways: *"Give, then, out of what We have provided for you."* (Verse 10) This reminds us of the source of all that we have. It is all from God in whom we believe and who instructs us to be generous

38

and charitable. Such giving should be done *"before death comes to any of you…"* It should be a result of the person's own action before death overtakes him and he leaves everything behind for others to enjoy. If he does not do so then he will look around only to discover that he has put nothing forward for his own salvation. This is the worst stupidity and the greatest loss.

He will then feel pangs of regret and wish he could have more time to be charitable and join with those people who are righteous. Such wishes benefit him nothing, for *"God does not grant a delay to any soul when its term has come."* (Verse 11) How can he now put forward anything when the chance is gone? *"God is fully aware of all that you do."* (Verse 11) Several touches within a short space are thus made at the right place, immediately after depicting the hypocrites' characteristics and their scheming against the believers. When the believers stand firm in God's own rank, they will be protected against the hypocrites. It serves them well, then, to fulfil the duties that their faith requires of them. They must never abandon their remembrance of God, as this is the source of their ultimate safety. Thus does God use the Qur'ān to educate and cultivate believers' minds and hearts.

SŪRAH 64

Al-Taghābun
(Mutual Loss and Gain)

Prologue

In subject matter, images and import, this *sūrah* is very similar to those revealed in Makkah, particularly in its opening section. Indeed, the overall atmosphere that characterizes the *sūrahs* revealed in Madīnah begins to appear only in its concluding section.

The verses from the beginning up to the direct address to the believers in verse 14 aim to establish the foundations of faith and to instil the Islamic concept. Employing the style of Makkan *sūrahs*, it addresses the unbelievers directly, presenting its theme to them. It uses the same universal and psychological effects and portrays images of the destruction of earlier communities that denied God's messages. It also presents images of the Day of Judgement, emphatically confirming resurrection. This indicates that the addressees denied it altogether.

The last verses, from 14 to 18, address the believers in a manner similar to that used in *sūrahs* revealed in Madīnah, urging them to spend their money in the service of God's cause, and warning them against failure in the test that their riches and children represent. Similar addresses can be found in many *sūrahs* of the Madīnah period, and this because of the problems faced by the fledgling Muslim community there. This address also includes a comforting aspect to help the Muslims bear with patience any reversals, calamities or burdens; all these are attributed to

41

God's will. This is the concept these *sūrahs* seek to confirm, particularly after the command given to the Muslim community to fight for God's cause and what this involves of sacrifice.

Several reports suggest that this *sūrah* was revealed in Makkah, but other reports, given more weight, state that it was in fact a Madīnan revelation. I almost leaned to the view that it was Makkan, because of the style of its earlier sections and its general ambience. Eventually, however, I decided to stick to the more preponderant view that its revelation was Madīnan. There is nothing to preclude those earlier sections from addressing the unbelievers after the Prophet's migration to Madīnah, whether those unbelievers were the people of Makkah or others living closer to Madīnah. Likewise, there is nothing to exclude the possibility that Madīnan *sūrahs* should at times clarify the fundamentals of faith and the Islamic concept of life, using the same style that we find in what was revealed in Makkah.

Al-Taghābūn
(Mutual Loss and Gain)

In the Name of God, the Lord of Grace, the Ever Merciful

All that is in the heavens and all that is on earth extol the limitless glory of God; all sovereignty belongs to Him and all praise is due to Him. He has power over all things. (1)

It is He who has created you, yet some of you are unbelievers and some do believe. God sees all that you do. (2)

He has created the heavens and the earth in accordance with the truth, and fashioned you, giving you a comely appearance. To Him all shall return. (3)

He knows what is in the heavens and the earth; and He knows what you conceal and what you reveal. God has full knowledge of the secrets of all hearts. (4)

Have you not heard of those who disbelieved in earlier times? They tasted the evil consequences of their own doings. Painful suffering still awaits them. (5)

بِسْمِ اللَّهِ الرَّحْمَنِ الرَّحِيمِ

يُسَبِّحُ لِلَّهِ مَا فِي السَّمَوَاتِ وَمَا فِي الْأَرْضِ لَهُ الْمُلْكُ وَلَهُ الْحَمْدُ وَهُوَ عَلَى كُلِّ شَيْءٍ قَدِيرٌ ﴿١﴾

هُوَ الَّذِي خَلَقَكُمْ فَمِنكُمْ كَافِرٌ وَمِنكُم مُّؤْمِنٌ وَاللَّهُ بِمَا تَعْمَلُونَ بَصِيرٌ ﴿٢﴾

خَلَقَ السَّمَوَاتِ وَالْأَرْضَ بِالْحَقِّ وَصَوَّرَكُمْ فَأَحْسَنَ صُوَرَكُمْ وَإِلَيْهِ الْمَصِيرُ ﴿٣﴾

يَعْلَمُ مَا فِي السَّمَوَاتِ وَالْأَرْضِ وَيَعْلَمُ مَا تُسِرُّونَ وَمَا تُعْلِنُونَ وَاللَّهُ عَلِيمٌ بِذَاتِ الصُّدُورِ ﴿٤﴾

أَلَمْ يَأْتِكُمْ نَبَأُ الَّذِينَ كَفَرُوا مِن قَبْلُ فَذَاقُوا وَبَالَ أَمْرِهِمْ وَلَهُمْ عَذَابٌ أَلِيمٌ ﴿٥﴾

That is because their messengers came to them with clear signs, but they said, 'Shall mere mortals be our guides?' So, they denied the truth and turned away. God is free of all need. God is self-sufficient, worthy of all praise. (6)

ذَٰلِكَ بِأَنَّهُۥ كَانَت تَّأْتِيهِمْ رُسُلُهُم بِٱلْبَيِّنَٰتِ فَقَالُوٓا۟ أَبَشَرٌ يَهْدُونَنَا فَكَفَرُوا۟ وَتَوَلَّوا۟ وَّٱسْتَغْنَى ٱللَّهُ وَٱللَّهُ غَنِىٌّ حَمِيدٌ ﴿٦﴾

The unbelievers allege that they will not be raised from the dead. Say, 'Yes indeed! By my Lord, you will certainly be raised from the dead, and then you will certainly be told of all that you have done. This is easy for God.' (7)

زَعَمَ ٱلَّذِينَ كَفَرُوٓا۟ أَن لَّن يُبْعَثُوا۟ قُلْ بَلَىٰ وَرَبِّى لَتُبْعَثُنَّ ثُمَّ لَتُنَبَّؤُنَّ بِمَا عَمِلْتُمْ وَذَٰلِكَ عَلَى ٱللَّهِ يَسِيرٌ ﴿٧﴾

Believe then in God and His Messenger, and in the light which We have bestowed from on high. God is fully aware of what you do. (8)

فَـَٔامِنُوا۟ بِٱللَّهِ وَرَسُولِهِۦ وَٱلنُّورِ ٱلَّذِىٓ أَنزَلْنَا وَٱللَّهُ بِمَا تَعْمَلُونَ خَبِيرٌ ﴿٨﴾

[Think of] the time when He will gather you all together for the Day of the Gathering, the day of mutual loss and gain. For anyone who shall have believed in God and done what is right, He will efface his bad deeds and will admit him into gardens through which running waters flow, where they will abide for ever. That is the supreme triumph. (9)

يَوْمَ يَجْمَعُكُمْ لِيَوْمِ ٱلْجَمْعِ ذَٰلِكَ يَوْمُ ٱلتَّغَابُنِ وَمَن يُؤْمِنۢ بِٱللَّهِ وَيَعْمَلْ صَٰلِحًا يُكَفِّرْ عَنْهُ سَيِّـَٔاتِهِۦ وَيُدْخِلْهُ جَنَّٰتٍ تَجْرِى مِن تَحْتِهَا ٱلْأَنْهَٰرُ خَٰلِدِينَ فِيهَآ أَبَدًا ذَٰلِكَ ٱلْفَوْزُ ٱلْعَظِيمُ ﴿٩﴾

But those who disbelieve and deny Our revelations are destined for the fire where they will abide. How miserable an end! (10)

وَٱلَّذِينَ كَفَرُوا۟ وَكَذَّبُوا۟ بِـَٔايَٰتِنَآ أُو۟لَٰٓئِكَ أَصْحَٰبُ ٱلنَّارِ خَٰلِدِينَ فِيهَا ۖ وَبِئْسَ ٱلْمَصِيرُ ۝

No calamity can ever befall anyone except by God's leave. He will guide the heart of anyone who believes in Him. God has full knowledge of all things. (11)

مَآ أَصَابَ مِن مُّصِيبَةٍ إِلَّا بِإِذْنِ ٱللَّهِ ۗ وَمَن يُؤْمِنۢ بِٱللَّهِ يَهْدِ قَلْبَهُۥ ۚ وَٱللَّهُ بِكُلِّ شَىْءٍ عَلِيمٌ ۝

So obey God, and obey the Messenger. If you turn away, know that Our Messenger's only duty is to deliver his message in full clarity. (12)

وَأَطِيعُوا۟ ٱللَّهَ وَأَطِيعُوا۟ ٱلرَّسُولَ ۚ فَإِن تَوَلَّيْتُمْ فَإِنَّمَا عَلَىٰ رَسُولِنَا ٱلْبَلَٰغُ ٱلْمُبِينُ ۝

God: there is no deity other than Him. In God, then, let the believers place their trust. (13)

ٱللَّهُ لَآ إِلَٰهَ إِلَّا هُوَ ۚ وَعَلَى ٱللَّهِ فَلْيَتَوَكَّلِ ٱلْمُؤْمِنُونَ ۝

Believers, some of your spouses and children are enemies to you; so beware of them. Yet if you overlook their faults, pardon and forgive, God is Much-Forgiving, Ever Merciful. (14)

يَٰٓأَيُّهَا ٱلَّذِينَ ءَامَنُوٓا۟ إِنَّ مِنْ أَزْوَٰجِكُمْ وَأَوْلَٰدِكُمْ عَدُوًّا لَّكُمْ فَٱحْذَرُوهُمْ ۚ وَإِن تَعْفُوا۟ وَتَصْفَحُوا۟ وَتَغْفِرُوا۟ فَإِنَّ ٱللَّهَ غَفُورٌ رَّحِيمٌ ۝

Your wealth and children are only a trial and a temptation, whereas with God there is a great reward. (15)

إِنَّمَآ أَمْوَٰلُكُمْ وَأَوْلَٰدُكُمْ فِتْنَةٌ ۚ وَٱللَّهُ عِندَهُۥٓ أَجْرٌ عَظِيمٌ ۝

Therefore, remain God-fearing as best as you can, listen, obey and be charitable. That will be best for you. Those that are preserved from their own meanness are the ones who will achieve success. (16)

فَٱتَّقُوا۟ ٱللَّهَ مَا ٱسْتَطَعْتُمْ وَٱسْمَعُوا۟ وَأَطِيعُوا۟ وَأَنفِقُوا۟ خَيْرًا لِّأَنفُسِكُمْ ۗ وَمَن يُوقَ شُحَّ نَفْسِهِۦ فَأُو۟لَٰٓئِكَ هُمُ ٱلْمُفْلِحُونَ ۝

If you make a goodly loan to God, He will repay you in multiples, and will forgive you your sins. God is ever thankful, forbearing. (17)

إِن تُقْرِضُوا۟ ٱللَّهَ قَرْضًا حَسَنًا يُضَٰعِفْهُ لَكُمْ وَيَغْفِرْ لَكُمْ ۚ وَٱللَّهُ شَكُورٌ حَلِيمٌ ۝

He knows all that is beyond the reach of human perception and all that is witnessed; the Almighty, the Wise. (18)

عَٰلِمُ ٱلْغَيْبِ وَٱلشَّهَٰدَةِ ٱلْعَزِيزُ ٱلْحَكِيمُ ۝

The Creator and His Creation

The first section of the *sūrah* aims to establish the proper concept of the universe based on faith, present the true bond between the Creator and the universe He has created, and mention some of God's names and attributes as well as their effect on the universe and on human life:

All that is in the heavens and all that is on earth extol the limitless glory of God; all sovereignty belongs to Him and all praise is due to Him. He has power over all things. It is He who has created you, yet some of you are unbelievers and some do believe. God sees all that you do. He has created the heavens and the earth in accordance with the truth, and fashioned you, giving you a comely appearance. To Him all shall return. He knows what is in the heavens and the earth; and He knows what you conceal and what you reveal. God has full knowledge of the secrets of all hearts. (Verses 1–4)

This concept is one hundred per cent accurate: it depicts what believers have always known and followed. All divine messages have preached the concept of God's oneness and His creation of everything in the universe. They all make it clear that God takes care of everyone and everything in the universe. We have no doubt about this, since the Qur'ān confirms the same about all God's messengers and the messages they advocated. Hence, we pay little attention to what we find today in distorted scriptures or to what is written on comparative religion by people who do not believe in the Qur'ān, in whole or in part. Deviation from the true divine faith is the result of what has been introduced by some followers of these messages, giving the appearance that they did not preach the pure concept of God's oneness, or that God is not in full control and direct contact with every creature. All this is deviation and does not belong to the original form of any divine religion, which remains the same from the first to the last of God's messages. It is impossible that God should have sent down a religion that is in conflict with these essential principles, as alleged by scriptures that have been distorted.

This pure concept allows the human mind to understand, as best as it can, the true nature of Godhead, feel the power of the Almighty, and recognize it in everything we see in the universe. We can thus see the work of this supreme power within ourselves, live within its scope, and appreciate its effects that cannot be removed from our senses or our minds. We see it encompassing everything, conducting all affairs, controlling all events, taking care of all. Nothing escapes it, small or large, trivial or important. This means that the human heart will always be highly sensitive, truly alert, entertaining feelings of apprehension and expectation, fear and hope. Thus man goes about life, looking up to God with every move and every action, feeling His power and realizing that He sees all, watches all and controls all. Yet He is also ever merciful to all and bestows His grace on everyone and in all situations.

Moreover, this concept enables us to feel that the entire universe turns to its Lord. So, we turn with the universe and join it in extolling God's limitless glory. We realize that the whole universe is controlled by God's will, subject to His wisdom, and so we submit to His law. This is why we describe it as a universal concept of faith. Its universality is emphasized in a variety of ways throughout the Qur'ān. A clear example can be found in the concluding verses of *Sūrah* 59, The Gathering, discussed in Volume XVI.

God's Limitless Power

"*All that is in the heavens and all that is on earth extol the limitless glory of God; all sovereignty belongs to Him and all praise is due to Him.*" (Verse 1) Everything in the heavens and the earth turns towards their Lord, extolling His limitless glory and praising Him. The heart of this universe is a believing heart, and the soul of everything that exists is a believer. God owns all, and they all know this truth. God is praised in Himself, glorified by all His creation. When man alone stands in the midst of this great universe rebelling against the truth, cold-hearted, spiritless, turning away from his Lord and Master, refusing to glorify Him, he is at odds with all, discarded by all.

"*He has power over all things.*" (Verse 1) His is absolute, limitless and unrestricted power. The Qur'ān impresses this truth on every believer's heart. As the believer recognizes its significance, he knows that placing his trust in God alone means that he relies on the power that can do and achieve everything, without limit or restriction. This understanding of God's power and His glorification and praise by all that exists is part of the universal concept of faith Islam formulates.

The second point penetrates deep into the human heart. It is man alone who stands in the midst of the universe in two states of belief and unbelief, while all the universe believes in its Creator, and extols His limitless glory and praise: "*It is He who has created you, yet some of you are unbelievers and some do believe.*" (Verse 2) It is by God's will and through His power that man was originated. He gave him the ability to turn to or away from faith. Thus man is distinguished among God's creation by this dual ability. Hence, he is assigned the great trust and momentous responsibility of faith. Therefore, God has honoured this creature by giving him the ability to distinguish truth from falsehood; furthermore, the choice is up to him. He has also given him the standard by which he can evaluate his own actions and determine his way. This standard is the religion God revealed to human messengers. In this way,

God has helped man to shoulder the trust assigned to him, depriving him of nothing that he needs. *"God sees all that you do."* (Verse 2) He watches man's actions, knows his true intentions and the direction he takes. Let man, then, go about life alert to the fact that he is watched by the One who sees all. This concept of man's nature is part of the clear and straightforward Islamic concept of man's position in the universe, as well as his abilities and responsibilities towards the Creator of the universe.

The third point emphasizes the truth that is inherent in the nature of the universe and which ensures the proper functioning of the heavens and the earth. It also highlights the fine beauty of God's creation as seen in the creation of man himself. It also makes it clear that all creatures will ultimately return to Him: *"He has created the heavens and the earth in accordance with the truth, and fashioned you, giving you a comely appearance. To Him all shall return."* (Verse 3)

The first sentence in this verse, *"He has created the heavens and the earth in accordance with the truth,"* implants in a believer's mind that the truth is firmly established in the very foundation of this universe. It is neither transitory nor incidental. The very structure of the universe is founded on this basis. This is stated by none other than God who created the heavens and the earth and knows what foundation He has given them. When this fact is firmly settled in our consciousness, it gives us total reassurance about the basis of our faith: it is the same truth that serves as the foundation of the universe. This means that this faith must inevitably triumph, and must remain pure and well established. Whatever else is false and will certainly be swept away.

Another fact is stated in the same verse, *"and [He] fashioned you, giving you a comely appearance."* This gives man the feeling that he has special privilege with God who has bestowed on him the blessing of a comely appearance, both physically and spiritually. Man is the most perfected creature on earth in respect of his physical constitution and his spiritual qualities, which also entails marvellous secrets. Hence, he has been placed in charge of the earth, which is a vast area by human standards. A careful glance at man's general physical constitution, or at any of his physical systems, is sufficient to portray this fact most clearly: God *"fashioned you, giving you a comely appearance."* It is an

49

appearance that combines beauty and perfection. The beauty varies between one physical form and another, but the design itself is so beautiful and so well executed, that it enables all functions and qualities that distinguish man above all other living creatures to work together perfectly.

"*To Him all shall return.*" Every thing, situation and creature will return to Him. The ultimate destiny of the universe and with it the ultimate destiny of man is with Him. It is from His will that they originated and to Him they will return. He is the First and the Last who holds every thing from its both ends, the beginning and the end. He, in His limitless glory, is not restricted by anything.

The fourth point in the opening section of the *sūrah* describes God's perfect knowledge that includes all and every thing. He is fully aware of what man declares and what he conceals, and knows what is even more deeply hidden than the deepest and closest of secrets. He knows what people entertain deep in their hearts: "*He knows what is in the heavens and the earth; and He knows what you conceal and what you reveal. God has full knowledge of the secrets of all hearts.*" (Verse 4) When this fact is firmly established in man's mind it gives him a better knowledge of his Lord, contributing to his concept of the universe. It influences his feelings. He leads his life fully aware that God knows all there is to know about him, including his most secret thoughts and unexpressed feelings.

The three verses that follow the first are enough to enable man to live with the full awareness of the truth of his existence and that of the universe around him. He will also be aware of the bond he has with his Lord, how he should behave towards Him and how to fear Him in every situation in which he finds himself.

The Unbelievers' Objections

The second section reminds us of the fate of earlier communities that denied God's messages and the signs He gave them. They objected to the fact that God assigned His messages to human messengers, in the same way as the idolaters in Makkah objected to the Prophet Muḥammad (peace be upon him) and denied all the clear proof he put before them:

Have you not heard of those who disbelieved in earlier times? They tasted the evil consequences of their own doings. Painful suffering still awaits them. That is because their messengers came to them with clear signs, but they said, 'Shall mere mortals be our guides?' So, they denied the truth and turned away. God is free of all need. God is self-sufficient, worthy of all praise. (Verses 5–6)

The addressees here are, most probably, the unbelievers. They are reminded of the fates suffered by earlier communities who denied the truth, and warned against a similar fate. The interrogative form is adopted either as a denunciation of their stubbornness after they have been given such information or it is used to draw their attention to this same history that relates to them. They were fully aware of what happened to some of these communities, such as the 'Ād, Thamūd and the towns of Sodom and Gomorrah. In fact, they passed by them in their trips to the north and south of Arabia.

The Qur'ān mentions their fate in this life and states what awaits them in the life to come: "*Painful suffering still awaits them.*" (Verse 5) It then explains why they deserved what happened to them and what they are still to face: "*That is because their messengers came to them with clear signs, but they said, 'Shall mere mortals be our guides?'*" (Verse 6) It is the same objection voiced by the Makkan idolaters to the Prophet. It is an arrogant objection that betrays a total ignorance of the nature of the divine message and its being a code to be implemented in human life. Hence, it must be practically represented in a human being, in the Messenger who lives according to it and presents a model of its implementation. Thus, others will then be able to mould their own lives in the same way, and to the best of their abilities. Were the Messenger to belong to any other than the human race, people would not have had a practical example against which to mould their feelings and lives. Moreover, this objection betrays ignorance of the true nature of man and his elevated status, which enables him to receive and deliver a divine message instead of God assigning it to an angel, as the unbelievers frequently suggested. Man carries the spirit of God breathed into him when God first created Adam. This prepares him to receive God's message and to deliver it complete as he receives it from

51

on high. This is an honour bestowed on the human race, rejected only by those who are ignorant of the high status God gives to man when, within his own personal world, he gives full effect to this breath of God's spirit in him. Furthermore, the objection reflects the arrogance and false pride of those who refuse to follow a human messenger, as if such following would detract from the status of those ignorant, arrogant unbelievers. To them, it is acceptable to follow a messenger who belongs to a different kind of creature, but to follow one from their own ranks is too unbecoming.

Therefore, they disbelieved in God's messengers and turned away from them, rejecting the clear proofs and signs that they brought them. Their pride, combined with their ignorance of human nature, stood as a barrier preventing them from accepting the truth. Thus, they chose to turn away from God's guidance and to disbelieve in Him. "*So, they denied the truth and turned away.*" (Verse 6)

"*God is free of all need. God is self-sufficient, worthy of all praise.*" (Verse 6) He does not need that they should accept His guidance, nor does He need their worship. Indeed, He needs nothing from them or from anyone else. He is free of all need.

Such is the story of those who in earlier times denied God's messages and were made to taste the fruits of their unbelief. It also explains the reasons behind what happened to them and what awaits them in the life to come. How can present generations follow in their footsteps and deny the truth now? How can they risk a similar fate?

The Truth of Resurrection

The third section carries the theme of the previous one further, stating the situation of those unbelievers who deny the resurrection. It is clearly apparent that these were the idolaters whom the Prophet addressed, calling on them to believe in his message. This section instructs the Prophet to confirm, most emphatically, to them that the resurrection will certainly take place. Indeed, it adds a scene from the Day of Judgement that depicts the fates of the two groups who either deny or accept it. It calls on them to believe, obey and attribute everything that happens in the world to God Almighty:

The unbelievers allege that they will not be raised from the dead. Say, 'Yes indeed! By my Lord, you will certainly be raised from the dead, and then you will certainly be told of all that you have done. This is easy for God.' Believe then in God and His Messenger, and in the light which We have bestowed from on high. God is fully aware of what you do. [Think of] the time when He will gather you all together for the Day of the Gathering, the day of mutual loss and gain. For anyone who shall have believed in God and done what is right, He will efface his bad deeds and will admit him into gardens through which running waters flow, where they will abide for ever. That is the supreme triumph. But those who disbelieve and deny Our revelations are destined for the fire where they will abide. How miserable an end! No calamity can ever befall anyone except by God's leave. He will guide the heart of anyone who believes in Him. God has full knowledge of all things. So obey God, and obey the Messenger. If you turn away, know that Our Messenger's only duty is to deliver his message in full clarity. God: there is no deity other than Him. In God, then, let the believers place their trust. (Verses 7–13)

Right from the start the *sūrah* describes the unbelievers' argument as an 'allegation', thereby branding it as a lie. It follows this with a directive to the Prophet to assert his message of resurrection most emphatically, swearing by his Lord to its truth. Nothing can be more emphatic than an oath the Prophet makes by his Lord. "*Say: Yes indeed! By my Lord, you will certainly be raised from the dead, and then you will certainly be told of all that you have done.*" (Verse 7) Nothing of it will suffer neglect. God knows their deeds better than they do, so He will tell them all about it on the Day of Resurrection. "*This is easy for God.*" He knows all that is in the heavens and the earth, open and secret, as well as what is in people's hearts, expressed or otherwise. He also has power over all things, as stated earlier in the *sūrah*.

The *sūrah* then calls on them to believe in God and His Messenger, and in the light He has given His Messenger, which is the Qur'ān and the faith embodied in the Qur'ān. It is indeed light, since it comes from God, and "*God is the light of the heavens and the earth.*" (24: 35) The Qur'ān enlightens the heart to make it shine, able to see the truth inherent within it: *"Believe then in God and His Messenger, and in the light which We have bestowed from on high."* (Verse 8) This call on them to believe is followed by a comment that makes them realize that their situation is fully observed by God: *"God is fully aware of what you do."* (Verse 8)

The next verse continues to draw the scene of the Day of Resurrection: *"[Think of] the time when He will gather you all together for the Day of the Gathering, the day of mutual loss and gain."* (Verse 9) It is called the Day of the Gathering because all creatures from all generations are gathered together on that day, which is also attended by the angels. Only God knows the numbers of the angels, but we may have a sense of it when we reflect on the following *ḥadīth* in which Abū Dharr quotes the Prophet as saying: "I see and hear what you do not. The heavens is noisily bustling, and rightly so: there is not a four-finger width in it but occupied by an angel with his forehead placed low in prostration before God. Were you to know what I know, you would have laughed but a little and wept much, and you would not have enjoyed being in bed with women. You would have gone up the hills and mountains earnestly appealing to God. I wish I were a tree to be felled." [Related by al-Tirmidhī.] The heaven in which there is an angel in every little space of four fingers is this great expanse for which we know no limit, and in which a sun like ours appears to be no more than a fine particle floating in the air. Does this then give us an approximation for the number of angels in it? Furthermore, all these angels will form part of the assembled mass of creatures on the Day of Gathering.

It will be in front of this great assembly that the loss and gain will take place: the believers will take all happiness purely for themselves while the unbelievers will be totally deprived of it before being sent to hell. These are two greatly different lots. The sense we receive is that of a competition where the winners take all. Hence, each side wants to deprive its competitors. The believers end up winners and the unbelievers losers. This is what is meant by 'mutual loss and gain', as explained in the same verse and that which follows: *"For anyone who shall have believed in God and done what is right, He will efface his bad deeds and will admit him into gardens through which running waters flow, where they will abide for ever. That is the supreme triumph. But those who disbelieve and deny Our revelations are destined for the fire where they will abide. How miserable an end!"* (Verses 9–10)

Before completing the call to them to believe, the *sūrah* states one of the main elements of the Islamic faith, which is to believe in God's will and the effect of belief in God on the human heart: *"No calamity can ever befall anyone except by God's leave. He will guide the heart of anyone who believes in Him. God has full knowledge of all things."* (Verse 11)

Perhaps this fact is stated here only to put it clearly within the context of the faith they are called upon to adopt. It is a belief that attributes everything to God, and whatever good or evil takes place occurs only by God's will. This is an essential fact without which faith is incomplete. It is indeed the basis of all feelings a believer may have when facing life events and situations, good and happy or bad and miserable. On the other hand, this fact is stated here in response to something that took place and was clear in people's minds at the time of the revelation of this *sūrah* or this verse. Regardless of the exact situation, this fact represents an important aspect of the concept Islam implants in a believer's consciousness. He thus feels God's hand behind every event and every move. He receives with a calm heart whatever happens to him, whether it brings him happiness or adversity. He expresses his gratitude in the first case and demonstrates patience in the second. Alternatively, he may rise to a higher level, expressing his thanks to God in both cases of happiness and adversity, feeling that both bring him God's blessings. He then sees adversity as a reminder for him or an occasion that may bring him forgiveness of past sins or an increase in his reward. In an authentic *ḥadīth*, the Prophet is quoted as saying: "Amazing is the believer's situation: whatever God determines is good for him. Should he meet with adversity, he resorts to patience and this is good for him, while if he meets with what is pleasant, he expresses his gratitude to God, and this is good for him. This situation applies to no one other than a believer." [Related by al-Bukhārī and Muslim.]

"He will guide the heart of anyone who believes in Him." (Verse 11) Some commentators explain this as meaning belief in God's will and being resigned to it in the event of facing a calamity. Ibn 'Abbās, however, takes this statement as indicating complete guidance granted to believing hearts, making them recognize the absolute truth. Thus

55

they attribute all things and all events to God, their source and goal. This provides them with reassurance and comfort. With such a complete and comprehensive vision, they are not encumbered by a partial view that may be deficient or erroneous. Hence, the comment at the end of the verse: *"God has full knowledge of all things."* (Verse 11) It is, then, guidance to a share of God's knowledge. God grants this guidance to a person who truly believes, thus earning the prize of knowing something of what lies beyond this limited human life.

The *sūrah* continues with its call on people to believe, calling them now to obey God and His Messenger: *"So obey God, and obey the Messenger. If you turn away, know that Our Messenger's only duty is to deliver his message in full clarity."* (Verse 12) The *sūrah* has already shown them the end suffered by earlier communities who turned away. Now it tells them that the role of God's Messenger is only to deliver His message. When he has done this, he has fulfilled the trust assigned to him and put the proof before them. What remains is the fate merited by those who are stubborn in disobedience and rejection. They have already been reminded of this.

This section concludes by restating the truth of God's oneness, which they persistently deny. It also states the believers' attitude in dealing with God: *"God: there is no deity other than Him. In God, then, let the believers place their trust."* (Verse 13) The truth of God's oneness is the essence of faith. Its practical import is to place one's total trust in God and to rely on Him alone. This verse provides a bridge between these sections of the *sūrah* and its final one which comes as an address to the believers.

Spouses and Children as Enemies

In the final section the *sūrah* addresses the believers, warning them against failure in the test represented in the temptation spouses, children and riches offer. They are required to remain God-fearing, be obedient to Him and give willingly for His cause. They are warned against being stingy. They are further promised the doubling of their provisions, forgiveness of their sins and success. They are finally reminded of God's all-encompassing knowledge, power and wisdom:

Believers, some of your spouses and children are enemies to you; so beware of them. Yet if you overlook their faults, pardon and forgive, God is much-forgiving, ever merciful. Your wealth and children are only a trial and a temptation, whereas with God there is a great reward. Therefore, remain God-fearing as best as you can, listen, obey and be charitable. That will be best for you. Those that are preserved from their own meanness are the ones who will achieve success. If you make a goodly loan to God, He will repay you in multiples, and will forgive you your sins. God is ever thankful, forbearing. He knows all that is beyond the reach of human perception and all that is witnessed; the Almighty, the Wise. (Verses 14–18)

A man asked Ibn 'Abbās about the first verse in this section and it is reported that he told him that there were some people in Makkah who accepted Islam and wanted to join the Prophet in Madīnah, but their spouses and children prevented them. When they ultimately joined him, they realized that those who were already with the Prophet had acquired insight in their religion. Therefore, they wanted to punish their spouses and children for having kept them away. God then revealed this verse telling them: "*If you overlook their faults, pardon and forgive, God is much-forgiving, ever merciful.*" (Verse 14) This *ḥadīth* is related by al-Tirmidhī who describes it as authentic. The same opinion is expressed by 'Ikrimah, Ibn 'Abbās's disciple.

The Qur'ānic statement is wider in scope and import than this particular situation represents. For this warning is the same as that in the following verse: "*Your wealth and children are only a trial and a temptation.*" (Verse 15) Both caution against the temptation that wives, children and wealth present. The warning that some spouses and children may be one's enemies refers to a true fact in human life. In this way, the verses touch upon some intricate and complex ties in man's emotions and how they are influenced by life's circumstances. Spouses and children may divert a person's attention from God's remembrance. They may also make a man fall short of discharging the responsibilities required of his faith; this in order to spare himself the troubles that he may face as a result of fulfilling such responsibilities. A person who strives for God's cause may be exposed to much loss and may have to sacrifice a great deal. He and his family may have to withstand much hardship. He may be willing to face such hardship himself, but cannot bear that such hardship be suffered by his wife and children. As a result, he may be tight-fisted and cowardly in order to ensure that they are safe, free of trouble and financially secure. Thus, they become his enemies as they turn him away from doing what is good and stop him from fulfilling the ultimate objective of his existence. Indeed, they may even stand in his way, stopping him from fulfilling his duty. In doing so, they may wish to spare themselves what may happen as a result, or they may not share his belief. In this way, man finds himself unable to separate himself from them and dedicate himself to God's cause. This is also a form of enmity that may vary in degrees. Furthermore, such situations are faced by believers at all times.

This very complex situation merits such a caution from God as to alert believers' hearts so that they do not allow such feelings and pressures to creep into their minds. The caution is stated again, this time as a warning against the temptation presented by wealth and children. The Arabic word used here is *fitnah*, which conveys two meanings. The first is 'trial', which makes the verse mean that God puts you to trial by giving you riches and children. He tests you in this way, so always be on the alert in order to pass your test and dedicate yourself to God. The second meaning is 'temptation', and in this sense the verse means that riches and children present temptations for you to indulge in sin. Beware then and do not allow such temptations to distract you from the way that leads to God's acceptance. Both meanings are acceptable.

Imām Aḥmad relates on the authority of Buraydah, a Companion of the Prophet: "The Prophet was delivering a sermon when al-Ḥasan and al-Ḥusayn came wearing two red shirts and tripping as they walked. The Prophet got down from the pulpit and took them up, placing them next to him. He then said: 'God and His Messenger speak the truth: *Your wealth and children are only a trial and a temptation.* I saw these two young boys tripping as they walked, and I could not wait. I had to interrupt my speech to lift them up." Thus did the Prophet do with his two grandchildren. It is, then, a very serious matter. Therefore alerting people to it and making them aware of what it may lead to is necessary, as God, who created people and gave them their natural feelings, knows. They can then restrain themselves so as not to allow such feelings to dictate their behaviour, knowing that such loving bonds could end up causing them what an enemy tries to cause. Therefore, when the warning is given and the encouragement is made to pass the test and to overcome the temptation, they are reminded of what God has in store for them: "*whereas with God there is a great reward.*" (Verse 15)

The believers are admonished to do their best to remain God-fearing and to obey God's orders: "*Therefore, remain God-fearing as best as you can, listen, obey and be charitable.*" (Verse 16) Here we see an aspect of God's care as He restricts what is expected of the believers to that which remains within their power and ability. He knows the limit of what they can do in obedience of Him. The Prophet says: "When I give you an order, do it as best you can, and when I prohibit something, refrain from it completely." [Related by al-Bukhārī and Muslim.] Limits cannot be set on obeying an order to do something. Therefore, what is within one's ability and power is sufficient. On the other hand, prohibition cannot be divided. It is required in full.

They are also called upon to be generous in what they donate: "*And be charitable. That will be best for you.*" (Verse 16) Normally, they spend their money on their own needs. God instructs them to spend in charity what is good for themselves. Thus, when they are charitable, they are actually spending their money on what is good for themselves. The *sūrah* also depicts meanness as a plague, one they must try to get rid of. He is happy who manages to achieve this: "*Those that are preserved from their own meanness are the ones who will achieve success.*" (Verse 16)

The *sūrah* goes on encouraging them to be charitable, making it desirable for them. It describes such charity as a loan given to God. Who would want to lose the opportunity to give his Master a loan? God accepts the loan, repays it many times over, forgives the lender his sins, thanks the lender and forbears with him when he falls short of thanking Him: "*If you make a goodly loan to God, He will repay you in multiples, and will forgive you your sins. God is ever thankful, forbearing.*" (Verse 17) Blessed be God's name: how generous and great He is! It is He who creates man, His servant, and then gives him all his provisions. He then asks him to give him as a loan some of what is surplus to his needs. He repays this loan in multiples and thanks His servant and forbears when His servant is not as grateful to Him as he should be.

God thus teaches us how to rise above our weaknesses and shortcomings and how to aspire to the sublime, trying to be like Him, albeit within our limited abilities. God has breathed of His spirit into man, so that man will always aspire to achieve this ideal, within the scope of his nature and ability. Therefore, the sublime remains open for man always to aspire to. He can try to rise step after step so that he can meet God presenting what He likes him to present and what earns him His pleasure.

The section then concludes with a statement of God's knowledge and wisdom: "*He knows all that is beyond the reach of human perception and all that is witnessed; the Almighty, the Wise.*" (Verse 18) Everything is within His knowledge, subject to His power, conducted according to His wisdom. As they go through life, people should realize that they remain under God's watchful eye, are subject to His power, and that everything takes place by His will. When this truth is appreciated by people, they will remain God-fearing and respond to Him only as they should.

SŪRAH 65

Al-Ṭalāq
(Divorce)

Prologue

This *sūrah*, Divorce, is an outline by God of the rules governing divorce, discussing in detail those cases that were not discussed in the other *sūrah* that tackles this important issue, *Sūrah* 2, The Cow. The *sūrah* also deals with a number of other family issues that result from divorce. It specifies the time when divorce may take place if it is to gain God's approval and to follow His law: "*Prophet! When you divorce women, divorce them with a view to their prescribed waiting period.*" (Verse 1) It states the divorced woman's right and duty to stay in her family home, i.e. her divorcing husband's home, during her waiting period. She cannot be turned out and should not leave of her own accord except in situations where a woman has committed an act of gross indecency: "*Do not drive them out of their homes, nor shall they themselves leave, unless they commit a flagrant indecency.*" (Verse 1) It also specifies the woman's right to leave home after the end of her waiting period and her freedom to do what she likes, unless her husband has reinstated the marriage within the waiting period. Should this occur, it should only be to resume normal married life between them. It cannot be done to cause the woman any harm or to deprive her of the chance to marry a different man: "*When they have completed their appointed term, either retain them in fair manner or part with them in fair manner.*" (Verse 2) Whichever

61

option is followed, retaining the marriage or allowing the break up to be complete, it should be in the presence of witnesses: *"Call to witness two persons of known probity from among yourselves."* (Verse 2)

In *Sūrah* 2, the waiting period of a woman who has not yet reached the menopause is specified as three cycles, counting either the time of menstruation or the time of cleanliness. The scholarly difference here is based on the linguistic meaning of the term used in the *sūrah*, *qur'*, which applies to either period. In this *sūrah*, the waiting period of a divorced woman who has passed the menopause or who is too young to have a period is specified: *"As for those of your women who are beyond the age of monthly courses, as well as for those who do not have any courses, their waiting period, if you have any doubt, is three months."* (Verse 4) Likewise, the waiting period of a pregnant divorcee is specified: *"As for those who are with child, their waiting term shall end when they deliver their burden."* (Verse 4)

The *sūrah* also includes rulings on the home where a divorced woman lives during her waiting period and, if she is pregnant, her right to maintenance until she has delivered the baby: *"Let them dwell wherever you dwell, according to your means, and do not harass them so as to make their lives a misery. If they are with child, maintain them until they have delivered their burden."* (Verse 6) The *sūrah* then goes on to give detailed rules about the breast-feeding of a divorcee's child and her right to financial compensation if she so breast-feeds the child, if the two parents agree this is in the child's best interests, as also provisions for the child's breast-feeding by another woman if the two cannot agree: *"If, after that, they suckle your infants, pay them for it. Take counsel with one another in a fair manner. If some of you make things difficult, let another woman suckle the child."* (Verse 6) The *sūrah* then adds further details on maintenance and compensation in all cases, making it commensurate with the financial means of the divorcing husband: *"Let the one who has ample means spend in accordance with his means; and let the one whose provisions are restricted spend according to what God has given him. God does not burden anyone with more than He has given them."* (Verse 7)

Thus, the *sūrah* takes up all divorce situations. providing detailed legislation for each context. It caters for every problem that results from the collapse of the family, providing a comfortable solution that combines clarity with care, ease and attention to detail.

Taking Divorce Seriously

This *sūrah* is remarkable in the way it tackles divorce and the situations that may result from it. It brings together many aspects of encouragement and warning, and gives comments on every order and ruling. It links the question of divorce to God's will as it works in the heavens and the earth, and to God's law that brings destruction to those who stubbornly disobey Him. By the same token, it also provides comfort and increased provisions to those who remain God-fearing. It repeats its directive to treat the other party with kindness, forbearance and mutual consideration, always preferring to do a good turn. It holds out the prospect of people receiving better results, reminding them of God's will and how it applies to creation, the provision of sustenance, and in cases of ease and affliction.

We can only look with amazement at the numerous universal truths brought together in a *sūrah* that primarily deals with divorce. The theme is taken so seriously that the *sūrah* begins making its address to the Prophet personally, although it is intended as a general address to all believers. The *sūrah* is also remarkable in the way it deals with each situation in great detail, requiring that its provisions and rulings be implemented while maintaining a fear of God. We also note that the comments given are numerous, coupled with promises of reward and warning against punishment. These comments, long and frequent as they are, give the impression that this question is the total sum of Islam. It is the question determined by God who watches how His instructions are put into effect. Those who implement them with a genuine God-fearing sense need fear no harm, while those who procrastinate, evade or try to harm others are threatened with the sternest punishment. It raises the hope of good prospects to the community that deals with such situations in a fair, reasonable and kind manner.

We read in this *sūrah* statements like: "*Be conscious of God, your Lord... These are the bounds set by God. Whoever transgresses God's bounds wrongs his own soul. You never know; after that, God may bring about some new situation.*" (Verse 1) "*Call to witness two persons of known probity from among yourselves; and do yourselves bear witness before God. Thus is admonished everyone who believes in God and the Last Day. For everyone who fears God, He will grant a way out, and will provide for him whence he does not expect. God will be sufficient for everyone who puts his trust in Him. God always attains His purpose. God has set a measure for everything.*" (Verses 2–3) "*For everyone who is God-fearing, God makes things easy. Such is God's commandment which He has revealed to you. God will pardon the bad deeds of everyone who is God-fearing and will grant him a richl reward.*" (Verses 4–5) "*After hardship, God will grant ease.*" (Verse 7)

We also read the following stern, long and detailed warning: "*Many a community that insolently defied the commandment of their Lord and His messengers We have brought to account in a severe manner and inflicted on them terrible suffering. Thus they tasted the outcome of their own conduct. Yet the end of their conduct was ruin. God has prepared a severe punishment for them.*" (Verses 8–10) We note how it is followed with a strong caution against doing what leads to such a fate, and a reminder of the great blessing of sending God's Messenger with the light that he brings and with the promise of great reward: "*So, you who are endowed with insight, you who have faith, fear God. God has bestowed on you a reminder from on high. [He has sent you] a Messenger who recites to you God's revelations that make things clear, so that He may lead those who believe and do righteous deeds out of the depths of darkness into the light. God will admit everyone who believes in Him and does righteous deeds into gardens through which running waters flow, where they will abide for ever. God will have granted them a most excellent provision.*" (Verses 10–11) We then read how it is all concluded with a note that opens up the whole universe before us: "*It is God who has created seven heavens and likewise of the earth. His command descends through them all, so that you may learn that God has power over all things, and that God encompasses all things with His knowledge.*" (Verse 12)

All this is contained in a comment on the rulings regarding divorce. We also note that a whole *sūrah* of the Qur'ān is devoted to regulating this situation and the consequences that result from it. In this way, we see how divorce is linked to the most fundamental and essential facts of faith, both at the level of the universe and the level of the human soul, even though divorce is a situation of ruin, not building, a severance, not initiation, and its subject matter is a family, not a state. Yet the *surah* gives us the impression that it is more serious than establishing a state.

What does all this signify? Its significance is varied, but in its totality it points to the sublime nature of this religion, its seriousness and its divine origin. This is clear even though nothing else points to it other than this *surah*. Hence, we see how the Islamic system approaches the family question with much seriousness. Islam is a system based on the family. The family home is a shelter that gives comfort. People live there nurturing ties of love, affection, mutual sympathy and care while observing values that maintain purity and the absence of lewdness. Within the family home children are reared and looked after.

> Relations within the family are shown in an atmosphere of clarity that radiates with mutual sympathy and genuine care: "*And among His signs is that He creates for you spouses out of your own kind, so that you might incline towards them, and He engenders love and tenderness between you.*" (30: 21) "*They are as a garment for you, as you are for them.*" (2: 187) Marriage, then, is a bond between two souls, based on mutual inclination, love and tenderness. It establishes a unit within which relations reflect mutual care and kindness. The very words the Qur'ān uses in reference to the family generate an air of ease and tenderness as they express the type of bond Islam wants to see within this unit, recognizing its noble objectives of helping life to continue through procreation. Therefore, these objectives are shown to be clean, pure and serious. It describes them very aptly in the following way: "*Your wives are your tilth.*" (2: 223) This description also implies fertility and increase in numbers.
>
> In keeping with its total approach to all aspects, Islam provides this homely unit with all its care and warrantees. It does not limit itself to spiritual inspiration, but also adds legal provisions and guarantees.[1]

---

1. Sayyid Quṭb (1982), *Al-Salām al-'Ālamī wal-Islam*, (Islam and World Peace), Beirut and Cairo, pp. 67–68.

When we look at Islamic family legislation in the Qur'ān and the *Sunnah* regarding all situations, and consider the directives accompanying the legal provisions, as well as the different influences brought to bear, and the fact that the whole question is given a direct link to God at every step, as is the case in this *sūrah* and in others, we then realize how important an institution the family is in the Islamic system. We appreciate the value God assigns to the question of the family when we remember that in the opening verse of *Sūrah* 4, Women, God states in the same sentence the requirement of fearing Him and being mindful of family ties: *"Mankind, fear your Lord, who has created you from a single soul, and from it created its mate, and from the two of them spread abroad so many men and women. Fear God, in whose name you appeal to one another, and be mindful of your ties of kinship. Indeed, God is ever watching over you."* (4: 1) He also combines worshipping God alone with kindness to parents: *"Your Lord has ordained that you shall worship none but Him, and that you must be kind to your parents."* (17: 23) In another *sūrah*, gratitude to God is coupled with gratitude to one's parents: *"Be grateful to Me and to your parents."* (31: 14)

That we should take such great care is consistent with God's will that has established human life on the basis of the family. He willed that the first unit in human existence was a family made of Adam and his wife. All mankind is the progeny of this first family unit. God could have created millions of human individuals at the same time, but He chose to let all humanity begin with a single unit because He wished to give the family a momentous role in human life. Family life meets the requirements of human nature and allows human abilities and character to develop. It also nurtures the child's talents and strengthens his potential. The most profound influences on man are seen within the family. Therefore, the Islamic system, which represents the final and complete divine code for human life, fits perfectly with God's will that brought man into existence. Such harmony is observed in everything that comes from God.

The second message that the *sūrah*'s serious approach to marital and family matters delivers is how the Islamic system wishes to elevate these human ties to a sacred level that sees them linked to God. In essence, they are made a means for spiritual purification. This contrasts with the way they have been viewed in idolatrous beliefs and in distorted religion that has moved far away from dealing with human nature.

> Islam neither suppresses natural feelings nor considers them dirty. It only regulates, purifies and elevates them above the physical level so that they become central to many psychological and social values. By contrast, adultery, and prostitution in particular, removes from such natural desires all the exquisite feelings, attractions and values that have been refined over the long history of human life. It leaves such desires naked, dirty and coarser than in animals. In many animal and bird species, couples live together in a regulated life. They do not have the sort of sexual chaos that adultery spreads in some human communities, particularly where prostitution is rife.[2]

Islam considers marriage a means to maintain one's purity. It calls on the Muslim community to facilitate the marriage of men and women, should money become an obstacle to marriage: *"Marry the single from among you as well as such of your male and female slaves as are virtuous. If they are poor, God will grant them sufficiency out of His bounty. God is Munificent, All-Knowing. As for those who are unable to marry, let them live in continence until God grants them sufficiency out of His bounty."* (24: 32–33) It calls marriage *iḥsān*, which means protection. Thus, believers develop the concept that staying without protection, even for a short period, does not earn God's favour. 'Alī explained the reason for his marriage shortly after the death of his first wife, Fāṭimah, the Prophet's daughter thus: "I feared to meet God when I was without a wife." Marriage is, then, one of the acts of obedience to God, and by which a believer hopes to improve his position with God. The marital tie becomes to him a sacred one since it is part of obeying God.

---

2. Sayyid Qutb (2006), *In the Shade of the Qur'ān,* Leicester, Islamic Foundation, Vol. XII, p. 269.

A Realistic Approach to Marriage

This *sūrah* and similar ones like it indicate the realistic nature of the Islamic approach to life and to human nature. It accepts human nature as it is and works upon its potentials and circumstances. Therefore, it does not stop at either providing detailed legislation on a matter that is left to people's consciences or issuing directives. Instead, it uses both in its approach to the human soul and to practical life.

To start with, the marriage bond is meant to be permanent and well established. Islam adds a host of guarantees to ensure that it remains so, raising it to the level of fulfilling God's orders. It enables state funds to be used to help poor men and women marry. It legislates for the observance of values that prevent exposing physical charms so as to tempt the other sex, this so that desires are settled within a proper and legitimate framework. It prescribes punishments for adultery and false accusations of adultery. It protects the sanctity of homes by requiring people to ask permission before entering, and defines that people inside the home should ask permission before entering other rooms. Islam also regulates marital ties with specific rules and laws. It establishes the family system on the basis that one of the two partners is responsible for taking full care of the family, the man, as he is better suited for this responsibility. In this way, Islam prevents conflict and disorder within the family. Further safeguards are put in place to work together with directives utilizing people's emotions. It adds to all this the fact that this bond and its preservation are an essential aspect of being God-fearing.

Yet practical human life shows that there are situations that end in ruin, despite all the guarantees and safeguards. These must be faced in a practical way. Denial is of no use when the continuity of marital life becomes almost impossible. To hold on to marriage in such cases serves no purpose.

Islam does not rush to enforce a break-up of the marriage once conflict erupts. On the contrary, it tries hard to hold on to it, allowing it to break only when there is no other way.

Islam addresses men: "*Consort with them in a goodly manner. Even if you are averse to them, it may well be that you are averse to something in which God has placed much good.*" (4: 19) Thus it encourages them to take things easy and to persevere, even when they are averse to their wives. It opens up a window for them as regards something they may not know: "*It may well be that you are averse to something in which God has placed much good.*" These women to whom they are averse may bring them much good, which they are unaware of. If God has this good in store for them, they must not let it go to waste. Nothing is more effective in working on emotions so as to control feelings of hate and moderate them.

Should the matter go beyond feelings of like or dislike and reach a point of incompatibility and irreconcilability, Islam does not rush to recommend divorce. Rather, it recommends an attempt by well-wishers to achieve reconciliation: "*If you have reason to fear that a breach may occur between a (married) couple, appoint an arbiter from among his people and an arbiter from among her people. If they both want to set things aright, God will bring about their reconciliation. God is indeed All-Knowing, aware of all things.*" (4: 35) "*If a woman has reason to fear ill-treatment or desertion by her husband, it shall not be wrong for the two of them if they should try to set things peacefully to rights between them; for peace is best.*" (4: 128)

If all such intermediation fails, and there appear to be things that prevent a tolerably peaceful life, then the split is serious. To retain the marriage in such circumstances would inevitably lead to failure. The pressures involved would compound the already adverse effects on the people involved. Hence, it is wise to accept the facts and put an end to the marriage. Islam in no way likes this, but views it as necessary. We should always remember that of all lawful things, God dislikes divorce most.[3]

Even if the man wants to divorce his wife, this is not instantaneously possible. The proper thing is for divorce to take place when the woman is not in her monthly period, and provided that no sexual intercourse had taken place between the couple. This means that a delay takes

---

3. Sayyid Quṭb (1982), *Al-Salām al-ʿĀlamī wal-Islam*, (Islam and World Peace), Beirut and Cairo, pp. 84–85.

place, which could overcome the anger and provide an opportunity for the couple to review their situation. In this way, they may reflect and be more inclined to make peace. Divorce may then not take place as a result of this initial delay.

Moreover, there is the waiting period: three monthly cycles, or three months in the case of a divorced woman who has passed the menopause or until childbirth if the woman is pregnant. During this waiting period, the reinstatement of the marriage is possible if a change of heart takes place and the couple want to resume their married life.

Yet all these attempts do not negate the fact that a total split may occur and that there are situations that need to be practically regulated. Islam addresses these situations putting in place legislation to take care of all the aspects involved. Hence, we have the detailed provisions included in this *sūrah*, which show the practical Islamic approach to life's problems in a way that ensures progress and maintains purity.

Eradicating Traces of *Jāhiliyyah*

This *sūrah* with all that it includes of encouragement, warnings, emphasis, detailed provisions and telling comments clearly indicates that it was addressing certain situations that continued to carry traces of the days of ignorance, marked by the ill-treatment of women and gross injustice towards them. Hence, strong influences are brought to bear on people's minds together with detailed provisions to close any loopholes that may allow evasion of the rules and a return to the old ignorant concepts that led to unhealthy marital relations.

This did not apply to Arabia only. It was common throughout the world. Women were treated in the same way as slaves, or worse than slaves, in almost all parts of the world. In some communities, sex was viewed as filthy and women were thought of as evil, tempting men to indulge in such filth. It was from such depths of global ignorance that Islam raised women and marital relations to their high and pure levels, giving women their rightful positions of honour and putting in place safeguards to protect their rights. No little girl would now be the victim of infanticide. Furthermore, when she reached a marriageable age, she could no longer be forced into marriage against her will. Whether virgin or mature, a woman must give her consent before she can be married. As a wife, a woman has full and protected rights, and she further enjoys the safeguards provided by Islamic law. If divorced, a woman has the rights detailed in this *sūrah* and in *Sūrah* 2, The Cow, as also revealed elsewhere in the Qur'ān and *Sunnah*.

At its own initiative, Islam put all these legislative provisions in place. It was not a response to a feeling among women in Arabia or anywhere else in the world that their situation was unsatisfactory, or to a twinge of conscience among men that required fairness to women. There was no association of women in Arabia or anywhere else for that matter demanding reforms; nor were there any female members of any consultative or legislative assembly. Indeed, not a single voice demanded an improvement in women's status. These legal provisions were part of the code made in heaven for implementation on earth, to ensure fairness to all its people. It was God's will to raise human life from the depth of ignorance into which it had sunk, purge marital relations from their shameful status and to give to man and woman, created originally from a single soul, all their human rights that preserve their honour and dignity.

Islam is a noble religion. Only a perverted ignorant will stand in opposition to it. For, no one abandons God's law in preference for human law except through the pressures of desire and a clinging to worldly pleasures.

Having reviewed the subject matter of the *sūrah* in general terms, we will now discuss the provisions it puts in place. When we look at them within the context of the *sūrah*, we find that they reflect life and movement and that they are full of inspiration. This is the difference between looking at such provisions within their Qur'ānic context and studying them in books of Islamic law.

Al-Ṭalāq (Divorce)

In the Name of God, the Lord of Grace, the Ever Merciful

Prophet! When you[4] divorce women, divorce them with a view to their prescribed waiting period, and reckon the period accurately. Be conscious of God, your Lord. Do not drive them out of their homes, nor shall they themselves leave, unless they commit a flagrant indecency. These are the bounds set by God. Whoever transgresses God's bounds wrongs his own soul. You never know; after that, God may bring about some new situation. (1)

When they have completed their appointed term, either retain them in fair manner or part with them in fair manner. Call to witness two persons of known probity from among yourselves; and do yourselves bear witness before God. Thus is admonished everyone who believes in God and the Last Day. For everyone who fears God, He will grant a way out, (2)

---

4. The plural form is used here indicating that the address is to the Muslim community as a whole.

72

and will provide for him whence he does not expect. God will be sufficient for everyone who puts his trust in Him. God always attains His purpose. God has set a measure for everything. (3)

وَيَرْزُقْهُ مِنْ حَيْثُ لَا يَحْتَسِبُ وَمَن يَتَوَكَّلْ عَلَى اللَّهِ فَهُوَ حَسْبُهُ إِنَّ اللَّهَ بَالِغُ أَمْرِهِ قَدْ جَعَلَ اللَّهُ لِكُلِّ شَيْءٍ قَدْرًا ٣

As for those of your women who are beyond the age of monthly courses, as well as for those who do not have any courses, their waiting period, if you have any doubt, is three months. As for those who are with child, their waiting term shall end when they deliver their burden. For everyone who is God-fearing, God makes things easy. (4)

وَاللَّائِي يَئِسْنَ مِنَ الْمَحِيضِ مِن نِّسَائِكُمْ إِنِ ارْتَبْتُمْ فَعِدَّتُهُنَّ ثَلَاثَةُ أَشْهُرٍ وَاللَّائِي لَمْ يَحِضْنَ وَأُولَاتُ الْأَحْمَالِ أَجَلُهُنَّ أَن يَضَعْنَ حَمْلَهُنَّ وَمَن يَتَّقِ اللَّهَ يَجْعَل لَّهُ مِنْ أَمْرِهِ يُسْرًا ٤

Such is God's commandment which He has revealed to you. God will pardon the bad deeds of everyone who is God-fearing and will grant him a rich reward. (5)

ذَلِكَ أَمْرُ اللَّهِ أَنزَلَهُ إِلَيْكُمْ وَمَن يَتَّقِ اللَّهَ يُكَفِّرْ عَنْهُ سَيِّئَاتِهِ وَيُعْظِمْ لَهُ أَجْرًا ٥

Let them dwell wherever you dwell, according to your means, and do not harass them so as to make their lives a misery. If they are with child, maintain them until they have delivered their burden. If, after that, they suckle your infants, pay them for it.

أَسْكِنُوهُنَّ مِنْ حَيْثُ سَكَنتُم مِّن وُجْدِكُمْ وَلَا تُضَارُّوهُنَّ لِتُضَيِّقُوا عَلَيْهِنَّ وَإِن كُنَّ أُولَاتِ حَمْلٍ فَأَنفِقُوا عَلَيْهِنَّ حَتَّى يَضَعْنَ حَمْلَهُنَّ فَإِنْ أَرْضَعْنَ لَكُمْ فَآتُوهُنَّ

73

Take counsel with one another in a fair manner. If some of you make things difficult, let another woman suckle the child. (6)

أُجُورَهُنَّ وَأْتَمِرُوا بَيْنَكُم بِمَعْرُوفٍ وَإِن تَعَاسَرْتُمْ فَسَتُرْضِعُ لَهُۥٓ أُخْرَىٰ ﴿٦﴾

Let the one who has ample means spend in accordance with his means; and let the one whose provisions are restricted spend according to what God has given him. God does not burden anyone with more than He has given them. After hardship, God will grant ease. (7)

لِيُنفِقْ ذُو سَعَةٍ مِّن سَعَتِهِۦ وَمَن قُدِرَ عَلَيْهِ رِزْقُهُۥ فَلْيُنفِقْ مِمَّآ ءَاتَىٰهُ ٱللَّهُ لَا يُكَلِّفُ ٱللَّهُ نَفْسًا إِلَّا مَآ ءَاتَىٰهَا سَيَجْعَلُ ٱللَّهُ بَعْدَ عُسْرٍ يُسْرًا ﴿٧﴾

Many a community that insolently defied the commandment of their Lord and His messengers We have brought to account in a severe manner and inflicted on them terrible suffering. (8)

وَكَأَيِّن مِّن قَرْيَةٍ عَتَتْ عَنْ أَمْرِ رَبِّهَا وَرُسُلِهِۦ فَحَاسَبْنَٰهَا حِسَابًا شَدِيدًا وَعَذَّبْنَٰهَا عَذَابًا نُّكْرًا ﴿٨﴾

Thus they tasted the outcome of their own conduct. Yet the end of their conduct was ruin. (9)

فَذَاقَتْ وَبَالَ أَمْرِهَا وَكَانَ عَٰقِبَةُ أَمْرِهَا خُسْرًا ﴿٩﴾

God has prepared a severe punishment for them. So, you who are endowed with insight, you who have faith, fear God. God has bestowed on you a reminder from on high. (10)

أَعَدَّ ٱللَّهُ لَهُمْ عَذَابًا شَدِيدًا فَٱتَّقُوا ٱللَّهَ يَٰٓأُوْلِي ٱلْأَلْبَٰبِ ٱلَّذِينَ ءَامَنُوا قَدْ أَنزَلَ ٱللَّهُ إِلَيْكُمْ ذِكْرًا ﴿١٠﴾

[He has sent you] a Messenger who recites to you God's revelations that make things clear, so that He may lead those who believe and do righteous deeds out of the depths of darkness into the light. God will admit everyone who believes in Him and does righteous deeds into gardens through which running waters flow, where they will abide for ever. God will have granted them a most excellent provision. (11)

رَسُولًا يَتْلُواْ عَلَيْكُمْ ءَايَـٰتِ ٱللَّهِ مُبَيِّنَـٰتٍ لِّيُخْرِجَ ٱلَّذِينَ ءَامَنُواْ وَعَمِلُواْ ٱلصَّـٰلِحَـٰتِ مِنَ ٱلظُّلُمَـٰتِ إِلَى ٱلنُّورِ وَمَن يُؤْمِنۢ بِٱللَّهِ وَيَعْمَلْ صَـٰلِحًا يُدْخِلْهُ جَنَّـٰتٍ تَجْرِى مِن تَحْتِهَا ٱلْأَنْهَـٰرُ خَـٰلِدِينَ فِيهَآ أَبَدًا قَدْ أَحْسَنَ ٱللَّهُ لَهُۥ رِزْقًا ۝

It is God who has created seven heavens and likewise of the earth. His command descends through them all, so that you may learn that God has power over all things, and that God encompasses all things with His knowledge. (12)

ٱللَّهُ ٱلَّذِى خَلَقَ سَبْعَ سَمَـٰوَٰتٍ وَمِنَ ٱلْأَرْضِ مِثْلَهُنَّ يَتَنَزَّلُ ٱلْأَمْرُ بَيْنَهُنَّ لِتَعْلَمُوٓاْ أَنَّ ٱللَّهَ عَلَىٰ كُلِّ شَىْءٍ قَدِيرٌ وَأَنَّ ٱللَّهَ قَدْ أَحَاطَ بِكُلِّ شَىْءٍ عِلْمًۢا ۝

The Process of Divorce

Prophet! When you divorce women, divorce them with a view to their prescribed waiting period, and reckon the period accurately. Be conscious of God, your Lord. Do not drive them out of their homes, nor shall they themselves leave, unless they commit a flagrant indecency. These are the bounds set by God. Whoever transgresses God's bounds wrongs his own soul. You never know; after that, God may bring about some new situation. (Verse 1)

This is the first stage and the first rule. It is addressed in the first instance to the Prophet, but it is soon realized that it is a general rule applicable to every Muslim, not to the Prophet in isolation. In the sentence starting with, *'when you divorce women'*, the pronoun 'you' is used in the plural form throughout. This stylistic form is employed to alert attention and imply the seriousness of the matter under discussion. God addresses it to the Prophet in person, giving him His instructions and directives, so that he will, in turn, deliver it to those who follow him. The psychological impact achieved in this way is both strong and clear.

"When you divorce women, divorce them with a view to their prescribed waiting period." (Verse 1) An authentic *ḥadīth* related by al-Bukhārī explains this directive: "'Abdullāh ibn 'Umar divorced his wife when she was in the midst of her menstrual period. 'Umar mentioned this to the Prophet who was clearly angry. He said to 'Umar: 'Tell him to take her back and keep her until she has finished her period, then through her cleanliness cycle and her next menstrual period. When she is clean again if he still wants to divorce her, he should do so before he has intercourse with her. This is when the waiting period which God has ordained starts." Muslim also relates this *ḥadīth* but the last sentence in his version runs as follows: "This is the start of the waiting period which God ordered that women should be divorced with a view to."

It is clear, then, that there is a time when the divorce process can rightly start. A man cannot divorce his wife at any time; he can only do so when his wife is in a period of cleanliness from menstruation during which they have had no sexual intercourse. Other statements indicate that there is another time when the divorce process can be started, which is if the woman is clearly pregnant. The purpose behind limiting the time to these two situations is to delay the divorce for a while after the man has decided to so separate from his wife. During this time, tension may subside if it is of a transitory type and the couple may resume a normal life together. On the other hand, it also ensures that the woman is not pregnant before they embark on divorce. After all, a man may be inclined not to divorce his wife when he learns that she is pregnant. If he still resorts to divorce when he has become aware of her pregnancy, this means that his mind is made up. To sum up, the condition that the wife should be in cleanliness from menstruation without any intervening sexual intercourse is so as to ensure that she is not pregnant, and the condition that the pregnancy should be clearly determined is to ensure that the man is aware of it. This, then, is the first attempt to deal with cracks in the family structure, and to stop the axe that seeks to destroy it.[5]

Yet this does not mean that divorce does not occur except in these two periods; it occurs whenever it is pronounced,[6] but it will be frowned upon by God, and it will incur the anger of God's Messenger. This is sufficient for a good believer to hold on and not to pronounce the word of divorce until the appropriate time, leaving the matter to God to determine its outcome as He pleases.

"And reckon the period accurately." This is important, so that the waiting period is not made too long as to harm the divorcee, preventing her from remarriage after her waiting period is over. On the other hand, the first purpose of making sure that she is not pregnant will not be properly fulfilled if the waiting period is cut short. Moreover, this directive implies the seriousness of the matter and that God watches us and requires those involved to be careful at every step.

"Be conscious of God, your Lord. Do not drive them out of their homes, nor shall they themselves leave, unless they commit a flagrant indecency." (Verse 1) This is the first caution that follows the address. It is given by God to emphasize the need to maintain fear of Him in all situations. This caution is stated before the order not to turn divorced women out of their homes. Although these are their husbands' homes, they are called here 'their homes' so as to emphasize the woman's right to stay there during the waiting period. Women must not be driven out of these homes; nor should they leave of their own accord, except in a situation where a divorcing woman commits a flagrant indecency. Reports suggest that such an indecency might entail adultery and the need for the woman

---

5. Some readers may wonder about the woman's right to initiate a termination of the marriage. Islam legislates separately for this situation. Verse 229 of *Sūrah* 2 includes a provision for it, and the *Sunnah* provides more details. Such termination at the wife's request is called *khul'* in Islamic law. Hence, the provisions related to divorce are related to the husband, because he is the one required to take care of all complications resulting from divorce. – Editor's note.

6. This is the view of the majority of scholars, but a minority hold that it does not occur unless it takes place in one of these two periods only.

to receive her punishment, or it might entail her causing harm to her husband's family, or rebellion against her husband and doing what harms him, even though he is a divorcing husband. The purpose of the woman staying in her husband's home is to allow every chance for reconciliation and the reawakening of tender feelings and memories of shared things between the couple. This situation means that the couple will be apart because of the divorce that has been set in process, yet they are close physically. Should she sink so low that she commits adultery, or should she cause harm to her husband's family or rebel against him, this leaves no room for the reawakening of compassionate feelings. Nor is there any need for her to stay with her husband any longer. In fact, their proximity would only deepen the break, rather than heal it.

"*These are the bounds set by God. Whoever transgresses God's bounds wrongs his own soul.*" (Verse 1) This is the second warning. It is God who watches the implementation of this rule. Would any believer deliberately contravene the bounds God sets in place? To do so would be to bring ruin to those involved. "*Whoever transgresses God's bounds wrongs his own soul.*" He exposes himself to God's anger. He wrongs himself by wronging his wife, when the two are created from a single soul. Thus any wrong that befalls her rebounds on him also. Besides, "*you never know; after that, God may bring about some new situation.*" (Verse 1) This is an inspiring statement. Who knows how God's order to divorced woman to observe a waiting period during which she stays in her husband's home will work to fulfil His will? This order gives a little hope and kindles a faint light that may yet bring about an immeasurably good result. Things may change, and conflict may give way to reconciliation and contentment. God's will is always active, changing things and creating new situations. To submit to His will and observe His orders is for the better. Being conscious of Him and always on our guard lest we do what is sinful ensures an abundance of goodness.

People tend to think only of the present moment and the situation they are in with all its circumstances and difficulties. They may not look up to the future, remaining imprisoned within the present moment feeling that it will continue for ever. They feel that what they are going through now will be their permanent lot. This sort of psychological imprisonment can be terribly detrimental. Yet the truth is different, because God's will always changes things and brings about what people have never thought possible. It opens up hope, bringing ease after hardship. God initiates at any moment situations that might never have been dreamt of.

God wants this truth to be clearly understood by us so that we will continue to look up with hope to what He puts before us. We must always be optimistic, thinking of what He may grant us and what prospects He opens before us. We should always remember that the next moment can bring something beyond our wildest dreams: "*You never know; after that, God may bring about some new situation.*" (Verse 1)

Fairness in All Situations

When they have completed their appointed term, either retain them in fair manner or part with them in fair manner. Call to witness two persons of known probity from among yourselves; and do yourselves bear witness before God. Thus is admonished everyone who believes in God and the Last Day. For everyone who fears God, He will grant a way out, and will provide for him whence he does not expect. God will be sufficient for everyone who puts his trust in Him. God always attains His purpose. God has set a measure for everything. (Verses 2–3)

These two verses deal with the next stage, stating its rulings. Completing the term means the end of the waiting period. While the divorced woman is in her waiting period, whatever its length be, her husband may take her back in marriage and she regains her status as his wife. This is what is referred to in the verse as 'retain them'. Likewise, he may allow the waiting period to reach its specified end when his divorced wife will part with him and she cannot be lawful to him again unless they go through a fresh marriage contract, just as if he had taken a new wife. In either situation, the divorcing husband is commanded to behave in fairness. He is prohibited from retaining her so as to harm her. A man may retain his divorced wife shortly before the end of her waiting period then divorce her a second and a third time to prevent her from marrying someone else. He may also retain her to leave her, as it were, in a state of suspense, and so put further pressure on her causing her to offer to forgo her rights in order to gain her divorce. Both situations were common practice at the time this *sūrah* was revealed. They continue to take place when people deviate from the path of fearing God, which is the most important guarantee of the implementation of His rules governing cases of family relations and break ups. Husbands are also forbidden to harm their divorcees by verbal abuse of any sort. The marriage bond is set in place on the basis of fairness and must end, when it is terminated, in a fair manner, so that the couple retain good feelings towards each other. They may, for all they know, resume life together in the future, and they will not then want to have any painful memory of verbal abuse that may cast a shadow on their new relation. Besides, this is the sort of good manners that Islam wants all its followers to abide by.

In either case of complete parting or reinstatement of the marriage, two witnesses of known probity are required, so that no doubt about the marriage status should remain. People may learn of the divorce, but the reinstatement of the marriage may escape their attention, which may lead to doubts and gossip. Islam wants all marital matters to remain clean and clear, in reality, in people's feelings and in their conversations. According to some scholars, but not others, the reinstatement of the marriage, as well as the full divorce, are completed without witnesses, but some make it a condition for the reinstatement of the marriage only. It is agreed, however, that witnesses are needed after or at the time of complete parting or the reinstatement of the marriage. Both views are expressed.

Having established the ruling, comments and directives follow in succession: "*Do yourselves bear witness before God.*" (Verse 2) The issue is one in which God is concerned, and the witnesses are called in for His sake. It is He who has ruled that witnesses are needed, and He watches how this is done and gives rewards for it. The witnesses are dealing with Him directly, not with either of the divorcing couple or with the general public. "*Thus is admonished everyone who believes in God and the Last Day.*" (Verse 2) These rulings are addressed to people who believe in the Day of Judgement. The *sūrah* tells them this admonition applies to them in particular. If they truly believe in God and the Last Day, they will be admonished. This is the test of their faith. It proves whether their claims to be believers are true or not.

"*For everyone who fears God, He will grant a way out, and will provide for him whence he does not expect.*" (Verses 2–3) He will grant God-fearing people a way out of any tight situation in this present life and in the life to come. He will also give them their provisions from where they neither know nor expect. This is a general statement describing a permanent situation. However, stating it here in the context of the rulings concerning divorce suggests that this is particularly true when people remain God-fearing in dealing with this particular situation. This is when the most important means of control come from within oneself and from one's own conscience. There is much scope for misuse of resources and for the appropriation of what does not rightfully belong to oneself. Only fear of God and a sensitive conscience provide effective restraint.

"*God will be sufficient for everyone who puts his trust in Him. God always attains His purpose.*" (Verse 3) Again, wicked scheming has wide scope and can take different routes in this relationship. Indeed, trying to avoid wicked scheming by one party may make the other resort to wicked scheming of their own. This statement impresses on people that they should not attempt anything of the sort. Rather, they should place their trust in God; this is sufficient for anyone. God always accomplishes what He wants. Whatever He has willed has already taken place. Therefore, to rely on Him is to rely on the One who is able, powerful and always brings about the results He seeks. It should be noted that this Qur'ānic statement is general and aims to instil into people the right concept with regard to God's will and power. Including it here with the rulings on divorce suggests that it has important significance and effect in this very crucial social matter.

"*God has set a measure for everything.*" (Verse 3) Everything is given its due measure, accomplished at the place, time and with the circumstances set for it. Hence, it is the result of its particular causes and produces its own results. Nothing is the result of blind coincidence, either within man and his life or in the universe at large. This is an important aspect of the Islamic concept.[7] Yet mentioning it here relates it to the rulings God has given concerning divorce, its timing, waiting period and witnesses.

---

7. We spoke in detail about this truth in our commentary on verse 2, *Sūrah* 25, in Vol. XII, pp. 379–382, and also in commenting on verse 49, *Sūrah* 54, in Vol. XVI.

All these rulings are thus given an extra aspect of being part of God's overall law and give us the feeling that the serious view Islam takes of divorce is part of the seriousness of the system God has established for the universe.

More on the Waiting Period

As for those of your women who are beyond the age of monthly courses, as well as for those who do not have any courses, their waiting period, if you have any doubt, is three months. As for those who are with child, their waiting term shall end when they deliver their burden. For everyone who is God-fearing, God makes things easy. Such is God's commandment which He has revealed to you. God will pardon the bad deeds of everyone who is God-fearing and will grant him a rich reward. (Verses 4–5)

These verses specify the length of the waiting period for women who do not have a monthly cycle and for pregnant women. It includes women who are past the menopause and those who do not as yet have a menstrual cycle because they have not attained puberty or because of a malfunction in their system. The length of the waiting period for women generally is determined in verse 228, *Sūrah* 2, as three menstrual periods or three periods of cleanliness from menses. Hence, there remained the question of how long a woman who does not have a monthly cycle should wait. This verse removes all doubt, setting the waiting period for such women at three months. Pregnant women wait until they have delivered their child, regardless of whether this provides a short or a long waiting period. Once a woman has given birth, it is absolutely certain that she is not pregnant. Hence, there is no need for her to have any extended waiting period. If such a woman is divorced, her divorce is complete once she has given birth. The process of her divorce is completed and the marriage cannot be reinstated without a fresh marriage contract. God has set a measure for everything, and every ruling of His has its wise purpose.

This ruling is followed by inspiring comments: "*For everyone who is God-fearing, God makes things easy.*" (Verse 4) Ease is the ultimate blessing that anyone hopes for. When God bestows this great favour on His servants, making things easy for them so that they encounter neither difficulty nor hardship, they will approach matters gently, achieve what they desire easily through their endeavours and happily accept the outcome. Thus they live in ease and comfort until they are due to meet their Lord. Do we see here a temptation for people to approach divorce with ease and in return their life will generally become easy?

"*Such is God's commandment which He has revealed to you.*" (Verse 5) This is a totally different touch, alerting us to the source of the order. It is given by God to those who believe in Him. To obey the order is to make the belief and the bond with God a practical reality. Then we have further emphasis on the need to remain always God-fearing, particularly in connection with what people may do in cases of divorce: "*God will pardon the bad deeds of everyone who is God-fearing and will grant him a rich reward.*" (Verse 5) The first reward is to make things easy for us, and the second is to forgive us our sins and to increase our reward for good deeds. It is a very generous and exciting offer, yet it is made in the form of a general statement and a promise that applies to all. However, it imparts a particular colour to the question of divorce and gives us a reminder of God's great bounty. Why would anyone, then, make things hard and complicated when God promises such a great reward for making things easy?

Maintenance and Breast-Feeding

Let them dwell wherever you dwell, according to your means, and do not harass them so as to make their lives a misery. If they are with child, maintain them until they have delivered their burden. If, after that, they suckle your infants, pay them for it. Take counsel with one another in a fair manner. If some of you make things difficult, let another woman suckle the child. Let the one who has ample means spend in accordance with his means; and let the one whose provisions are restricted spend according to what God has given him. God does not burden anyone with more than He has given them. After hardship, God will grant ease. (Verses 6–7)

83

These verses state the final provisions concerning the issue of a divorcee staying in her home, which is the home she has shared with her husband, and her maintenance during the waiting period, whatever its length be. Husbands are commanded to provide them with a dwelling of the standard they can afford. They cannot give them an inferior home to their own or to what they can afford. They must not intentionally try to harass them by giving them a sub-standard dwelling place or by ill-treating them. Pregnant women are given special mention with regard to maintenance – which is due by right to every divorced woman – because the extra length of her waiting period may lead some people to think that maintenance is due for only a part of the waiting period, or that it may go further than the waiting period should it be very short. Hence, clarification is needed, requiring the maintenance to be paid until the end of the waiting period.

Breast-feeding of the child is also discussed in detail. It is not made a duty of the mother that gives her no return. As long as she continues to breast-feed the child, which belongs to them both, she is entitled to receive some wages to help her with life's necessities and to ensure that her milk continues to flow for the benefit of the child. We see how Islamic law takes care of every aspect of the mother's needs. At the same time, both parents are commanded to consult with each other in a fair manner concerning their child, ensuring what is best for it. The child is a trust given to both of them. Their failure to maintain their relation as sound and healthy should not be made to rebound on their child.

Such is the easy approach that God calls on them both to pursue. Should they take a hardened attitude and be unwilling or unable to agree on the child's breast-feeding and the compensation due for it, the child's rights are guaranteed: "*If some of you make things difficult, let another woman suckle the child.*" (Verse 6) The mother must not object to such an arrangement in a way that jeopardizes the child's right to breast-feeding. This arrangement is resorted to only because she and the child's father take a hard attitude and cannot agree on suitable arrangements.

Further details are then given concerning the level of maintenance, which should ensure ease, fairness and cooperation. The man must be fair and the woman must not be unreasonable: "*Let the one who has ample means spend in accordance with his means; and let the one whose provisions are restricted spend according to what God has given him."* (Verse 7) The person to whom God has given in plenty should be generous in what he gives to his divorced wife in respect of her housing, maintenance and compensation for breast-feeding their child. The one who has limited provisions is not to be blamed for giving according to his means. God does not require anyone to spend above their means. It is He who gives us what we have. No one can have anything other than what God has given him, because there is no other source from which people may take anything. His is the only treasure on which all creatures depend: *"God does not burden anyone with more than He has given them."* (Verse 7)

Then follows a gentle touch that is bound to please and open a window of hope for both parties: *"After hardship, God will grant ease."* (Verse 7) It is through God alone that hardship is followed by ease and generous provisions are given after means have been restricted. It behoves both parties then to pin their hopes on Him alone, watching Him in their dealings with each other and maintaining an attitude based on fearing Him in all their affairs. It is to Him that they look up with hope, and it is He who provides comfort and ease after difficulty and hardship.

A Holistic Approach to Divorce

By this point, the *sūrah* has completed its discussion of all rulings concerning divorce and its effect on the family. It has dealt with all consequences, providing a clear provision for each. The split in the family home thus leaves neither ruins nor dust that settles over hearts and souls. No problem is left unsolved. The split family is not left in lingering turmoil.

Thus the *sūrah* deals with all thoughts and fears that may occur. The husband is assured that he will not suffer poverty or loss of fortune if he provides his divorcee with a good home and proper maintenance, or gives generous compensation for the breast-feeding of his child. The same fears are removed from the woman's mind so that she is not worried about a life of poverty. Likewise, she must not entertain thoughts of receiving an unfair share of her ex-husband's money. Both are assured that a God-fearing approach will see them in ease after hardship, comfort after difficulty and provisions that come from where they do not expect.

85

What is more is that God will grant such God-fearing people ample reward in the life to come. It is a promise that will see their sins wiped out and their reward multiplied.

The *sūrah* also deals with the after-effects of the dispute that has led to the divorce. There may be lingering feelings of resentment, anger and bitterness. All these are cleared with a gentle, comforting touch and replaced with hope in God's mercy. The *sūrah* here taps feelings of fairness and compassion, relying on the God-fearing value it implants in people's hearts and the desire to win His pleasure.

This holistic approach and its inspiring touches, together with confirmed and repeated assurances, provide the only guarantees to implement these legal provisions Islam puts in place. The only control is that brought about by a sensitive conscience and a God-fearing heart. Each of the divorcing couple can cause the other no end of heartache and problems if they have nothing to limit their area of manoeuvre other than the limits of the law. Some of the Qur'ānic commandments given in the *sūrah* are so flexible as to address all aspects of this whole area. Take, for example, the order: "*Do not harass them.*" (Verse 6) This prohibits all aspects of harassment which no legal provision, however wide in scope, can incorporate. Its implementation is attached to conscience which is profoundly influenced by the approach the *sūrah* takes and to the enhanced God-fearing sense it instils in both parties. They realize that God is aware even of their innermost thoughts. His knowledge encompasses all. Besides, they will hope to receive the compensation He grants to His God-fearing servants in both this life and in the life to come, particularly in relation to provisions and livelihood. This message is repeated in different ways in the *sūrah* because it has a telling effect in easing the hardship that divorce generates and softens the attitudes of both parties.

When they bear all these rulings and directives in mind, a divorcing couple retain on parting some seeds of their old mutual affection and cordial feeling which may yet send up new shoots. In all these rulings and provisions we see the high moral standard that Islam wants to impart to the life of the Muslim community.

The Fate of the Disobedient

When the *sūrah* has completed all this, it provides the ultimate lesson referring to the fates of those communities that defied God's commandments and disobeyed His messengers. They neither listened to admonition, nor responded to calls given them by their prophets. The lessons derived from their fates are thus placed before us, reminding all of the miserable fate that awaits those who do not fear God and who disobey Him. It also reminds people of the grace God bestows on believers, to whom the legislation is addressed:

Many a community that insolently defied the commandment of their Lord and His messengers We have brought to account in a severe manner and inflicted on them terrible suffering. Thus they tasted the outcome of their own conduct. Yet the end of their conduct was ruin. God has prepared a severe punishment for them. So, you who are endowed with insight, you who have faith, fear God. God has bestowed on you a reminder from on high. [He has sent you] a Messenger who recites to you God's revelations that make things clear, so that He may lead those who believe and do righteous deeds out of the depths of darkness into the light. God will admit everyone who believes in Him and does righteous deeds into gardens through which running waters flow, where they will abide for ever. God will have granted them a most excellent provision. (Verses 8–11)

This is a long warning incorporating detailed scenes and images. It is also a profound reminder of God's grace, represented by faith and the light He grants through it. A further reminder is given of His reward in the life to come, which is the best and most generous of all provisions.

To start with, the punishment God metes out to those who defy His orders and do not respond to His messengers is a law He has set in operation: "*Many a community that insolently defied the commandment of their Lord and His messengers We have brought to account in a severe manner and inflicted on them terrible suffering.*" (Verse 8) The verse mentions more details about the way in which they were brought to account, highlighting its severity and the terrible suffering inflicted on them. This is followed by the final outcome of their actions: *"Thus they tasted the outcome of their own conduct. Yet the end of their conduct was ruin."* (Verse 9) The image given of this outcome is delayed to the next verse: *"God has prepared a severe punishment for them."* (Verse 10) All this serves to make the scene longer and provide details of its steps and stages. This is one of the ways the Qur'ān employs to enhance the effects of the message it wants to give.

We need to reflect a little on this warning. We realize that God brought different communities to account, one at a time, whenever they defied His commandments and disobeyed His messengers. We note that this warning is given here in the context of outlining the rulings on divorce. Thus, a link between divorce and this divine law is established. This suggests that the divorce issue is not merely one of couples and families; it is an issue for the entire Muslim community, which is responsible for implementing God's law. To disobey God in this question, or indeed in other aspects of the divine law, or rather the code of living God has given, is an act of defiance which merits punishment, not only for the individuals who commit such disobedience, but also for the community or the country where such defiance takes place. Such defiance means setting up a life system that differs from what God has legislated. The religion of Islam has been bestowed from on high so that it will be obeyed and implemented in a way that regulates life as a whole. Therefore, defying it, even in the area of an individual's personal affairs, exposes the defiant to what earlier communities suffered of God's punishment.

Those communities tasted the results of their own conduct, and the end to which their actions led was utter ruin, which they suffered in this life, before the final reckoning on the Day of Judgement. Cities, peoples and nations tasted such outcomes when they defied God and refused to adopt the code of living He revealed to them. Today, we witness, as did our predecessors, such an outcome being suffered in the form of corruption, loose morality, poverty, drought, injustice and a life of fear that is devoid of peace and security. We see with our own eyes the truth of this warning.

On top of this, there will be grievous suffering that awaits those who defy God's orders and discard the way of life He has laid down. He, the most truthful of all, says: "*God has prepared a severe punishment for them.*" (Verse 10)

In Volume XVI, we explained in our discussion of *Sūrah* 61, the Ranks, that Islam aims to create a Muslim community distinguished by its special system. It is, therefore, a collective system that conducts all the life affairs of its community. Hence, the community as a whole is responsible for putting it into practice and enforcing its laws. When the community discards the laws and rulings Islam puts in place, it leaves itself exposed to a fate which it is warned about here, just like it befell earlier defiant communities.

The *sūrah* follows the long warning and its detailed images with an address to believers endowed with insight. They are called upon to remain God-fearing: "*So, you who are endowed with insight, you who have faith, fear God. God has bestowed on you a reminder from on high.*" (Verse 10) The *sūrah* gives life to this reminder embodying it in the Prophet (peace be upon him). Thus, God's Messenger in person is the reminder: "*A Messenger who recites to you God's revelations that make things clear.*" (Verse 11)

Here we have a superb example of the Qur'ānic style giving us a profound and true image and that imparts more than one meaning. It first indicates that this reminder, which has been issued to them by God, has been given to them through the person of God's Messenger. It is as if the reminder was given directly to them. Nothing of it was screened by the Prophet. It also means that God's Messenger, in person, is a reminder. His personality has become an embodiment of this reminder, and his actions are a true translation of the Qur'ān. Thus, indeed, was the Prophet Muḥammad (peace be upon him). 'Ā'ishah, his wife, describes him in these words: "His morals and manners were the Qur'ān." The Qur'ān was always in his mind as he faced life, and he himself was the Qur'ān addressing life.

In addition to the blessings of the reminder, and the light and guidance given by God, we also have a promise of admission to heaven where believers will enjoy its everlasting bliss. There is a reminder here making clear that this is the best of all provisions, and that whatever people are given in this present life cannot be compared to it: "*God will have granted them a most excellent provision.*" (Verse 11) It is God who grants all provisions in the life of this world and in the life to come, but some provisions are better than others. His choice of what is best is the right choice. We see how the point of good provisions is mentioned here again so as to impress on people that the provisions in heaven are immeasurably better than what is provided here. Yet this is in addition to the true promise made earlier of giving good provisions to those who remain God-fearing.

The Creator of All

The *sūrah*'s concluding note refers to the great universe, thus linking the theme of the *sūrah*, its legislation and directives to God's will, power and knowledge that encompass the entire universe:

> *It is God who has created seven heavens and likewise of the earth. His command descends through them all, so that you may learn that God has power over all things, and that God encompasses all things with His knowledge.* (Verse 12)

We do not know to what the term 'seven heavens' really refers, nor are we aware of their sizes and dimensions. Likewise, we do not know what the seven earths are. This earth of ours may be one of them and the others are known to God alone. Yet the term *mithluhunn*, translated here as 'likewise' may not be a reference to number, but to the fact that the earth is made of the same material or qualities as the heavens. Whichever is the case, it is unnecessary to try to apply our own knowledge to Qur'ānic statements of this type. Our knowledge does not extend to everything in the universe so as to enable us to learn what exactly the Qur'ān refers to. To claim such precise knowledge is possible only when man acquires absolutely certain knowledge of the entire universe. While this is impossible, we can still benefit by the Qur'ānic reference to this fact and its psychological effect and its bearing on our understanding of the proper Islamic concept of the universe.

This reference to the creation of the vast universe, "*seven heavens and likewise of the earth,*" is awe inspiring. It presents us with a great image of the Creator's limitless power, the vastness of His kingdom. When compared to the universe, the entire earth seems a tiny little place. How do we see those living on it, and how do we estimate an event that takes place on it? What value should we give to a little sum of money a man gives his divorced wife in maintenance, or that a woman forgos?

God's command descends in between, or through, these seven heavens and the earth or the seven earths. A part of His command is the sum of these rulings concerning the subject matter of this *surah*, i.e. divorce. It is, then, a great issue, even by human standards and our concept of time and place. To defy it is to be in defiance of a command that resounds throughout the heavens and the earths. It is a command that those on high hear of, as do other creatures in the heavens and the earths. Defying it, then, becomes a ghastly offence that no wise believer would even contemplate, and particularly when God's messenger has recited to him God's precise revelations, enlightening him on this matter so as to take him from darkness into light.

This command descends through the heavens and the earth so that it implants in believers' hearts the belief that God has the power to do what He wills. Nothing is beyond Him. He also knows everything throughout His great kingdom. Nothing escapes His knowledge, not even the best guarded secrets of the heart.

This truth is relevant here in two ways: the first is that these rulings on divorce are given by God who knows everything. He has issued them knowing all their situations, circumstances, interests and abilities. Hence, they are better to be followed with diligence, for they are better suited for human life. Secondly, the implementation of these rulings in particular is left to people's consciences. Therefore, realizing the extent of God's knowledge and His awareness of everything, including people's feelings and intentions, ensures that such consciences remain sensitive in an area where nothing is more important than fearing God Almighty.

Thus the *surah* concludes on this awe-striking note, which also makes people's minds ready to listen and obey. All praise is due to the Creator of these hearts who knows how to inspire and influence them.

SŪRAH 66

Al-Taḥrīm

(Prohibition)

Prologue

God has willed that Islam should be His final message, and the code of living it outlines should be the one suitable for the rest of human life. Furthermore, the life of those who believe in Islam should be consistent with the law that governs the universe, and Islam should be the faith to guide human life and shape all its activities. Therefore, He made this code of living comprehensive and perfect, catering for all human abilities and potentials. At the same time, this code elevates such abilities and potentials to the level suited for the creature God has placed in charge of the earth, honouring him above many of His other creatures, and blowing into him of His own spirit. Consistent with this will of His, God has made Islam naturally forward-looking. It enables life to grow while at the same time elevating it to the highest standard of purity. It does not stop any creative aspect or suppress a useful potential. On the contrary, it awakens and enhances these while ensuring a proper balance between forward movement and rising to a higher horizon. It is this which prepares the human spirit in this life for the superior happiness and bliss of the life to come, and the human mortal for a life everlasting.

God has also willed that the Messenger who delivers this final message should be a man who reflects the faith, with all its distinctive

93

characteristics and its special nature. Thus, as he goes through life, the Prophet becomes a true and practical translation of this faith, its nature and direction. He is an ordinary human being whose human abilities have attained a high standard: physically strong, with perfect constitution, sound senses, alert, able to perfectly feel all there is to feel. At the same time, he is full of emotion, naturally alert and sensitive, appreciates beauty, and is receptive and responsive. Moreover, he is of great intelligence, broad-minded, strong-willed, and he controls his feelings and reactions. Above all this, he is the Prophet whose soul reflects pure light, able to undertake the night journey from Makkah to Jerusalem and his subsequent ascendance to heaven. He is the one who is addressed from on high, sees the light of his Lord, and whose nature is in touch with the nature of everything in the universe: small and large stones greet him, the branches of trees yearn for contact with him, and Uḥud, the mountain, shakes at his presence. All these powers and potentials are balanced within his personality in such a way as to reflect the balance of the faith he has been chosen to present to humanity.

God has made the Prophet's life, its private and public aspects, an open book for the benefit of his followers and humanity at large. They can read in it all aspects of the Islamic faith and its practical implementation. Hence, there is nothing in it that is secret or limited to a closed circle. Indeed, many of its aspects are stated in the Qur'ān, revealing things that for an ordinary person are normally kept private. Indeed, even those aspects of human weakness, which are beyond our control, are left open for all to see. We almost see the wisdom behind so revealing such aspects of the Prophet's life to mankind. Nothing in his person or in his life belongs exclusively to him. He and all aspects of his life belong to his message. Why should, then, any aspect of his life be hidden? His life is the Islamic faith, something that is both close to us and easy to implement. The Prophet is assigned the task of presenting it in practice in his own life, just as he presents it by word and directive. This is the role assigned to him.

His Companions – may God be pleased with them and reward them well – conveyed to us all the details of his life. Nothing, whether of little or great importance in his daily life, is left unrecorded. It was part of God's will to have such a detailed record of His Messenger's life, or rather to have a detailed record of Islam as lived by the Prophet. What his Companions reported is added to what the Qur'ān records of the Prophet's life and both form an everlasting record of this noble life, which benefits all humanity.

The Prophet's Wives

In its opening section, this *sūrah* presents an episode of life in the Prophet's home, showing some of the reactions and responses between some of his wives, and between them and himself. It also shows how these reactions and responses were reflected in the life of the Muslim community as a whole. This is followed by directives given to the community on the basis of what took place in the Prophet's homes, between his wives.

The time when these events took place is not precise, but reference to the various reports detailing them confirm that they definitely occurred after the Prophet's marriage to Zaynab bint Jaḥsh.

It may also be useful to give here a summary of the Prophet's marriages and his home life at that time. This will enable us to visualize the events referred to in the *sūrah*. This brief outline is based on *Jawāmiʿ al-Sīrah* by Ibn Ḥazm and the Prophet's biography by Ibn Hishām. We will also add some brief comments as appropriate.

The Prophet's first wife was Khadījah bint Khuwaylid. He was 25, or perhaps 23,[1] when he married her. She was 40 or even older.[2] She died three years before the Prophet's migration to Madīnah. He did not marry another wife during her lifetime, and by then he was over 50 years of age.

After Khadījah's death, the Prophet married Sawdah bint Zimaʿh. There are no reports to suggest that she was either pretty or young. She was a widow of al-Sakrān ibn ʿAmr ibn ʿAbd Shams. Her husband

---

1. Other figures of the Prophet's age are mentioned in different reports: the lowest year of age is 21 and the highest is 30. – Editor's note.

2. Khadījah is commonly thought to have been 40 at the time of her marriage to the Prophet. This is highly unlikely as she gave the Prophet six children over a period of ten years. Other reports suggest that she was 25, 28, 30, 35 and even 45 years of age. One of the lower figures is more likely. – Editor's note.

was one of the early Muslims, and he was among the first migrants to Abyssinia. When he died, the Prophet married her.

He then married 'Ā'ishah bint Abū Bakr. She apparently was young, and he did not hold his wedding with her until he had settled in Madīnah. She was the only virgin he married, and she was the one he loved most. It is said that she was only nine years of age at the time of her marriage.[3] By the time he passed away, she had been with him nine years and five months.

The Prophet then married Ḥafṣah bint 'Umar, just over two years after settling in Madīnah. She had been married before. Her father had offered her in marriage to Abū Bakr and to 'Uthmān, but they both declined. The Prophet had promised her father something better for her so he married her himself.

He then married Zaynab bint Khuzaymah. Her first husband, 'Ubaydah ibn al-Ḥārith ibn 'Abd al-Muṭṭalib, was killed at the Battle of Badr. Zaynab died during the Prophet's lifetime. It is also reported that her first husband was 'Abdullāh ibn Jaḥsh who fell a martyr at the Battle of Uḥud. Perhaps this report is more accurate.

The Prophet also married Umm Salamah. Her first husband, Abū Salamah, was wounded at the Battle of Uḥud, and his wound did not heal until he died. The Prophet then married her, looking after her children by her first husband.

Zaynab bint Jaḥsh was his next wife. He himself had given her in marriage to Zayd ibn Ḥārithah, his former servant whom he had adopted as a son, but marital life between her and Zayd was fraught with difficulties. So, he divorced her. We related their story when discussing verses 36–40 of *Sūrah* 33, The Confederates, in Volume XIV.[4] She was pretty. Indeed, she was the one 'Ā'ishah felt most able to compete with because she was the Prophet's cousin, born to his paternal aunt, and because of her beauty.

---

3. This is again highly unlikely. She is mentioned among the early Muslims, which suggests that she was old enough to accept the new faith nine years before her marriage. Different reports of her reaction to events and statements suggest that she was perhaps twice this age at the time of her marriage. – Editor's note.

4. Sayyid Quṭb (2006), *In the Shade of the Qur'ān*, Vol. XIV, Leicester, Islamic Foundation, pp. 82–91.

Juwayriyyah bint al-Hārith was the next wife to be taken by the Prophet. This was in the middle of the sixth year of the Islamic calendar. Ibn Ishāq attributes the following report to 'Ā'ishah: "When the Prophet distributed the women taken slaves after the Expedition of al-Mustalaq, Juwayriyyah fell to Thābit ibn Qays ibn Shammās or his cousin. She made an agreement with him to buy her own freedom. She was very pretty. Anyone who saw her felt very attracted. She went to the Prophet seeking his help in paying what she owed for her freedom. When I saw her at my doorstep, I hated her, realizing that the Prophet would see of her beauty what I saw. She entered his room and said to him: 'Messenger of God. I am Juwayriyyah bint al-Hārith. My father is the chief of his tribe. You are not unaware of the trouble that has befallen me. I am here to seek your help in paying for my freedom after I had made an agreement to so buy myself.' He said to her: 'What about something better?' She asked him: 'What is that, Messenger of God?' He said: 'I will pay for your freedom and marry you.' She said: 'I accept.' He said: 'It is a deal.'"

The Prophet married Umm Habībah bint Abū Sufyān after the al-Hudaybiyah Peace Treaty. She had migrated to Abyssinia, but her husband, 'Ubaydullāh ibn Jahsh, converted to Christianity there and left her. The Prophet proposed marriage to her. It was King Negus who officiated at the marriage and paid her dowry on behalf of the Prophet.[5] She then returned to Madīnah.

Following the Battle of Khaybar, the Prophet married Safiyyah bint Huyayy ibn Akhtab. Her father was the chief of the Jewish tribe, al-Nadīr. She had been married to Kinānah ibn Abī al-Huqayq, a Jewish leader. Ibn Ishāq reports that "she was brought to him with another woman who had fallen prisoner. Bilāl walked them through the battlefield passing a number of Jews who had been slain. The other woman cried out loud as they passed by, throwing dust over her own head. The Prophet said: 'Take this devil woman away from me.' He

---

5. The Prophet sent a messenger to Negus to arrange this marriage on his behalf, when he heard of Umm Habībah's plight after she had lost her husband. This was some time before al-Hudaybiyah's peace treaty. However, she only arrived in Madīnah after that event. – Editor's note.

ordered that Ṣafiyyah be kept behind him, throwing his robe over her. His Companions thereby realized that he would take her himself. The Prophet is reported to have said to Bilāl: 'Are you devoid of compassion? How can you walk two women through the grounds where their menfolk have been killed?'"

Maymūnah bint al-Ḥārith ibn Ḥazn was the last of the Prophet's wives. She was the maternal aunt of Khālid ibn al-Walīd and 'Abdullāh ibn 'Abbās. Before marrying the Prophet she was married to Abū Ruḥm ibn 'Abd al-'Uzzā, or perhaps Ḥuwayṭib ibn 'Abd al-'Uzzā.

Thus, we see the special reasons that made it necessary for the Prophet to marry each of his wives. Apart from Zaynab bint Jaḥsh and Juwayriyyah bint al-Ḥārith, none were young or particularly attractive to men.[6] 'Ā'ishah was the one he loved most. Even in the case of those wives who were young and beautiful, there were psychological and humanitarian factors involved in their marriages. These increased their attraction. I do not deny or disregard the physical attraction, or beauty 'Ā'ishah felt the moment she saw Juwayriyyah, while Zaynab's beauty was also known to all. There is no need to deny that such human elements were a part of the Prophet's life. These cannot, however, form the basis for accusations levelled by the Prophet's enemies and which were denied by his followers. He was chosen as a human being, but with superior qualities and characteristics. Different as they were, his motives for whatever he did in his life, including his marriages, matched his superior qualities. In his home, he lived with his wives as a human being entrusted with the delivery of God's message. Indeed, God commanded him to declare the fact: "*Say, 'Limitless in His glory is my Lord. Surely I am only a man and a Messenger.'*" (17: 93)

He enjoyed life with his wives, as so did they. 'Ā'ishah states: "When the Prophet was alone with his wives, he was the most lenient and generous of people, always smiling and laughing." [Related by al-Suyūṭī and Ibn 'Asākir.] Yet this applied to what he himself could offer out of his character, compassion, manners and behaviour. As for their material life, it was mostly a life of poverty, even after the Muslim community

---

6. We should perhaps add Ṣafiyyah bint Ḥuyayy as well, who was also young at the time the Prophet married her. – Editor's note.

achieved several victories and made plentiful gains. In commenting on *Sūrah* 33, The Confederates, we discussed the crisis that took place in the Prophet's home when his wives asked for more housekeeping money.[7] The problem ended with a choice put to them in the following terms: *"Prophet! Say to your wives: 'If you desire the life of this world and its charms, I shall provide for you and release you in a becoming manner; but if you desire God and His Messenger and the life of the hereafter, know that God has readied great rewards for those of you who do good.'"* (33: 28–29) They all chose God, His Messenger and the life of the hereafter.

Nevertheless, life in the Prophet's home was not such as to stifle normal human feelings and jealousies in his wives' minds. Sometimes they had their disagreements, just like those that may occur among women in similar circumstances. We have seen how the moment 'Ā'ishah saw Juwayriyyah, she hoped that the Prophet would not see her because she was certain he would appreciate her beauty. She was right. 'Ā'ishah herself mentions a situation involving her and Ṣafiyyah: "I said to the Prophet: 'It is enough that Ṣafiyyah is so and so,' [meaning, she was short]. He said to me: 'You have said a word which could colour an entire sea.'" [Related by Abū Dāwūd.] She also reports that when the verses giving the Prophet's wives the choice referred to above, she was the first to be asked, and she chose to stay with the Prophet. She also requested that he not tell his other wives of her choice should any of them so ask. He said to her: "God has not sent me to make things hard for people. He sent me as a teacher who makes things easier. I will tell anyone of them about your choice should any care to ask." [Related by Muslim.]

These reports given by 'Ā'ishah about herself, reflecting her truthfulness and her shining Islamic education, are only examples of many others reflecting the normal way ordinary people behave in such a situation. They also show how the Prophet delivered his message through good example, cultivating the better characteristics of his household members, just as he delivered it by good example within his community.

---

7. This discussion is included in Volume XIV, pp. 61–66.

Al-Taḥrīm (Prohibition)

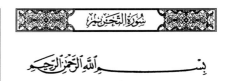

In the Name of God, the Lord of Grace, the Ever Merciful

يَـٰٓأَيُّهَا ٱلنَّبِيُّ لِمَ تُحَرِّمُ مَآ أَحَلَّ ٱللَّهُ لَكَ تَبۡتَغِي مَرۡضَاتَ أَزۡوَٰجِكَۚ وَٱللَّهُ غَفُورٞ رَّحِيمٞ ١

Prophet, why do you prohibit yourself something that God has made lawful to you in your desire to please your wives? God is much-forgiving, ever merciful. (1)

قَدۡ فَرَضَ ٱللَّهُ لَكُمۡ تَحِلَّةَ أَيۡمَٰنِكُمۡۚ وَٱللَّهُ مَوۡلَىٰكُمۡۖ وَهُوَ ٱلۡعَلِيمُ ٱلۡحَكِيمُ ٢

God has already ordained for you [believers] a way to release you from such oaths. God is your Lord Supreme. He alone is the All-Knowing, the Wise. (2)

وَإِذۡ أَسَرَّ ٱلنَّبِيُّ إِلَىٰ بَعۡضِ أَزۡوَٰجِهِۦ حَدِيثٗا فَلَمَّا نَبَّأَتۡ بِهِۦ وَأَظۡهَرَهُ ٱللَّهُ عَلَيۡهِ عَرَّفَ بَعۡضَهُۥ وَأَعۡرَضَ عَنۢ بَعۡضٖۖ فَلَمَّا نَبَّأَهَا بِهِۦ قَالَتۡ مَنۡ أَنۢبَأَكَ هَٰذَاۖ قَالَ نَبَّأَنِيَ ٱلۡعَلِيمُ ٱلۡخَبِيرُ ٣

The Prophet told something in confidence to one of his wives. When she divulged it, and God made this known to him, he spoke of a part of it and passed over a part. When he thus let her know of that, she asked, 'Who has told you this?' He said: 'The All-Knowing, the All-Aware told me.' (3)

إِن تَتُوبَآ إِلَى ٱللَّهِ فَقَدۡ صَغَتۡ قُلُوبُكُمَاۖ وَإِن تَظَٰهَرَا عَلَيۡهِ فَإِنَّ ٱللَّهَ هُوَ مَوۡلَىٰهُ وَجِبۡرِيلُ وَصَٰلِحُ ٱلۡمُؤۡمِنِينَۖ وَٱلۡمَلَـٰٓئِكَةُ بَعۡدَ ذَٰلِكَ ظَهِيرٞ ٤

Would that you two turn to God in repentance, for your hearts have swerved! But if you support each other against him, know that God is his protector, and that, therefore, Gabriel, all righteous believers and the angels will stand behind him. (4)

Were he to divorce you, his Lord may well give him in your stead spouses better than you: women who surrender themselves to God, true believers, devout, penitent, who worship in humility and reflect thoughtfully, be they women previously married or virgins. (5)

عَسَىٰ رَبُّهُۥٓ إِن طَلَّقَكُنَّ أَن يُبۡدِلَهُۥٓ أَزۡوَٰجًا خَيۡرًا مِّنكُنَّ مُسۡلِمَٰتٍ مُّؤۡمِنَٰتٍ قَٰنِتَٰتٍ تَٰٓئِبَٰتٍ عَٰبِدَٰتٍ سَٰٓئِحَٰتٍ ثَيِّبَٰتٍ وَأَبۡكَارًا ۝

Believers! Guard yourselves and your families against a fire fuelled by people and stones, over which are appointed angels, stern and mighty, who never disobey God in whatever He commands them and always do what they are bidden to do. (6)

يَٰٓأَيُّهَا ٱلَّذِينَ ءَامَنُوا۟ قُوٓا۟ أَنفُسَكُمۡ وَأَهۡلِيكُمۡ نَارًا وَقُودُهَا ٱلنَّاسُ وَٱلۡحِجَارَةُ عَلَيۡهَا مَلَٰٓئِكَةٌ غِلَاظٌ شِدَادٌ لَّا يَعۡصُونَ ٱللَّهَ مَآ أَمَرَهُمۡ وَيَفۡعَلُونَ مَا يُؤۡمَرُونَ ۝

Unbelievers! Make no excuses today. You will only be requited for what you used to do. (7)

يَٰٓأَيُّهَا ٱلَّذِينَ كَفَرُوا۟ لَا تَعۡتَذِرُوا۟ ٱلۡيَوۡمَ إِنَّمَا تُجۡزَوۡنَ مَا كُنتُمۡ تَعۡمَلُونَ ۝

Believers! Turn to God in sincere repentance. It may well be that your Lord will efface your bad deeds and admit you into gardens through which running waters flow, on a day when God will not disgrace the Prophet or those who believed with him. Their light will spread out before them, and on their right. They will say: 'Our Lord! Perfect our light for us and forgive us. You certainly have power over all things.' (8)

يَٰٓأَيُّهَا ٱلَّذِينَ ءَامَنُوا۟ تُوبُوٓا۟ إِلَى ٱللَّهِ تَوۡبَةً نَّصُوحًا عَسَىٰ رَبُّكُمۡ أَن يُكَفِّرَ عَنكُمۡ سَيِّـَٔاتِكُمۡ وَيُدۡخِلَكُمۡ جَنَّٰتٍ تَجۡرِى مِن تَحۡتِهَا ٱلۡأَنۡهَٰرُ يَوۡمَ لَا يُخۡزِى ٱللَّهُ ٱلنَّبِىَّ وَٱلَّذِينَ ءَامَنُوا۟ مَعَهُۥ نُورُهُمۡ يَسۡعَىٰ بَيۡنَ أَيۡدِيهِمۡ وَبِأَيۡمَٰنِهِم يَقُولُونَ رَبَّنَآ أَتۡمِمۡ لَنَا نُورَنَا وَٱغۡفِرۡ لَنَآ إِنَّكَ عَلَىٰ كُلِّ شَىۡءٍ قَدِيرٌ ۝

Prophet, strive hard against the unbelievers and the hypocrites, and press hard on them. Their ultimate abode is hell, and how vile a journey's end. (9)

يَـٰٓأَيُّهَا ٱلنَّبِىُّ جَٰهِدِ ٱلۡكُفَّارَ وَٱلۡمُنَٰفِقِينَ وَٱغۡلُظۡ عَلَيۡهِمۡۚ وَمَأۡوَىٰهُمۡ جَهَنَّمُۖ وَبِئۡسَ ٱلۡمَصِيرُ ۝

God has given examples of unbelievers: Noah's wife and Lot's wife. They were married to two of Our righteous servants but betrayed them. Their husbands could be of no avail to them against God. They were told: 'Enter both of you the fire with all those who will enter it.' (10)

ضَرَبَ ٱللَّهُ مَثَلٗا لِّلَّذِينَ كَفَرُوٓاْ ٱمۡرَأَتَ نُوحٖ وَٱمۡرَأَتَ لُوطٖۖ كَانَتَا تَحۡتَ عَبۡدَيۡنِ مِنۡ عِبَادِنَا صَٰلِحَيۡنِ فَخَانَتَاهُمَا فَلَمۡ يُغۡنِيَا عَنۡهُمَا مِنَ ٱللَّهِ شَيۡـٔٗا وَقِيلَ ٱدۡخُلَا ٱلنَّارَ مَعَ ٱلدَّٰخِلِينَ ۝

God has also given examples of believers: Pharaoh's wife, who said: 'My Lord! Build me a mansion in heaven near You, and save me from Pharaoh and his doings, and save me from the wrongdoing folk.' (11)

وَضَرَبَ ٱللَّهُ مَثَلٗا لِّلَّذِينَ ءَامَنُواْ ٱمۡرَأَتَ فِرۡعَوۡنَ إِذۡ قَالَتۡ رَبِّ ٱبۡنِ لِي عِندَكَ بَيۡتٗا فِي ٱلۡجَنَّةِ وَنَجِّنِي مِن فِرۡعَوۡنَ وَعَمَلِهِۦ وَنَجِّنِي مِنَ ٱلۡقَوۡمِ ٱلظَّٰلِمِينَ ۝

And Mary, the daughter of 'Imrān, who guarded her chastity; and We breathed of Our spirit into her. She accepted the truth of her Lord's words and His revealed books. She was truly devout. (12)

وَمَرۡيَمَ ٱبۡنَتَ عِمۡرَٰنَ ٱلَّتِيٓ أَحۡصَنَتۡ فَرۡجَهَا فَنَفَخۡنَا فِيهِ مِن رُّوحِنَا وَصَدَّقَتۡ بِكَلِمَٰتِ رَبِّهَا وَكُتُبِهِۦ وَكَانَتۡ مِنَ ٱلۡقَٰنِتِينَ ۝

The Event

The opening section of the *sūrah* speaks of an event in the lives of the Prophet and his wives. Although there are a number of reports giving different versions of what actually took place, we will leave these for now and return to them a little later. Based on this incident and the directives issued in connection with it, particularly the request that the two conspirators among the Prophet's wives repent, the *sūrah* also calls on believers to repent of their sins and requires that heads of families ensure their families are well brought up. They are specifically urged to protect themselves and their families from hell. A direct image of hell is also included here. The *sūrah* then concludes by citing various examples. Noah's and Lot's wives are shown as examples of unfaith in a house emanating belief, while Pharaoh's wife is depicted as someone holding to right faith while living in a house full of unbelievers. Mary is also shown as a pure woman who received a breath of God's spirit and believed in God's words and scriptures.

Prophet, why do you prohibit yourself something that God has made lawful to you in your desire to please your wives? God is much-forgiving, ever merciful. God has already ordained for you [believers] a way to release you from such oaths. God is your Lord Supreme. He alone is the All-Knowing, the Wise. The Prophet told something in confidence to one of his wives. When she divulged it, and God made this known to him, he spoke of a part of it and passed over a part. When he thus let her know of that, she asked, 'Who has told you this?' He said: 'The All-Knowing, the All-Aware told me.' Would that you two turn to God in repentance, for your hearts have swerved! But if you support each other against him, know that God is his protector, and that, therefore, Gabriel, all righteous believers and the angels will stand behind him. Were he to divorce you, his Lord may well give him in your stead spouses better than you: women who surrender themselves to God, true believers, devout, penitent, who worship in humility and reflect thoughtfully, be they women previously married or virgins. (Verses 1–5)

The Reports

There are several reports about the event in question, one of which is related by al-Bukhārī, which means that it is authentic. On 'Ā'ishah's authority, al-Bukhārī relates: "The Prophet used to have a honey drink at Zaynab bint Jaḥsh's home and then stay for some time with her. Ḥafṣah and I secretly agreed that when he came to either of us we would say to him: 'You have eaten *Maghāfīr*[8]; I can smell it.' When this occurred, he said: 'No. I only had a honey drink at Zaynab's. I will not do it again, and I have made an oath to this effect. Do not tell anyone of this.' This is what he prohibited himself, even though it was permissible for him to have."

It seems that either 'Ā'ishah or Ḥafṣah told her co-conspirator of the Prophet's decision to no longer take this honey drink. God then informed him of the same. He went back to her and mentioned some of what went on between the two of them, but without recounting it all in order not to embarrass her. He only touched upon the subject so that she realized that he was aware of it all. Surprised, she asked him: 'Who told you all this?' It might have occurred to her that his other wife was the one to tell him. He, however, said to her: '*The All-Knowing, the All-Aware told me.*' (Verse 3) His information, then, was given by the One who knows it all, which, in turn, implies that the Prophet was also aware of it *in toto*, not merely what he mentioned to her.

This incident angered the Prophet, exposing as it did that intrigue was going on in his home. He, therefore, swore that he would not touch any of his wives for a full month. People in the Muslim community also heard that the Prophet was thinking of divorcing his wives. This *sūrah* was then revealed and the Prophet's anger subsided. Subsequently, he resumed his life with his wives. We will presently mention how this happened, but we will first give a different version of the incident.

This second version is related by al-Nasā'ī on Anas's authority: "The Prophet had a bondswoman with whom he had sex. His wives, 'Ā'ishah and Ḥafṣah, put pressure to bear on him until he prohibited himself from doing so. God revealed the verses starting with *"Prophet, why do you*

---

8.   *Maghāfīr* is a glue-like type of food with a sweet taste and bad smell.

prohibit yourself something that God has made lawful to you in your desire to please your wives?" (Verse 1) Another report given by Ibn Jarīr and Ibn Isḥāq mentions that the Prophet had sex with Maria, the mother of his son Ibrahīm, in Ḥafṣah's home. Ḥafṣah was very angry, considering this to be an insult against her person. The Prophet promised her he would banish Maria from him, swearing to this, and he asked Ḥafṣah to keep this a secret, but she told 'Ā'ishah.

Either one of these two incidents may have taken place. However, the second report involving Maria may be closer to what we can understand from the text of the *sūrah* and the consequences that led to the Prophet being so angry that he even considered divorcing his wives. Taken together, this suggests that the matter was very sensitive and involved. The first report concerning the Prophet's favourite honey drink is more authentic with regard to its transmission. While it is not as serious as the second incidence implies, it might have led to such serious consequences if we take into account the high moral standards prevailing in the Prophet's home. Regardless though of what actually did happen, we should place our trust in God for He knows the truth of it all.

The Outcome

What, then, were the effects of this incident and the Prophet's decision to stay away from his wives for a month? This is best described in a *ḥadīth* related by Imām Aḥmad in *Al-Musnad,* which quotes 'Abdullāh ibn 'Abbās:

> I was keen to ask 'Umar about the Prophet's two wives in reference to whom God says in the Qur'ān: '*Would that you two turn to God in repentance, for your hearts have swerved.*' When 'Umar went on pilgrimage, I went with him. As we were travelling, he moved from the rest and I went with him, carrying a water container. He relieved himself and came back to me. I poured water for him to do his ablution. I then asked him: 'Which two of the Prophet's wives are referred to in God's statement, '*Would that you two turn to God in repentance, for your hearts have swerved*'?' He said: 'I wonder at you, Ibn 'Abbās!' [Al-Zuhrī comments here that 'Umar disliked

being asked about this, but he did not withhold the information.] 'Umar said: 'They were 'Ā'ishah and Ḥafṣah.' He then told me the story.

We, the Quraysh, used to have complete authority over our wives. When we settled in Madīnah, however, we found its people more submissive to their wives. Our women started to learn from their women. I used to live in Umayyah ibn Zayd's home in the highlands. One day, I was angry with my wife, as she objected to something I said. I disliked the fact that she should object to me. She said: 'Why are you so surprised that I should object? God's Messenger's own wives may object to something he says, and any of them may not speak to him the whole day, until night time.' I, therefore, went straight to Ḥafṣah[9] and asked her: 'Do you sometimes object to what the Prophet says?' She confirmed that she did. I asked: 'Would any of you refrain from speaking to him throughout the day, until nightfall?' She again answered in the affirmative. I said: 'Ill-advised and a loser indeed is any of you who does that! Do you not consider that any of you might incur God's anger as a result of His Messenger being angry, and then you end in ruin? Do not object to God's Messenger in anything he says, and do not ask anything from him. Take from me instead whatever you want. Do not be deluded by the fact that your friend [meaning 'Ā'ishah] is more pretty and is loved best by the Prophet.'

I had a neighbour from the Anṣār, with whom I took turns in going down to see the Prophet. He would go one day and I the next day. Each of us would inform the other of any new Qur'ānic revelations and of any events or developments. At the time, we were aware that the Ghassān[10] were preparing to invade us. My neighbour went to the Prophet one day and then came to me in the evening, knocking on my door. He called out and I went to see him. He said: 'A very serious matter took place.' I asked whether the Ghassān army was approaching. He said: 'No, something more serious than

9. Ḥafṣah was 'Umar's daughter, married to the Prophet. – Editor's note.
10. The Ghassān was a major Arab tribe living in southern Syria and Palestine, as part of the Byzantine Empire. – Editor's note.

that. The Prophet has divorced his wives.' I said: 'Ill-advised and lost is Ḥafṣah! I thought that this might happen.'

In the morning, after I had prayed *Fajr*, I put on my clothes and went to Ḥafṣah. I found her crying. I asked her whether the Prophet had divorced his wives. She said: 'I do not know. He has shut himself in this room close by.' I went there and found a black servant. I said to him: 'Seek permission for 'Umar to enter.' He went in and came back, and said: 'I mentioned you to him but he did not reply.' I went away, and I found close to the pulpit in the mosque a few men sitting down, some of whom were in tears. I sat there for a short while and I was then overcome by my own grief. I went back to the servant and told him to seek permission for me to enter. He again went in and told me as he came out that he mentioned my name but the Prophet remained silent. Once more I went to sit near the pulpit until I was overcome by my feelings. I went a third time to the servant and told him to seek permission for me to see the Prophet. Yet he again told me when he came out that he mentioned my name but the Prophet did not reply. I went away, but soon the servant called me. He said: 'You can go in. He has given you permission.' As I went in, I greeted the Prophet. I found him sitting on a straw mat which had left its mark on his side. I asked him whether he had divorced his wives. He lifted his head and said: 'No.' I said: 'God is Supreme.'

I then said: 'Messenger of God. If you could but see us, the Quraysh, when we used to have complete authority over our wives. When we settled in Madīnah, however, we found its people more submissive to their wives. Our women started to learn from their women. I used to live in Umayyah ibn Zayd's home in the highlands. One day, I was angry with my wife, as she objected to something I said. I disliked the fact that she should object to me'. She said: 'Why are you so surprised that I should object? God's Messenger's own wives may object to something he says, and any of them may not speak to him the whole day, until night time.' I then said to Ḥafṣah: 'Ill-advised and a loser indeed is any of you who does that! Do you not consider that any of you might incur God's anger as a result of His Messenger being angry with you, and

107

so end in ruin?' The Prophet smiled as I said this. I then told him that I said to my daughter that she should not to be deluded by the fact that her friend [meaning 'Ā'ishah] was prettier and loved the best by the Prophet. The Prophet smiled again. I asked whether I could sit down with him and he invited me to so sit.

As I lifted my head, looking around his home, I found absolutely nothing of note, apart from his dignified presence. I said: 'Messenger of God. Pray to God to give your community abundance of things. He has given abundance to the Persians and the Byzantines while they do not worship God.' He sat up and said to me: 'Are you in doubt, Ibn al-Khattab? These are people who have been given their good shares in this present life.' I said: 'Please pray to God to forgive me.' The Prophet had vowed not to come near his wives for a month, because he was so aggrieved by them. Because of this, God took issue with him. [This report is related by al-Bukhārī, Muslim, al-Tirmidhī and al-Nasā'ī on al-Zuhrī's authority, with different chains of transmission.]

The Qur'ānic Discussion

Such is the reporting of the incident in historical sources. We will now look at its treatment in the Qur'ān. The *sūrah* begins with a mild reproach by God to His Messenger:

Prophet, why do you prohibit yourself something that God has made lawful to you in your desire to please your wives? God is much-forgiving, ever merciful. God has already ordained for you [believers] a way to release you from such oaths. God is your Lord Supreme. He alone is the All-Knowing, the Wise. (Verses 1–2)

The reproach is mild but effective. It is not proper for a believer to prohibit himself something that God has made lawful. The Prophet had not imposed a legal prohibition on himself with regard to the honey drink he liked or to Maria. He only decided to refrain from enjoying either. This gentle reproach makes it clear that it is not right to deliberately deprive oneself of what God has made lawful in order to appease someone else. The comment at the end of the verse is: '*God is much-forgiving, ever merciful.*' This suggests that such deliberate action would require questioning unless it was overlooked by an act of God's forgiveness and grace.

As for the oath that the Qur'ānic text suggests the Prophet made, God stated a way for him to release himself from it. This means that an oath that establishes a situation other than what is best should be atoned for so as to release oneself from it and then take up the better option. "*God is your Lord Supreme.*" (Verse 2) He helps you to overcome your weaknesses and to cope with what may be hard for you. Hence, he has ordained for you a way out of your oaths so as to ensure that you do not incur unnecessary hardship. "*He alone is the All-Knowing, the Wise.*" (Verse 2) He legislates for you on the basis of His absolute knowledge and perfect wisdom. He only commands you to do what is within your power and what is best suited for you. Therefore, do not prohibit yourselves anything other than what He has forbidden, and continue to make lawful only what He has made lawful. It is clear that the comment here fits perfectly with the directive already stated.

The *sūrah* then refers to what the Prophet said to one of his wives, but mentions neither its subject matter nor its details. None of this is important. What is important, however, is what it signified and the knock-on effects it generated: "*The Prophet told something in confidence to one of his wives.*" (Verse 3) What we are looking at here is something unique in human history. We are looking at a period when there was direct contact between heaven and ordinary people. Here is a direct, public and detailed intervention by heaven in human affairs. God informs the Prophet of a conversation between two of his wives concerning something he had told one of them in confidence. When the Prophet mentioned this to the wife who had divulged it, he only hinted at a certain aspect of it, rather than giving her a detailed account. At the same time, he also informed her of the source of his information: it was the One solid source that could not be mistaken: "*When she divulged it, and God made this known to him, he spoke of a part of it and passed over a part. When he thus let her know of that, she asked, 'Who has told you this?' He said: 'The All-Knowing, the All-Aware told me.'*" (Verse 3)

The choice of God's attributes of perfect knowledge and complete awareness of everything particularly suit the conspiratory situation under discussion. Thus, the one who asked the question is reminded of that which she might have forgotten or overlooked. We are all so reminded whenever we read the Qur'ān.

A change of style then follows. The *sūrah* is no longer reporting an incident; it is now addressing the two women involved, as if the matter is taking place at this very moment: "*Would that you two turn to God in repentance, for your hearts have swerved! But if you support each other against him, know that God is his protector, and that, therefore, Gabriel, all righteous believers and the angels will stand behind him.*" (Verse 4) They are, thus, invited to turn to God in repentance after their hearts had swerved from rightful action.

We so realize that the incident had such a profound effect on the Prophet as to require the statement that he is given full protection by God. Furthermore, Gabriel, the believers and all angels stand ready to give him their full support. The Prophet is thus reassured and comforted after this serious breach of confidence. Indeed, the whole situation must have been considered as very serious, implying far-reaching consequences for it to have necessitated such assurances. We can appreciate this for ourselves from the reports mentioned earlier, particularly the answer given by the Anṣārī man when 'Umar asked him about whether the Ghassān army was approaching. In fact his answer states that the matter was even more serious than that threat. Ghassān was an autonomous region in the tutelage of the Byzantine Empire, bordering the Arabian Peninsula. An attack by Ghassān on the Muslim community would have been very serious, yet the other matter was felt by Muslims to be even far more serious and far-reaching. They felt that the Prophet's own comfort and the maintenance of serenity and peace in his noble home were more important than anything else. This, then, gives us a clear indication of how the Muslim community viewed these developments, a view in line with how heaven treated it. It is, then, a correct view.

The next verse provides similar import. It details the qualities of the women whom God may give to His Messenger, should he divorce his current wives. This is addressed to all his wives by way of an implicit threat: "*Were he to divorce you, his Lord may well give him in your stead spouses better than you: women who surrender themselves to God, true believers, devout, penitent, who worship in humility and reflect thoughtfully, be they women previously married or virgins.*" (Verse 5) They are, thus, indirectly called upon to adopt these qualities. The first quality is full submission to God and the fulfilment of all religious obligations. Next, is complete faith that leads to surrendering oneself to God, which is the literal meaning of the Arabic word *islam*. Devotion, the third quality, means conscious obedience of God. The Prophet's wives should also be penitent, which means that they should regret any slip into sin and follow this by turning to do God's bidding. To worship in humility is another quality they should possess. It is the means by which to communicate with God and express our submission to Him. Thoughtful reflection is how we have translated the quality the *sūrah* refers to by the Arabic word *sā'ihāt,* which literally means 'wandering, contemplating'. What it means here is that they always reflect on God's creation and contemplate the great universe He has created. Having all these qualities, these new wives would be either virgins or previously married, in the same way as the Prophet married those wives already with him.

This warning was apparently necessary because of the telling effect their conspiracy had on the Prophet, incurring his anger. He was never given to anger, but the matter was clearly serious. The Prophet felt comforted and reassured when these verses were revealed, addressing him personally as also members of his household. Thereafter, the atmosphere in his blessed home regained its serenity as a direct result of God's statements. This was an honour given to the Prophet and his household, given their important role in the solid implementation of God's code for human life.

We have thus seen a picture of the home life of the man who was entrusted with establishing a nation and a state on hitherto unknown lines. This nation was to be entrusted with the fulfilment of divine faith in its final form. It was to be the practical establishment of a devout society that sets the example for future generations. We see also a picture of a man of exceptional greatness and nobility. Yet, he lived his humanity just as he fulfilled the tasks of his prophethood; the two were intertwined. It was God's will that he should be a human Messenger delivering His last message to mankind, outlining a perfect code for all humanity.

It is a perfect message delivered by a perfect Messenger. One aspect of its perfection is that its every adherent remains a human being: none of his abilities or talents are suppressed or prevented from developing and flourishing. At the same time, it cultivates and educates him so as to attain the highest standard within his power.

Thus has been the method of Islam with those who understood it well and who have moulded their lives on the basis of its teachings. They became living examples of Islam. The Prophet's practical life, with all that it involved of human experience, endeavours, strengths and weaknesses, was intertwined with the divine message. As we see in the case of those who were closest to him and his own family, his life was the practical example of how to live Islam. It set the model for those who wish to learn an easy and practical way of implementing God's message. It also steered away from theoretical assumptions that have no practical effect.

God's purpose was thus fulfilled: the final message to mankind was revealed in full, the Messenger who could receive it and give it its practical form was chosen, and his life was left as an open book for all, studied and reviewed by one generation after another.

A Believer's Responsibility

Now the *sūrah* addresses the believers enjoining them to fulfil their family duties, providing good education, admonition and reminders so that they protect themselves and their families from hell. It provides an image of the fire and how the unbelievers stand before it. In line with the call to those involved in the earlier event to turn to God in repentance, the same call is made to the believers, adding an image of heaven which awaits those who repent of their sins. This second section of the *sūrah* concludes with a call on the Prophet to strive hard against the unbelievers and the hypocrites:

Believers! Guard yourselves and your families against a fire fuelled by people and stones, over which are appointed angels, stern and mighty, who never disobey God in whatever He commands them and always do what they are bidden to do. Unbelievers! Make no excuses today. You will only be requited for what you used to do. Believers! Turn to God in sincere repentance. It may well be that your Lord will efface your bad deeds and admit you into gardens through which running waters flow, on a day when God will not disgrace the Prophet or those who believed with him. Their light will spread out before them, and on their right. They will say: 'Our Lord! Perfect our light for us and forgive us. You certainly have power over all things.' Prophet, strive hard against the unbelievers and the hypocrites, and press hard on them. Their ultimate abode is hell, and how vile a journey's end. (Verses 6–9)

A believer's responsibility with regard to himself and his family is heavy and awesome. He and his family are liable to punishment in the fire of hell and it is his responsibility to protect himself and his family from such a dreadful fate. It is a terrible fire, *"fuelled by people and stones."* (Verse 6) People there are treated in the same way as stones: cheap, abject and thrown away with a total disregard as to what may happen to them. A fire fuelled by stones must blaze fiercely, and a torment that combines its scourge with humiliation compounds the suffering. Everything about it is absolutely terrible: *"over [it] are appointed angels, stern and mighty,"* so that they suit the punishment they are required to administer. They *"never disobey God in whatever He commands them and always do what they are bidden to do."* (Verse 6) By nature they always obey every command God gives them, and are well able to carry out any such assignment. Possessing such qualities, they are chosen to guard the fire of hell, while every believer is responsible for protecting himself and his family from it. He has to attend to his responsibility now, in this life, before it is too late. When the chance is gone, no excuse is acceptable. The unbelievers will try to present excuses, but they are confronted with the facts that leave them in utter despair: *"Unbelievers! Make no excuses today. You will only be requited for what you used to do."* (Verse 7) That day is not a time for presenting excuses. It is the day when reward and punishment are given. The unbelievers will only take what their own actions incur.

How are the believers to protect themselves and their families from the fire of hell? The way is mapped out for them, and they are further equipped with great hope: *"Believers! Turn to God in sincere repentance. It may well be that your Lord will efface your bad deeds and admit you into gardens through which running waters flow, on a day when God will not disgrace the Prophet or those who believed with him. Their light will spread out before them, and on their right. They will say: 'Our Lord! Perfect our light for us and forgive us. You certainly have power over all things.'"* (Verse 8) The way, then, begins with sincere repentance setting the heart on an honest course that allows no deception. This means genuine regret for past sins and a commitment to do what is good and required. Such repentance is certain to rid a person's heart of any residue sin may leave behind and encourages only what is good. Both qualities are necessary to make the repentance sincere and effective.

When repentance is sincere, it brings with it a hope that God will forgive the repentant their sins and admit them into heaven on the day when the unbelievers are given their humiliating punishment. No disgrace will on that day attach to the Prophet or those who followed him and accepted his message. This prospect is very tempting as it brings about great honour, with the believers being joined to the Prophet as one group treated with dignity when others are shamed. Furthermore, they are given light that *"spreads out before them and on their right."* Thus they are identified among the great multitude, and they can find their way to their ultimate goal, which is heaven.

In that fearful position when everyone is in the grip of worried anticipation, they are inspired with a humble prayer: *"Our Lord! Perfect our light for us and forgive us. You certainly have power over all things."* (Verse 8) The fact that they say such a prayer when the situation makes everyone speechless is a sign that their prayer will be answered. God inspires believers to offer such a prayer only when He will be pleased to answer it. This means that their very prayer is a blessing God bestows on them in addition to the honour and the light already given to them.

How different all this is from the fire fuelled by people and stones! However, both reward and punishment highlight the responsibility of every believer to protect himself and his family from the fire and to place them in a position where they deserve to receive the reward of heaven. In the light of the event that took place in the Prophet's home, we can appreciate the message given in these verses. A believer is responsible for setting his household on the right way, just as he is responsible for ensuring that he purges his heart of sin and follows divine guidance.

As we said in our commentary on the previous *sūrah*, Divorce, Islam is a faith that takes care of the family. Therefore, it sets certain duties and responsibilities a believer must fulfil with regard to his home and family. The home is the nucleus of the Muslim community. Muslim families are the cells that make up the Muslim society. Every single home is a fortress of faith that must have no flaw in its internal structure. Everyone inside guards their positions so that no external enemy can infiltrate them. Otherwise, the whole society would be penetrated from within, and so would fall apart should any external attack occur. It is the first duty of a believer to attend to his home and family so that it is internally solid and well guarded. Before he tries to present his message to others, he must close any loophole within.

In this set up, a Muslim mother has an essential role to play; a Muslim father cannot on his own ensure the security of the fortress. Together, the two must cooperate fully in the upbringing of their sons and daughters. A group of men on their own can never succeed in establishing a Muslim society. Indeed, it is women who have a more important role to play in taking care of the new generation and safeguarding the future of the Muslim community. Hence, the Qur'ān addressed both men and women. It set out a system for the Muslim home, placing on believers a clear responsibility for their families, in the same way as they are responsible for themselves: "*Believers! Guard yourselves and your families against a fire fuelled by people and stones.*" (Verse 6)

Advocates of Islam must be fully aware of this and ensure that they put it into practice. Their first efforts must be addressed to their homes: to their wives and mothers first, and to their children and the rest of their families. Great importance should be attached to the education of the Muslim woman, so that she can make her family home a Muslim home. Anyone who wants his home to be Islamic must start by choosing a Muslim wife. Otherwise, the formation of a Muslim community will take far too long and its structure will remain weak and flawed.

Our Own Hard Task

The situation with the first Muslim community was easier than it is in our present day. A Muslim society was already established in

Madīnah, where Islam, its vision of a clean, virtuous human life and its laws based on this vision were the driving force. Men and women looked up to God and His Messenger for judgement. When judgement was given, it was accepted as final. In such a society, it was easy for women to mould themselves as Islam wanted them to be. Likewise, it was easy for husbands to advise their wives and bring up their children in line with the Islamic system.

We are now in a totally different situation, as we have sunk back into a state of *jāhiliyyah* that influences our society, its laws, morality, traditions, systems, manners and culture. Women find themselves in the midst of this society and feel its crushing pressures as they try to bring their lives in line with Islam, whether on their own initiative or guided by their fathers, husbands or brothers.

In that first Muslim community, the man, the woman and society all had the same perspective and looked to the same source for judgement. In our own time, the man is looking up to a theoretical abstract while the woman writhes under the heavy pressure of a society that is extremely hostile to her perspective. There is no doubt that the pressures society brings to bear on women are many times greater than its pressure on men. Hence, a believing man has a double duty: he must not only protect himself from the fire but also protect his family that is exposed to such pressures.

A Muslim man must realize the size of his responsibility in order to address it properly. This requires that he exert much greater efforts than a Muslim man in the first Muslim community. This is why it is essential for anyone who wants to establish a Muslim home to look first of all for a partner who can guard his fort. She must be a woman who derives her perspective from the same source, Islam. He will have to sacrifice certain things. He must sacrifice superficial attractions that society presents, looking instead for a woman of firm belief who will help him in building a Muslim family. Muslim fathers who want to be part of the Islamic revival must also realize that the new cells in this revival are a trust they must safeguard. It is their task to educate, cultivate and bring them up on Islamic lines before they address their message to anyone else. Only in this way can they fulfil God's orders as He bids them to protect themselves and their families from the fire.

Once more we refer to the nature of Islam that requires the establishment of a community that runs its affairs according to Islam and gives it a practical presence. Islam is based on the need to establish a community that believes in it and adopts it as a way of life and a code of law. It is from Islam, the complete and perfect system, that this community derives all its concepts and perspectives. Such a community is the fertile soil where Islam finds its practical model. Within this community, people look at this model and feel free of the pressures of an un-Islamic society. Moreover, the Muslim community ensures that its members are not subjected to any persecution.

We, thus, see the importance of establishing a Muslim community where Muslim girls and women live, protected from the crushing pressures of the un-Islamic society around them. In such a community they are no longer torn apart by their own Islamic perspective and traditions that are un-Islamic. A young Muslim man will find in that community a woman who will share life with him in a family nest, or a fortress, which is the first and primary unit of the Islamic camp.

It is essential rather than merely desirable for an Islamic community to be established along Islamic lines, adopting Islamic ideas, morality, manners and life concepts and implementing them within its own ranks. Only such a community can safeguard its concepts and values, advocating them in a practical way, seen by all. Thus individuals in an un-Islamic society, who are addressed by the advocates of Islam, will look at Islamic life and be motivated to come out of the darkness in which they live and replace it with the light Islam provides. Eventually, when God wills that Islam should triumph, new generations will be raised under its care, protected from the *jāhiliyyah* that has long prevailed.

It was to protect the first Muslim community that the command was issued to the Prophet to strive hard against those who take a hostile stand towards it: *"Prophet, strive hard against the unbelievers and the hypocrites, and press hard on them. Their ultimate abode is hell, and how vile a journey's end."* (Verse 9) This is particularly significant in light of the earlier command to the believers to protect themselves and their families against the fire of hell. It is also significant in respect of the invitation given to them to sincerely repent of their sins so that their bad deeds are erased and they are admitted into heaven. It highlights the importance

117

of safeguarding the environment where protection from the fire takes place. Thus, oppressive and wicked elements are not allowed to attack the Muslim community whether from outside, as the unbelievers used to do, or from within as the hypocrites did.

In its order to strive hard against the enemies of Islam, the Qur'ānic statement groups together both the unbelievers and the hypocrites because they shared the same mission – the destruction of the Muslim community, or at least its disintegration. To strive against them is, then, the sort of effort that protects from the fire, and to be hard against them is the proper response required of the Prophet and the believers in this present life. As for the life to come, "*their ultimate abode is hell, and how vile a journey's end.*" (Verse 9)

We note that the harmonious tune this second section of the *sūrah* sings of its message is also in perfect harmony with the first section that dealt with a particular event in the Prophet's own home.

Contrasting Examples

The third and final section of the *sūrah* sounds as if it is a direct continuation of its first section. It speaks of unbelieving women married to prophets and women believers in the midst of unbelievers:

> God has given examples of unbelievers: Noah's wife and Lot's wife. They were married to two of Our righteous servants but betrayed them. Their husbands could be of no avail to them against God. They were told: 'Enter both of you the fire with all those who will enter it.' God has also given examples of believers: Pharaoh's wife, who said: 'My Lord! Build me a mansion in heaven near You, and save me from Pharaoh and his doings, and save me from the wrongdoing folk.' And Mary, the daughter of 'Imrān, who guarded her chastity; and We breathed of Our spirit into her. She accepted the truth of her Lord's words and His revealed books. She was truly devout. (Verses 10–12)

Reports speaking of the betrayal of Noah and Lot by their wives suggest that it was a betrayal of their messages, rather than their being unfaithful to their marriage bonds. Noah's wife used to join the unbelievers in his community in making fun of him, while Lot's wife used to inform his people when he received guests, knowing what they tried to do with such visitors.

Similarly, reports concerning Pharaoh's wife make it clear that she lived in his palace as a believer in God Almighty, and suggest that she was of Asian origin following a divine religion that was revealed before Moses' time. Historical reports mention that the mother of Eminhuteb IV, the Pharaoh who advocated belief in one god, making the sun a symbol of the divine being, calling himself Ekhnaton, was Asian and believed in a religion other than that known in Egypt. God only knows if she is the one referred to in this *sūrah*, or whether the reference is made to the Pharaoh challenged by Moses and his wife. Moses' Pharaoh is definitely different from Eminhuteb IV. We need not, however, be particularly concerned about the exact identity of Pharaoh's wife. What is important is that the Qur'ānic statement confirms a permanent fact in which individual people are only examples.

Having made an order to believers to protect themselves and their families from incurring punishment in hell, the *sūrah* now highlights the principle of individual responsibility. The Prophet's wives, and indeed wives of all believers, are told here that ultimately they are personally accountable for what they do and the decisions they make. Their individual responsibility cannot be waived merely because they are married to a prophet or to a devout believer. Both Noah's and Lot's wives *"were married to two of Our righteous servants but betrayed them. Their husbands could be of no avail to them against God. They were told: 'Enter both of you the fire with all those who will enter it.'"* (Verse 10) When the question is one of belief or unbelief, or one of betrayal of faith, there can be no special privilege for anyone, not even for prophets' wives.

Pharaoh's wife gives the perfect contrast. She was living in the midst of sweeping unbelief, but that did not deter her from seeking her own personal safety. She disowned all connection with Pharaoh's palace, praying to God to grant her a home in heaven. She disavowed any relation with Pharaoh, praying that God grant her safety from him. Realizing that as Pharaoh's wife she was the closest person to him and his actions, she feared that some blame might attach to her. She, therefore, made it clear that she had nothing to do with all this, further praying to God that He keep her away from it: "*And save me from Pharaoh and his doings.*" (Verse 11) She disowned Pharaoh's people while at the same time living in their midst: "*And save me from the wrongdoing folk.*" (Verse 11)

Pharaoh's wife's prayer and her overall position is a shining example of rejecting all temptation that the life of this world can offer, even at its most splendid. Pharaoh was the most powerful king on earth, and his palace offered the best that a woman could desire. Yet his wife chose faith in preference to all this. She did not merely treat it with contempt; she considered it evil and sought refuge with God from yielding to it, praying to be saved from it and its consequences. Yet Pharaoh's wife was a woman standing on her own in the midst of a great kingdom, which makes her all the more admirable and gives her an even greater position. As we have stated earlier, women are more sensitive and responsive to social pressures. However, this woman, on her own, resisted the pressures exerted by society, the palace, the throne, the courtiers and her own royal position, lifting her head to heaven seeking its light. She certainly provides a great example of submission to God, resisting all temptations and overcoming all impediments. Hence she deserved her special mention in God's book, the words of which are echoed throughout the universe as they are revealed from on high.

"*And Mary, the daughter of 'Imrān,*" provides another example of total dedication. Her story is given from its early beginnings elsewhere in the Qur'ān. Her distinctive quality mentioned here is her purity, "*who guarded her chastity.*" (Verse 12) Thus, her innocence is made absolutely clear, refuting the vile accusations the Jews levelled at her. "*And We breathed of Our spirit into her.*" (Verse 12) It was from this breathing of God's spirit into her that Jesus, her son, was born, as detailed in *Sūrah* 19, Maryam. We will not go into the details of his birth here, limiting ourselves only to the discussion of the present text which highlights Mary's purity, complete faith and total obedience of God: "*She accepted the truth of her Lord's words and His revealed books. She was truly devout.*" (Verse 12)

The fact that Pharaoh's wife is the one chosen to be mentioned here together with Mary is indicative of her own sublime status; a status enhanced by the special circumstances of her own life. Both ladies are splendid examples of women who combined firm faith with purity of behaviour and total devotion. God sets these two examples for the Prophet's own wives in the context of the event reported in the first section of the *sūrah*. They are also examples set before believing women in all generations.

This *sūrah* gives us a glimpse of the Prophet's own life, drawn in the inspiring style of the Qur'ān. No human report speaking of the period can give us a similar picture. This because Qur'ānic expressions are more inspiring and far-reaching. In this way, a single event is cited to state the truth that remains valid for the rest of time.

SŪRAH 67

Al-Mulk

(Dominion)

Prologue

Whereas the revelation of the previous ten *surahs* (57–66) took place in Madīnah, this *sūrah* and all nine that follow in this volume were revealed in Makkah. Each type has its own features and leaves its special impressions on the reader. Makkan revelation generally deals with belief in God, revelation and the Day of Judgement, as well as establishing concepts about life, the universe and its relation with its Creator based on such beliefs. It speaks about God, the Creator, in such a way that makes our hearts feel His presence and outlines the sort of emotions and manners that are appropriate for a human being who addresses his Lord and looks up to Him. It clearly sets the standards and values a Muslim adopts in judging events, situations and people. As we discuss the remaining *surahs* in this volume, we will see examples of such treatment, to be added to what we have already seen in other Makkan *surahs*.

Revelations given in Madīnah address the implementation of such beliefs, concepts, standards and values in practical life. They urge people to live up to their faith, which is the trust assigned to them. They must fulfil their obligations both within themselves and in their public lives.

The present *sūrah* seeks to formulate a new concept of the universe and its relation with its Creator. It is a broad, comprehensive concept that transcends the world we live in and our limited lifespans to include the universe at large and the life to come. It speaks of creatures living on earth alongside man, such as the *jinn* and the birds, or belonging to the hereafter, such as hell and its guards. Furthermore, it refers to worlds beyond the reach of our human perception bringing these closer to our feelings so that we do not focus solely on our present life on earth. It invites us to reflect on what we see in our lives and within ourselves but which we tend to take for granted.

It awakens within man all images and impressions that have long been stagnant as a result of holding on to *jāhiliyyah* concepts. It removes the dust that has gathered over our feelings, opens windows and releases minds, and frees senses and perceptions so that they can look at the wide horizon, the vast space, the deep oceans, the inner soul and the world beyond, reflecting on God's marvellous creation. It invites us to look at how the universe moves on by God's will. We thus realize that the whole thing is far greater and its scope much wider than we could possibly have imagined. Then, we no longer focus on our earth, but instead look up to heaven; we move from what we see to the truth beyond and we are able to see how God's will both brings life and controls it.

Life and death are two familiar phenomena. Yet the *sūrah* invites us to look at what lies beyond these two phenomena of God's will, wisdom, and the way He sets tests and conducts all affairs. It is God: "*who has created death as well as life, so that He may put you to a test to show who of you is best in conduct. He alone is Almighty, Much-Forgiving.*" (Verse 2) The skies above are creatures people see with their eyes. Yet they do not look beyond them to see God's hand that brought them into existence, nor the perfection they manifest. The *sūrah*, however, initiates action so that we contemplate such beauty and perfection as well as the ultimate objective of creation: "*He created seven heavens in layers. No fault will you see in what the Lord of Grace creates. Turn up your eyes: can you see any flaw? Then look again, and again: your vision will come back to you dull and weary. We have adorned the lowest heaven with lamps and made them missiles to pelt the devils with.*" (Verses 3–5)

To those who live in a state of ignorance, or *jāhiliyyah*, the life of this world appears to be the ultimate objective. The *sūrah*, however, presents another world to devils and unbelievers, a world that is full of movement and expectation. It stands in waiting: "*We have prepared for them suffering through the blazing fire. Suffering in hell awaits those who deny their Lord: an evil destination. When they are thrown in it, they will hear it drawing in its breath as it boils up, almost bursting with fury. Every time a group is thrown in it, its keepers will ask them, 'Did no one come to warn you?' 'Yes,' they will reply, 'a warner did indeed come to us, but we did not believe him. We said, "God has revealed nothing. You are in total error."' They will further say, 'Had we but listened, or reasoned, we would not now be among the inhabitants of the blazing fire.' Thus they shall confess their sins. Far be the inhabitants of the blazing fire [from God's mercy].*" (Verses 5–11)

In a world of *jāhiliyyah*, people hardly ever look beyond their immediate life or think of a world beyond what they can perceive. They are, as it were, locked within the cage of their current life on earth. The *sūrah*, therefore, directs their minds and sights to look to what is beyond, to the heavens and the divine will which, though unseen by any human eye, can do whatever it wills, whenever and wherever it chooses. Thus, the earth, stable as it appears before their eyes, is strongly shaken: "*Whether you keep your words secret or state them openly, He has full knowledge of what is in all hearts. How could it be that He who has created should not know all? He is indeed Most Gracious, All-Aware. He it is who has made the earth easy to live upon. Go about, then, in all its highlands and eat of His provisions. To Him you will be resurrected. Do you feel secure that He who is in heaven will not cause the earth to swallow you up when it quakes? Or do you feel secure that He who is in heaven will not let loose against you a sandy whirlwind. You will come to know the truth of My warning.*" (Verses 13–17)

They look at birds, an aspect of creation they see frequently but which they rarely contemplate its marvellous creation. The *sūrah* again fixes their eyes on this and lets their minds appreciate God's power as He shapes and fashions His creation: "*Do they not see the birds above them, spreading their wings and drawing them in? None but the Lord of Grace holds them up. He sees everything.*" (Verse 19)

125

They feel safe and secure on earth, but this is only the false sense of one who is oblivious to what God's will and power may bring about. Having shaken the earth under their feet, including all that forms their environment, the *sūrah* then shakes them even harder so that they realize that nothing can ever withstand God's power, which they hardly ever even take into account: "*What army is there to come to your aid, except for the Lord of Grace? The unbelievers are truly lost in self-delusion.*" (Verse 20)

They feel that the provisions they have are close at hand, and that they can compete for them as they please. The *sūrah*, however, directs their attentions to look far beyond the elements they think to be involved in securing their provisions: "*Who will provide for you, if He were to withhold His provision? Yet they persist in their arrogance and in rebellion.*" (Verse 21)

As they pursue their erring ways, thinking they are well guided, the *sūrah* paints them a vivid, inspiring image showing their own condition and that of those who truly follow correct guidance: "*Is he who goes grovelling on his face better guided than the one who walks upright on a straight path?*" (Verse 22)

They do not benefit by what God has placed in their make-up of talents, faculties and perceptions. They do not go beyond what they perceive so as to look at what lies beyond their immediate world. The *sūrah* reminds them of God's grace as He has given them these abilities, and directs them to use these in a way that tries to divine the future and determine the ultimate objective: "*Say: 'It is He who has brought you into being, and given you hearing, sight and hearts. Yet seldom are you thankful. And He it is who caused you to multiply on earth; and to Him you shall be gathered.*" (Verses 23–24)

Even in their persistent denial of the resurrection, they still constantly ask about its timing. The *sūrah* depicts this as a true and imminent event, one that will approach them all of a sudden. Hence, they have nothing but distaste for it: "*They say: 'When is this promise to be fulfilled, if what you say be true?' Say: 'God alone has knowledge of this. I am only a plain warner.' When they see it close at hand, the unbelievers' faces will be stricken with grief, and it will be said: 'This is what you were calling for.*'" (Verses 25–27)

They hope that the Prophet and those who follow him will perish, as this will silence this voice that has for long irritated them by the warnings it delivers. They would rather revert to their foolish slumber. The *surah* reminds them that whether this group of believers perish or flourish, it cannot affect their own destiny that is determined by a persistent rejection of faith. Hence, they are better advised to look at their own situation and to make amends before it is too late: "*Say: 'Just think: whether God destroys me and those who follow me, or bestows mercy upon us, who will protect the unbelievers from painful suffering?' Say: 'He is the Lord of Grace: in Him we believe, and in Him we place our trust. You will come to know who is in manifest error.'*" (Verses 28–29)

Finally, the *surah* warns them that water, which is essential for life, may be taken away by God, whom the unbelievers deny: "*Say: Just think: if all your water were to sink underground, who would give you clear flowing water?*" (Verse 30)

The key to the whole *surah* and the axis of the movement it sets in our hearts, minds, senses and feelings are found in its inspiring opening: "*Blessed be He in whose hand all dominion rests; who has power over all things.*" (Verse 1) It is from the truth of God's dominion and power that all images presented in the *surah*, as well as all hidden and apparent movements to which it alludes, branch out. Thus, the creation of life and death, testing people through them, the creation of the heavens and their adornment with lamps that serve as missiles pelting devils, the preparation of hell as it is described, the knowledge of what is secret and public, making the earth easy for humans to live upon, the destruction of early communities who rejected divine guidance, holding birds in the sky, God's overwhelming power and His exaltation, providing sustenance to all as He pleases, His creation of people and granting them hearing, eyesight and hearts, causing them to multiply on earth and then gathering them all, His full knowledge of the hereafter which is His own preserve, the meting out of punishment to the unbelievers, the provision of water, which is essential to life, and the ability to take it away whenever He wishes all emanate from the fact that to God belongs all dominion in the universe. He has power over all things.

The *sūrah* states a long sequence of truths that flow uninterruptedly with successive impressions and ideas to explain its concise, yet comprehensive, opening. It is, therefore, difficult to divide into passages. Let us, then, look at it as it develops its theme from start to finish.

I

The Sovereign of the Universe

Al-Mulk (Dominion)

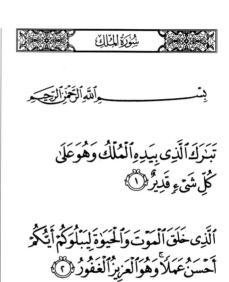

In the Name of God, the Lord of Grace, the Ever Merciful

Blessed be He in whose hand all dominion rests; who has power over all things; (1)

who has created death as well as life, so that He may put you to a test to show who of you is best in conduct. He alone is Almighty, Much-Forgiving. (2)

He created seven heavens in layers. No fault will you see in what the Lord of Grace creates. Turn up your eyes: can you see any flaw? (3)

Then look again, and again: your vision will come back to you dull and weary. (4)

We have adorned the lowest heaven with lamps and made them missiles to pelt the devils with. We have prepared for them suffering through the blazing fire. (5)

وَلَقَدْ زَيَّنَّا ٱلسَّمَآءَ ٱلدُّنْيَا بِمَصَٰبِيحَ وَجَعَلْنَٰهَا رُجُومًا لِّلشَّيَٰطِينِ وَأَعْتَدْنَا لَهُمْ عَذَابَ ٱلسَّعِيرِ ٥

Suffering in hell awaits those who deny their Lord: an evil destination. (6)

وَلِلَّذِينَ كَفَرُوا۟ بِرَبِّهِمْ عَذَابُ جَهَنَّمَ وَبِئْسَ ٱلْمَصِيرُ ٦

When they are thrown in it, they will hear it drawing in its breath as it boils up, (7)

إِذَآ أُلْقُوا۟ فِيهَا سَمِعُوا۟ لَهَا شَهِيقًا وَهِيَ تَفُورُ ٧

almost bursting with fury. Every time a group is thrown in it, its keepers will ask them, 'Did no one come to warn you?' (8)

تَكَادُ تَمَيَّزُ مِنَ ٱلْغَيْظِ كُلَّمَآ أُلْقِىَ فِيهَا فَوْجٌ سَأَلَهُمْ خَزَنَتُهَآ أَلَمْ يَأْتِكُمْ نَذِيرٌ ٨

'Yes,' they will reply, 'a warner did indeed come to us, but we did not believe him. We said, "God has revealed nothing. You are in total error."' (9)

قَالُوا۟ بَلَىٰ قَدْ جَآءَنَا نَذِيرٌ فَكَذَّبْنَا وَقُلْنَا مَا نَزَّلَ ٱللَّهُ مِن شَىْءٍ إِنْ أَنتُمْ إِلَّا فِى ضَلَٰلٍ كَبِيرٍ ٩

They will further say, 'Had we but listened, or reasoned, we would not now be among the inhabitants of the blazing fire.' (10)

وَقَالُوا۟ لَوْ كُنَّا نَسْمَعُ أَوْ نَعْقِلُ مَا كُنَّا فِىٓ أَصْحَٰبِ ٱلسَّعِيرِ ١٠

Thus they shall confess their sins. Far be the inhabitants of the blazing fire [from God's mercy]. (11)

فَٱعْتَرَفُوا۟ بِذَنۢبِهِمْ فَسُحْقًا لِّأَصْحَٰبِ ٱلسَّعِيرِ ١١

Those who stand in awe of their Lord although He is beyond the reach of human perception will have forgiveness and a rich reward. (12)

إِنَّ ٱلَّذِينَ يَخْشَوْنَ رَبَّهُم بِٱلْغَيْبِ لَهُم مَّغْفِرَةٌ وَأَجْرٌ كَبِيرٌ ۝١٢

Whether you keep your words secret or state them openly, He has full knowledge of what is in all hearts. (13)

وَأَسِرُّوا۟ قَوْلَكُمْ أَوِ ٱجْهَرُوا۟ بِهِۦٓ إِنَّهُۥ عَلِيمٌۢ بِذَاتِ ٱلصُّدُورِ ۝١٣

How could it be that He who has created should not know all? He is indeed Most Gracious, All-Aware. (14)

أَلَا يَعْلَمُ مَنْ خَلَقَ وَهُوَ ٱللَّطِيفُ ٱلْخَبِيرُ ۝١٤

He it is who has made the earth easy to live upon. Go about, then, in all its highlands and eat of His provisions. To Him you will be resurrected. (15)

هُوَ ٱلَّذِى جَعَلَ لَكُمُ ٱلْأَرْضَ ذَلُولًا فَٱمْشُوا۟ فِى مَنَاكِبِهَا وَكُلُوا۟ مِن رِّزْقِهِۦ وَإِلَيْهِ ٱلنُّشُورُ ۝١٥

Do you feel secure that He who is in heaven will not cause the earth to swallow you up when it quakes? (16)

ءَأَمِنتُم مَّن فِى ٱلسَّمَآءِ أَن يَخْسِفَ بِكُمُ ٱلْأَرْضَ فَإِذَا هِىَ تَمُورُ ۝١٦

Or do you feel secure that He who is in heaven will not let loose against you a sandy whirlwind. You will come to know the truth of My warning. (17)

أَمْ أَمِنتُم مَّن فِى ٱلسَّمَآءِ أَن يُرْسِلَ عَلَيْكُمْ حَاصِبًا فَسَتَعْلَمُونَ كَيْفَ نَذِيرِ ۝١٧

Those who lived before them also disbelieved. How terrible was My rejection of them? (18)

وَلَقَدْ كَذَّبَ ٱلَّذِينَ مِن قَبْلِهِمْ فَكَيْفَ كَانَ نَكِيرِ ۝١٨

131

Do they not see the birds above them, spreading their wings and drawing them in? None but the Lord of Grace holds them up. He sees everything. (19)

أَوَلَمْ يَرَوْا إِلَى ٱلطَّيْرِ فَوْقَهُمْ صَنَفَّتٍ وَيَقْبِضْنَّ مَا يُمْسِكُهُنَّ إِلَّا ٱلرَّحْمَنُ إِنَّهُۥ بِكُلِّ شَيْءٍ بَصِيرٌ ﴿١٩﴾

What army is there to come to your aid, except for the Lord of Grace? The unbelievers are truly lost in self-delusion. (20)

أَمَّنْ هَٰذَا ٱلَّذِى هُوَ جُندٌ لَّكُمْ يَنصُرُكُم مِّن دُونِ ٱلرَّحْمَٰنِ إِنِ ٱلْكَٰفِرُونَ إِلَّا فِى غُرُورٍ ﴿٢٠﴾

Who will provide for you, if He were to withhold His provision? Yet they persist in their arrogance and in rebellion. (21)

أَمَّنْ هَٰذَا ٱلَّذِى يَرْزُقُكُمْ إِنْ أَمْسَكَ رِزْقَهُۥ بَل لَّجُّوا فِى عُتُوٍّ وَنُفُورٍ ﴿٢١﴾

Is he who goes grovelling on his face better guided than the one who walks upright on a straight path? (22)

أَفَمَن يَمْشِى مُكِبًّا عَلَىٰ وَجْهِهِۦٓ أَهْدَىٰٓ أَمَّن يَمْشِى سَوِيًّا عَلَىٰ صِرَٰطٍ مُّسْتَقِيمٍ ﴿٢٢﴾

Say: 'It is He who has brought you into being, and given you hearing, sight and hearts. Yet seldom are you thankful. (23)

قُلْ هُوَ ٱلَّذِىٓ أَنشَأَكُمْ وَجَعَلَ لَكُمُ ٱلسَّمْعَ وَٱلْأَبْصَٰرَ وَٱلْأَفْـِٔدَةَ قَلِيلًا مَّا تَشْكُرُونَ ﴿٢٣﴾

And He it is who caused you to multiply on earth; and to Him you shall be gathered.' (24)

قُلْ هُوَ ٱلَّذِى ذَرَأَكُمْ فِى ٱلْأَرْضِ وَإِلَيْهِ تُحْشَرُونَ ﴿٢٤﴾

They say: 'When is this promise to be fulfilled, if what you say be true?' (25)

وَيَقُولُونَ مَتَىٰ هَٰذَا ٱلْوَعْدُ إِن كُنتُمْ صَٰدِقِينَ ﴿٢٥﴾

Say: 'God alone has knowledge of this. I am only a plain warner.' (26)

قُلْ إِنَّمَا ٱلْعِلْمُ عِندَ ٱللَّهِ وَإِنَّمَآ أَنَا۠ نَذِيرٌ مُّبِينٌ ٢٦

When they see it close at hand, the unbelievers' faces will be stricken with grief, and it will be said: 'This is what you were calling for.' (27)

فَلَمَّا رَأَوْهُ زُلْفَةً سِيٓـَٔتْ وُجُوهُ ٱلَّذِينَ كَفَرُواْ وَقِيلَ هَٰذَا ٱلَّذِى كُنتُم بِهِۦ تَدَّعُونَ ٢٧

Say: 'Just think: whether God destroys me and those who follow me, or bestows mercy upon us, who will protect the unbelievers from painful suffering?' (28)

قُلْ أَرَءَيْتُمْ إِنْ أَهْلَكَنِىَ ٱللَّهُ وَمَن مَّعِىَ أَوْ رَحِمَنَا فَمَن يُجِيرُ ٱلْكَٰفِرِينَ مِنْ عَذَابٍ أَلِيمٍ ٢٨

Say: 'He is the Lord of Grace: in Him we believe, and in Him we place our trust. You will come to know who is in manifest error.' (29)

قُلْ هُوَ ٱلرَّحْمَٰنُ ءَامَنَّا بِهِۦ وَعَلَيْهِ تَوَكَّلْنَا فَسَتَعْلَمُونَ مَنْ هُوَ فِى ضَلَٰلٍ مُّبِينٍ ٢٩

Say: 'Just think: if all your water were to sink underground, who would give you clear flowing water?' (30)

قُلْ أَرَءَيْتُمْ إِنْ أَصْبَحَ مَآؤُكُمْ غَوْرًا فَمَن يَأْتِيكُم بِمَآءٍ مَّعِينٍ ٣٠

God's Power of Creation

Blessed be He in whose hand all dominion rests; who has power over all things. (Verse 1)

Coming as it does at the outset of the *sūrah*, this glorification imparts a feeling of the multiplication of God's blessings and their continued outflowing. The fact that dominion is mentioned alongside it suggests that this blessing flows over God's kingdom. Hence, it is glorified throughout the universe, as it is glorified with God Himself. It sounds like a hymn echoed throughout the universe and within every creature's heart. It begins with the divine word in God's glorious book, the Qur'ān, inscribed in a well-guarded record, and which spreads throughout the universe.

"*Blessed be He in whose hand all dominion rests.*" (Verse 1) He is the Sovereign who has full control over the universe; He conducts its affairs. When this truth is established in the human heart, its direction and destination become well defined. It no longer turns to anyone or relies on anyone other than the Sovereign to whom all dominion belongs. It feels free from submission to anyone else. It, thus, addresses its worship to none other than Him.

"*Who has power over all things.*" (Verse 1) Nothing escapes Him, and no one diverts or limits His will. He creates and does what He wants. He has full power over everything. His will is subject to neither limitation nor restriction. As this truth becomes well established, the human mind is free to perceive God's will and action that are free of any restriction our senses, perception of reality or what lies beyond it, or indeed our imagination can visualize. God's power extends far beyond anything that a human mind can entertain. After all, human imagination is restricted in its expectation of change by what is familiar to it. Appreciation of the truth of God's limitless power removes this restriction. Hence, a believer expects God's power to accomplish anything, without limit or restriction.

> *Who has created death as well as life, so that He may put you to a test to show who of you is best in conduct. He alone is Almighty, Much-Forgiving.* (Verse 2)

One of the results of His complete dominion of the universe and absolute power over all things is that He created death and life. The term 'death' in this context includes the death that precedes life and the one that follows its end, whereas 'life' includes this first life and the life to come. All these are of God's creation as stated in this verse. In this way, it establishes this truth in the human mind, alerting it to the test it aims to set. Nothing, then, comes by blind coincidence or without purpose. The test aims to establish, in reality, what God knows in advance of people's behaviour on earth and the reward they merit for their actions: "*so that He may put you to a test to show who of you is best in conduct.*" (Verse 2) Thus, man should always be on the alert, considering every thought and every action. He should not be oblivious to anything. This also means that he is unable to rest. Hence, the verse ends with the comment, "*He alone is Almighty, Much-Forgiving.*" It thus gives reassurance to every God-fearing servant. God is certainly Almighty, but He is at the same time Much-Forgiving. When a person's heart is alert, aware that this life is a test, and tries to keep on the right track, he is reassured of God's forgiveness and grace. This gives man all the rest and comfort he needs.

The truth Islam establishes in people's hearts does not depict God as chasing humans to afflict or punish them. He only wants them to be aware of the purpose behind their existence and of their true nature. He wants them to rise to the level worthy of His honour when He blew of His own spirit into them, elevating them above many of His other creations. When they have absorbed this truth and hold to it, they will find that His grace, mercy and forgiveness are always available to them.

In the Wide Universe

This great truth is then anchored to the universe at its broadest and highest. At the same time, the universe is shown to be related to the truth of reward and requital in the life to come:

> *He created seven heavens in layers. No fault will you see in what the Lord of Grace creates. Turn up your eyes: can you see any flaw? Then look again, and again: your vision will come back to you dull and weary. We have adorned the lowest heaven with lamps and made them missiles to pelt the devils with. We have prepared for them suffering through the blazing fire. Suffering in hell awaits those who deny their Lord: an evil destination. When they are thrown in it, they will hear it drawing in its breath as it boils up, almost bursting with fury. Every time a group is thrown in it, its keepers will ask them, 'Did no one*

come to warn you?' 'Yes,' they will reply, 'a warner did indeed come to us, but we did not believe him. We said, "God has revealed nothing. You are in total error."' They will further say, 'Had we but listened, or reasoned, we would not now be among the inhabitants of the blazing fire.' Thus they shall confess their sins. Far be the inhabitants of the blazing fire [from God's mercy]. (Verses 3–11)

Everything this passage mentions is a result of the first verse and is an aspect of the complete sovereignty God exercises over His dominion and of His free, unrestricted power. Everything it contains confirms what the second verse states of the creation of death and life to test people and then their reward according to what their test proves.

"He created seven heavens in layers." (Verse 3) We cannot, on the basis of astronomical theories, exactly ascertain the meaning of the expression *'seven heavens in layers'*. These theories are subject to amendment and correction with every new generation of telescopes and other machines and tools. It is not right, therefore, to attach the meaning of the Qur'ānic statement to discoveries that remain subject to amendment and correction. It is sufficient for us to know that there are seven heavens, and that they are placed in layers of different dimensions.

Whilst the Qur'ān always turns our attentions to God's creation generally, it also specifically directs us to the heavens above. The perfection of His creation is enough to make our eyes turn back in absolute amazement: *"No fault will you see in what the Lord of Grace creates."* (Verse 3) No flaw, no defect, no imbalance is ever seen in God's creation. *"Turn up your eyes,"* and look again. *"Can you see any flaw?"* (Verse 3) Can you detect anything out of place? *"Then look again, and again."* (Verse 4) You might have overlooked something in your first perusal, so make sure by looking again and again. *"Your vision will come back to you dull and weary."* (Verse 4)

Posing such a challenge heightens the importance of what people are being directed towards. In this way, they are made to look seriously at the heavens and at God's creation in general. It is precisely such a contemplating, examining look that the Qur'ān wants people to cast. Familiarity breeds contempt, and our long presence in this world takes much away from its fascinating perfection and meticulous cohesion.

Yet a careful look will not tire of examining the beauty of the world around us; our hearts will want more of its inspiration, and our minds will reflect endlessly on the universe's perfect balance. When we cast such a reflective and examining look at the universe we see it as an overwhelmingly amazing festival of wonders. Every time we so look our eyes and minds see something new.

Anyone who knows even a little about the nature of the universe and its system, some aspects of which have been uncovered by modern science, is bound to be absolutely fascinated. Yet appreciation of the universe's miraculous beauty does not need such scientific discoveries. One aspect of God's blessings is that He has given man the ability to interact with the universe by merely looking at it and contemplating its many different facets. Our hearts directly receive the tune of this awesomely beautiful universe and can respond to it as living creatures respond to each other.

Therefore, the Qur'ān invites people to look at the universe and reflect on its wonders. The Qur'ān addresses all people, across all generations: it addresses those who live in the jungle or the desert, as well as city dwellers and sea travellers. It presents its truth to the person who cannot read or write just as it does to astronomers, physicists and scientists. Everyone of these find in the Qur'ān what invites him to establish contact with the universe. It is that that alerts his heart to reflect on and enjoy what he sees.

Like perfection, beauty is also deliberately placed in the universe. Indeed, the two stem from the same truth. When perfection is attained, beauty is a part of it. Hence, having drawn our attention to the perfection in the creation of the heavens, the Qur'ān now mentions their beauty: "We have adorned the lowest heaven with lamps." (Verse 5) What is the lowest heaven? Perhaps it is the one nearest to the earth and its people to whom the Qur'ān is addressed. The lamps mentioned here may refer to the stars and planets that we see with the naked eye as we look up to the sky. This fits with the invitation to look at the sky at a time when they had nothing other than their eyes and what they saw of shining stars.

Undoubtedly, the sight of stars in the sky is immensely beautiful. Such beauty is always renewed, emanating different aspects at different times, morning or evening, sunrise or sunset, a moonlit night or a moonless one, clear skies or overcast ones. Indeed, its beauty differs from one hour to the next, from one observatory or angle to another. Yet the sky is always awesome in its beauty. Look at that single star flickering at a distance, as though it is a beautiful eye, shining with the appeal of love. Those two other stars appear removed from the rest, as though they are two lovers whispering to each other, away from the crowd. Look around and you see clusters joining together here and there, as if they are a group enjoying a night out in the great and vast open space. They seem to come together or go their separate ways like those attending a night performance in the open air. The moon appears in full splendour one night, dreamy on another, feeling low and dispirited on a third, and looking like a newborn starting life one night and like an elderly expecting the end on another. Look also at this vast space that stretches way beyond what our eyes can see. It is all part of the beauty of this universe; a beauty we can only look at and enjoy, but about which we do not have the words and expressions to describe.

The Qur'ān directs our hearts to reflect on the beauty of the skies and the universe as a whole, because appreciating such beauty is the closest way to comprehend their Creator's own beauty. It is this comprehension that elevates man to the highest level he can attain. When he reaches this, he is ready for an eternal life in a splendid world that is free from the shackles of earthly life. The happiest moments for a human heart are those in which it appreciates the beauty of God's creation in the universe. These are the moments that make it possible for him to feel and appreciate divine beauty.

Pelting Lamps

The *sūrah* states that the lamps which adorn the lowest heaven also have another function: *"And made them missiles to pelt the devils with."* (Verse 5) We have established a rule in this commentary that we do not try to add any explanation to any matter relating to the world beyond our faculties of perception. We limit ourselves only to whatever God tells us about them, leaving the Qur'ānic text as it is. This is certainly enough to state whatever is needed for our comprehension. We certainly believe that a different type of creation is the devils. Some description of them is given in the Qur'ān, and we have referred to these in our commentary wherever they occur. We have though added nothing to what the Qur'ān states. We, therefore, believe that these lamps, which God placed as adornments of the lowest heaven, are also used as missiles to pelt devils with. This may be in the form of shooting stars, as mentioned in another *sūrah*: "*We have adorned the skies nearest to the earth with stars, and have made them secure against every rebellious devil... If any of them stealthily snatches away a fragment, he will be pursued by a piercing flame.*" (37: 6–7 and 10) How? In what form and of what size? God has told us nothing of this and we have no other source to refer to in such matters. Therefore, we have all we need to know and we should believe in this as it is. This is all there is to it. Had God known that further details or explanations would have benefited us, He would have given us these. Why, then, should we try to reach to what God knows to be of no use to us in such a matter as the pelting or shooting of devils?

The *sūrah* speaks further about what God has in store for such devils, other than these pelting missiles: "*We have prepared for them suffering through the blazing fire.*" (Verse 5) This means that they will be pelted with missiles in this present life and that they will suffer the blazing fire in the life to come. Perhaps this comes as a follow up to what the *sūrah* says about the heavens and prior to what it says about the unbelievers. The relation between devils and unbelievers is obvious. Thus, having mentioned the heavens and their lamps, the *sūrah* refers to these lamps' other function, as missiles for pelting devils. Then, as it speaks of what is prepared for these devils in the life to come, the *sūrah* mentions what is made ready for the unbelievers who follow those devils: "*Suffering in hell awaits those who deny their Lord: an evil destination.*" (Verse 6) It then carries on to give us an image of hell, full of rage and anger, as it receives the unbelievers: "*When they are thrown in it, they will hear it drawing in its breath as it boils up, almost bursting with fury.*" (Verses 7–8)

Praised by All Creatures

Hell seems here to be a living creature, one suppressing its fury, but as a result of which draws its breath and boils over. Its anger is so immense that it almost bursts with hate for the unbelievers. Although

139

this may appear to some as an allegorical description of hell, to my mind, it describes a reality. Every creature of God is a living creature, with a life suited to its kind. Every creature knows its Lord and addresses Him with glorifications and praises. They are amazed at man when he denies his Creator and feel anger as a result. This is mentioned in several places in the Qur'ān, suggesting that it is an established reality in the universe.

For example, the following clear statement occurs in the Qur'ān: "*The seven heavens extol His limitless glory, as does the earth, and all who dwell in them. Indeed every single thing extols His glory and praise, but you cannot understand their praises. He is indeed Forbearing, Much Forgiving.*" (17: 44) The Qur'ān also says: "*We graced David with Our favour. We said: 'You mountains, sing with him God's praises! And likewise you birds!'*" (34: 10) These statements are so clear that they admit no interpretation other than what they literally say. Another Qur'ānic statement says: "*Then, He applied His design to the sky, which was but smoke; and said to it and to the earth: 'Come, both of you, willingly or unwillingly.' They both said: 'We do come willingly.'*" (41: 11) This last statement may be said to be an allegory of how the skies and earth submit to God's law, but there is no need to make such an interpretation. It is further removed than the direct and clear meaning intended.

We have the present description of hell, but a similar statement describes the surprise and anger expressed by different creatures at the thought of attributing to God a son: "*They say: 'The Most Merciful has taken to Himself a son!' Indeed you have said a most monstrous falsehood, at which the heavens might be rent into fragments, and the earth be split asunder, and the mountains fall down in ruins! That people should ascribe a son to the Most Merciful, although it is inconceivable that the Most Merciful should take to Himself a son.*" (19: 88–92)

All these statements refer to the truth that the universe believes in its Creator, and that everything extols His glory and praise. They also confirm that all creatures shudder at the thought that man departs from this norm, disbelieving in his Lord. All these creatures feel anger when someone close and dear to them is badly hurt. It is no different from the anger a person is ready to vent at the one who committed such behaviour. He is almost bursting with fury, just like hell is described here: "*It boils up, almost bursting with fury.*" (Verses 7–8)

The same is expressed by the angels who guard hell: "*Every time a group is thrown in it, its keepers will ask them, 'Did no one come to warn you?'*" (Verse 8) It is clear that the question is meant as a rebuke. They share hell's anger and they participate in meting out punishment. Nothing hurts a person in distress more than a rebuke. The answer is given in humility, acknowledging their own lack of judgement and utter stupidity when they denied God's oneness, relying on no evidence whatsoever. Furthermore, they make a wild accusation against God's messengers, who have always stated the truth, clear and simple: "*We said, "God has revealed nothing. You are in total error."*" (Verse 9)

"*Thus they shall confess their sins. Far be the inhabitants of the blazing fire [from God's mercy].*" (Verse 11) This is a prayer made by God against them. This after they have acknowledged their guilt, at a time and place they denied would ever occur. Prayer by God denotes a judgement. Thus, they are far removed from God's mercy. They cannot hope for forgiveness or exemption from punishment. They dwell in the blazing fire. What a fate!

Such torment in the blazing fire that draws its breath as it boils is truly fearsome. God does not treat anyone unfairly. We think – but God knows best – that a person who denies his Lord, when God has instilled the truth of faith and its evidence in his very nature, is one that is devoid of all goodness. Such a person deprives himself of every quality that gives him a position in this universe. He is like the stones that are the fuel of hell. He ends up in the middle of the fire, with no hope of reprieve.

The one who denies God during his life on earth sinks further every day into the darkness of disbelief, until he ends up in an ugly shape, derived from hell. It is so ugly an image that it is unlike anything else in this universe. Everything in the universe has a believing soul that extols God's praises. In everything and every creature there is this element of goodness and this tie which pulls it towards the centre of existence, with the exception of those unbelievers who run loose, severing their ties with the rest of the universe, rebelling against all standards and values. Where will they end up in this universe when they have no bond with anything in it? They can only end up in hell, which rages in fury against them. They have deprived themselves of all right, meaning and dignity. Hence, in hell they receive none.

It is customary in the Qur'ān to portray images of the Day of Judgement in two contrasting scenes. Hence, we now have a scene showing the believers as compared with the unbelievers. In this way, we have the full meaning of the statement at the *surah*'s outset: "*He may put you to a test to show who of you is best in conduct.*" (Verse 2) Having mentioned the test, the *surah* completes its account by speaking of the reward: "*Those who stand in awe of their Lord although He is beyond the reach of human perception will have forgiveness and a rich reward.*" (Verse 12)

The phrase '*beyond the reach of human perception*' expresses the meaning of the Qur'ānic word *ghayb*. In its use in this verse it includes their fear of God whom they have never seen, as well as their fear of Him when they are alone, unseen by any human eye. Both are fine qualities, reflecting a pure feeling and a profound understanding which together qualify a person to receive what the *surah* expresses in general terms as "*forgiveness and a rich reward.*"

To watch God when one is alone, unseen by any other human being is the gauge of a heart's sensitivity and the quality that keeps conscience alive. Anas ibn Mālik reports that some of the Prophet's Companions said to him: "Messenger of God! When we are with you we are at a certain standard, but when we depart we are at a different one." He asked: "How do you feel with regard to your Lord?" They answered: "God is our Lord in secret and open situations." He said: "Yours is not a case of hypocrisy." The bond of God is, then, the essential criterion. Once it is firm in one's heart, one is a true believer.

All in the Open

This last verse provides a bridge linking what precedes it with what comes after. It emphasizes God's knowledge of everything, whether it is said in public or private. He, thus, challenges mankind. It is He who created them and He who knows their inner souls:

Whether you keep your words secret or state them openly, He has full knowledge of what is in all hearts. How could it be that He who has

created should not know all? He is indeed Most Gracious, All-Aware.
(Verses 13–14)

They are told they can say what they like, in whatever way they like; it is all equally known to God, for He knows what is concealed deeper even than secrets. *"He has full knowledge of what is in all hearts."* (Verse 13) Even those thoughts that are kept deep within one's breast, unexpressed, are also known to Him. It is He who created these thoughts, just as He created the breasts that keep them. *"How could it be that He who has created should not know all?"* (Verse 14) The One who has created them must surely know all about them. *"He is indeed Most Gracious, All-Aware."* (Verse 14) His knowledge encompasses every little detail and every hidden feeling and thought.

Yet people try to hide themselves from God, by making a move here, keeping a secret there or by hiding their intentions. How ludicrous! Their minds in which they try to hide their intentions, are created by God, and He knows all their pathways and hidden corners. Indeed, the intentions they seek to hide are also God's creation; He knows how they are formulated and where they are lodged. So, what can people hide, and where will they turn to?

The Qur'ān makes sure of instilling this truth in people's minds because this gives them the correct understanding. Additionally, it keeps people alert and conscious of God, able to fulfil the trust believers are assigned in this world. This is the trust of faith, maintaining justice and dedication to God in both action and intention. Such understanding cannot be achieved until we clearly realize that we, our hearts and minds, our secrets and intentions, are all of God's creation; it is all fully known to Him. When a believer attains such realization, he purges his heart of bad intentions and fleeting thoughts just as he keeps his open behaviour and expressed statements on the right track. He deals with God in all situations, public or private, open or secret.

Mankind's Abode

The *sūrah* now refers to the earth, which God has created for man to live on. He smoothed it and provided in it all the means that enable it to support human life:

He it is who has made the earth easy to live upon. Go about, then, in all its highlands and eat of His provisions. To Him you will be resurrected. (Verse 15)

Man has lived long on earth finding it easy to settle upon, walk along and utilize its potentials – including its soil, water, air, minerals and all other natural resources. Hence, people forget God's blessing as He made the earth easy for them to live on and to benefit by what it contains. The *sūrah* reminds them of this great blessing, putting it before their eyes, in a fine expression that everyone, regardless of when do they live, can understand according to their knowledge of the earth and its potentials.

The description of the earth as easy to live upon meant for those generations of old the surface of the earth and its being smoothed out so that people and animals could walk upon it, and boats could sail through its seas. It also meant for them that it has been made suitable for cultivation and harvest, and given the sorts of atmosphere, water and soil to make life possible. These, however, are general notions. Scientific discoveries, up to the present day, provide further details that give a much broader sense to this Qur'ānic statement.

The Arabic term used in the *sūrah* to describe the earth as 'easy to live upon' is *dhalūl*, which is normally used to describe an animal that is 'broken' so that man can use it as a mount. Science tells us that use of this term is apt, because the earth which we see as stable and motionless is nonetheless certainly moving. What is more is that it is running at a fast pace, without stopping. Nevertheless, it is broken so as not to throw off its rider and not to trample him as it goes along. It does not shake him as it moves, but rather gives him an easy ride. Moreover, it is just like a mount that produces milk, yielding much.

The earth, this mount man rides, revolves at a speed of 1,000 miles per hour, and, at the same time, moves in its orbit around the sun at a speed of approximately 65,000 miles per hour. Furthermore, the earth, the sun and the solar system travel in space at a speed of around 20,000 miles per hour. Despite such speedy movements, man stays in perfect comfort and stability on the earth's surface. Nothing tears him apart, nor are his belongings thrown in the air. Indeed, he suffers neither dizziness nor concussion. Instead, he remains firmly on his mount.

These three movements have a definite purpose. We know the effect of two of these movements on human life, and on life on earth in general. As the earth revolves, the day and night alternate. Had night been the permanent condition, all life on earth would have been frozen out. By contrast, a permanent day condition would result in everything being burnt. The earth's orbiting of the sun causes the four seasons we enjoy each year. Had any of these seasons been permanent, life would not have been possible in the form God has willed. We have not as yet discovered the purpose of the third movement in the solar system, but it must relate to the overall harmony clearly noticeable in the universe.

Despite these three exceedingly fast movements, this broken mount, the earth, maintains the same position defined by the position of its axis at an angle of 23.5 degrees. This position of the earth's axis is instrumental in producing, along with the earth's orbit, the four seasons. A change in the axis angle would disrupt the cycle of the four seasons. Yet maintaining this cycle is essential for the life of plants, and indeed for all life on earth.

God has made the earth easy for man to live upon by giving it a gravity which keeps people steady and in balance, while it makes its three speedy movements. He also determined the degree of its atmospheric pressure to make man's overall movement easy. Had this pressure been heavier, man would have found moving about much harder, or even impossible, depending on the level of such pressure. For certain, heavy atmospheric pressure would either hinder man's movement or crush him completely. Had it been lighter, man's movement would have lacked stability. Indeed, he would have suffered implosions within his body, because his body pressure would be high in relation to the atmospheric pressure: this does indeed sometimes happen to those who climb to high altitudes.

Furthermore, God has stretched the surface of the earth, giving it its soft soil. Had its surface been made of hard rock, as scientific theories suppose should have been the case following the earth's cooling and hardening, walking on its surface would have been very difficult, and it would not have produced any plant life. Rain, wind and other atmospheric elements managed to crush this solid surface so as to form, by God's will, this fertile soil, allowing plant life to flourish for the benefit of man and animal alike. God also made the air above the earth's surface, putting in it the elements necessary for life in all their accurate proportions. Had these proportions been different, life would have been disturbed, even been impossible. Oxygen constitutes 21% of the element air, while nitrogen forms 78% of it. The remainder is made up of carbon monoxide at a rate of 3 portions out of 10,000, as well as other elements. These are the exact proportions vital for supporting life on earth. In addition, thousands of other correlations have been established by God so as to make life on earth possible. These include the sizes of the earth, the sun and the moon, the distance between these three, the level of the sun's temperature, the thickness of the earth's crust, its speed, the angle of its axis, the proportion of sea water to dry land, the density of air covering it, and so forth. Maintaining all these together is what 'breaks' the earth, making it ready to support life, allowing it to produce sustenance and enabling life in general, and human life in particular, to flourish.

The *sūrah* refers to these facts so that they are understood and appreciated by every individual and every generation as they are able to do so, and as their levels of knowledge and observation put before them. Thus, they realize that God's hand, in which all dominion rests, takes care of them and of all around them, makes the earth easy for them to live upon, keeping them and the earth safe and secure. Should this divine care be withheld for just one moment, the whole universe would reel out of control, leading to its destruction along with all those living on it.

When man's heart is alert to this great fact, God, the Creator, the Lord of Grace, the Ever Merciful, allows him to go about wherever he wishes, and to eat of His provisions: "*He it is who has made the earth easy to live upon. Go about, then, in all its highlands and eat of His provisions.*" (Verse 15) Permission to go about the highlands incorporates walking along its plains and valleys. When the more difficult enterprise is allowed, the easier one goes without saying. The provisions available on earth are all of God's creation and belong to Him. What God has provided is much wider in its significance than what we understand from the term 'provision', even when it is used in the plural form. It does not refer to the money one has in hand to pay for one's needs and enjoyments. Rather, it refers to everything God has placed on the earth that man can use to earn something that contributes to his livelihood. Essentially, these are part of the earth's composition of the elements that are present in their relative proportions, as also the ability God gave to plant, animal and man to use these elements and benefit by them:

As is well known, all vegetable life is dependent upon the almost infinitesimal quantity of carbon dioxide in the atmosphere which, so to speak, it breathes. To express this complicated photosynthetic chemical reaction in the simplest possible way, the leaves of the trees are lungs and they have the power when in the sunlight to separate this obstinate carbon dioxide into carbon and oxygen. In other words, the oxygen is given off and the carbon retained and combined with the hydrogen of the water brought up by the plant from its roots. By magical chemistry, out of these elements nature makes sugar, cellulose, and numerous other chemicals, fruits and flowers. The plant feeds itself and produces enough more to feed every animal on earth. At the same time, the plant releases the oxygen we breathe and without which life would end in five minutes... So, all the plants, the forests, the grasses, every bit of moss, and all else of vegetable life, build their structure principally out of carbon and water. Animals give off carbon dioxide and plants give off oxygen. If this interchange did not take place, either the animal or the vegetable life would ultimately use up practically all the oxygen or all of the carbon dioxide, and the balance, being completely upset, one would wilt or die and the other would quickly follow. It has recently been discovered that carbon dioxide in small quantities is also essential to most animal life, just as plants use some oxygen.

Hydrogen must be included, although we do not breathe it. Without hydrogen water would not exist, and the water content of animal and vegetable matter is surprisingly great and absolutely essential.[1]

Nitrogen also plays an important part in the provisions the earth yields:

> Without nitrogen in some form not a food plant could grow. One way in which nitrogen can get into the soil is through the activities of certain bacteria which inhabit the roots of leguminous plants, such as clover, peas, beans, and many others. These bacteria take atmospheric nitrogen and turn it into combined nitrogen, and when the plant dies some of this combined nitrogen is left in the soil. Another way in which nitrogen gets into the soil is through thunderstorms. Whenever a flash of lightening rushes through the atmosphere, it combines a very small quantity of the oxygen with the nitrogen and the rain brings it to the earth as combined nitrogen.[2]

Thus nitrogen is brought down in the form plant life can absorb. Plants cannot absorb pure nitrogen as it exists in the air.

Solid and liquid metals buried inside the earth are other types of provisions resulting from the way the earth was formed and the conditions it went through. We need not go into any details here. All we say is that the Arabic term *rizq*, or provisions, appears, in the light of our brief discussion, to be wider in scope and significance than what people normally associate with this word. It is more significantly related to the way the earth is made and to the design of the universe as a whole. When God has permitted mankind to eat of it, He has granted them the facility to make use and partake of it and of the earth as a whole: "*Go about, then, in all its highlands and eat of His provisions.*" (Verse 15)

This is, however, all limited to a period of time known only to God as He set the time allowed for testing people through life and death. It

1. Morrison, A. Cressy (1959), *Man Does Not Stand Alone*, Kingswood, Surrey: The World's Work (1913) Ltd., pp. 31–33.
2. Ibid., p. 35.

is further confined to all that God makes available for man in this life. When the time of the test is over, death occurs, ushering in what comes after it: "*To Him you will be resurrected.*" (Verse 15) To Him, certainly. It is He who has the dominion over the universe, and with Him all refuge lies. He is able to accomplish anything. If not to Him, to whom would resurrection be?

When the Earth is Shaken

At this moment, as they are safe on the face of the earth that has been made easy to live upon, and as they enjoy all this ease that flows by God's leave, this stable earth is shaken violently from under their feet. They feel it quake. The atmosphere surrounding them is suddenly disturbed and a whirlwind engulfs them, hitting their faces and breasts. All this takes place so that they wake up, look up to heaven, try to discern what is in the realm beyond, and be watchful of what God's will may bring about:

> *Do you feel secure that He who is in heaven will not cause the earth to swallow you up when it quakes? Or do you feel secure that He who is in heaven will not let loose against you a sandy whirlwind. You will come to know the truth of My warning. Those who lived before them also disbelieved. How terrible was My rejection of them?* (Verses 16–18)

The people who live on earth enjoying the way it has been smoothed out for their living and who take out of its wealth of resources what they need, realize that it may at times become rebellious, hard for man's living. This takes place when God permits a small disturbance of its system, and things on its surface are severely shaken or destroyed. Whatever happens to be on the surface quakes and can no longer hold its place. We see this when earthquakes occur or volcanoes erupt, revealing an unwieldy beast within the broken mount. Yet God reins it in so that its violent rebellion is brought swiftly under control. It rebels merely for a few seconds, but this is enough to bring about destruction to the structures man has built on its surface; or it may open its mouth to swallow a whole portion of its surface. When it quakes, people are simply helpless, unable to do anything to stop it. In the face of earthquakes, volcanoes and earth subsidence, people run about aimlessly, like terrified mice in a cage. Yet only seconds before, they were enjoying themselves, oblivious to the Supreme Power that holds everything in place.

People have also experienced whirlwinds, tornadoes and hurricanes that cause much destruction and fire. They can do little to protect themselves against these. When such a storm blows fiercely, hitting faces and breasts with the sand it carries, carrying away with it whatever is in its way, man is clearly powerless, helpless, unless God reins it in.

The Qur'ān reminds people who have long felt secure in their life on earth that such events can always come about and that they can do nothing to stop or control them. Therefore, a telling warning is issued to them: "*You will come to know the truth of My warning.*" (Verse 17) Examples are cited for them from the history of ancient, unbelieving communities: "*Those who lived before them also disbelieved. How terrible was My rejection of them?*" (Verse 18) God rejected that those people of old should disbelieve. He now asks the present unbelievers: "*How terrible was My rejection of them?*" (Verse 18) They were fully aware of how terrible it was. The ruins and other traces of destruction were vivid evidence of how terrible His scourge was.

Moreover, the sense of security that God objects to is that which makes people oblivious of Him, His will and power. This is not the same as the sense of reassurance that believers have about His care and compassion being granted. The two are totally different. A believer always has trust in his Lord, praying for His grace and bounty, but this does not lead him to forgetfulness or to thoughtless indulgence of the earth's pleasures. On the contrary, it makes him always alert, wary that he may incur God's displeasure, keen to avoid any adversity that His will may bring about. Yet, at the same time, he willingly submits himself to God, reassured of His mercy.

'Ā'ishah reports: "I never saw God's Messenger laughing heartily so as to be able to see the inside of his mouth. He only smiled. When God's Messenger saw clouds gathering or felt a wind, he would look worried. I said to him: 'Messenger of God! When people see clouds, they are pleased, hoping that they bring them rain; yet I see you worried when you see clouds gathering.' He said: 'What would assure me, 'Ā'ishah, that it would not bring suffering? People in the past were punished by means of storms. Others saw the suffering about to overtake them, yet they thought that it was clouds bringing rain'." [Related by Aḥmad, al-Bukhārī and Muslim.] Such is the alertness to what God's will may bring, and the lesson to be learnt from the stories mentioned in the Qur'ān. This does not, however, contradict the feeling of reassurance that God's grace and bounty can always be bestowed.

Besides, this is all part of attributing all apparent causes to the main one. The decision in all matters belongs to the One in whose hand rests all dominion. He has power over all things. Avalanches, sandy whirlwinds, tornadoes, hurricanes, earthquakes, volcanoes and other natural forces and phenomena are in no way subject to man; they are totally controlled by God. All that people say about these are merely attempts to explain how they occur. They cannot intervene in bringing them about or in preventing their occurrence. All that they can build on the earth's surface may be wiped out in just a moment, like a house of cards, whether by an earthquake or a hurricane. Hence, they better turn to the Creator of the universe, who has set its laws in operation and who placed in it the forces that occasionally manifest in such events. They should look up to the heavens, the symbol of exaltation, and remember the Sovereign to whom all dominion belongs.

Man's power extends to the limit God has given him. By the same token, knowledge extends by the measure God has assigned man. The controls of this great universe are in the hand of its Creator who has set its laws and powers. These powers operate in accordance with His laws and according to His will. What happens to man as a result of these and what he knows of them are set according to a particular measure. Universal events may at times put man in a position of helplessness towards these great powers. Then, he can do nothing more than remember the Creator and Controller of all these forces and powers, looking up to Him for help, and praying to Him to enable him to use what he can of them.

When man forgets this truth, deluded by what God has granted him of knowledge and ability to use some of these natural forces and powers, he becomes a small creature, isolated from true knowledge that elevates his soul to its sublime origin. He is then attached to the earth, alienated from the rest of the universe. By contrast, a scientist who believes in God submits with the universe to the Almighty Creator, enjoying a sense of happiness that no one experiences except by God's will.

However, the great forces of nature bring man forcibly into a position of helplessness when he can do nothing other than submit to God, whether he is allowed to enjoy such a sense of happiness or be deprived of it. Man may make discoveries, produce inventions, and acquire much power, yet when he faces the great power of nature, he stands helpless. He may be able to protect himself from a hurricane, but the hurricane will take its course and man cannot stop it. All that his knowledge and planning can achieve is sometimes to enable him to move away from its course. Yet, at times, the hurricane will kill him even though he hides within strong walls. At sea, when a hurricane gathers force, man's largest and best built ships are no more than a doll facing a whirlwind. Earthquakes and volcanoes, on the other hand, remain the same as they have always been. It is only blindness that make some miserable individuals assert that man stands alone in the universe, or that he is the master of the universe.

It is by God's will that man has been assigned trusteeship over the earth, and given the power, ability and knowledge he needs for this task. It is God who takes care of him, and gives him his provisions. Should God abandon him, he would be crushed by even the smallest forces placed at his disposal. Flies, and even smaller creatures, would eat him. It is only by God's care that he is protected and honoured. He should know from where he derives his honour and who bestows on him such great bounty.

An Invitation to Reflect

This strong warning now gives way to a call to reflect on something that man often sees but rarely considers and contemplates. It is yet another aspect of God's great design of creation and of His limitless power:

> Do they not see the birds above them, spreading their wings and drawing them in? None but the Lord of Grace holds them up. He sees everything. (Verse 19)

This is a miracle that takes place at every moment, yet because of its familiarity we tend to overlook its testimony of God's great power. Yet, look at the birds: how they spread their wings and then draw them in, but in both situations remain airborne, floating easily and smoothly. Moreover, at times, they make certain movements that appear to be for show, adding beauty to their flight, rising high or diving down at speed. Neither eye nor heart tires of looking at this scene and following each type of bird perform their characteristic movements. It is certainly an enjoyment that invites contemplation of God's beautiful creation. We see here how beauty and perfection go hand in hand.

The *sūrah* first suggests that people should look at this beautiful sight: "*Do they not see the birds above them, spreading their wings and drawing them in?*" (Verse 19) It follows this with a clear indication of God's perfect design: "*None but the Lord of Grace holds them up.*" God holds them up by the laws of nature He has set in operation, maintaining a high standard of harmony that is apparent in all creatures, large and small. To achieve such harmony, every little cell or particle is taken into account. These laws of nature ensure that aspects of balance are set in place, in their thousands, on the earth's surface, in the air and in the shape of birds. Thus, this miracle is achieved and it continues to replicate itself with perfect regularity.

God, the Lord of Grace, holds them up in position with His infinite power that admits no weakening and with His care that never loses sight of His creation. It is His will that keeps the laws of nature working regularly, accurately and harmoniously. Thus, they never slow down even for a wink unless God wills otherwise: "*None but the Lord of Grace holds them up.*" The way this statement is phrased suggests that God's hand holds every bird and every wing in the air, whether the bird is spreading its wings out or drawing them in.

"*He sees everything.*" (Verse 19) He sees them all, knows every minute detail about them, coordinates matters and takes care of every little thing, at every moment. Holding the birds in the air is the same as holding the creatures that walk on earth as it moves in its orbit. It is the same method by which God holds all celestial bodies in place. Who could hold them in position other than God? The *sūrah*, however, presents for us a scene that we see at all times, allowing its message to touch our hearts. If we look carefully, we realize that everything God makes is miraculous and truly inspirational. Every heart and every generation can feel and see of this miraculous truth what they can understand.

Who Else?

The next verse, however, returns unbelievers to fear. Thus they alternate between feelings of fear and admiration of God's creation:

What army is there to come to your aid, except for the Lord of Grace? The unbelievers are truly lost in self-delusion. (Verse 20)

They have been warned lest they be swallowed up by the earth or be overwhelmed by a sandy whirlwind, and they have been reminded of the fate of earlier communities whom God rejected for their disbelief. Now the *sūrah* asks them: who other than He can give them protection against Him? Who can ward off His might other than the Lord of Grace Himself? "*The unbelievers are truly lost in self-delusion.*" Such self-delusion gives them the false feeling of safety and security. They rely on this false sense of security at the very moment they are exposed to His might. They have neither faith nor good action to put forward in support of any plea for mercy from the Lord of Grace.

Next, the *sūrah* mentions the provisions they enjoy but the source of which they overlook. They do not fear that this might be withheld, but instead continue to behave arrogantly:

Who will provide for you, if He were to withhold His provision? Yet they persist in their arrogance and in rebellion. (Verse 21)

As we have already said, all people's provisions come, first and foremost, by God's will and the way He designed the universe and made the earth and the atmosphere as they are. All these factors are absolutely beyond mankind's control and cannot be influenced in any way by them. They predate man's creation. They are more powerful than man, and are better able to erase all traces of life as and when God so wills. Who, then, will provide for mankind, should God withdraw water, or withhold air from them, or indeed any of the elements that are essential for life?

Included under this broad and profound sense of provisions are all the meanings that readily spring to mind when the term is used, and which man tends to treat as of his own making, such as work, invention and production. All these are closely linked to primary causes on the one hand and are dependent on what God grants to individuals and communities on the other. Every breath a worker draws and every movement he makes is part of God's provisions. Is He not the One who originated him, gave him all his abilities and powers, created for him the breath he draws in and the substance that is consumed by his body enabling movement? Every mental endeavour man makes is part of God's provision. Is He not the Creator who gave man the ability to think and invent? Besides, what can anyone produce unless he uses a substance initially made by God, and utilizes natural and human factors provided by Him? "*Who will provide for you, if He were to withhold His provision?*" (Verse 21)

"*Yet they persist in their arrogance and in rebellion.*" (Verse 21) Having established the nature of the provisions people have and made it clear that mankind are totally dependent on God for all this, the *sūrah* paints a picture of people bearing themselves in total arrogance. All arrogance is ugly, but its ugliest form is that demonstrated by those who are dependent on the One who gives them their food, clothing and all that they have. Indeed, they have nothing other than what He bestows on them; yet they persist in their haughty arrogance.

This is indeed a very true picture of those who turn away from the divine message in arrogant rebellion, forgetting that God is their Maker and that they can only survive by His grace. They control nothing whatsoever of their lives or their provisions.

What Guidance?

On top of all this, they described the Prophet and those who followed him as having gone astray, claiming that they were better guided than them. The same is levelled at the advocates of faith by unbelievers in

155

every community. Therefore, the *surah* paints a true to life image of the status of both parties: *"Is he who goes grovelling on his face better guided than the one who walks upright on a straight path?"* (Verse 22) The one who grovels on his face is either someone who actually walks on his face instead of the right way using his feet and legs, or is someone who trips as he walks, falling on his face. He then lifts himself up only to trip again. Both are miserable conditions, beset with affliction and hardship. Neither leads to proper guidance or goodness. How far removed such conditions are from that of one who walks upright, steady along a way that is free of pitfalls and crookedness, fully aware of the goal towards which he moves.

The first is the situation of a miserable person who has deviated from God's way and, as such, become deprived of His guidance. He is on a collision course with God's laws and creatures, taking up a way different from theirs. Therefore, he is always falling and tripping, tired and lost. The second situation is that of a happy person, benefiting by God's guidance and enjoying travelling along the way charted by believers who always glorify and praise Him. Thus, he joins the procession of the entire universe and of all living and inanimate creatures.

The life of faith is that of ease, straightforwardness and clear objectives. By contrast, the life of disbelief is marked by hardship and error. Which, then, is better guided? Does the question require an answer? It is a rhetorical question, designed to drive its message home.

Both question and answer fade away, giving way to a moving image in which we see two groups of people. The first either grovel or fall on their faces, lacking a goal or charted line. The second group walk with their heads held high. They are steady of step, following a straight path that takes them to a set destination.

In connection with following guidance or error, the *surah* reminds people of the means God has provided for them and the faculties of understanding He has equipped them with, yet still they do not put these to good use:

Say: It is He who has brought you into being, and given you hearing, sight and hearts. Yet seldom are you thankful. (Verse 23)

The truth that man was originated by God presses hard on the human mind. It affirms itself in a way that is hard to refute. Man exists in a world in which he is the highest and noblest species known to him. Among all creatures, mankind are equipped with the highest knowledge and the most extensive abilities. Man has not created himself. There must be, then, someone higher, nobler, more able and more knowledgeable than him who brought him into existence. Man must inevitably acknowledge this truth: his very existence puts it before his eyes. To continue trying to deny it is both unworthy and futile.

The *sūrah* mentions this truth here in order to add a reminder about the means of learning, which God has equipped man with: "*Say: It is He who has brought you into being, and given you hearing, sight and hearts.*" How does man receive such great favours and blessings: "*Yet seldom are you thankful.*" (Verse 23)

Hearing and sight are two great miracles about which we have learnt some remarkable aspects. 'Heart' is often used in the Qur'ān in reference to the faculty of knowledge acquisition and understanding. This is an even greater and more remarkable miracle about which we only know very little. It is one of God's secrets in man's creation. Science has made significant attempts to understand the nature of hearing and sight, and here it is perhaps useful to mention briefly some of its findings:

> The hearing system begins with the outer ear, but only God knows where it ends. Science says that sound vibration is carried through the air which directs its entry through the auditory canal to the eardrum, which then transmits it to the labyrinth inside the ear. The labyrinth includes the cochlea and semicircular canals. In the cochlea part there are four thousand minute arches connected to the auditory nerve. Can we imagine the length and size of these arches, and how each of these thousands of arches is fitted in place? What space do they occupy? Yet in this hardly visible labyrinth there are some tiny bones. The ear contains 100,000 hearing cells. The hair cells trigger nerve impulses. Such microscopic accuracy in organization is most amazing.[3]

---

3. Nawfal, Abd al-Razzaq, (n.d.), *Allah wal-'Ilm al-Hadīth*, Cairo, p. 57.

157

The central part of the visual system is the eye, which includes 130 million light receptors... The eye consists of the sclera, the cornea, the choroid and the retina and a large number of tiny nerves and canals.[4]

The retina is composed of nine separate layers, all of which together are no thicker than thin paper. The inmost layer is made up of rods and cones, which are said to number thirty million rods and three million cones. These are all arranged in perfect relation to each other and to the lens, but, strangely enough, they turn their backs upon the lens and look inward, not outward... The lens of our eye varies in density so that all rays are brought into focus. Man finds this unattainable in any homogeneous substance, such as glass.[5]

'Heart', which is often used in the Qur'ān interchangeably with 'mind', is the quality that makes man what he is. It denotes the faculty of understanding, distinction and knowledge which qualifies man to take charge of the earth and to shoulder the great trust. This is the trust that the heavens, the earth and the mountains feared to bear. It is to believe by choice and to discern guidance by self motivation. It signifies the diligent observance, by will and choice, of the code God has laid down. No one knows the nature of this faculty, or its centre, or whether it is inside or outside the human body. It is a secret God has not given anyone.

Yet despite having all such grace and gifts to fulfil his momentous trust, man is ungrateful to God: "*Yet seldom are you thankful.*" (Verse 23) Man should feel ashamed of himself when he is thus reminded. He does not thank God for all the blessings He has favoured him with. Had man devoted all his life to expressing gratitude to God, it still would not thank Him enough.

---

4. Ibid., p. 58.
5. Morrison, op. cit., p. 60.

The Promise Fulfilment

A reminder follows making it clear that God has not created mankind and given them all their distinctive qualities haphazardly, without a definite purpose: it is all for the purpose of initiating life that incorporates a test and then the administering of reward and requital at the end: *"And He it is who caused you to multiply on earth; and to Him you shall be gathered."* (Verse 24)

The Arabic term *dhar'*, used in the verse to denote multiplication also signifies 'spreading far and wide', which provides a contrast in both image and meaning with the second action of gathering. The *sūrah* gives both images in a short verse so as to present these vividly before our eyes. Thus, people who have spread all over the earth will realize that they are moving towards an end that brings them all together for an ultimate purpose: one that brings the test of life and death to its final goal.

The *sūrah* then mentions their doubts concerning this promised gathering: *"They say: 'When is this promise to be fulfilled, if what you say be true?'"* (Verse 25) Such a question is put only by one who is in serious doubt or one who is in stubborn denial. Knowing the exact time of the fulfilment of the promise adds nothing to its truth. It has nothing to do with the fact that it is the time appointed for requital after the test has been completed. It is the same to them whether it takes place tomorrow or after millions of years. What is certain is that it is going to happen. Then they will be gathered to receive what they deserve for what they have done in their lives.

God has not imparted knowledge of the Day of Judgement to anyone of His creatures, because such knowledge serves none of their interests. Indeed, imparting such information is against the very nature of this day and has no bearing on the duties people are asked to fulfil in preparation for it. On the contrary, withholding such information from all creatures and keeping it with God Almighty is an act of wisdom that serves human interests. Hence the answer: *"Say: God alone has knowledge of this. I am only a plain warner."* (Verse 26)

This answer clearly reflects the great difference between the Creator and His creation. God is seen in His absolute oneness: no one bears any similarity to Him and He has no partner. All knowledge belongs to

Him alone. All creatures, including prophets and angels, stand before Him in complete humility: *"Say: God alone has knowledge of this. I am only a plain warner."* I have a mission and a task, to warn and to make things plain. Knowledge belongs solely to the All-Knowing.

We see them here putting forward questions that imply doubts and being given firm and decisive answers. The *sūrah* then presents an image depicting the subject of their questioning, this day has now arrived. The promise they have seriously doubted is fulfilled and they face it here and now: *"When they see it close at hand, the unbelievers' faces will be stricken with grief, and it will be said: 'This is what you were calling for.'"* (Verse 27) Here is this day that you have always claimed will never take place; it is staring you in the face.

The Qur'ān often uses this method of painting in the present what is to happen in future. The purpose is to counter the state of doubt with an element of surprise. The doubter is shown a scene of something happening which he has denied will ever happen. But it is a true image. This day is present in God's knowledge. The time gap separating it from us is true in relation to us. This is a relative matter that does not represent the plain truth of this day as it is in God's sight. If God wills, they will see it now as it is in His knowledge. Thus, what the *sūrah* does, moving suddenly from this present life to that of the hereafter, and from the attitude of doubt to suddenly facing the truth represents a reality that, had God so willed, they would see now. The *sūrah* paints this reality in a clear and effective way.

Awaiting the Prophet's Death

The unbelievers hoped that the Prophet and the small group that followed him would soon perish, thereby ridding them of a problem that caused much anxiety. They counselled each other to persist until he so died, when they would be able to patch things up and resume their life as before. Sometimes they voiced the claim that God would take Muḥammad and his followers away because they were in error, fabricating lies against God! Hence, as the *sūrah* puts before them the scene of gathering and requital on the Day of Judgement, it alerts them to the fact that even if their wish were fulfilled, they would not be immune from facing the consequences of their disbelief. Therefore, it is far better for them to be well prepared for this appointed day, shown to them as though it were taking place there and then:

> *Say: Just think: whether God destroys me and those who follow me, or bestows mercy upon us, who will protect the unbelievers from painful suffering?* (Verse 28)

They will be well advised to think of their own situation and their own future. What benefit would accrue to them if the Prophet and his followers died? Likewise, should God bestow His mercy on the Prophet and his followers, this would not by itself protect the unbelievers from their inevitable fate. God, who let them multiply on earth and who will eventually gather them, is eternal. He never dies. Yet the *sūrah* does not say to them, 'who will protect you from suffering?' It does not specify that they are unbelievers. It simply tells them of the painful suffering that awaits unbelievers. This is a wise approach, instilling fear in their hearts on the one hand, and on the other giving them the chance to review their situation. Had the *sūrah* described them as unbelievers and that they would be certain to suffer painful punishment, they might have retorted with outright rejection and stubborn insolence. It is often the case that dropping a hint is far more effective than making a blunt statement.

The *sūrah* then outlines the believers' attitude, one based on faith, and how they place their full trust in God, relying on Him. They are very confident, assured that they are on the right course, well guided, and that the unbelievers are in manifest error:

> *Say: He is the Lord of Grace: in Him we believe, and in Him we place our trust. You will come to know who is in manifest error.* (Verse 29)

That God is mentioned here by His great attribute, the Lord of Grace, refers to His profound and infinite mercy which He grants to His Messenger and the believers who follow him. He will not destroy them as the unbelievers wish He would.

The *sūrah* instructs the Prophet to highlight the bonds they have with their Lord, the Lord of Grace. The first is the bond of faith, "*in*

161

Him we believe," and this is followed by one of total reliance, "*and in Him we place our trust.*" The phraseology of this verse suggests a close relation between them and God who favours His Messenger and the believers with the permission to announce this close relationship. Indeed, God instructs the Prophet to announce it, as if He is saying to him: 'Do not be afraid of what the unbelievers say. You and those with you are attached to Me, and you are permitted by Me to declare that you are the recipient of this honour, so announce it to them.' What a great gesture of honour!

This is followed by an implicit warning: "*You will come to know who is in manifest error.*" (Verse 29) This is phrased in such a way that should make them ashamed of their stubborn rejection of the divine faith. It also invites them to review their positions, lest they be the ones who are in complete error. If they are, this inevitably makes them subject to painful suffering, as clearly stated in the previous verse: "*who will protect the unbelievers from painful suffering?*" (Verse 28) At the same time, the *sūrah* does not outrightly brand them as being in error, so as not to harden their attitude. This method of advocacy is one that works well with some people.

The Final Note

The *sūrah* ends with a note that mentions punishment in this present life in the form of depriving the unbelievers of the most essential thing of life, namely, water:

> *Say: Just think: if all your water were to sink underground, who would give you clear flowing water?* (Verse 30)

This is something so close and necessary for people's lives. They should therefore consider this move carefully if they cannot think of the Day of Judgement as certain. All dominion rests in God's hand and He is able to accomplish anything. What will their position be should He will that they be deprived of this most essential life element? They are left to contemplate this unthinkable eventuality, should God will it to happen.

Thus, this *sūrah* concludes, having taken us on a grand tour reaching up to great horizons and profound depths. Almost every verse provides a distinct beat. It can be seen as a journey into the unknown, or indeed into a close, visible world that is often overlooked. It is a grand *sūrah*, much greater than its length or the number of its verses. It is like arrows pointing far into the distance, with each aiming at a separate world.

The *sūrah* addresses a number of very important Islamic concepts. It establishes the truth of God's absolute power and His absolute sovereignty; the trial of death and life as a prelude to resurrection and requital; the beauty and perfection of God's design; His absolute knowledge of secrets and inner thoughts: of God being the source of all provisions; of His guardianship of all His creatures; of His presence with every creature, as well as a number of other truths that are part of a believer's concept of God, the universe and life. It is from this concept that a believer derives his code of living and his attitude towards God, himself, the rest of mankind, living creatures and the universe. It is this concept that shapes a believer's conscience, feelings, personality, values and standards.

Al-Qalam
(The Pen)

Prologue

Time of Revelation

It is practically impossible to date the revelation of this *sūrah*, and this applies to its opening as well as to the *sūrah* as a whole. Nor is it possible to say for certain that its opening was revealed first and the rest after the lapse of some time. We cannot even say that this was more probable, because the opening and the ending of the *sūrah* tackle the same point, namely, the unbelievers' rude claims about the Prophet, denouncing him as a madman.

There are many reports that suggest that this was the second *sūrah* to be revealed after *Sūrah* 96. Where different editions of the Qur'ān mention an order of revelation, they all suggest that this is the second *sūrah*. Yet the style of the *sūrah*, the way it tackles its subject matter and its drift point to something else. In fact, these aspects almost confirm that it was revealed sometime after the call to Islam went public. It is well known that for three years the Prophet addressed his message to people privately, on an individual basis. In other words, this *sūrah* was most probably revealed during that time, when the Quraysh was determinedly opposed to the new message of Islam, resorting to all means to prevent it, including levelling defamatory allegations against the Prophet.

By way of response, the Qur'ān began to denounce such tactics, repelling unfounded allegations and issuing threats and warnings of the type this *sūrah* includes.

As we have said, it has been suggested that only the opening of the *sūrah* was revealed early on, soon after the first revelation of *Sūrah 96*. It is further suggested that the negation of any madness attributed to the Prophet, which occurs in the opening, "*you are not, by your Lord's grace, a madman,*" was in order to calm his own fears about whether such revelations were signs of madness. This is again unlikely, because the reports mentioning any such fears the Prophet may have had are exceedingly lacking in authenticity. Moreover, the way the *sūrah* is built as a single whole makes it clear that this negation is meant to refute the allegation mentioned at its conclusion: "*The unbelievers well-nigh trip you up with their eyes when they hear this reminder. They say, 'He is surely mad.'*" (Verse 51) It is this allegation that is negated at the *sūrah's* very outset. This is clearly understood when we read all the *sūrah* and appreciate how closely interlinked it is throughout.

Some reports also suggest that certain passages, specifically verses 17–23 and 42–52, were revealed in Madīnah. The first of these passages mentions the test endured by the owners of the garden, and the second refers to the Prophet Jonah. Again, we believe this not to be the case. Instead, we suggest that the whole *sūrah* was revealed in Makkah, because its style is very much Makkan. Indeed, this is more likely, considering the style, the features and the overall unity of the *sūrah*.

Our own stance, therefore, is that the *sūrah* was not the second to be revealed, but rather that its revelation took place after the lapse of some considerable time after the start of the Prophet's mission. It was certainly after the divine instruction was given to the Prophet to "*warn your nearest kindred,*" (26: 214), and after the revelation of a substantial portion of the Qur'ān speaking about earlier communities. Such reports have been described by some unbelievers as 'fables of the ancients'. It was clearly revealed then at a time when the Quraysh had already been called upon to accept Islam and whence it started its resistance to the call. Indeed, so determined had it become in its opposition at this point that it did not hesitate to level false allegations against the

Prophet and his mission. It is such opposition that necessitated the very strong denunciation the *sūrah* makes of the unbelievers and the strong warnings it issues both early on and towards its end. Such timing of its revelation is also confirmed by the last image it portrays: "*The unbelievers well-nigh trip you up with their eyes when they hear this reminder. They say, 'He is surely mad.'*" (Verse 51) This is an image of a public address calling on large groups of people to accept the message. Such gatherings most certainly did not take place during the early years of the Islamic message. Indeed, the first such public address was only made three years after the Prophet began to receive Qur'ānic revelations.

The *sūrah* refers to some of the offers the unbelievers made to the Prophet, suggesting a compromise over the central issue in dispute, namely that of faith. It says: "*They would love that you compromise with them, so that they will also compromise.*" (Verse 9) Needless to say, such an offer would not have been made at a time when the message was only advocated in private, presented to a few individuals. In such circumstances, it would not have been felt to represent any danger. It is more likely that such offers would only have been made later, when the message advocated itself in public and when the unbelievers realized its far-reaching significance.

We see how several indications confirm that the *sūrah* was not revealed in the very early days of the Islamic message, and that at least three years had passed before its revelation. It is highly unlikely that no Qur'ānic revelations were made during these three years. On the contrary, it is much more likely that many *sūrahs* and passages were revealed in the intervening period, presenting the Islamic faith without strongly denouncing the unbelievers in the way we find in this *sūrah*. Having said all this, however, one can still not say that this *sūrah*, as well as *Sūrahs* 73 and 74, were revealed late into the Islamic period.

A Wide Gulf

The tree of the Islamic faith, in its real, clean and pure form, was being planted on earth. It was totally unfamiliar to the prevailing state of ignorance, or *jāhiliyyah*, not only in the Arabian Peninsula but throughout the globe. Indeed there was a great gulf between it and the deviant and colourless form of the Abrahamic faith, mixed with local superstitions, which the Arab idolaters upheld. What Muḥammad (peace be upon him) advocated was a clear, straightforward, simple, yet comprehensive and profound faith that was fully in line with the original pure faith preached by Abraham, but to a standard of perfection that fits its being the last message to mankind, addressing them in their stage of maturity and remaining intact to the end of time. Take, for example, the notion of multiple deities that assigns partners to God: in this respect, the Arabs worshipped angels, statues, the *jinn* and spirits. Their beliefs were a medley of corrupt and hollow notions. Compare these with the noble picture the Qur'ān paints of God and His majestic power that takes care of every creature. The gulf between the two is immense.

Similarly wide is the gulf between the class system that prevailed in Arabia, the clerical nature of its religion and the monopoly of privileges, such as custodianship of the Ka'bah, on the one hand and the equality of all people preached by Islam and every individual's direct relation with God as explained in the Qur'ān on the other. Likewise, the morality advocated by the Prophet Muḥammad was a world apart from the values that prevailed in Arabia's *jāhiliyyah* society.

This great gulf between the new faith and the Quraysh's beliefs, values and practices was sufficient to bring about direct conflict between the two camps. There were, however, other factors which perhaps were, to the Quraysh, more serious than the issue of faith. There were, for example, social factors, some of which prompted them to suggest what is reported in the Qur'ān: "*They also say, 'Why was not this Qur'ān revealed to some great man of the two cities?'*" (43: 31) The two cities mentioned here are Makkah and Ṭā'if. Despite the fact that the Prophet was a descendent of the noblest family in the Quraysh, the very fact that he was not the chief of his clan made it very difficult for their chiefs to accept his leadership. In that social environment, position in one's clan was of paramount importance.

Family factors also played their part. We see such significance in the fact that 'Amr ibn Hishām, better known as Abū Jahl, stubbornly refused to accept the truth of the Islamic message, despite his being certain of it, because the Prophet preaching it belonged to the 'Abd Manāf clan. This is recounted in the story of Abū Jahl, Abū Sufyān and al-Akhnas ibn

Sharīq who each went out individually, on three consecutive nights, to listen to the Qur'ān being recited by the Prophet. Every morning, they met on their way back home and started blaming each other, pledging that they would never do this again, lest their actions encourage others to listen to the Qur'ān. When al-Akhnas asked Abū Jahl what he thought of what he heard Muḥammad reciting, the latter answered: "We have competed with the clan of 'Abd Manāf for honours: they fed the poor, and we did the same; they provided generous support to those who needed it and we did the same. When we were together on the same level, like two racehorses running neck and neck, they said that one of their number was a Prophet receiving revelations from on high! When can we attain such an honour? By God, we shall never believe in him."[1]

There were also other interests and psychological factors determined to uproot this new tree before it could firmly establish its roots and stretch forth its branches. Such efforts were particularly heightened once the new message had moved on from private and individual advocacy to the open, public stage, outlining the essential features of the new faith, Islam. The Qur'ān spoke in clear terms, showing the absurdity of polytheism and its deviant concepts and traditions.

His position as a Prophet receiving revelations from on high notwithstanding, Muḥammad was a man who experienced normal human feelings. He was at the receiving end of such determined opposition that culminated in an all out fight against him, his message and the small band of his followers. He and his Companions could not help but hear the false allegations the unbelievers levelled at him. "*They say, 'He is surely mad.'*" (Verse 51) This was but one of the many types of ridicule they levelled on him, as is reported in the Qur'ān. Such ridicule, added to the abuse and persecution many of his followers suffered at the hands of their own relatives and clansmen, pained Muḥammad, God's Messenger, greatly.

We see in Makkan *sūrahs* how God bestows His abundant care on His Messenger and this small group of followers, consoling and commending him and those who accepted his message. In this respect, God gives

---

1. Ibn Hishām, *Al-Sīrah al-Nabawiyyah*, Dar al-Qalam, Beirut, Vol. 1, pp. 337–338. Also, Adil Salahi (2002), *Muhammad: Man and Prophet*, Leicester, The Islamic Foundation, pp. 172–173.

prominence to the moral aspect embodied in the Islamic message and its bearer, Muḥammad (peace be upon him). He refutes what the unbelievers alleged about him. He reassures the persecuted believers that He is on their side, so they do not have to think about their enemies, powerful and wealthy as they may seem.

We find in this *sūrah* many examples of how God comforts and reassures the Prophet: "*Nūn. By the pen, by all they write, you are not, by your Lord's grace, a madman. And indeed you shall have a never-ending reward. Most certainly, yours is a sublime character.*" (Verses 1–4) He also says of the believers: "*For the God-fearing there shall be gardens of bliss with their Lord. Should We treat those who submit themselves to Us as We treat the guilty? What is the matter with you? On what basis do you judge?*" (Verses 34–36) Of one of the Prophet's more prominent enemies, God says: "*Pay no heed to any contemptible swearer, slanderer, going about with defaming tales, hinderer of good, aggressor, sinful, cruel and, on top of all that, given to evil. Just because he has wealth and children, when Our revelations are recited to him, he says, 'Fables of the ancients!' We shall brand him on the snout.*" (Verses 10–16) The Almighty then speaks about the war against those who deny the truth generally: "*Therefore, leave to Me those who deny this revelation. We shall bring them low, step by step, in ways beyond their knowledge. I will allow them more time: My scheme is truly firm.*" (Verses 44–45) This is different from the punishment of the hereafter when the arrogant will be humiliated: "*On the day when matters become so dire, they will be asked to prostrate themselves, but they will not be able to do so. Their eyes will be downcast, with ignominy overwhelming them. They were invited to prostrate themselves when they were safe.*" (Verses 42–43)

The *sūrah* cites the example of those people who had a garden, but were too greedy. This serves as a warning directed against the elders of the Quraysh who, feeling powerful on account of their wealth and families, schemed against the new message, trying to bring it down. At the end, the *sūrah* enjoins the Prophet to remain steadfast in adversity: "*So, await in patience your Lord's judgement; and do not be like the man in the whale...*" (Verse 48)

Through such comforting, praise and reassurance, coupled with fearsome warnings and an uncompromising attack on the unbelievers,

God Himself takes up the fight. We can discern the features of that period when the believers were few, weak, suffering persecution and hardship and facing a determined effort to uproot the tree of their new faith. In the *sūrah*'s style, the words it uses and in its themes we identify certain features of the environment in which the new message functioned. Essentially, it was characterized by naïve concepts, petty concerns, and the lack of any profound thinking.

Such naïvety is seen in the unbelievers' crude methods to counter the Prophet's message. They describe him as a madman, but this is an allegation that lacks even elementary tact. It is crude abuse levelled by uncouth, unrefined and ill-mannered people.

Their naïvety is brought into focus by the way God refutes their false allegations. First of all, the line it takes is the most suited to their own conditions: "*You are not, by your Lord's grace, a madman. And indeed you shall have a never-ending reward. Most certainly, yours is a sublime character. You shall before long see, as they will see, which of you is the one afflicted.*" (Verses 2–6) Secondly, the *sūrah* adds a clear warning: "*So pay no heed to those who deny the truth. They would love that you compromise with them, so that they will also compromise.*" (Verses 8–9) Thirdly, the refutation turns their abusive words against one of their own number: "*Furthermore, pay no heed to any contemptible swearer, slanderer, going about with defaming tales, hinderer of good, aggressor, sinful, cruel and, on top of all that, given to evil.*" (Verses 10–13) Fourthly, the focus increases as the *sūrah* tells the story of those owners of a garden who lacked all refinement despite their wealth. In their arrogance, they whisper to each other that they will make sure that no poor people will be allowed into their garden to disrupt their harvest.

Furthermore, the unbelievers' naïvety is clearly shown in the argument put to them: "*Or have you a divine book which you study, and in which you find that you shall have all that you choose? Or have you received solemn oaths, binding on Us till the Day of Resurrection, that you will get whatever you yourselves decide? Ask them which of them will vouch for this.*" (Verses 37–40)

We see all these features through the expressions used in the *sūrah*. They are of benefit in our study of the events that took place during the Prophet's lifetime and as we follow the progress of the Islamic message.

171

They explain how the Qur'ān elevated that social environment and the Muslim community towards the end of the Prophet's mission, and how far removed from such crudeness and naïvety the Muslim community became. To appreciate the wide gulf between the two situations we only need to study the mode of address the Qur'ān adopts in speaking to the Muslim community at the time. We need also to look at the changes in the situation of that Muslim community, its concerns, feelings and attitudes brought about within no more than 20 years, a period that is no more than a glance in the life of nations. Such a change in the social fabric of the community was both profound and firmly established, yet accomplished in such a short time. It enabled that community to assume mankind's leadership, attaining at the same time a sublime standard of morality that no other human leadership has ever attained. It was a unique standard in the very nature of the faith it preached, its practical effects on human life, its broad outlook that views all mankind with love and compassion, and its meeting all the community's needs: emotional, intellectual and social.

All in all, the progress so achieved was miraculous, elevating the community from such naïvety to a high standard of refinement and broadness of vision. It was such an enormous transformation that entailed much more than a minority becoming the majority, or the weak becoming strong. Building character and imparting depth to a people's way of thinking are far more difficult than just increasing numbers and marshalling armies.

Al-Qalam (The Pen)

سُورَةُ الْقَلَمِ

In the Name of God, the Lord of Grace, the Ever Merciful

بِسْمِ اللَّهِ الرَّحْمَٰنِ الرَّحِيمِ

Nūn. By the pen, by all they write, (1)

نٓ ۚ وَٱلْقَلَمِ وَمَا يَسْطُرُونَ ﴿١﴾

you are not, by your Lord's grace, a madman. (2)

مَآ أَنتَ بِنِعْمَةِ رَبِّكَ بِمَجْنُونٍ ﴿٢﴾

And indeed you shall have a never-ending reward. (3)

وَإِنَّ لَكَ لَأَجْرًا غَيْرَ مَمْنُونٍ ﴿٣﴾

Most certainly, yours is a sublime character. (4)

وَإِنَّكَ لَعَلَىٰ خُلُقٍ عَظِيمٍ ﴿٤﴾

You shall before long see, as they will see, (5)

فَسَتُبْصِرُ وَيُبْصِرُونَ ﴿٥﴾

which of you is the one afflicted. (6)

بِأَييِّكُمُ ٱلْمَفْتُونُ ﴿٦﴾

Your Lord knows best who has strayed from His path, as He knows the ones who are rightly guided. (7)

إِنَّ رَبَّكَ هُوَ أَعْلَمُ بِمَن ضَلَّ عَن سَبِيلِهِۦ وَهُوَ أَعْلَمُ بِٱلْمُهْتَدِينَ ﴿٧﴾

So pay no heed to those who deny the truth. (8)

فَلَا تُطِعِ ٱلْمُكَذِّبِينَ ﴿٨﴾

They would love that you compromise with them, so that they will also compromise. (9)

وَدُّوا لَوْ تُدْهِنُ فَيُدْهِنُونَ ۝

Furthermore, pay no heed to any contemptible swearer, (10)

وَلَا تُطِعْ كُلَّ حَلَّافٍ مَّهِينٍ ۝

slanderer, going about with defaming tales, (11)

هَمَّازٍ مَّشَّاءٍ بِنَمِيمٍ ۝

hinderer of good, aggressor, sinful, (12)

مَّنَّاعٍ لِّلْخَيْرِ مُعْتَدٍ أَثِيمٍ ۝

cruel and, on top of all that, given to evil. (13)

عُتُلٍّ بَعْدَ ذَٰلِكَ زَنِيمٍ ۝

Just because he has wealth and children, (14)

أَن كَانَ ذَا مَالٍ وَبَنِينَ ۝

when Our revelations are recited to him, he says, 'Fables of the ancients!' (15)

إِذَا تُتْلَىٰ عَلَيْهِ ءَايَٰتُنَا قَالَ أَسَٰطِيرُ الْأَوَّلِينَ ۝

We shall brand him on the snout. (16)

سَنَسِمُهُ عَلَى الْخُرْطُومِ ۝

We try them as We tried the owners of a certain garden, who vowed that they would harvest its fruits on the morrow, (17)

إِنَّا بَلَوْنَٰهُمْ كَمَا بَلَوْنَا أَصْحَٰبَ الْجَنَّةِ إِذْ أَقْسَمُوا لَيَصْرِمُنَّهَا مُصْبِحِينَ ۝

and made no allowance. (18)

وَلَا يَسْتَثْنُونَ ۝

A visitation from your Lord came upon that garden while they were asleep, (19)

فَطَافَ عَلَيْهَا طَآئِفٌ مِّن رَّبِّكَ وَهُمْ نَآئِمُونَ ﴿١٩﴾

so that by morning it was stripped bare and looked desolate. (20)

فَأَصْبَحَتْ كَالصَّرِيمِ ﴿٢٠﴾

At daybreak they called out to one another: (21)

فَتَنَادَوْاْ مُصْبِحِينَ ﴿٢١﴾

'Go early to your tilth if you wish to gather all its fruits.' (22)

أَنِ اغْدُواْ عَلَىٰ حَرْثِكُمْ إِن كُنتُمْ صَٰرِمِينَ ﴿٢٢﴾

So they went off, whispering to one another, (23)

فَانطَلَقُواْ وَهُمْ يَتَخَٰفَتُونَ ﴿٢٣﴾

'Make sure that no needy person enters the garden today.' (24)

أَن لَّا يَدْخُلَنَّهَا الْيَوْمَ عَلَيْكُم مِّسْكِينٌ ﴿٢٤﴾

Early they went, strongly bent on their purpose. (25)

وَغَدَوْاْ عَلَىٰ حَرْدٍ قَٰدِرِينَ ﴿٢٥﴾

When they saw it, they exclaimed: 'Surely we have lost our way! (26)

فَلَمَّا رَأَوْهَا قَالُوٓاْ إِنَّا لَضَآلُّونَ ﴿٢٦﴾

No! We are utterly ruined.' (27)

بَلْ نَحْنُ مَحْرُومُونَ ﴿٢٧﴾

The wisest among them said, 'Did I not tell you, "Will you not extol God's limitless glory?"' (28)

قَالَ أَوْسَطُهُمْ أَلَمْ أَقُل لَّكُمْ لَوْلَا تُسَبِّحُونَ ﴿٢٨﴾

They said, 'Limitless in His glory is our Lord! Truly, we were doing wrong.' (29)

قَالُواْ سُبْحَٰنَ رَبِّنَآ إِنَّا كُنَّا ظَٰلِمِينَ ﴿٢٩﴾

Then they turned upon each other with mutual reproach. (30)

فَأَقْبَلَ بَعْضُهُمْ عَلَىٰ بَعْضٍ يَتَلَوَمُونَ ۝

They said: 'Woe betide us! We have done great wrong. (31)

قَالُوا يَٰوَيْلَنَآ إِنَّا كُنَّا طَٰغِينَ ۝

It may be that our Lord will grant us something better instead. To our Lord we truly turn in hope.' (32)

عَسَىٰ رَبُّنَآ أَن يُبْدِلَنَا خَيْرًا مِّنْهَآ إِنَّآ إِلَىٰ رَبِّنَا رَٰغِبُونَ ۝

Such is the suffering [in this life], but greater indeed is the suffering in the life to come, if they but knew it. (33)

كَذَٰلِكَ ٱلْعَذَابُ وَلَعَذَابُ ٱلْءَاخِرَةِ أَكْبَرُ لَوْ كَانُوا يَعْلَمُونَ ۝

For the God-fearing there shall be gardens of bliss with their Lord. (34)

إِنَّ لِلْمُتَّقِينَ عِندَ رَبِّهِمْ جَنَّٰتِ ٱلنَّعِيمِ ۝

Should We treat those who submit themselves to Us as We treat the guilty? (35)

أَفَنَجْعَلُ ٱلْمُسْلِمِينَ كَٱلْمُجْرِمِينَ ۝

What is the matter with you? On what basis do you judge? (36)

مَا لَكُمْ كَيْفَ تَحْكُمُونَ ۝

Or have you a divine book which you study, (37)

أَمْ لَكُمْ كِتَٰبٌ فِيهِ تَدْرُسُونَ ۝

and in which you find that you shall have all that you choose? (38)

إِنَّ لَكُمْ فِيهِ لَمَا تَخَيَّرُونَ ۝

Or have you received solemn oaths, binding on Us till the Day of Resurrection, that you will get whatever you yourselves decide? (39)

أَمْ لَكُمْ أَيْمَنٌ عَلَيْنَا بَلِغَةٌ إِلَىٰ يَوْمِ ٱلْقِيَمَةِ إِنَّ لَكُمْ لَمَا تَحْكُمُونَ ﴿٣٩﴾

Ask them which of them will vouch for this. (40)

سَلْهُمْ أَيُّهُم بِذَلِكَ زَعِيمٌ ﴿٤٠﴾

Or have they partners? Let them produce their partners, if what they say is true. (41)

أَمْ لَهُمْ شُرَكَاءُ فَلْيَأْتُوا بِشُرَكَائِهِمْ إِن كَانُوا صَدِقِينَ ﴿٤١﴾

On the day when matters become so dire, they will be asked to prostrate themselves, but they will not be able to do so. (42)

يَوْمَ يُكْشَفُ عَن سَاقٍ وَيُدْعَوْنَ إِلَى ٱلسُّجُودِ فَلَا يَسْتَطِيعُونَ ﴿٤٢﴾

Their eyes will be downcast, with ignominy overwhelming them. They were invited to prostrate themselves when they were safe. (43)

خَشِعَةً أَبْصَرُهُمْ تَرْهَقُهُمْ ذِلَّةٌ وَقَدْ كَانُوا يُدْعَوْنَ إِلَى ٱلسُّجُودِ وَهُمْ سَلِمُونَ ﴿٤٣﴾

Therefore, leave to Me those who deny this revelation. We shall bring them low, step by step, in ways beyond their knowledge. (44)

فَذَرْنِي وَمَن يُكَذِّبُ بِهَذَا ٱلْحَدِيثِ سَنَسْتَدْرِجُهُم مِّنْ حَيْثُ لَا يَعْلَمُونَ ﴿٤٤﴾

I will allow them more time: My scheme is truly firm. (45)

وَأُمْلِي لَهُمْ إِنَّ كَيْدِى مَتِينٌ ﴿٤٥﴾

Do you [Prophet] demand a payment from them [and so they fear] that they would be burdened with debt? (46)

أَمْ تَسْـَٔلُهُمْ أَجْرًا فَهُم مِّن مَّغْرَمٍ مُّثْقَلُونَ ﴿٤٦﴾

Do they have knowledge of the hidden reality so that they can write it down? (47)

أَمْ عِندَهُمُ ٱلْغَيْبُ فَهُمْ يَكْتُبُونَ ﴿٤٧﴾

So, await in patience your Lord's judgement; and do not be like the man in the whale who called out in distress. (48)

فَٱصْبِرْ لِحُكْمِ رَبِّكَ وَلَا تَكُن كَصَاحِبِ ٱلْحُوتِ إِذْ نَادَىٰ وَهُوَ مَكْظُومٌ ﴿٤٨﴾

Had not grace from his Lord reached him, he would have been left upon that barren shore in a state of disgrace. (49)

لَّوْلَآ أَن تَدَٰرَكَهُۥ نِعْمَةٌ مِّن رَّبِّهِۦ لَنُبِذَ بِٱلْعَرَآءِ وَهُوَ مَذْمُومٌ ﴿٤٩﴾

His Lord, however, chose him and made him one of the righteous. (50)

فَٱجْتَبَٰهُ رَبُّهُۥ فَجَعَلَهُۥ مِنَ ٱلصَّٰلِحِينَ ﴿٥٠﴾

The unbelievers well-nigh trip you up with their eyes when they hear this reminder. They say, 'He is surely mad.' (51)

وَإِن يَكَادُ ٱلَّذِينَ كَفَرُوا۟ لَيُزْلِقُونَكَ بِأَبْصَٰرِهِمْ لَمَّا سَمِعُوا۟ ٱلذِّكْرَ وَيَقُولُونَ إِنَّهُۥ لَمَجْنُونٌ ﴿٥١﴾

Yet it is but a reminder to all mankind. (52)

وَمَا هُوَ إِلَّا ذِكْرٌ لِّلْعَٰلَمِينَ ﴿٥٢﴾

Issues Spelled Out

"Nūn. By the pen, by all they write." (Verse 1) The *sūrah* begins with an oath by God Almighty. The oath is by the letter *nūn*, the pen and writing. The relationship between this letter of the alphabet and the other two, i.e. the pen and writing, is clear. As God swears by these He gives them due importance, highlighting this and presenting it to a community where learning through this approach was not valued. In fact, writing was very rare and primitive in that community while the role it was destined to play required that such ability develop and become widespread. This was the only way through which it could advocate its faith and the systems it laid down for human life. It would then be required to provide wise leadership for humanity. Writing is no doubt a basic element in fulfilling such tasks.

This point is endorsed by the fact that Islamic revelations started with the order to read: *"Read in the name of your Lord who has created – created man out of a germ-cell. Read – for your Lord is the most Bountiful One, Who has taught the use of the pen, taught man what he did not know."* (96: 1–5) This instruction was given to the unlettered Prophet, whom God in His infinite wisdom willed to be unable to read and write. Yet the revelations vouchsafed to him began with such emphasis on learning through reading and writing with the pen. This importance is reiterated here by the oath using the letter *nūn*, the pen and the writing. All this should be seen as part of the divine system of cultivating the Muslim community and preparing it for the universal role God assigned to it.

God Almighty states this oath by *nūn*, the pen and writing to refute the unbelievers' false allegation. He shows how improbable it is, since it is He who bestowed His grace on His Messenger: *"You are not, by your Lord's grace, a madman."* (Verse 2) This short verse also identifies God's grace bestowed on the Prophet in an expression that confirms his closeness to Him. At the same time, the verse refutes the alleged condition, one that cannot combine with God's grace bestowed on His chosen servant.

Anyone who studies the Prophet's relations with his people will be utterly astonished that any should level such a description at him. They knew him to be very wise. Several years before his prophethood, they accepted his arbitration in a dispute over which of their clans should be honoured with placing the Black Stone in its position in the Ka'bah. It was they who nicknamed him *al-Amīn*, meaning the trustworthy. They also continued to deposit their valuables with him for safekeeping, and this despite their fierce enmity towards him and his message, throughout his time in Makkah. Indeed, so trustworthy was the Prophet that he entrusted his cousin, 'Alī, with the task of returning such deposits to them when he migrated to Madīnah. The unbelievers also confirmed that he never told a lie even before the start of his prophethood. Heracules, the Byzantine Emperor, asked Abū Sufyān, the Quraysh leader, whether they ever accused Muḥammad of lying before he became a prophet. Abū Sufyān, who was his sworn enemy at the time, said that they did not. Heracules then said: "He would not refrain from lying to people and then start lying to God."

It is absolutely astounding that the hatred felt by the Quraysh unbelievers was of such a magnitude that they should make allegations of this sort against a noble man distinguished among them by his wisdom and high standards of morality. Yet grudges can blind people to the truth. The perpetrator of such falsehood is the first to know that he is a wicked liar.

This spiteful lie by the unbelievers is countered with a gesture of compassionate honour: "*You are not, by your Lord's grace, a madman.*" (Verse 2) Moreover, "*And indeed you shall have a never-ending reward.*" (Verse 3) This never-ending reward is granted by your Lord who has bestowed on you the honour of prophethood. This gives solace and abundant compensation for any type of isolation or allegation the unbelievers may hurl at him. What loss could be incurred by the one whose Lord kindly and benevolently assures him of a continuing reward, one that never ends?

A Testimony by God

This is followed by a great testimony and abundant honour: "*Most certainly, yours is a sublime character.*" (Verse 4) The whole universe echoes this unique praise of the Prophet. No writer can describe the value of this great testimony by the Creator of the universe; no imagination can give it its worth. It is a testimony by God, according to His own measure, given to His servant, in His own words: "*Most certainly, yours is a sublime character.*" A sublime character has, according to God's measure, its own unique value which no other creature can imagine.

This testimony confirms Muhammad's greatness in several ways. First of all, by the fact that it is God's own testimony, given in His majesty, and appreciated by the whole universe and echoed by everyone on high. Secondly, his greatness is seen by virtue of the fact that Muhammad (peace be upon him) was able to receive God's testimony, live with it and know who was saying it. It was God Almighty, in His absolute power and knowledge, that stated it. The Prophet knew his own position in relation to such absolutely great power. He could appreciate this position as no one else could. The fact that Muhammad (peace be upon him) held his position firmly as he received this word, from its sublime source, without being crushed by the pressure it brought on him, and that he remained calm and stable is the best evidence of his own greatness.

There are many reports about the Prophet's greatness given by his Companions. Indeed, his practical conduct is better evidence than anything reported about him. However, this testimony, given by God Almighty, is greater still than any reported evidence. God knows best whom to entrust with His final message. Muhammad, (peace be upon him), in his sublime character, was indeed the one to deliver this message, which is the noblest in history. He was a match for it, and a living example of its greatness. The message of Islam is so perfect, beautiful, comprehensive and truthful that it could only be delivered by a man who deserved such testimony from God, and by one who would receive such divine testimony with confidence. At the same time, however, God remonstrated with the Prophet for some of his actions but all the while imbibing the same confidence and reassurance. He declared both aspects to all people, hiding nothing. In both situations, he was a noble Prophet, an obedient servant and a trusted deliverer of the divine message.

The greatness of Muhammad (peace be upon him) mirrors the greatness of the Islamic message: both go further in scope than the most powerful telescope can reach. The most that anyone who wants to monitor this dual greatness can do is to look at it without assigning limits to it, and point to its field in the universe, without setting parameters on it.

Once more I feel the need to stress the broad significance of the fact that the Prophet received this testimony from his Lord and that he remained firm, confident and reassured. He himself, a human being, would praise one of his Companions and that person, as well as those close to him, would feel so excited and overwhelmed with joy. Yet all involved, the one making the statement of praise, the praised person and the ones who heard of it knew that the Prophet was human. It is true that he was a Prophet, yet he remained within the human circle, with its well-known limitations. In his case, the praise came from God Almighty, and he knew of God what no one else could know. Yet he remained firm and continued his mission. How this must have felt is beyond imagination.

It was Muḥammad alone who could attain such a sublime level of greatness and human perfection that matched the spirit God breathed into man. Muḥammad alone matched this ultimate divine message to mankind so that it is reflected in him alive, taking the form of a man. Muḥammad alone was the one God knew to be worthy of this position and further knew that his character was sublime. It was God who declared here His testimony that he had a sublime character, as also declared elsewhere in the Qur'ān that He, the Lord of all the worlds, showered His blessings on him: "*God and His angels bless the Prophet. Believers! Bless him and give him greetings of peace.*" (33: 56) Only God can grant one of His own servants such a great and unique favour.

Emphasis on Morality

We also note here that the moral element is given considerable weight in God's measure. It is a fundamental element in the Islamic message, just as it is fundamental in the Prophet's own character. Indeed, we note its prominence in both. In fact, both legislative and educational aspects of the Islamic message rely on moral values. The strongest emphasis in what it advocates is laid on purity, cleanliness, honesty, truth, justice, mercy, compassion, kindness, fulfilment of promises and commitments, actions matching words and both consistent with intentions and thoughts. It forbids injustice, dishonesty, cheating, taking other people's property unlawfully, violating other people's rights and honour and spreading immorality in any way or form. Its laws are geared to protecting these principles and safeguarding the moral element in people's consciences and behaviour, as well as in personal, social and international dealings.

The Prophet says: "I have been given the message that perfects noble morality." He thus sums up the objective of his message. His teachings are highly consistent in emphasizing the importance of morality and good manners. His own behaviour provides a shining picture as well as a practical noble example that merits a record in God's eternal book: "*Most certainly, yours is a sublime character.*" (Verse 4) Thus God praises His Messenger as well as the morality aspect of His message. With such praise God sets out a strong bond pulling the earth towards heaven. He makes this aspect the one to which believers' hearts, those who look up to His reward, are strongly attached. He thus identifies for them which values He would like them to possess.

This is the unique aspect of Islamic morality. It does not stem from the local environment, or indeed from any earthly consideration. Nor does it draw on any tradition, interest or bond that was at play in that generation. Instead, it comes from heaven and relies on it. It responds to the call coming from heaven so that those on earth look up to a high horizon. It derives from God's own absolute attributes, which people are asked to emulate. This so that ordinary human beings can achieve their utmost level of humanity and be worthy of God's honour, bestowed on them as they are placed in charge of the earth. It is in this way only that they will merit a more sublime life, "*in a seat of truth, in the presence of an all-powerful Sovereign.*" (54: 55) This means that Islamic morality is not restricted by any earthly limitation. It rather aspires to the highest level that people can achieve.

Moreover, Islamic morality is not a set of individual values, such as truthfulness, honesty, justice, mercy, kindness, etc. Rather, it is a complete system in which personal education collaborates with the legal code; a system that deals with life as a whole and defines its direction. It ultimately seeks God's pleasure, and nothing else. This morality, in its perfection, beauty, balance, consistency, straightforwardness and unity was reflected in the person of Muḥammad, (peace be upon him), as he deservedly earned the praise granted by none other than God Almighty: "*Most certainly, yours is a sublime character.*" (Verse 4)

Reassurance About the Future

God then reassures His Messenger about the immediate future and how things will develop with those unbelievers who hurled such lies at him. He warns them that their true situation will be publicized and their falsehood be made public:

> *You shall before long see, as they will see, which of you is the one afflicted. Your Lord knows best who has strayed from His path, as He knows the ones who are rightly guided.* (Verses 5–7)

The afflicted person whom God assures the Prophet will be identified to all is the one that has gone astray, or the one subjected to a test that reveals his true condition. The two meanings are not much apart. This promise reassures the Prophet and the believers in his message and at the same time it warns those who oppose and abuse him, regardless of whatever type of madness they attribute to him. Most probably they did not mean that he was insane, because they realized that this could not be the case. They probably meant that he had associates from among the *jinn*, who perhaps inspired him with the fine words he recited. They used to say that every poet had someone from the *jinn* assisting their efforts. This was, however, far from the case with the Prophet. Nor does it fit with the nature of his revelations that are both consistent and truthful.

This promise by God confirms that the future will make clear the true nature of the Prophet and those who denied his message. The future will prove which party was afflicted or had gone astray. God reassured him that his Lord "*knows best who has strayed from His path, as He knows the ones who are rightly guided.*" (Verse 7) It is his Lord who gave him his revelations. He indeed knows that he and his followers are rightly guided. This is enough to reassure the Prophet and set his enemies worrying about what the future will bring.

God then tells the Prophet of their true feelings as they continued to argue with him about the truth he preached and the abuse they levelled at him. They may appear determined to uphold their ignorant beliefs, but the truth is that they are fundamentally uncertain about them. They are ready to shed most of these if only the Prophet would abandon some of what he called on them to accept. They are prepared to compromise everything, retaining only some appearances in return for a gesture of compromise from him. They do not have a faith that they consider to embody the truth; they are only keen to retain some appearances:

So pay no heed to those who deny the truth. They would love that you compromise with them, so that they will also compromise. (Verses 8–9)

It is all subject to negotiation, then, with the aim of agreeing a meeting point somewhere in the middle, just like commercial transactions. Yet the difference between beliefs and commercial activities is vast. A person with faith will not abandon any of its beliefs or values, because its minor points are the same as its major ones. Indeed, in faith there is nothing minor and nothing major: both are the same. A faith is a single unity with parts complementing each other. Its advocate will never discard any part of it in order to please someone else.

Islam and *jāhiliyyah* can never meet halfway, or indeed in any way. This is true of Islam everywhere and across all generations. All states of ignorance, or *jāhiliyyah*, are the same: past, present or future. The gulf that separates the two states is unbridgeable and admits no compromise. The two are diametrically opposed.

Several reports speak of what the unbelievers in Makkah tried to achieve by way of compromise with the Prophet so that he would stop criticizing their worship methods. They hoped that he would give them something that would save their faces if they were to follow him. In this, they were no different from any negotiator seeking a compromise. The Prophet, however, maintained a decisive firmness, refusing to give up even a small part of his faith. Additionally, he was extremely well mannered, kind and benevolent towards his tribesmen, eager to make things easy for them. With regard to faith, he was committed, obedient of God's instructions: *"So pay no heed to those who deny the truth."* (Verse 8)

The Prophet did not compromise an iota of his faith even during the direst period of his life in Makkah, where he and his few followers were under siege, suffering immense persecution. He never withheld a word that needed to be uttered in the face of such tyrants. He never sought to soften their stance or to avoid their persecution by such compromise. Nor did he ever hesitate to clarify any point that was closely or remotely relevant to his faith.

Ibn Hishām reports in his biography of the Prophet:

> It should be said in fairness that the chiefs of Makkah did not take any action worth noting against the Prophet in the early stages. When he started to criticize their pagan faith and ridicule their idols, however, they began to think that the matter was much too serious to ignore. Yet, they could not do much about it because Abū Ṭālib protected his nephew against all threats. To ignore such protection by the Makkan chiefs would contravene one of the basic conventions of their social set-up. Therefore, a small delegation, composed of a number of the most influential people in Makkah, went to Abū Ṭālib complaining about his nephew's behaviour. The delegation included the two brothers 'Utbah and Shaybah, sons of Rabī'ah from the clan of 'Abd Shams; Abū Sufyān Sakhr ibn Ḥarb from Ummayah; Abū al-Bakhtarī al-'Āṣ ibn Hishām and al-Aswad ibn al-Muṭṭalib from Asad, Abū Jahl 'Amr ibn Hishām and al-Walīd ibn al-Mughīrah from Makhzūm; the two brothers Nabīh and Munnabih sons of al-Ḥajjāj from Sahm and Al-'Āṣ ibn Wā'il, also from Sahm. They made their complaint clear to Abū Ṭālib and they offered him the choice of either telling Muḥammad not to criticize their ways and ridicule their idols or allowing them to take such effective measures as they might deem necessary to end the trouble. Abū Ṭālib, who continued to follow the religion of his people, spoke to them gently and calmed them down. He did not promise them much.

The Prophet continued to preach his message regardless. The crisis with his people increased in intensity. Feelings of hostility spread. So the delegation went again to Abū Ṭālib and said to him: "Abū Ṭālib, you enjoy a position of honour and respect among us. We have requested you to stop your nephew, but you have not taken any action. We certainly cannot just sit and do nothing when he continues to speak ill of our forefathers and to ridicule us and our gods. You have to stop him or we will fight him and you over this question until one of the two parties is destroyed."

Abū Ṭālib was in a dilemma. He did not like to quarrel with his people, yet he could not bear to let his nephew down. So he called Muḥammad and explained to him what had taken place between him and his visitors. He then said to him: "You see the difficulty of my situation. Do not put my life and your life at risk, and do not burden me with what I cannot bear."

The Prophet felt that his uncle might be contemplating withdrawing his protection so he stated his own position with the greatest emphasis he could muster: "Uncle, should they give me the sun in my right hand and the moon in my left hand in return for abandoning my call, I would not do anything of the sort until God has brought this message to triumph or until I have perished." The Prophet was under the pressure of such strong emotions that tears sprang to his eyes. He started to walk away, but his uncle called him back, saying reassuringly: "My nephew, you may go and say whatever you like. I will never withdraw my protection from you, and never will I let you down."[2]

This is an image of the Prophet's commitment to his message at the precise moment when his uncle and protector, who was his last resort on earth, seemed on the verge of letting him down. It is a powerful image in its very nature, connotations and implications, as well as in its words and expressions. It is as new and powerful as this faith is. It is a reflection of the truth of God's description of the Prophet: *Most certainly, yours is a sublime character.* (Verse 4)

Another image also reported by Ibn Hishām, through Ibn Isḥāq relates a direct attempt at compromise offered by the unbelievers. This

---

2. Ibn Hishām, ibid., pp. 282–285. Also, Adil Salahi, ibid., pp. 95–96.

they did when they realized that the Prophet continued to be as firm as ever, despite their persecution of his Companions and their attempts to force them to renounce Islam.

'Utbah ibn Rabī'ah, one of the leading figures in Makkah, was one day sitting with a group of the Quraysh notables when he noticed the Prophet sitting alone close to the Ka'bah. 'Utbah suggested to his friends: "Shall we go to Muḥammad and make him some offers? He may accept one or the other. If he does we will give him that and put an end to our problem with him."

This idea was greeted with unanimous approval. As 'Utbah sat with the Prophet he addressed him: "My nephew, you know you command a position of high esteem and noble birth among us. You have brought into the life of your community something very serious indeed. You have thus caused disunity to creep into their ranks; you have belittled their ideals, ridiculed their gods and their religion and spoken ill of their forefathers. Now listen to me. I am making you some offers which I would like you to consider. You may, perhaps, find some of them acceptable."

The Prophet asked him to make his proposals, and listened attentively. 'Utbah said: "My nephew, if you have started this affair hoping to make money out of it, we are all willing to give you some of our own wealth so that you would be the richest among us. If it is honour and position you want, we will make you our master and seek your advice in all matters. If it is a throne you are after, we will make you our king. If, on the other hand, you are possessed and are unable to resist what overwhelms you, we will spare no expense in seeking a medical cure for you."

When 'Utbah stopped, the Prophet asked him whether he had finished. As 'Utbah affirmed that he had, the Prophet asked him to listen to what he had to say. The Prophet then recited the first 38 verses of *Sūrah* 41 of the Qur'ān. 'Utbah listened attentively. When the Prophet finished his recitation, he prostrated himself in humble devotion to God, before saying to 'Utbah: "You have heard what I have to say and you can make up your own mind."

'Utbah left quietly and went to his people, who realized as they saw him approaching that a change had come over him. They looked up at him curiously, listening to his words: "I have heard something the like of which I have never heard in my life. It is neither poetry nor sorcery. Take up the suggestion I am making to you, and lay the blame for the outcome at my door. Leave this man alone. What I have heard from him will certainly bring about great events. Should the rest of the Arabs kill him, you would have been spared the trouble. If he wins, whatever glory he achieves will be yours." They retorted: "He has certainly bewitched you." He said: "I have stated my opinion, and you can do as you wish."[3]

A different report suggests that when 'Utbah listened to the Prophet's recitation, he stopped him when the Prophet read the verse saying: "*If they turn away, say: 'I warn you of a thunderbolt like the thunderbolt that struck the 'Ād and Thamūd.'*" (41: 13) He was terrified and put his hand on the Prophet's mouth, and said to him: "I appeal to you, Muḥammad, by God and our kinship not to do that." He feared that the warning may come true. He then left him and went to his people suggesting that they leave Muḥammad alone.

Be that as it may, this was another way of trying to achieve compromise. Yet it also portrays an image of the Prophet's sublime character. We see him listening to 'Utbah's hollow offers, without stopping him, even though whatever 'Utbah had to offer did not deserve a moment's thought from Muḥammad (peace be upon him), considering his own vision of the universe and its values, and his understanding of the truth and what life on earth is worth. Yet his manners would not allow him to interrupt his interlocutor or to display any sign of annoyance with his worthless offers. Instead, he listened to him with full attention until he had finished. Then he asked him whether he had finished what he had to say. His attitude throughout was that of one who is certain of the truth, reassured and at the same time very polite.

A third form of the Quraysh's attempts to reach a compromise is seen in the following report by Ibn Isḥāq:

---

3.   Ibn Hishām, ibid., pp. 313–314, Also, Adil Salahi, ibid., pp. 113–114.

189

One day as the Prophet was doing the *ṭawāf* at the Ka'bah, he was stopped by a group of the Quraysh elders including al-Aswad ibn al-Muṭṭalib, al-Walīd ibn al-Mughīrah, Umayyah ibn Khalaf and al-'Āṣ ibn Wā'il. They said to him: 'Muḥammad! Let us worship the God you worship, and you worship the deities we worship. Thus, we will be together at the same level. If your God is better than ours, we will have benefited by that, and if our deities are the better ones, you will have made the benefit.' He answered as God instructed him: "*Say: 'Unbelievers! I do not worship what you worship, nor do you worship what I worship. I shall never worship what you worship, nor will you ever worship what I worship. You have your own religion and I have mine.'*"[4] (109: 1–6)

God thus put an end to this absurd offer, and the Prophet replied to them as God so instructed him.

What Sort of Nobility

The importance of the moral element is again stressed when the Prophet is ordered not to obey one particular unbeliever. We have a full list of the terrible and shameful qualities of this person, who is then threatened with humiliation:

Furthermore, pay no heed to any contemptible swearer, slanderer, going about with defaming tales, hinderer of good, aggressor, sinful, cruel and, on top of all that, given to evil. Just because he has wealth and children, when Our revelations are recited to him, he says, 'Fables of the ancients!' We shall brand him on the snout. (Verses 10–16)

It is said that this person was al-Walīd ibn al-Mughīrah, to whom the following passage in *Sūrah* 74 also refers: "*Leave to me the one I created alone, to whom I have granted vast wealth, and sons by his side, making life smooth and easy for him; yet he greedily desires that I give him more. No! He has set himself stubbornly against Our revelations. I will constrain him*

---

4. Ibn Sayyid al-Nas (1996), *'Uyūn al-Athar*, Dar al-Turath, Madīnah, p. 197.

to endure a painful uphill climb! He thought and he schemed. Damn him, how he schemed! Again, damn him, how he schemed! He looked around, then he frowned and glared, then he turned his back and gloried in his arrogance, and said, 'This is just sorcery handed down from olden times! This is nothing but the word of a mere mortal!' I will cast him into the scorching fire." (74: 11–26) There are many reports that speak of al-Walīd's repeated scheming against the Prophet and his opposition to the message of Islam, trying to turn people away from it. It is also reported that the verses in the present *sūrah* refer to al-Akhnas ibn Sharīq, another of the Prophet's determined opponents. The present denunciation of the man, whether he was al-Walīd or al-Akhnas, and the stern warnings given in the other *sūrah*, suffice as evidence of this person's wicked role in the fight against the Prophet and the Islamic message. They also indicate his evil intentions and that he was devoid of all goodness.

The Qur'ān lists here nine of his bad characteristics. He is a 'swearer', which suggests that he always does so. Only a liar swears much because he feels that people do not believe him. Therefore, he resorts to swearing to persuade people to accept what he says. Moreover, he is 'contemptible', someone who does not even respect himself. Nor do people trust his word. This is proven by the fact that he feels the need to swear all the time to overcome people's mistrust. Despite the fact that he has wealth, sons and position, he remains contemptible. It is often the case that a tyrant remains contemptible even though he holds power and authority. Likewise, dignity is a personal trait which remains distinctive of its possessor even though he has nothing of the material luxuries of this world.

He is a 'slanderer' who disrespects people and tries to insult them by word and gesture, in their presence or absence. This is a characteristic that Islam brands as most hateful because it is contrary to gallantry, self-respect and propriety of conduct towards others in so far as respecting their dignity, regardless of their social position. The Qur'ān denounces this characteristic in several places: *"Woe to every taunting, slandering backbiter."* (104: 1) *"Believers! No men shall deride other men: it may well be that those [whom they deride] are better than themselves. And no women [shall deride other] women: it may well be that those [whom they deride] are better than themselves. And neither shall you defame yourselves, nor insult one another by [opprobrious] epithets."* (49: 11) All the actions mentioned in this verse are types of slander.

Another characteristic of this person is that he 'goes about with defaming tales'. He goes around, telling people what will spoil their relations, create rancour in their hearts and destroy their ties. This is an evil and contemptible quality that no one who respects himself and wants to be respected will entertain. People realize that the one who tells tales about others is unworthy of respect. Even those who listen to him will not respect him, because they know he is evil.

The Prophet instructed his Companions not to tell him anything that would cause him to change his attitude towards any of them. He said: "Let no one tell me any negative thing about any of my Companions. I love to come out to you with no ill-feeling in my heart." [Related by Abū Dāwūd and al-Tirmidhī.] In an authentic *ḥadīth*, 'Abdullāh ibn Mas'ūd reports that "the Prophet passed by two graves. He said that the two buried in them are suffering punishment for no cardinal sin. One of them used not to cover himself when urinating, and the other used to go about with defaming tales." [Related by al-Bukhārī and Muslim.] Hudhayfah quotes the Prophet as saying: "No one who goes about with defaming tales will be admitted into heaven." [Related by Aḥmad, al-Bukhārī, Muslim and others.] Yazīd ibn al-Sakan reports that "the Prophet said to his Companions: 'Shall I tell you who are the best among you?' They said: 'Please do.' He said: 'They are the ones who, when seen, the name of God is glorified.' He then said: 'Shall I tell you who are the worst among you? They are the ones who go about with defaming tales, who spoil relations between friends and try to get innocent people defamed.'" [Related by Aḥmad.]

Islam naturally denounces this despicable and shameful characteristic in strong terms. It spoils people's hearts and destroys friendships. It degrades the one who does it before it spoils relations between others. It undermines the person's own character even before undermining society. It creates mistrust between people and often lands the innocent in trouble.

Moreover, this person is a 'hinderer of good', preventing it from reaching him and others. He used to prevent people from accepting the divine faith, even though it is the sum of all goodness. Furthermore, whenever he noticed that any of his children or clansmen leaned towards the Prophet, he would say to them: 'If any of you were to follow Muḥammad's religion, I would never give him an iota.' Thus he tried his utmost to prevent them from accepting Islam. Hence, the Qur'ān records this as one of his characteristics.

He is also an 'aggressor', stepping over the limits of right and justice. His aggression is levelled against the Prophet and the Muslims on the one hand, and against his own family and clan on the other, given he prevented them from accepting Islam. Aggression is an evil quality which the Qur'ān and the Prophet denounce in clear terms. Islam forbids it in any form, even in one's approach to food and drink: "*Eat of the wholesome things which We have provided for you and do not transgress.*" (20: 81) Both justice and moderation are essential qualities of the Islamic code.

What is more is that he is 'sinful', committing all sorts of sins so as to earn this description, without specifying what it is he does. Thus, committing sin becomes his essential characteristic.

The next characteristic is stated in translation as 'cruel', but in the Arabic original this is *'utull*, which by its very sound connotes a host of features that no group of words can adequately describe. The one who is *'utull* is cruel, unfriendly, gluttonous, heavy handed, mean, given to treating others badly. Abū al-Dardā', a Companion of the Prophet, defined an *'utull* person as 'the one who is covetous, ill-mannered, gluttonous, greedy for money, tight-fisted.' The word *'utull* thus reveals a hateful character.

On top of all these evil qualities, this enemy of Islam is also described as 'given to evil'. The Arabic word used here is *zanīm*, which has more than one meaning. One of these denotes someone who is attached to a group of people, but he is of suspect descent. None of them knows his parentage. Another meaning denotes a person who lacks morality and who is known by his many evil deeds. This second meaning is perhaps more true of al-Walīd ibn al-Mughīrah, but the use of this word here makes him contemptible even though he was also proud and arrogant.

These personal qualities are followed with a denunciation of this person's attitude to divine revelations: "*Just because he has wealth and children, when Our revelations are recited to him, he says, 'Fables of the ancients!'"* (Verses 14–15) How ungrateful! How can anyone enjoy God's favours of children and wealth and then deride His revelations, ridicule His Messenger and denounce His message? By itself, this is equal to all the evil qualities already mentioned.

Hence a warning is issued to him by the Almighty. The warning hits at the very position of pride on account of his wealth and children, in the same way as the earlier mention of his personal characteristics hit at his pride in his position among his people. He hears now a threat that will inevitably be fulfilled: *"We shall brand him on the snout."* (Verse 16)

The Arabic word *khurṭūm*, translated here as snout, means, among other things, the nose of a wild pig. Perhaps this is the meaning intended here, denoting his nose. In Arabic, the nose connotes dignity. People refer to an honourable person as one of high nose, while a humiliated one is described as having his nose in the dust. Hence, the threat of branding him on his nose connotes double humiliation: being branded like slaves used to be, and his nose being referred to as a snout or pig's nose.

Undoubtedly, these verses fell like a fatal blow for al-Walīd. He belonged to a community which attached much importance to avoiding abuse by a poet, even though the abuse was no more than false allegations. How about such a truthful description by the Creator of the universe, in such an inimitable style, and in the Qur'ān which is echoed throughout the universe for the rest of time! It was a fatal blow that this enemy of Islam and its noble Prophet deserved.

The People of the Garden

A reminder of the outcome of the greed and denial of other people's rights then follows. This in a reference to a group of people who owned a garden. It seems that the story was well known to the Arabs addressed by the Qur'ān. The reminder makes it clear that what people have of wealth and children is only a means to test them, in the same way as the people of the garden were put to trial. The result of all such tests will inevitably be revealed:

We try them as We tried the owners of a certain garden, who vowed that they would harvest its fruits on the morrow, and made no allowance. A visitation from your Lord came upon that garden while they were asleep, so that by morning it was stripped bare and looked desolate. At daybreak they called out to one another: 'Go early to your tilth if you wish to gather all its fruits.' So they went off, whispering to one another, 'Make sure that no needy person enters the garden today.' Early they went, strongly bent on their purpose. When they saw it, they exclaimed: 'Surely we have lost our way! No! We are utterly ruined.' The wisest among them said, 'Did I not tell you, "Will you not extol God's limitless glory?"' They said, 'Limitless in His glory is our Lord! Truly, we were doing wrong.' Then they turned upon each other with mutual reproach. They said: 'Woe betide us! We have done great wrong. It may be that our Lord will grant us something better instead. To our Lord we truly turn in hope.' Such is the suffering [in this life], but greater indeed is the suffering in the life to come, if they but knew it. (Verses 17–33)

This story may well have been well known, but its narration in the Qur'ān reveals what lies behind its episodes of God's power, the tests He sets for some of His servants and their requital at the end. This is, then, what is new in its presentation in the Qur'ān. As it unfolds, we see a group of naïve people who appear to us in their thoughts and actions like simple rural people. Perhaps this type of person was closer to the addressees who were stubborn in their rejection of the faith, but who were not particularly sophisticated characters. Rather, they tended to be simple folk.

From an artistic point of view, the narrative represents one of the methods of story-telling in the Qur'ān. It includes an element of surprise that captures the listener's interest. It shows the ludicrous nature of human scheming as compared with God's planning. Moreover, the events are brought alive as if we see them unfolding.

We see the owners of a garden agreeing to a plan. According to reports, the previous owner of the garden was a good man who had allocated a portion of its harvest to the poor. His heirs, however, wanted to keep all its fruits and yield for themselves, depriving the poor of their customary share.

The story now unfolds: "*We try them as We tried the owners of a certain garden, who vowed that they would harvest its fruits on the morrow, and made no allowance.*" (Verses 17–18) They made up their minds to harvest its fruits very early in the morning, taking all for themselves and making no allowance for the poor. They swore to this and even went to bed with this evil intention. We leave them in their slumber to look at what takes place during the night when they are totally unaware. God certainly does not sleep. His scheme is different from theirs: "*A visitation from your Lord came upon that garden while they were asleep, so that by morning it was stripped bare and looked desolate.*" (Verses 19–20) We then leave the garden to look at the plotters and what they are now doing.

They wake up very early, calling each other to get ready: "*At daybreak they called out to one another: 'Go early to your tilth if you wish to gather all its fruits.'*" (Verses 21–22) Thus they remind and counsel one another. The *sūrah* carries its ridicule further, showing them on their way, speaking in whispers to ensure that no one learns of their plot to deprive the poor of their legitimate share: "*So they went off, whispering to one another, 'Make sure that no needy person enters the garden today.'*" (Verses 23–24) We, the reader and listener, know something unknown to the owners of the garden. We have seen the subtle hand making away with all its fruits, leaving it stripped bare. We, therefore, hold our breath to look at what these plotters do.

The *sūrah* adds more ridicule: "*Early they went, strongly bent on their purpose.*" (Verse 25) They certainly felt able to deprive others, or at least to deprive themselves. Now for the surprise: "*When they saw it, they exclaimed: 'Surely we have lost our way!'*" (Verse 26) This is certainly not our garden. We seem to have lost our way. However, they soon make sure: "*No! We are utterly ruined.*" (Verse 27) This is the truth of the matter.

Now that they are facing the results of their scheme that aimed to deprive the needy, the middle one among them, who was their best and wisest, reminds them of his earlier counsel. He apparently had a different point of view, but when he could not persuade them to accept it, he went along with them instead of holding on to the truth. Hence, he suffered the same fate as they. Hence, too, his reminder: "*The wisest among them said: 'Did I not tell you, "Will you not extol God's limitless glory?'"'"* (Verse 28) Now, when it is too late, they listen to sound counsel: *"They said, 'Limitless in His glory is our Lord! Truly, we were doing wrong.'"* (Verse 29)

As happens in every situation when results turn bad, everyone tries to shift the blame away from himself: *"Then they turned upon each other with mutual reproach."* (Verse 30) Then, they finally stop blaming each other and acknowledge their common fault, hoping that God will forgive them and replace their lost harvest: *"They said: 'Woe betide us! We have done great wrong. It may be that our Lord will grant us something better instead. To our Lord we truly turn in hope.'"* (Verses 31–32)

Before the curtains are drawn on the last scene we have the *sūrah's* parting comment: *"Such is the suffering [in this life], but greater indeed is the suffering in the life to come, if they but knew it."* (Verse 33) This, then, is a test of affluence. The people of Makkah should learn this lesson for they are being tested in the same way as the owners of the garden were tested. They should consider what their own test will bring in its wake. They should take heed and avoid what is certainly greater than any test and suffering endured in this present world: *"Greater indeed is the suffering in the life to come, if they but knew it."*

The *sūrah* cites this well-known story, given it deals with their own environment. In this way it establishes a clear link between the application of God's law to communities of olden times and to the generation being addressed. It touches their hearts with what is close to their own lives. At the same time it tells the believers that the wealth they see the unbelievers enjoying is nothing but a test God sets for them. It has its own consequences. It is part of God's law that He tests people either with luxuries and comforts or with hardship. Those who behave with arrogance, deprive others of their share, and feel that what they are given is theirs by right may always face a result of the type suffered by those owners of the garden. Yet, *"greater indeed is the suffering in the life to come, if they but knew it."* (Verse 33) Believers who watch God in all their actions enjoy a different outcome: *"For the God-fearing there shall be gardens of bliss with their Lord."* (Verse 34) The contrast between the two ends echoes the contrast between their behaviour and reality. Two opposite lines of action lead to two contrasting ends.

Can They Be Equal?

At this point, the *sūrah* puts a simple, uncomplicated argument to them, challenging them, putting to them one question after another, on matters that can have only one answer. It warns them, showing them a fearsome scene of the life to come, and threatens them that, in this present life, they could face a war against God Almighty:

> *Should We treat those who submit themselves to Us as We treat the guilty? What is the matter with you? On what basis do you judge? Or have you a divine book which you study, and in which you find that you shall have all that you choose? Or have you received solemn oaths, binding on Us till the Day of Resurrection, that you will get whatever you yourselves decide? Ask them which of them will vouch for this. Or have they partners? Let them produce their partners, if what they say is true. On the day when matters become so dire, they will be asked to prostrate themselves, but they will not be able to do so. Their eyes will be downcast, with ignominy overwhelming them. They were invited to prostrate themselves when they were safe. Therefore, leave to Me those who deny this revelation. We shall bring them low, step by step, in ways beyond their knowledge. I will allow them more time: My scheme is truly firm. Do you [Prophet] demand a payment from them [and so they fear] that they would be burdened with debt? Do they have knowledge of the hidden reality so that they can write it down?* (Verses 35–47)

The warning against punishment in the life to come and a war in this present life is made within the argument and challenge this passage delineates. This has the effect of heightening the argument and increasing the pressure the challenge represents. The passage starts with a rhetorical question: *"Should We treat those who submit themselves to Us as We treat the guilty?"* (Verse 35) This question refers to the outcome of the two parties that has already been stated. This is a question that admits only one answer. No, it cannot be! Those who submit to God can never be treated on the same footing as those who are knowingly guilty. No logic and no standard of justice allows that the guilty and those who submit to God should face the same result. Hence, the *sūrah* puts a second rhetorical question to them: *"What is the matter with you? On what basis do you judge?"* (Verse 36) How do you judge matters so as to make the two equal? This certainly cannot be.

The *sūrah* moves on to add an element of sarcasm: *"Or have you a divine book which you study, and in which you find that you shall have all that you choose?"* (Verses 37–38) It is a sarcastic question that asks whether or not they have a book and if their studies lead them to make a judgement that no logic or fair standard would accept. A book that tells them that those who submit to God and the guilty are treated in the same way is indeed a funny sort of book that seeks to please them and fan their desires. It provides them with whatever rulings they like. Needless to say, such a book has nothing to do with truth, reason, justice or human tradition.

"Or have you received solemn oaths, binding on Us till the Day of Resurrection, that you will get whatever you yourselves decide?" (Verse 39) If they do not have a book to rely on in their judgement, then they must have the alternative spelled out in this verse: a binding pledge by God that remains in force until the Day of Judgement, one to the effect that they will have whatever they decide. They may choose as they please. But this is not the case: they have no such oaths or pledges. How can they, then, assert their claims? On what basis do they make such claims?

"Ask them which of them will vouch for this." (Verse 40) Who of them can pledge his word of honour that they have such an agreement with God, or that the pledges He has made them will remain in force until the Day of Judgement? This is again a sarcastic question that should place them in endless embarrassment.

"Or have they partners? Let them produce their partners, if what they say is true." (Verse 41) They used to associate partners with God, but the *sūrah* makes these their own partners, not God's. It challenges them to invoke these partners if they believe that what they say is true. The question here is when will they invoke such partners? *"On the day when matters become so dire, they will be asked to prostrate themselves, but they will not be able to do so. Their eyes will be downcast, with ignominy overwhelming them. They were invited to prostrate themselves when they were safe."* (Verses 42–43) The *sūrah* puts this scene before them as if

it is taking place at the moment of address. Thus, they are challenged to bring in their alleged partners, when this day appears as a reality, unattached in God's knowledge to a particular time. To put it before the addressees in this way gives it a very strong and profound effect. So, on the Day of Judgement, when matters are so dire and people are in great distress, these arrogant people will be asked to prostrate themselves, but they will be unable to do so, either because the time for this has lapsed, or because their bodies are so tense they will not respond. Be that as it may, the image here is one of extreme distress.

The *sūrah* continues painting their sorry picture: "*Their eyes will be downcast, with ignominy overwhelming them.*" (Verse 43) Such arrogant, tyrannical people with downcast eyes and overwhelming ignominy are shown in perfect contrast to the attitude they displayed in this life when they were extremely arrogant. This reminds us of the threat mentioned earlier in the *sūrah*: "*We shall brand him on the snout.*" (Verse 16) The impression of humiliation and ignominy is clear and deliberate. Yet in their humble position, enduring much humiliation, they are reminded of the arrogance that brought about this suffering: "*They were invited to prostrate themselves when they were safe.*" (Verse 43) When they were able to do it willingly, they arrogantly refused to prostrate themselves before God. Now, in the hereafter, when the life of this world is behind them, they wish they could respond to the invitation, but they cannot so prostrate themselves.

In their utterly dire situation, they face a stern warning: "*Therefore, leave to Me those who deny this revelation.*" (Verse 44) The warning shakes their very foundations. It is God Almighty who says to His Messenger that he should leave to Him those who deny His revelations. He will settle the matter with them. Who denies God's revelations other than such a weak, small creature devoid of all strength? Indeed, he is no more than a little ant, or a tiny particle. Nay, he is much less when he has to face the might of God, the All-Powerful. The Prophet is told to leave God alone with such a person and to go and rest with his fellow believers. That person's fight is not with the Prophet and the believers, but with God. He is God's enemy and God will deal with him. How terrifying! Who, then, would want to be an unbeliever! At the same time, how reassuring for the Prophet and the believers!

The Almighty then discloses the fighting plan against this little, weak creature: "*We shall bring them low, step by step, in ways beyond their knowledge. I will allow them more time: My scheme is truly firm.*" (Verses 44–45) These unbelievers and all dwellers on earth are too small and weak to warrant God making such a plan for them. God is only warning them so that they may save themselves before it is too late. They should realize that their apparent security is the trap they fall into. If God allows them time when they indulge in aggression and injustice and persist in error, this is merely to lead them on to their miserable end. They will thus carry their full burdens. They will come on that day burdened with sin, deserving all humiliation and ignominy.

Nothing is fairer or more merciful than a timely warning that places the outcome before them. God in His limitless glory offers His justice and mercy to His enemies and the enemies of His faith and Messenger. They are offered this warning when they still have the perfect chance to choose for themselves. All matters are laid bare. It is up to them.

God – limitless is He in His glory – gives chances, but He does not ignore anything. He allows an unjust tyrant respite, but then when He takes him, He does not let go. Here God speaks of the plan He in His wisdom has chosen. He tells His Messenger to leave those who deny His revelations to Him. They are the ones who take pride in their wealth, power, children and position. God will allow them respite, making all these favours their lure. He thus reassures His Messenger and warns His enemies. They are then left to consider their position.

The scene of the Day of Judgement, with all that it involves of stress and hardship, and the strong warning are followed with a continuation of the argument that wonders at their singular attitude: "*Do you [Prophet] demand a payment from them [and so they fear] that they would be burdened with debt?*" (Verse 46) Is it that you, Prophet, demand a hefty fee for providing guidance to them, and is it this fee that causes them to turn away and deny the divine faith, preferring to face such a miserable end? Could it be this or, "*Do they have knowledge of the hidden reality so that they can write it down?*" (Verse 47) Are they so certain of what is in store for them and, as a result, have no worry about it? Have they already written it down, or was it written according to what they wish? No answer is needed here. How, then, can they adopt such an attitude?

What Type of Fight?

A remarkable statement, *"Leave to Me those who deny this revelation,"* carries with it a terrible threat. It is then followed by an outline of the battle between God and His enemies. Together, the two statements make it clear that the Prophet and the believers have no part in the battle between faith and unfaith, truth and falsehood. This is indeed true, even though the Prophet and the believers may think that they have a genuine role to play in this battle. Whatever role they do play, when God so facilitates it for them, is only a part of God's will in His battle against His enemies. They are merely a tool, which God may or may not use. In either case, He does what He wants to do. In both cases, it is He who conducts the battle according to His laws ascertained as He chooses.

This statement was revealed when the Prophet and his followers were still in Makkah, a small minority unable to do much. Hence, it served as reassurance to those weak elements suffering persecution, and it struck fear in the hearts of those who thought they were powerful, having much at their disposal. In Madīnah, the situation completely changed. God willed then that the believers should play a prominent role in the battle. Yet at the same time, He also reiterated what He had said earlier, when they were in Makkah, weak and helpless. When they achieved their resounding victory at Badr, He said to them: *"It was not you who slew them, but it was God who slew them. When you threw [a handful of dust], it was not your act, but God's, so that He might put the believers through a fair test of His own making. Indeed, God hears all and knows all."* (8: 17)

God wants this truth of the battle being His battle to be firmly understood by the believers. It is His issue and He settles it. When He assigns a role in it to the believers, it is only because He wants to put them to a fair test, for which they earn a good reward. As for the war itself, it is He who fights it, and it is He who assigns its victory. He is able to conduct this war without them. When they participate in it, they are one of the tools He uses, not the only tool. There are many Qur'ānic texts that assert this truth in all situations. It also fits well with the Islamic concept of God's will, rules and laws, as well as the nature of human efforts made to accomplish God's will. These efforts are no more than a tool in God's hand.

This truth gives believers great reassurance in their two conditions of weakness and strength, provided they are sincere in their efforts, placing their trust in God when they fight for His cause. It is not their own power that ensures victory in the battle between truth and falsehood, faith and unfaith. It is God who ensures their victory. Their weakness does not lead to defeat because God's power supports them. God, however, may give respite to the unbelievers and lead them step by step. He determines events according to His will, wisdom, justice and mercy.

At the same time, this truth is bound to strike fear in the hearts of the enemy, whether the believers they are confronting are in a state of weakness or in a state of strength. Those believers are not the actual opponent. It is God who is conducting this war, with His own might. It is God who says to the Prophet to leave such miserable enemies to Him. It is He who leads them on step by step so that they fall into the fearful trap. Even if this enemy is equipped with all its strength, the same applies, because His power is indeed what sets the trap: "*I will allow them more time: My scheme is truly firm.*" (Verse 45) As for the timing of when all this will happen, this is something only God knows. Hence, no one should be deluded by a false sense of security. Only a transgressor allows such a false feeling to take hold of him.

The Value of Patience

Now the Prophet is directed to remain patient in adversity. He should persevere in his efforts to deliver his message, and face all obstacles including people's twisted minds, the harm they cause him and their denial of the truth. He must remain patient facing all this adversity until God judges as He pleases at the time of His choice. The Prophet is here reminded of the experience of a brother of his who lived in former times. That prophet was impatient and felt fed up with all the opposition. Had he not been granted God's grace, he would have been left in a state of disgrace:

So, await in patience your Lord's judgement; and do not be like the man in the whale who called out in distress. Had not grace from his Lord reached him, he would have been left upon that barren shore in a state of disgrace. His Lord, however, chose him and made him one of the righteous. (Verses 48–50)

The man in the whale was the Prophet Jonah, as mentioned in *Sūrah* 37. God reminds the Prophet Muḥammad, the last of all prophets, of Jonah's experience so that he can benefit by it. All prophets preceded Muḥammad and he, the one charged with delivering God's final message to all mankind, should benefit from all their experiences. His task is not to address a particular tribe, town or nation, but to put God's message to all communities and all generations. His example should provide guidance for them all. Thus he should set a code of living that remains suitable for all mankind's needs, in all situations and all conditions, despite the fact that every day brings something new.

The gist of Jonah's experience is that God sent him to the people of a town said to be Nineveh, near Mousil in today's Iraq. When they were slow in responding to his call, he was terribly upset. He left them in anger, thinking that God would not leave him to bear all the opposition those people presented. God would be kind to him and send him to others who would be less stubborn. In his distress, he went towards the coast where he took a boat. When they were far out at sea, the boat became shaky and seemed about to sink. It thus became necessary to throw someone overboard so as to reduce the load. They drew lots to choose that person. Jonah was the one, and they threw him overboard. Subsequently, a whale swallowed him. Finding himself in such terrible distress, in layers of darkness, inside the whale in the depths of the sea, Jonah appealed to God, saying: "*There is no deity other than You! Limitless are You in Your glory! I have done wrong indeed.*" (21: 87) God bestowed His grace on him and the whale threw him out, leaving him skinless on the shore. His skin had melted inside the whale. God preserved his life by His will, which is unrestricted by any law that is familiar or unfamiliar to man.

Here, in this *sūrah*, God says that had it not been for the grace He bestowed on him, Jonah would have been abandoned, disgraced by

God because of his lack of patience. He had acted on his own initiative, without waiting for God's permission. He was though only spared by God's grace. God accepted Jonah's repentance just as he demonstrated what deserves acceptance. Hence, God chose him and made him one of His righteous servants.

God reminds the Prophet Muḥammad of Jonah's experience in the whale so as to reassure him at a time he was facing stubborn rejection. This reminder comes after He has told him to leave the battle to Him, to conduct as He determines in the way He wishes. What the Prophet is required to do, is to remain patient in adversity and to await God's judgement as and when it comes.

The true hardship the advocates of the divine message face is that of remaining patient in adversity until God makes His judgement at the right time, as His wisdom dictates. Along the way they face many types of adversity such as accusations of lying, physical persecution, stubborn rejection, the apparent power of falsehood as it seems to be victorious, and the need to remain steadfast in the face of all this, reassured that God's promise will be fulfilled. They must not hesitate to travel along their charted way, no matter what hardship they have to face. This requires great effort, determination and patience, as well as support from God. As for the battle itself, God has determined its nature and willed to conduct it Himself. It is He who has decided to give the unbelievers time and to lead them step by step, for a purpose of His own. Thus did He promise His Messenger, and He fulfilled the promise in good time.

To All Mankind

The *sūrah* concludes with an image of the unbelievers as they received the Prophet's call. They are full of hatred and grudges shown in the way they look at him as though they want to do away with him. The Qur'ān gives the best description of their looks:

The unbelievers well-nigh trip you up with their eyes when they hear this reminder. They say, 'He is surely mad.' (Verse 51)

Their looks almost affect the Prophet's feet so as to make him lose his balance and trip. It is a superb image describing the hatred embedded in these looks that boil with anger. Added to these hateful looks is their false allegation: "*They say: He is surely mad.*" (Verse 51) The image is taken from a scene of public address when the message is openly presented to people and they are called upon to accept it. It cannot be anywhere other than a public place where some of the most determined opponents are present, reacting with such looks that reflect a deep-seated hatred.

The final comment in the *sūrah* says: "*Yet it is but a reminder to all mankind.*" (Verse 52) Such a reminder cannot be presented by a madman. God tells the truth, while falsehood emanates from lying fabricators.

We conclude our commentary with highlighting the phrase '*to all mankind*', used at the end of the *sūrah*. We should remember that this revelation was Makkan, occurring in the early days of Islam, when the message was met with hard denial and the Prophet received such spiteful looks, when the unbelievers were fighting it with all their might. At this low ebb in its fortunes, the message of Islam declares its universal nature. Thus, its address to all mankind was in no way something it acquired later in Madīnah, when it achieved several victories, as some present-day fabricators allege. Right from its early days in Makkah, Islam declared its universal nature because this is part of its essence, right from its very first day. Thus did God will it to be and thus did He determine its direction from its early days. Thus will it remain until the end of time. God has willed it to be so, and He is its sponsor who protects and defends it. It is He who fights its battle against its opponents. As for its advocates, they only have to remain steadfast, patient in adversity until God, the best of judges, makes His judgement.

Al-Ḥāqqah
(The Inevitable Truth)

Prologue

This is an awesome *sūrah*, one that strikes terror in our hearts, shaking us up. From start to finish it focuses on something that is very serious, showing one awesome image after another. Some of these are frightening, some are majestic and others depict suffering, yet they are all characterized by strong movements. As a whole, the *sūrah* enhances the feeling that faith and religion are very serious; they admit no frivolity. The profundity of such questions is serious here in this life as also in the life to come. Furthermore, it is no less serious in God's own measure. Indeed, it is so serious that it permits no distraction. For, to turn away from faith and religion is to incur God's displeasure and all that is attendant with that, even though the one who turns away may happen to be God's Messenger. It is larger than God's Messenger, indeed all mankind, because it is the question of the truth absolute, laid down by the Lord of all the worlds.

This impression is heightened by the very name given in this *sūrah* to the Day of Judgement and which gives it its title, *al-Ḥāqqah*. The very sound of the word imparts a feeling of decisiveness, seriousness and a grounding stability. It sounds like a heavy object being lifted some considerable distance before being placed firmly into position. The strongly aspirated '*ḥ*' sound appears to be lifted by the elongated '*ā*' before it is firmly placed at the doubled '*q*' and then finally stabilized with the final '*h*' sound.

We see such great seriousness in the fates of those who denied the truth of faith and the Day of Judgement. One community after another suffered such severe punishment that each were utterly destroyed: "*The people of Thamūd and 'Ād denied the Striker. The Thamūd were destroyed by an overwhelming event, while the 'Ād were destroyed by a furiously howling wind, which He caused to rage upon them for seven nights and eight decisive days. You could see their people lying dead, like uprooted trunks of hollow palm trees. Can you see any trace of them now? Pharaoh, too, and those before him, and the ruined cities – all indulged in sin, and disobeyed their Lord's messenger; and so He took them to task with an ever-tightening grip. When the waters rose high, We carried you in the floating Ark, making it all a lasting reminder for you, so that attentive ears may take heed.*" (Verses 4–12) Thus, all those who turned away from faith suffered such grave and sudden punishments, as befit their approach to this decisive and serious requirement. It is important to realize then that this question of faith and religion admits no frivolity of approach and allows no distraction.

Such seriousness is also seen in the picture the *sūrah* draws of the resurrection, the terrible end of the universe, and the even more majestic scene of the angels carrying the Throne: "*When the trumpet is sounded a single time, and the earth and mountains are lifted up and with one mighty crash are flattened, that which is certain to happen will on that day have come to pass. The sky will be rent asunder, for, it will have become frail on that day. The angels will stand on all its sides and, on that day, eight of them will bear aloft the Throne of your Lord.*" (Verses 13–17)

Such awesomeness and majesty impart added seriousness to the scene of accounting for the all-important question of faith. Both help to deepen its effect on us, as do the beats of the *sūrah* and the statements of those who are granted reward and those who are doomed to suffer: "*He who is given his record in his right hand will say, 'Come you all! Read this my record. I certainly knew that one day I would have to face my account.' He will be in a happy state of life, in a lofty garden, with its fruits within easy reach. 'Eat and drink to your hearts' content as a reward for what you have done in days gone by.' But he who is given his record in his left hand will say, 'Would that I had never been shown my record and knew nothing of my account! Would that death had been the end of me! Nothing has my wealth availed me. I am now bereft of all my power.'"* (Verses 19–29) This long lamentation gives us a strong impression of the terrible end suffered.

God's own words, spelling out His sentence in the middle of that solemn scene on that great day, add to the seriousness of the whole affair: *"Lay hold of him and shackle him, and burn him in the fire of hell, and then fasten him in a chain seventy cubits long."* (Verses 30–32) Each clause in this command sounds as if it carries the whole weight of the heavens and earth to strike the offender in what is a terrifying image. This sentence is then followed with an explanation of its justifying causes: *"He did not believe in God Almighty, and he never encouraged feeding the needy. So, no friend has he here today, nor any food except the filth that none other than the sinners eat."* (Verses 33–37)

A hint of a great oath is followed in God's own statement outlining the truth of this final religion: *"I need not swear by what you can see and what you cannot see: this [Qur'ān] is the word of a noble Messenger, not the word of a poet – how little you believe! nor the word of a soothsayer – how little you reflect! This [Qur'ān] is a revelation from the Lord of all the worlds."* (Verses 38–43)

Further seriousness is provided by the *sūrah's* last beat as it issues a decisive warning of a very severe punishment to be meted out to anyone who tries to introduce any alteration into this faith. This applies even to Muḥammad, God's Messenger: *"Had he attributed some fabrications to Us, We would indeed have seized him by the right hand and cut off his life-vein, and none of you could have saved him."* (Verses 44–47)

The *sūrah* concludes with another decisive statement making the question of the final divine message as it is embodied in the Qur'ān absolutely clear: *"This [Qur'ān] is indeed a reminder to the God-fearing. We well know that among you are some who deny its truth. Yet it will be a cause of bitter regret for the unbelievers. It is indeed truth absolute. Extol, then, the glory of the name of your Lord, the Supreme."* (Verses 48–52) It is a finale that leaves no room for anything further to be added.

The Style

The *sūrah* has a central theme, which it aims to make absolutely clear. The style and beat it employs and the images and scenes it draws work in unison to drive this home to us in a highly inspiring way. Thus, the *sūrah* gives us a great host of images indeed it surrounds us with them from all sides. We cannot fail to see them brought alive as if they are taking place in front of our very eyes. Here, we see the fates of the Thamūd, the 'Ād, Pharaoh, Sodom and Gomorrah and feel engulfed by their terrible effects. The scene of the great floods and the few human survivors carried in the Ark is painted in two short verses. Read, if you will, how the 'Ād suffered their terrible fate: *"The 'Ād were destroyed by a furiously howling wind, which He caused to rage upon them for seven nights and eight decisive days. You could see their people lying dead, like uprooted trunks of hollow palm trees. Can you see any trace of them now?"* (Verses 6–8) Can you fail to see in your mind's eye how this raging storm continued to vent its furious havoc for eight days and seven nights leaving the 'Ād utterly destroyed and resembling hollow, uprooted tree trunks? It is such a vivid scene that we cannot help but see it with our eyes and paint it with our minds. The same applies to all images of the terrible fates suffered by unbelievers of old.

Then again the images of the terrible end of the universe are brought before us; we hear the noise accompanying them and we are filled with terror and distress. Listen to this verse: *"The earth and mountains are lifted up and with one mighty crash are flattened."* (Verse 14) Do you not hear that mighty crash after having seen the lifting up and then the fall? Listen again: *"The sky will be rent asunder, for, it will have become frail on that day."* (Verse 16) Does this sad end, with a beautiful sky torn apart, present itself clearly before you? Keep listening: *"The angels will stand on all its sides and, on that day, eight of them will bear aloft the Throne of your Lord. On that day you shall be brought to judgement and none of your secrets will remain hidden."* (Verses 17–18) The majesty of this awesome scene can only but fill your imagination.

Then look at the image of the person receiving his record in his right hand. The whole world is too small for his joy. He cheerfully calls on all creatures to come and read his record: *"Come you all! Read this my record.*

I certainly knew that one day I would have to face my account." (Verses 19–20) Contrast this with the image of the one whose record is given to him in his left hand: his words, tone and expression reflect his heart-felt grief: *"Would that I had never been shown my record and knew nothing of my account! Would that death had been the end of me! Nothing has my wealth availed me. I am now bereft of all my power."* (Verses 25–29)

Who of us will fail to shudder when we listen to the judgement in the case of the latter person: *"Lay hold of him and shackle him, and burn him in the fire of hell, and then fasten him in a chain seventy cubits long."* (Verses 30–32) We almost see those receiving the command rushing to carry it out, and we visualize his situation there as we read: *"So, no friend has he here today, nor any food except the filth that none other than the sinners eat."* (Verses 35–37) Finally, who of us will not experience fear when our minds receive this stern warning: *"Had he attributed some fabrications to Us, We would indeed have seized him by the right hand and cut off his life-vein, and none of you could have saved him."* (Verses 44–47) Combined, all these images and scenes are so powerful, clear and effective as to require our pressing attention.

The *sūrah*'s verse endings and their variation contribute to its clearly profound effect. At the very beginning, we have a very long '*a*' followed by a doubled plosive '*q*' sound and a fricative '*h*'. Then we have a long stretch in which all the verses end with a clear '*yah*' final syllable. This passage takes us through the scenes of ruin in this world and in the life to come, as well as those of joy and lamentation when personal records are given. Then the ending changes to '*ooh*' when the judgement is pronounced. When the basis of the judgement is outlined in all seriousness, the ending again changes to give us a firm and final sound formed of a long '*e*' followed by either '*m*' or '*n*'. This change of the last consonant and the vowel preceding it, as well as the beat, is a clear phenomenon that parallels the change of scene, image and aura. It fits perfectly with the subject matter and the images drawn. It contributes to the powerful effect the *sūrah* has generally. Having said all this, I would like to conclude by saying that the *sūrah* itself is far more powerful than can be shown by any analysis or comment anyone can make.

Al-Ḥāqqah
(The Inevitable Truth)

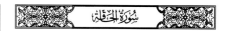

In the Name of God, the Lord of Grace, the Ever Merciful

The Inevitable Truth! (1)

What is the Inevitable Truth? (2)

Would that you knew what the Inevitable Truth is! (3)

The people of Thamūd and ʿĀd denied the Striker. (4)

The Thamūd were destroyed by an overwhelming event, (5)

while the ʿĀd were destroyed by a furiously howling wind, (6)

which He caused to rage upon them for seven nights and eight decisive days. You could see their people lying dead, like uprooted trunks of hollow palm trees. (7)

Can you see any trace of them now? (8)

Pharaoh, too, and those before him, and the ruined cities – all indulged in sin, (9)

213

and disobeyed their Lord's messenger; and so He took them to task with an ever-tightening grip. (10)

فَعَصَوۡاْ رَسُولَ رَبِّهِمۡ فَأَخَذَهُمۡ أَخۡذَةً رَّابِيَةً ﴿١٠﴾

When the waters rose high, We carried you in the floating Ark, (11)

إِنَّا لَمَّا طَغَا ٱلۡمَآءُ حَمَلۡنَٰكُمۡ فِي ٱلۡجَارِيَةِ ﴿١١﴾

making it all a lasting reminder for you, so that attentive ears may take heed. (12)

لِنَجۡعَلَهَا لَكُمۡ تَذۡكِرَةً وَتَعِيَهَآ أُذُنٌ وَٰعِيَةٌ ﴿١٢﴾

When the trumpet is sounded a single time, (13)

فَإِذَا نُفِخَ فِي ٱلصُّورِ نَفۡخَةٌ وَٰحِدَةٌ ﴿١٣﴾

and the earth and mountains are lifted up and with one mighty crash are flattened, (14)

وَحُمِلَتِ ٱلۡأَرۡضُ وَٱلۡجِبَالُ فَدُكَّتَا دَكَّةً وَٰحِدَةً ﴿١٤﴾

that which is certain to happen will on that day have come to pass. (15)

فَيَوۡمَئِذٍ وَقَعَتِ ٱلۡوَاقِعَةُ ﴿١٥﴾

The sky will be rent asunder, for, it will have become frail on that day. (16)

وَٱنشَقَّتِ ٱلسَّمَآءُ فَهِيَ يَوۡمَئِذٍ وَاهِيَةٌ ﴿١٦﴾

The angels will stand on all its sides and, on that day, eight of them will bear aloft the Throne of your Lord. (17)

وَٱلۡمَلَكُ عَلَىٰٓ أَرۡجَآئِهَا ۚ وَيَحۡمِلُ عَرۡشَ رَبِّكَ فَوۡقَهُمۡ يَوۡمَئِذٍ ثَمَٰنِيَةٌ ﴿١٧﴾

On that day you shall be brought to judgement and none of your secrets will remain hidden. (18)

يَوۡمَئِذٍ تُعۡرَضُونَ لَا تَخۡفَىٰ مِنكُمۡ خَافِيَةٌ ﴿١٨﴾

He who is given his record in his right hand will say, 'Come you all! Read this my record. (19)

I certainly knew that one day I would have to face my account.' (20)

He will be in a happy state of life, (21)

in a lofty garden, (22)

with its fruits within easy reach. (23)

'Eat and drink to your heart's content as a reward for what you have done in days gone by.' (24)

But he who is given his record in his left hand will say, 'Would that I had never been shown my record (25)

and knew nothing of my account! (26)

Would that death had been the end of me! (27)

Nothing has my wealth availed me. (28)

فَأَمَّا مَنْ أُوتِىَ كِتَٰبَهُۥ بِيَمِينِهِۦ فَيَقُولُ هَآؤُمُ ٱقْرَءُوا۟ كِتَٰبِيَهْ ۝

إِنِّى ظَنَنتُ أَنِّى مُلَٰقٍ حِسَابِيَهْ ۝

فَهُوَ فِى عِيشَةٍ رَّاضِيَةٍ ۝

فِى جَنَّةٍ عَالِيَةٍ ۝

قُطُوفُهَا دَانِيَةٌ ۝

كُلُوا۟ وَٱشْرَبُوا۟ هَنِيٓـًٔا بِمَآ أَسْلَفْتُمْ فِى ٱلْأَيَّامِ ٱلْخَالِيَةِ ۝

وَأَمَّا مَنْ أُوتِىَ كِتَٰبَهُۥ بِشِمَالِهِۦ فَيَقُولُ يَٰلَيْتَنِى لَمْ أُوتَ كِتَٰبِيَهْ ۝

وَلَمْ أَدْرِ مَا حِسَابِيَهْ ۝

يَٰلَيْتَهَا كَانَتِ ٱلْقَاضِيَةَ ۝

مَآ أَغْنَىٰ عَنِّى مَالِيَهْ ۝

I am now bereft of all my power.'
(29)

هَلَكَ عَنِّي سُلْطَـٰنِيَهْ ﴿٢٩﴾

'Lay hold of him and shackle him, (30)

خُذُوهُ فَغُلُّوهُ ﴿٣٠﴾

and burn him in the fire of hell, (31)

ثُمَّ الْجَحِيمَ صَلُّوهُ ﴿٣١﴾

and then fasten him in a chain seventy cubits long.' (32)

ثُمَّ فِي سِلْسِلَةٍ ذَرْعُهَا سَبْعُونَ ذِرَاعًا فَاسْلُكُوهُ ﴿٣٢﴾

He did not believe in God Almighty, (33)

إِنَّهُ كَانَ لَا يُؤْمِنُ بِاللَّهِ الْعَظِيمِ ﴿٣٣﴾

and he never encouraged feeding the needy. (34)

وَلَا يَحُضُّ عَلَىٰ طَعَامِ الْمِسْكِينِ ﴿٣٤﴾

So, no friend has he here today, (35)

فَلَيْسَ لَهُ الْيَوْمَ هَـٰهُنَا حَمِيمٌ ﴿٣٥﴾

nor any food except the filth (36)

وَلَا طَعَامٌ إِلَّا مِنْ غِسْلِينٍ ﴿٣٦﴾

that none other than the sinners eat. (37)

لَا يَأْكُلُهُ إِلَّا الْخَاطِئُونَ ﴿٣٧﴾

I need not swear by what you can see (38)

فَلَا أُقْسِمُ بِمَا تُبْصِرُونَ ﴿٣٨﴾

and what you cannot see: (39)

وَمَا لَا تُبْصِرُونَ ﴿٣٩﴾

this [Qur'ān] is the word of a noble Messenger, (40)

إِنَّهُ لَقَوْلُ رَسُولٍ كَرِيمٍ ﴿٤٠﴾

not the word of a poet – how little
you believe! (41)

وَمَا هُوَ بِقَوْلِ شَاعِرٍ قَلِيلًا مَّا تُؤْمِنُونَ ﴿٤١﴾

Nor the word of a soothsayer –
how little you reflect! (42)

وَلَا بِقَوْلِ كَاهِنٍ قَلِيلًا مَّا تَذَكَّرُونَ ﴿٤٢﴾

This [Qurʼān] is a revelation from
the Lord of all the worlds. (43)

تَنزِيلٌ مِّن رَّبِّ ٱلْعَٰلَمِينَ ﴿٤٣﴾

Had he attributed some fabrications to Us, (44)

وَلَوْ تَقَوَّلَ عَلَيْنَا بَعْضَ ٱلْأَقَاوِيلِ ﴿٤٤﴾

We would indeed have seized him
by the right hand (45)

لَأَخَذْنَا مِنْهُ بِٱلْيَمِينِ ﴿٤٥﴾

and cut off his life-vein, (46)

ثُمَّ لَقَطَعْنَا مِنْهُ ٱلْوَتِينَ ﴿٤٦﴾

and none of you could have saved
him. (47)

فَمَا مِنكُم مِّنْ أَحَدٍ عَنْهُ حَٰجِزِينَ ﴿٤٧﴾

This [Qurʼān] is indeed a reminder
to the God-fearing. (48)

وَإِنَّهُ لَتَذْكِرَةٌ لِّلْمُتَّقِينَ ﴿٤٨﴾

We well know that among you are
some who deny its truth. (49)

وَإِنَّا لَنَعْلَمُ أَنَّ مِنكُم مُّكَذِّبِينَ ﴿٤٩﴾

Yet it will be a cause of bitter
regret for the unbelievers. (50)

وَإِنَّهُ لَحَسْرَةٌ عَلَى ٱلْكَٰفِرِينَ ﴿٥٠﴾

It is indeed truth absolute. (51)

وَإِنَّهُ لَحَقُّ ٱلْيَقِينِ ﴿٥١﴾

Extol, then, the glory of the name
of your Lord, the Supreme. (52)

فَسَبِّحْ بِٱسْمِ رَبِّكَ ٱلْعَظِيمِ ﴿٥٢﴾

True and Inevitable

The Inevitable Truth! What is the Inevitable Truth? Would that you knew what the Inevitable Truth is! (Verses 1–3)

Most of this *sūrah* is taken up with scenes, images and events of the resurrection. Indeed, the *sūrah's* very title *al-Ḥāqqah*, or the Inevitable Truth resounds with the same. It is a name chosen for both its meaning and the sounds it delivers. *Al-Ḥāqqah* is something that falls due and then takes place, or it becomes inevitable and puts forward its judgement, or it manifests the truth. All these meanings are clear and decisive, fitting with the subject matter and drift of the *sūrah*. As we have already stated, the name chosen provides a powerful beat, one that is in harmony with the *sūrah's* meaning and which contributes to the intended atmosphere. It prepares us for what is about to befall the unbelievers in this world and in the life to come.

The ambience throughout the *sūrah* is one of seriousness, firmness, awe and fear. In addition to what we have said in the Prologue, it imparts to us a feeling of God's absolute power on the one hand and man's powerlessness on the other. It mentions how God's power can firmly take man to task, in this world and in the next, should he deviate from the code of living God wants man to implement. It is the code God's messengers outlined for people. This code is not laid down so that it can be ignored or abandoned; it is there to be respected and put into practice. Otherwise, God's painful punishment may be meted out at any time.

The words used here, their very sound, meaning and construction contribute to this ambience. The *sūrah* starts with one Arabic word, *al-Ḥāqqah*, translated here as 'the Inevitable Truth'. It is mentioned on its own as a subject that has no predicate. This is followed by a question that emphasizes the fact that the event referred to is extremely grave. This question is followed by the spreading of an air of mystery, so as to take the subject matter out of the area of man's knowledge, *"Would that you knew what the Inevitable Truth is!"* (Verse 3) The *sūrah*, however, does not answer the question. Instead, it leaves us stirring at this awesome event about which we know nothing. Indeed, we cannot know anything about it because it is beyond our knowledge.

Unbelievers' Fates

The *surah* begins with an account of the terrible fates met by different communities of unbelievers. They were all dealt with in a decisive and swift manner because the issue in question is very serious and does not allow denial. Those who persist with such denial cannot escape punishment:

> *The people of Thamūd and ʿĀd denied the Striker. The Thamūd were destroyed by an overwhelming event, while the ʿĀd were destroyed by a furiously howling wind, which He caused to rage upon them for seven nights and eight decisive days. You could see their people lying dead, like uprooted trunks of hollow palm trees. Can you see any trace of them now?* (Verses 4–8)

Al-Qāriʿah, or The Striker, is another name for Resurrection Day, complementing as it does *al-Ḥāqqah,* the Inevitable Truth. This means that in addition to its being true and inevitable, it also strikes like two solid objects hammering against each other. The Striker inflicts hearts with terror and delivers a crushing blow upon the universe. By its very sound, it strikes loudly, crushing everything and everyone around. Both the Thamūd and the ʿĀd denied it, saying that it was untrue. Let us see then what the result of such denial was:

"*The Thamūd were destroyed by an overwhelming event.*" (Verse 5) As mentioned elsewhere in the Qurʾān, the people of Thamūd used to live in the area of al-Ḥijr to the north of Ḥijāz, close to today's Palestine. They were destroyed by an event named elsewhere as a '*stunning blast*'. Here, the *surah* does not mention this blast but rather describes it as an '*overwhelming event*', as this fits better with the atmosphere of catastrophe that characterizes the *surah*. Moreover, the note the Arabic word *ṭāghiyah* strikes is consistent with the verse endings in the present passage. This short single verse is enough to completely engulf the Thamūd, leaving no trace of them.

The Thamūd's fate was swift and sudden, a single blast overwhelming them all. By contrast, the *surah* gives us a detailed account of the ʿĀd's fate, which was accomplished over seven nights and eight decisive days.

The 'Ād were destroyed by a howling, extremely cold wind described here as *ṣarṣar*. Whilst this carries strong connotations of such '*howling*', this is still not enough. Its howling is clearly described as furious, and fits with the fact that the 'Ād were arrogant and tyrannical in their dealings with others. They used to live at al-Aḥqāf in southern Arabia, in the area between Yemen and Ḥadramawt. This howling wind, furious as it was, "*He caused to rage upon them for seven nights and eight decisive days.*" (Verse 7) The *sūrah* gives the exact duration of this hurricane that hit for so long so as to draw an image of the scene after it was all over: "*You could see their people lying dead, like uprooted trunks of hollow palm trees.*" (Verse 7) The image is detailed, pressed on our minds so that we can see its every detail. The people of the 'Ād are '*lying dead*' everywhere, and they look '*like uprooted tree trunks*', but these trunks are '*hollow*', eaten from inside and no longer able to stand upright. They are thrown on the ground, lifeless. The sad silence of death now reigns after the furiously howling hurricane. So, what is left of them? The answer is expressed in a question for which no one bothers to hear an answer: "*Can you see any trace of them now?*" (Verse 8)

Such was the fates of the 'Ād and Thamūd. Other communities that denied the divine faith also suffered similar fates. In two short verses, the *sūrah* sums up several of these:

> *Pharaoh, too, and those before him, and the ruined cities – all indulged in sin, and disobeyed their Lord's messenger; and so He took them to task with an ever-tightening grip. (Verses 9–10)*

Pharaoh, in Egypt, was the one who opposed the Prophet Moses, but the *sūrah* gives no details of '*those before him*'. The '*ruined cities*' were those of Sodom and Gomorrah. The *sūrah* sums up the deeds of all these communities in a short phrase saying that they '*all indulged in sin*'. It explains that they all '*disobeyed their Lord's messenger.*' The fact is that these communities had several messengers whom they disobeyed, yet these messengers advocated the same truth, and their messages were essentially the same. Hence, they are like one messenger, representing a single truth. This is one of the most inspiring touches of the Qur'ānic style. Again the *sūrah* sums up their fates in a way that combines swiftness with strong and decisive action: "*He took them to task with an ever-tightening grip.*" (Verse 10)

The *sūrah* then gives us an image of the great floods and the floating Ark on the surface, in reference to the fate suffered by the people of Noah when they rejected God's message. Here the *sūrah* reminds people of God's favour as He saved their forefathers. Yet they do not take heed or give thanks:

When the waters rose high, We carried you in the floating Ark, making it all a lasting reminder for you, so that attentive ears may take heed. (Verses 11–12)

The images of the floods and the floating Ark fit well with the other scenes portrayed in the *sūrah*, and share the same verse endings so as to rhyme with other verses describing these fates. The fact is that the *sūrah* gives all this as "*a lasting reminder for you, so that attentive ears may take heed.*" This should inspire the hearts and ears of people who continue to deny the truth after all that happened before them and the warnings that were given to earlier communities. Indeed signs and lessons, as well as favours and blessings, have been given in abundance, but people need to wake up and take heed.

Greater Horrors

All such devastation and catastrophe seems, however, to be exceedingly small when compared to the horrors of the Striker, the Inevitable Truth, which those unbelievers deny, even though they have seen what befell earlier communities that denied it. These fates, terrible catastrophes in their own right, are of a limited nature compared to the absolute calamity that the Striker brings about on the day to be witnessed by all. Having thus introduced this horror in general terms, the *sūrah* now portrays its details:

When the trumpet is sounded a single time, and the earth and mountains are lifted up and with one mighty crash are flattened, that which is certain to happen will on that day have come to pass. The sky will be rent asunder, for, it will have become frail on that day. The angels will stand on all its sides and, on that day, eight of them will bear aloft the Throne of your Lord. (Verses 13–17)

We believe that there will be a single sounding of the trumpet and that this will be followed by these events. We do not know any details, however, because these events belong to a world about which we have no information except these texts. We have no other source to refer to. Moreover, no further details can add to the significance of these statements. To try to learn such details is a useless exercise which we are instructed not to resort to. When the trumpet is sounded once, a huge movement will take place: *"the earth and mountains are lifted up and with one mighty crash are flattened."* (Verse 14) The image of the earth and the mountains being lifted high and thrown so that they are crushed and levelled is absolutely terrifying. We walk over the earth in peace and reassurance, feeling that it is firm in its position. We look at the mountains and feel how stable and firmly placed they are. Yet both are lifted and sent crashing, as if they were a ball in a child's hand. How small man must feel, and how small is his world, compared with such great power.

What happens when all this takes place? It is the very thing the *sūrah* is speaking about: *"that which is certain to happen will on that day have come to pass."* (Verse 15) What is certain is the Day of Resurrection, which is called by many names such as *al-Ḥāqqah*, or the Inevitable Truth, *al-Qāri'ah*, or the Striker, *al-Wāqi'ah*, or the Happening, as if the certainty of its happening is part of its very nature. Using this last name here is deliberate, intended to give a particular impression countering all doubt and denial. Yet this is not all. The skies will also be seriously affected: *"The sky will be rent asunder, for, it will have become frail on that day."* (Verse 16) We do not know for certain to what the term 'the sky' refers to here, but this statement and similar ones referring to celestial events on that great day speak of a collapse of the order that keeps the universe functioning according to an accurate and fascinating plan. Once this perfect order collapses, all its different parts will be in chaos.

It is mere coincidence that astronomers are now predicting that something of this nature will take place bringing about an end to the world. Their predictions are based on scientific observations and the little they have come to know of the nature of the universe. We, for our part, almost witness these scenes as they unfold before us through the Qur'ānic texts informing us of things that are absolutely certain because they come from God, the Creator who knows what He has created. We almost see the earth being lifted high, with its mountains that are massive by our measure, but infinitely small when compared to the universe. We see them all sent crashing, being levelled. We see the sky torn apart, frail, while the planets are scattered everywhere. We see all this through the Qur'ān as it draws its images and plants them before our eyes.

An air of majesty then spreads over the entire stage. All the sounds of the trumpet, the crashing, the rending asunder and the scattering of stars then dies down, and we have an image of the Almighty's Throne: "*The angels will stand on all its sides and, on that day, eight of them will bear aloft the Throne of your Lord.*" (Verse 17) The angels are on all sides of the sky that has been torn and rent asunder, and the throne is there above them carried by eight of their number. Are they eight angels, or eight rows of angels, or eight classes, or some other eight known only to God? We do not know who or what they are, just as we do not know what the throne is like, or how it is carried. Knowledge of all these details has not been imparted to us, and God wants us to know of them only what He tells us. Therefore, we leave aside all details of these unknown matters and concentrate instead on the majestic aura they impart to the whole scene. This is what we are meant to feel as the events of that awesome day are reported.

On that day you shall be brought to judgement and none of your secrets will remain hidden. (Verse 18)

All are exposed: bodies, souls, consciences, actions and destinies. All curtains that used to hide secrets are lifted, and souls are laid bare just like bodies. What used to be concealed is now in full view. Man is without any of his precautions, schemings and plannings. What he was keen to conceal, even from himself, is there to be seen by all. Such disgrace and in front of everyone! As for God, He has always been fully

223

aware of every little thing, even that which is most deeply hidden, but man, accustomed to all sorts of concealment on earth, does not fully appreciate this. Now, on the Day of Judgement, when everything is laid bare throughout the universe, he realizes this. The earth is flattened and has no corner or protrusion to conceal anything; the sky is rent asunder showing what once was behind it; all bodies are without cover, and souls are left bare concealing no secret. The situation is very difficult indeed; harder to accept than the flattening of the earth and the mountains or the tearing of the sky apart. It leaves man bare in body, soul, history, and action. Not just this but he is also exposed in front of all these huge numbers of creatures – humans, *jinn* and angels – in front of the Almighty and under His majestic throne.

Man has a very complex nature. There are within his soul many corners and pathways where he hides his feelings, whims, yearnings, thoughts, secrets and private matters. Imagine how a snail quickly withdraws into its shell when it feels danger, hiding itself completely. Should man realize that an eye manages to see what he is keen to conceal, or that a glance exposes something he wants to remain hidden, he does much more than a snail sensing danger. He is deeply hurt when someone looks into his inner secrets. So how will man feel when he stands truly naked in body, heart, feeling and soul; when he has nothing to cover himself with, when he is under the throne of the Almighty and before this great assembly of creatures? This is the most painful of all situations.

Overwhelmed with Joy

The *sūrah* now presents two images, one of the winners and one of the losers. This is again done as though it is happening at this very instant:

> *He who is given his record in his right hand will say, 'Come you all! Read this my record. I certainly knew that one day I would have to face my account.' He will be in a happy state of life, in a lofty garden, with its fruits within easy reach. 'Eat and drink to your heart's content as a reward for what you have done in days gone by.'* (Verses 19–24)

Taking one's record with one's right or left hand, or behind one's back may be a statement expressing a material fact, or it may be an idiomatic expression, following standard rules of Arabic as it refers to the good direction as the right and the evil one as the left or the back. Whichever may be the case, the meaning remains the same. It merits no argument as any such argument spoils the effect of what takes place on this awesome day. What we see here is a person who is given his record and realizes that he has won. The hardship of the day is gone, and he moves along, overjoyed, among the great multitude. His happiness overflows and he calls to all people, saying: "*Come you all! Read this my record.*" (Verse 19) In his overwhelming delight, he says that he never thought that he would be spared. He expected to have to account for his deeds, and that means suffering. As one *ḥadīth* states, 'Ā'ishah quotes the Prophet as saying: "Whoever is held to account will be tormented." She then asked the Prophet: "How come, when God says: '*He who is given his record in his right hand will in time have a lenient reckoning and return rejoicing to his people.*'" (84: 7–9) He said: "This merely speaks of presentation. Whoever is questioned about his deeds on the Day of Judgement will indeed be in ruin." [Related by al-Bukhārī, Muslim, Abū Dāwūd and al-Tirmidhī.]

Another report on the authority of Abū 'Uthmān states: "A believer is given his record in his right hand where God gives him shelter. He reads first his bad deeds. Every time he reads such a negative item, his colour changes, then he begins to read his good deeds and his face regains its colour. He looks around and finds that his bad deeds have been replaced by good ones. It is at this point that such a person calls out to all people to come and read his record."

It is reported on the authority of 'Abdullāh ibn Ḥanẓalah, a Companion of the Prophet who was a martyr in the Battle of Uḥud: "God stops His servant on the Day of Judgement and shows him his evil deeds written on the back of his record. He asks him: 'Have you done this?' He confirms that he did. God says to him: 'I did not make it public during your life, and today I am forgiving you these.' He is then given his record of good deeds in his right hand. As for the unbelievers and the hypocrites, it is concerning these that "*witnesses shall say: 'These are they who lied against their Lord.' God's curse is on the wrongdoers.*"

(11: 18) The details of blessings made ready for such people are then announced before all. The account given here of these blessings includes some aspects of material comfort. This suited the state of those addressed by the Qur'ān at the time. They were still newcomers to Islam; it had not yet given its distinctive hue to their feelings, nor had they had the chance to appreciate luxuries higher than any material comfort: "*He will be in a happy state of life, in a lofty garden, with its fruits within easy reach. 'Eat and drink to your heart's ontent as a reward for what you have done in days gone by.'*" (Verses 21–24)

Such blessings and comforts are coupled with a special honour that is felt in the fact that the *sūrah* makes its address directly to those deserving of it, saying to them to eat and drink as they please. This type of blessing is the one those who were the first to be addressed by the Qur'ān could appreciate in the early stages of their new bond with God. Their feelings had not yet attained the sublime level that finds in being close to God what is much higher than any material comfort or luxury. Yet this type can satisfy the needs of many people across many generations.

At the Opposite End

> *But he who is given his record in his left hand will say, 'Would that I had never been shown my record and knew nothing of my account! Would that death had been the end of me! Nothing has my wealth availed me. I am now bereft of all my power.' 'Lay hold of him and shackle him, and burn him in the fire of hell, and then fasten him in a chain seventy cubits long.' He did not believe in God Almighty, and he never encouraged feeding the needy. So, no friend has he here today, nor any food except the filth that none other than the sinners eat.* (Verses 25–37)

"*But he who is given his record in his left hand,*" and knows that his bad deeds are reckoned against him realizes that his fate is one of suffering. He stands among this great multitude full of sorrow, broken. He will say: "*Would that I had never been shown my record and knew nothing of my account! Would that death had been the end of me! Nothing has my wealth availed me. I am now bereft of all my power.*" (Verses 25–29)

Long is his lamentation, miserable his tone and desperate his words. The *surah* presents his reaction at length and the listener almost feels his endless lamentation. This is another aspect of the Qur'ānic style: some situations are described at length while others are given a quick and short presentation, depending on the effect the Qur'ān wants to impart. In this case, the *surah* wants to bring this image of lamentation alive before us, so that we feel it thoroughly. Therefore, it harps long on its details. We see this miserable person wishing he had never witnessed this gathering, never been given his record, and knowing nothing of his account. He would have loved for the Striker to have spelt his absolute end, removing him from all existence. He bemoans that nothing of what he used to rate highly or treasure appears to be of any use or value: "*Nothing has my wealth availed me. I am now bereft of all my power.*" (Verses 28–29) The ending of these very short verses, with a strongly aspirated '*h*' preceded by a '*ya*' sound that comes after a long '*a*', adds to the tone of sorrow and grief. It is all part of the very clear ambience the *surah* generates.

This long, sorrowful lamentation is only interrupted by a decisive order given from on high:

> *Lay hold of him and shackle him, and burn him in the fire of hell, and then fasten him in a chain seventy cubits long.* (Verses 30–32)

A command is given by God Almighty, and everyone in the universe moves against this miserable creature. Those to whom the command is issued will move swiftly from all corners. A *ḥadīth* related by Ibn Abī Ḥātim states: "When God says, '*lay hold of him*,' seventy thousand angels swiftly take him. Each one of these angels can, in one gesture, cast seventy thousand creatures into hell."

"*And shackle him.*" The first angel to so hold him will immediately put the shackles around him. "*And burn him in the fire of hell.*" (Verse 31) We almost hear the sound of the fire as it burns such people. "*And then fasten him in a chain seventy cubits long.*" (Verse 32) One cubit of this chain is enough, but the impression intended here is one of elongation and the mention of '*seventy cubits*' gives us this sense of perpetuity.

Now that the command has been given, its justification is announced for all to know:

227

He did not believe in God Almighty, and he never encouraged feeding the needy. (Verses 33–34)

This is a person whose heart is devoid of faith and compassion. Thus, the only place fit for him is the fire. With a heart that has no trace of faith, he is ruined, like a barren land engulfed in darkness. He is below the level of animals, and indeed below the level of inanimate objects. Everything in the universe believes in God and glorifies Him, and as such they maintain their bond with their source of existence. This person, on the other hand, severed his ties with God, and therefore has no tie with the universe.

Likewise, his heart is devoid of compassion. A needy person is one who desperately needs compassion, but this one does not feel for his fellow humans in need. He does not encourage feeding them, which is a step further than simply providing the needy with food. It is a step that suggests a social duty that requires believers to encourage one another to undertake. It is closely related to faith, mentioned here after faith and given its value in God's measure:

So, no friend has he here today, nor any food except the filth that none other than the sinners eat. (Verses 35–37)

This complements the announcement from on high concerning the fate of such a miserable person. Since he had no faith in God and did not encourage the feeding of the needy, he has no friends, and he is deprived of all favours. His food is the filth that pours out of the people of hell. Such is the food that serves well those hardened hearts that are devoid of all compassion. It is a type of food that "*none other than the sinners eat.*" (Verse 37) He is essentially one of the sinners.

Such are the characteristics of the person that deserves the divine punishment of being cast into hell, tied with a chain seventy cubits long. This is the worst punishment meted out in hell. What will happen, then, to those who actually prevent giving food to the needy and who make women, children and the elderly people starve, hitting hard at those who give them something to eat or a piece of clothing to wear in the cold winter months? Such people do exist from time to time.[1] So how will God requite them?

Perhaps this terrifying scene was drawn because the Arabian environment was hard and cruel. It needed to have such shocking images to awaken its better feelings. Such environments do occur throughout history. Furthermore, these may exist side by side with softer and more responsive ones. The earth is wide, and on it a great variety of people, depicting a similarly great variety of psychologies, exist. The Qur'ān addresses every level and every soul in a way that finds its effect. Today, the population of the earth includes some very hardened, cruel hearts. These can only be influenced when addressed with words of fire, such as the ones used in this *sūrah*.

The Qur'ānic Revelations

The *sūrah* now makes a categorical statement defining the nature of the Qur'ān recited by God's noble Messenger, but received by the Arabs with derision and ridicule:

> *I need not swear by what you can see and what you cannot see: this [Qur'ān] is the word of a noble Messenger, not the word of a poet – how little you believe! Nor the word of a soothsayer – how little you reflect! This [Qur'ān] is a revelation from the Lord of all the worlds.* (Verses 38–43)

The statement is very clear, definite and certain. Hence, it requires no oath to prove it or to confirm its source. It comes from the truth. It requires no further confirmation. "*I need not swear by what you can see and what you cannot see.*" (Verses 38–39) This is an expression that imparts a sense of greatness to both the visible world and the world beyond. Needless to say, the universe is far greater than what people can say, and indeed what they can imagine. Indeed, all that humans

---

1. During Nasser's reign in Egypt, anyone who donated something to alleviate the plight of families of imprisoned members of the Muslim Brotherhood was liable to five years imprisonment. – Editor's note.

can see and imagine is what they need to fulfil their role of building the earth, as God has willed placing them in charge of it. Within the great universe, their planet, the earth, is no more than a barely visible particle. Humans cannot go beyond what they are allowed to see and comprehend of this vast universe, its laws and secrets.

"I need not swear by what you can see and what you cannot see." Such a statement tells us that beyond the reach of our faculties of perception there are worlds and secrets of which we know nothing. It thus broadens our vision of the universe and the truth. The universe is not confined to what we can see or comprehend with our limited faculties. After all, our task on earth is to build human life on it, and we have only been given what we need to fulfil this task. Yet when we appreciate this truth of our limited ability, and that there is a greater world beyond what we see, we can elevate ourselves above our needs and reach out to that source of perfect knowledge.

Those who confine themselves within what their senses can reach, using only their available tools, are wretched. They are imprisoned within a world that remains narrow despite its vastness. It is especially narrow when compared to the great universe. During different periods of history, some people, few or great in number, have been willing to imprison themselves, by their own hands, within the limits of their senses and what they see in the present world. They closed the windows of true light and knowledge that come from being in touch with the essential truth through faith. Some have gone even further and have sought to close these windows to all people. They did so in the name of *jāhiliyyah* at one time, and in the name of secularism at another. Both are types of imprisonment that bring endless misery, because they both involve isolation from the great sources of light and knowledge.

During the present century,[2] science has begun to rid itself of the fetters with which it shackled itself over the previous two centuries. It has started, through its own experiments, to regain its light. It had previously been on the loose, aiming to break from the confinement imposed on it by the Church. Now it knows its limits; it knows that its limited tools lead to what is beyond limit in this great universe. Now we

---

2. The author is referring here to the twentieth century. – Editor's note.

see a new call to faith made by scientists who have found their humility. All this appears to herald a new era of open-mindedness to end that of confinement in the narrow cell of materialism.

Alexis Carrel, a French surgeon and biologist who pioneered research in different areas and was the Nobel Prize winner for medicine in 1912, said: "This vast universe is full of active minds other than ours. If the human mind depends solely on its own guidance, it will be lost in the maze that surrounds it. Prayer is one method of communication with the minds around us and with the eternal mind that controls the destinies of all worlds, whether these are apparent to us or concealed from us."

"A feeling of holiness, together with other spiritual activities, have a special role in life because these bring us in contact with the spiritual world and its great mystery."[3]

Another French scientist who contributed to research in anatomy and physics, and who worked with the Curies, wrote:

Many intelligent and good intentioned people think that they cannot believe in God because they cannot imagine His nature. Yet an honest person who has the scientific drive does not need to imagine God's nature any more than a physicist needs to understand the nature of electricity. In both cases, our imagination remains deficient and invalid. It is impossible to imagine electricity in material terms, yet its effects are more concrete than a piece of wood.[4]

Sir Arthur Thomson, a famous Scottish naturalist and biologist, wrote: "We live at a time when the hard earth crust is becoming transparent, and the atmosphere is losing its material structure. Hence, our time is least suited to taking a too materialistic view." He also wrote:

A religious mind should not be sorry that a physicist does not move on from the study of nature to the Creator of nature, because this

---

3. This quotation is taken from an Arabic translation quoted by Al-ʿAqqād, A.M., *ʿAqāʾid al-Mufakkirīn fī al-Qarn al-ʿIshrīn*. Unfortunately, Sayyid Quṭb does not give further details of the title.

4. Ibid.

is not the line a physicist follows. The conclusion may be much bigger than the premise if scientists would draw on their study of physics to make conclusions on metaphysics. We should, however, be glad because physicists have enabled the religious tendency to breathe in a scientific environment. This was most difficult in our parents' and grandparents' time… If physicists have no business discussing God, as mistakenly advocated by Mr Langdon Davies in his book on man and his world, we say that the best service science has done is to lead man to formulate a more noble and sublime concept of God. We say literally that science has given man a new sky and a new earth, motivating him to exert his maximum mental effort. As a result, man often finds that he can only be at peace when he moves beyond the realm of understanding into the realm of certainty and reliance on God.[5]

A. Cressy Morrison, a former Head of the New York Academy of Sciences, wrote:

We do approach the vast abyss of the unknowable when we realize that all matter has scientifically become one by the acceptance of the theory that it is but a manifestation of a universal unit essentially electrical. But certainly chance has little place in the formation of the cosmos, for the mighty universe is governed by law.

The rise of man the animal to a self-conscious reasoning being is too great a step to be taken by the process of material evolution or without creative purpose.

If the reality of purpose is accepted, man as such may be a mechanism. But what operates this mechanism? For without operation it is useless. Science does not account for the operator, nor does Science say that it is material.

Progress has now been sufficient for us to see that God seems to be giving man a spark of His own intelligence.[6]

---

5. Ibid.
6. Morrison, A. Cressy (1962), *Man Does Not Stand Alone*, Kingswood, Surrey: The World's Work (1913) Ltd., pp. 113–114.

Thus, using its own tools, science has started to break through the prison walls of materialism to breathe the fresh air to which the Qur'ān refers in statements like, *"I need not swear by what you can see and what you cannot see."* (Verses 38–39) Yet in our own midst there are some who continue to try to close the windows with both their hands, to prevent the light from coming through, preferring to live in darkness. They do so in the name of science, without realizing that intellectually they lag behind science, and spiritually they lag behind religion. Moreover, they are backward, unable to move freely in pursuit of the truth. All this backwardness puts them in a position unworthy of man, the creature God has honoured.

God says that there is no need for an oath to prove the truth that *"this [Qur'ān] is the word of a noble Messenger, not the word of a poet – how little you believe! nor the word of a soothsayer – how little you reflect! This [Qur'ān] is a revelation from the Lord of all the worlds."* (Verses 40–43) One of the false allegations the unbelievers in Makkah fabricated against the Qur'ān and the Prophet alleged that Muḥammad was a poet or soothsayer. They based this on their recognition that the Qur'ān was superior to anything human beings could say or compose. They used to imagine that every poet had a friend from among the *jinn* who brought him his fine poetry, and that a soothsayer similarly had contacts with the *jinn*, giving him knowledge and information unavailable to humans. Yet a quick glance at the nature of the Qur'ān, and the nature of poetry and soothsaying is sufficient to show how hollow such claims are.

Poetry has its musical beat and it may be full of fine and beautiful images, but it can never be confused with the Qur'ān. There is a fundamental difference between the two. The Qur'ān establishes a complete concept of life based on truth, a holistic approach and clear notions of God's existence, the universe and life. Poetry, on the other hand, is an expression of a series of charged reactions that rarely reflects a consistent vision of life and this in situations of pleasure and anger, freedom and restriction, love and hate, as well as other changing influences.

Furthermore, this consistent concept the Qur'ān lays down is initiated in whole and in part by the Qur'ān itself, and attributed to its divine source. Every aspect of this concept suggests that it is not of man's making. It is not in the nature of human beings that they should come up with a complete concept of the universe. They have never done so in the past, nor will they ever be able to do so. We have a complete record of what human intelligence has come up with concerning the universe and the power that controls its system. It is all recorded in philosophical and intellectual works, as well as in poetry. When these are set side by side with the Qur'ānic concept, it is clearly apparent that the latter is not the work of a human mind. It is of a unique status, one that distinguishes it from all that the human intellect can produce.

The same applies to soothsaying. Never in human history, up to the present moment, has a soothsayer produced a complete code of living like the one delineated in the Qur'ān. All that soothsayers produce is limited to rhyming sentences containing some aspects of wisdom or ambiguous references.

Moreover, there are some Qur'ānic touches that are beyond man's ability to make. We discussed some of these when we commented on the relevant verses. For example, no one has ever portrayed comprehensive and accurate knowledge in images like those that follow: "*With Him are the keys to what lies beyond the reach of human perception: none knows them but He. He knows all that the land and sea contain; not a leaf falls but He knows it; and neither is there a grain in the earth's deep darkness, nor anything fresh or dry but is recorded in a clear book.*" (6: 59) "*He knows all that goes into the earth and all that comes out of it; all that descends from the skies and all that ascends to them. He is with you wherever you may be; and God sees all that you do.*" (57: 4) "*No female conceives or gives birth without His knowledge. No one attains to old age or has his life cut short unless it be thus laid down in [God's] decree. All this is easy for God.*" (35: 11)

No human being has ever, before or after the revelation of the Qur'ān, drawn an image of the power that holds the universe and conducts its affairs like this Qur'ānic verse: "*It is God alone who holds the celestial bodies and the earth, lest they deviate [from their courses]. If they should ever deviate, no one else could uphold them after Him.*" (35: 41) Nor has anyone ever attempted a description of the emergence of life in the universe and the deliberate balances that ensure its continuity in the universe similar to this Qur'ānic account: "*It is God who splits the grain and the fruit-stone. He brings forth the living out of that which is dead and the dead out of that which is alive. Such is God. How, then, are you deluded away from the truth? He is the One who causes the day to break. He has made the night to be [a source of stillness], and the sun and the moon for reckoning. All this is laid down by the will of the Almighty, the All-Knowing. It is He that has set up for you the stars, so that you may be guided by them in the deep darkness of land and sea. We have made Our revelations plain indeed to people who have knowledge. He it is who has brought you all into being from a single soul and has given you a dwelling and a place of sojourn. We have made Our revelations plain indeed to people of understanding. And He it is who sends down water from the sky with which We bring forth plants of every type and out of these We bring forth verdure from which We bring forth grain piled tight, packed on one another; and out of the spathe of the palm tree, dates in thick clusters; and gardens of vines; and the olive tree, and the pomegranate: all so alike, and yet so different. Behold their fruit when they come to fruition and ripen. Surely in these there are clear signs for people who truly believe."* (6: 95–99)

Such universal touches are found in plenty in the Qur'ān. They have no parallel in the way people tend to express similar thoughts and meanings. This is evidence enough to determine the source of this book, regardless of any other evidence that may be drawn from what the book says or the circumstances of its revelation. Indeed, the whole idea of the Qur'ān being like poetry or soothsaying is flimsy. Even when the Qur'ān was still in its early stages of revelation, having provided only a small number of *sūrahs* and verses with this distinctive divine colour, this idea did not cut any grounds. The elders of the Quraysh used to reflect on it from time to time, rejecting this notion, but they were blinded to the truth because of their own personal interests. It is just like the Qur'ān says: "*Since they refuse to be guided by it, they will always say, 'This is an ancient falsehood.'*" (46: 11)

Authoritative biographical works about the Prophet report several events when the elders of the Quraysh privately rejected this whole idea. Ibn Isḥāq reports a meeting attended by a large number of Makkans and chaired, as it were, by al-Walīd ibn al-Mughīrah, who was one of the more respected Quraysh elders. This was held shortly before the pilgrimage season and the idea was to agree an appropriate strategy:

In his opening address, al-Walīd said: "Now that the pilgrimage season is approaching, people will start arriving from all over the place. They must have heard about your friend [meaning the Prophet]. So you had better agree what to say when you are asked about him. We must guard against having too many opinions, particularly if they are mutually contradictory."

When his audience asked his advice as to what they should say, he preferred to listen to their suggestions first. What concerned al-Walīd most was that the opinion they would come out with should take account of the fact that Muḥammad was asking people to listen to the Qur'ān, God's message, expressed in beautiful language and powerful style. The description they would attach to Muḥammad should also account for his persuasive, eloquent argument.

Descriptions like 'fortune-teller', 'madman', 'poet' and 'magician' were proposed. None was considered convincing by al-Walīd, who pointed out weaknesses in each, one after the other. He told his people that what Muḥammad said was nothing like what was said by such men. When nobody could suggest anything more plausible, they asked al-Walīd if he had a better suggestion.

He said: "What Muḥammad says is certainly beautiful. It is like a date tree with solid roots and rich fruit. Every one of these suggestions you have made is bound to be recognized as false. The least disputable one is to claim that he is a magician who repeats magic words which make a man fall out with his father, mother, wife and clan." They all approved of al-Walīd's suggestion and set about preparing their propaganda campaign to make the pilgrims wary of Muḥammad and unwilling to meet him.[7]

Another prominent Quraysh figure to speak out about the Qur'ān was al-Naḍr ibn al-Ḥārith, when the Quraysh felt at a loss after having failed to win any compromise from the Prophet. He outlined their predicament in the following way:

7. Salahi, Adil (2002), *Muḥammad: Man and Prophet*, Leicester: The Islamic Foundation, pp. 119–120.

People of Quraysh, you are confronted with a problem for which you have not been able to find a solution. When Muḥammad was still a young man living among you, he won general admiration because he always spoke the truth and his honesty could not be faulted. When he had grown grey, and started to preach whatever he is preaching to you, you began to allege that he was a sorcerer. By God, he is no sorcerer. We have seen magicians and their tricks in the past. You also accused him of being a fortune teller. By God, he is not one, for we have seen fortune tellers and how they repeat their rhyming phrases. You also claimed that he was a poet. Again I say that, by God, he is not a poet, for we have seen poets and listened to all types of poetry. You claimed that he was also a madman, but he is far from being so. We have seen what madness has done to people, and how it causes them to say incoherent things. I say, people of Quraysh, you have to look at this question very carefully, for you have a big problem on your hands.[8]

The similarity between what the two prominent Quraysh figures state is almost complete. This is not surprising, considering their unresolved dilemma of how to deal with the Qur'ān. We also mentioned in our discussion of the previous *sūrah*, The Pen, how 'Utbah ibn Rabī'ah reacted to the Qur'ān, when he tried to make some offers to the Prophet in the hope that he would stop advocating his message. When they alleged that Muḥammad was a sorcerer or a soothsayer, that was nothing but a stratagem, crude at times and cunning at others. It only needed a little reflection to realize that it was all wrong. Hence, there was no need for an oath of any sort to confirm that the Qur'ān was the word of a noble Messenger and a revelation from on high.

The statement that the Qur'ān *"is the word of a noble Messenger,"* does not mean that it is of his own composition. It rather means that it is a different type of word, one not uttered by a poet or a soothsayer. It can only be said by a Messenger from God, carrying it from the One who sent him. What confirms this meaning is the word *'Messenger'* being sent with it. He is neither a poet nor a soothsayer composing his own

---

8. Ibid., pp. 161–162.

words alone or with the assistance of a *jinnee*. This is further confirmed by the categorical statement that follows: *"This [Qur'ān] is a revelation from the Lord of all the worlds."* (Verse 43)

In its negation of the Qur'ān being the word of a poet or a soothsayer, the *sūrah* uses the following two expressions: *"how little you believe!... how little you reflect!"* Thus, it completely negates their having any faith or resorting to any reflection. In a *ḥadīth*, the Prophet is described as 'little indulging in frivolous talk', which means that he did not say such things at all. Thus, the *sūrah* is describing those unbelievers as devoid of faith and reflection. No believer would say of the Prophet that he was a poet, and no man who reflects would say that he was a soothsayer.

A Very Serious Threat

As the *sūrah* draws to its conclusion, it issues a terrifying threat to anyone who fabricates something about the very serious matter of faith. The threat is issued so as to affirm the only possible scenario of the Prophet being very truthful and honest in delivering the message entrusted to him. The proof is that God has not punished him severely as He would have done so had the Prophet been anything other than that:

Had he attributed some fabrications to Us, We would indeed have seized him by the right hand and cut off his life-vein, and none of you could have saved him. (Verses 44–47)

The import of these verses is confirmation that Muḥammad (peace be upon him) only told them the truth. Had he invented something other than what was revealed to him from on high, God would have killed him in the way the verses describe. Since this did not take place, the inevitable conclusion is that he was truthful.

Yet this confirmation is given in a scene that goes much further than the actual statement, adding some fearsome connotations, action and life. We see here the violent, scary action of someone being seized by the right hand and his life-vein being cut. It makes a clear impression of God's limitless power and mankind's utter weakness in comparison.

It adds a suggestion that this question of faith is so serious that it allows no complacency or leniency towards anyone, not even Muḥammad in his close relation with God. Furthermore, these verses carry a strong beat, spreading an air of fear and submission to God.

The *surah* concludes with a statement of the true nature of the Qur'ān:

> *This [Qur'ān] is indeed a reminder to the God-fearing. We well know that among you are some who deny its truth. Yet it will be a cause of bitter regret for the unbelievers. It is indeed truth absolute.* (Verses 48–51)

This Qur'ān reminds God-fearing hearts and they remember. The truth the Qur'ān states is ingrained in people's hearts, but the reminder brings it to the fore in the minds of those who are God-fearing. Others continue to be preoccupied, unaware, and as such they benefit nothing by the reminder that this book, the Qur'ān, provides. It is a fact that the God-fearing find in the Qur'ān life, light, knowledge and remembrance, but none of these is experienced by other people.

"*We well know that among you are some who deny its truth.*" (Verse 49) Yet this is of no consequence, and it alters nothing of the reality. Those who reject the truth are of no importance whatsoever. "*Yet it will be a cause of bitter regret for the unbelievers.*" (Verse 50) It elevates the status of the believers and brings down the unbelievers. It establishes the truth and undermines the falsehood to which the unbelievers cling. Moreover, it provides the argument against them when they face the reckoning on the Day of Judgement. They will lament their fate to which their rejection of the truth of the Qur'ān has led them. Thus, it is a source of bitter regret for all unbelievers in this life and in the life to come.

In the face of all denials and rejection by the unbelievers, the Qur'ān is "*indeed truth absolute.*" (Verse 51) It is not merely the truth, but the truth absolute, reconfirmed in absolute terms. In fact, every word in the Qur'ān is profoundly true; every verse carries enough evidence that it originates with God, who Himself is the Truth.

At this point, an instruction is given from on high to the noble Messenger. It comes at the right time and during the right situation: "*Extol, then, the glory of the name of your Lord, the Supreme.*" (Verse 52)

This is the most suitable action as it reflects acknowledgement of God's glory and man's position as God's servant. To glorify God is the feeling that a believer experiences after the last statement explaining the nature of the Qur'ān is given and after the long discussion of God Almighty's greatness.

SŪRAH 70

Al-Ma 'ārij
(Ways of Ascent)

Prologue

This *sūrah* may be described as being part of the long, slow, yet accurate and profound treatment of the traces of *jāhiliyyah*, or ignorance, within the human soul. This was most evident as the Qur'ān was being revealed in Makkah but is true wherever *jāhiliyyah* reigns. There may be differences in different situations, but these are superficial affecting only appearances. Alternatively, we may say that this *sūrah* represents a round in the long, hard battle the Qur'ān fights within the human soul, going deep inside it to eradicate all lingering traces of *jāhiliyyah*. This battle is greater and longer lasting than the wars the Muslims later had to fight against their many enemies. Moreover, these traces are more persistent and harder in their resistance than the great forces that were marshalled against the Islamic message, or those which continue to be raised against it by different *jāhiliyyah* societies.

The major issue the *sūrah* focuses on is that of the hereafter and peoples requital for what they do during their lives on earth, particularly the punishment suffered by the unbelievers. In order to establish the truth of the hereafter, the *sūrah* speaks of how the human soul reacts to situations of hardship and comfort. Such reactions differ greatly between a believer and one who is devoid of faith. The *sūrah* also provides an outline of the believers' main features, their feelings and

241

behaviour, and it states how they deserve to be honoured. It also shows that the unbelievers are held in disregard by God, and gives a picture of the humiliation prepared for them. It is a humiliation the arrogant thoroughly deserve. Furthermore, the *sūrah* establishes the fact that values, standards and scales applied by God are different from those which human beings uphold.

The Qur'ān administered its long treatment and fought its hard battle within the human soul equipped with nothing other than its own powerful argument. It achieved its great victory within its followers even before it had a sword with which to defend those believers, let alone force its enemies into submission.

Whoever reads the Qur'ān bearing in mind the events that took place during the Prophet's lifetime will not fail to appreciate the overpowering effect the Qur'ān had on those people in Makkah until they willingly accepted its lead. We see the wide range of styles the Qur'ān employs. It may face the human soul with a great flood of inspiring proofs and powerful effects; or it may use a powerful tool that leaves nothing of the traces of ignorance without completely crushing it, or it may confront the human soul with something akin to a hard whip that kindles sensation so that the pain it inflicts is very hard to bear. It alternates its approaches between a calm friendly appeal that wins hearts, a loud terrifying outcry that warns of an impending and great danger, a clear presentation of powerful and irrefutable argument, and a raising of hopes with the prospect of an appealing outcome. At times the Qur'ān moves physically through the human soul, going along its alleyways and round its corners, shedding light on each of these. It, thus, puts these before man so that he looks at them, making him dislike certain aspects, feel ashamed at others, and alert to his own reactions, which he normally overlooked. The Qur'ān uses hundreds of such touches, appeals and influences in conducting its long battle and administrating its slow treatment. We can follow these as we read the Qur'ān and learn how it achieved its great victory against the stiff resistance the human soul put up from within. The present *sūrah* is one instalment of this Qur'ānic endeavour to establish the truth of the hereafter and other related truths.

The preceding *sūrah*, The Inevitable Truth, aimed to establish the same truth of the hereafter, but the methods employed in both *sūrahs* are widely different. The line followed in the preceding *sūrah* aimed to show the great universal upheaval taking place on the Day of Judgement through terror-striking images such as: "*When the trumpet is sounded a single time, and the earth and mountains are lifted up and with one mighty crash are flattened, that which is certain to happen will on that day have come to pass. The sky will be rent asunder, for, it will have become frail on that day.*" (69: 13–16) It also depicts the awesome nature of that day in a majestic scene: "*The angels will stand on all its sides and, on that day, eight of them will bear aloft the Throne of your Lord.*" (69: 17) It leaves us shaken as it describes how everything is laid bare: "*On that day you shall be brought to judgement and none of your secrets will remain hidden.*" (69: 18) The images so drawn of punishment add to the terrifying effect of the *sūrah*. This starts with the way judgement is announced: "*Lay hold of him and shackle him, and burn him in the fire of hell, and then fasten him in a chain seventy cubits long.*" (69: 30–32) Such feelings of terror are vividly reflected in the outcries of lamentation voiced by those receiving such judgement: "*Would that I had never been shown my record and knew nothing of my account! Would that death had been the end of me!*" (69: 25–27)

In the present *sūrah*, awesomeness is felt in the features, thoughts and movements of the human soul, rather than the universe and its great scenery. Even in the scenes of the universe presented in this *sūrah*, the fear appears to be almost psychological. It is certainly not the most prominent aspect. Indeed, such fear takes hold of the human soul, and its extent is reflected in the panic it produces: "*On the day when the sky will be like molten lead, and the mountains like tufts of wool, when no friend will ask about his friend, though they may be within sight of one another. The guilty one will wish he could ransom himself from the suffering on that day by sacrificing his own children, his wife, his brother, the kinsfolk who gave him shelter, and all those on earth, if it could save him.*" (Verses 8–14)

In this *sūrah*, hell itself has a soul, feelings and consciousness of its own. Like living creatures, it plays a part in producing the fright effect: "*It is the raging fire that tears the skin away. It will claim all who turn their backs, and turn away from the truth, amass riches and hoard them.*" (Verses 15–18) Even the punishment and suffering is more psychological than physical: "*the day when they shall come in haste from their graves, as if rallying to a flag, with eyes downcast, with ignominy overwhelming them. Such is the day they have been promised.*" (Verses 43–44)

The images, scenes and impressions in this *sūrah* are different from those of the preceding one because of the difference in their general outlooks, despite the fact that they address the same central theme. The *sūrah* also provides images of human psychology in positive and adverse situations, and in cases of embracing faith or otherwise. This fits perfectly with its special psychological emphasis. It describes man in the following terms: "*Man is born with a restless disposition: when misfortune befalls him, he is fretful; and when good fortune comes his way, he grows tight-fisted. Not so those who pray.*" (Verses 19–22) The *sūrah* goes on to provide a picture of believers and their apparent and inner characteristics. This is in line with the general style of the *sūrah*: "*Not so those who pray, and always attend to their prayers; who give a due share of their possessions to the one who asks [for help] and the one who is deprived; who believe in the Day of Judgement; who stand in fear of their Lord's punishment, for none may feel totally secure from their Lord's punishment; who guard their chastity except with those joined to them in marriage, or those whom they rightfully possess – for then, they are free of all blame, whereas those who seek to go beyond that [limit] are indeed transgressors; who are faithful to their trusts and to their pledges; who stand up for the truth when they bear witness; and who attend to their prayers without fail.*" (Verses 22–34)

The main drift in the preceding *sūrah* was to establish absolute seriousness in the question of faith. Hence the truth of the hereafter was one of several in the *sūrah*, alongside that of meting out swift punishment in this world to those who reject faith, and showing no leniency in the punishment of those who alter the principles of faith. By contrast, the drift in this *sūrah* is to establish the truth of the hereafter and the requital of all, as well as outlining the standards of such requital. This means that the hereafter is the main truth the *sūrah* speaks about. Hence, other truths mentioned here directly relate to the hereafter. An example of this is the difference in the way the *sūrah* mentions God's days and the reckoning of human days, and how God sees the Day of Judgement and how people see it: "*All the angels and the Spirit will ascend to Him, on a day the length of which is fifty thousand years. Therefore, endure all adversity with goodly patience. People think it to be far away, but We see it near at hand.*" (Verses 4–7) Another example is the difference affecting human psychology in the two cases of hardship and comfort when these are combined with faith or unfaith. Both are determinants of the type of requital received on the Day of Judgement. The *sūrah* also speaks of the unbelievers' arrogance as they entertain hopes of being admitted to gardens of bliss when they are of no importance in God's measure. They cannot evade His punishment. Thus we see that the *sūrah* is almost entirely devoted to the truth of the hereafter, which it aims to firmly establish in people's minds.

Another aspect of this *sūrah* is its particular musical rhythm that echoes its line of expression. The varied beat of the preceding *sūrah* responded to the change of the rhyme from one section to another, and the ambience of each. Here, the changes are wider in scope, because they incorporate the varied musical structure of the *sūrah*, not merely its varying rhyme. Here, every musical section is more complex and profound. This is particularly true of its first part where we have three melodies that differ in length and tune, but which share the same final beat. The first takes up verses 1–5, ending with a long '*a*' sound. This is repeated on two further occasions in the two short verses that follow. A second melody takes up three more verses, with the first two having different endings, but the third echoing the long '*a*' sound at the end. A third melody is composed of five verses, maintaining an '*eeh*' ending in the first four, but ending the fifth with another long '*a*'. Then we have six short verses, all ending with a long '*a*', but the rhyme in the first three is different from that of the other three. The remainder of the *sūrah* maintains an '*m*' or '*n*' ending preceded by a long '*e*' or '*o*'. The rhythm in the first section is both complex and profound. A sensitive ear will not fail to appreciate its sophistication, which is unfamiliar to those used to Arabic rhythm. However, the Qur'ānic style makes it easy to appreciate, moulding it in such a way as to overcome its unfamiliarity and so making it perfectly acceptable.

245

Al-Ma'ārij
(Ways of Ascent)

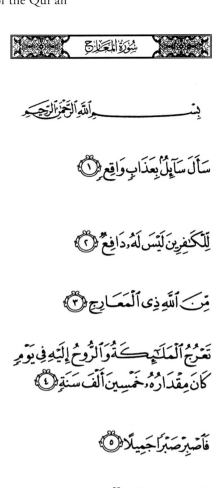

In the Name of God, the Lord of Grace, the Ever Merciful

An inquirer has asked about a suffering which is bound to befall (1)

the unbelievers. Nothing can ward it off, (2)

as it comes from God, the Lord of the Ways of Ascent. (3)

All the angels and the Spirit will ascend to Him, on a day the length of which is fifty thousand years. (4)

Therefore, endure all adversity with goodly patience. (5)

People think it to be far away, (6)

but We see it near at hand. (7)

On the day when the sky will be like molten lead, (8)

and the mountains like tufts of wool, (9)

when no friend will ask about his friend, (10)

وَلَا يَسۡـَٔلُ حَمِيمٌ حَمِيمٗا ۝

though they may be within sight of one another. The guilty one will wish he could ransom himself from the suffering on that day by sacrificing his own children, (11)

يُبَصَّرُونَهُمۡ يَوَدُّ ٱلۡمُجۡرِمُ لَوۡ يَفۡتَدِي مِنۡ عَذَابِ يَوۡمِئِذِۭ بِبَنِيهِ ۝

his wife, his brother, (12)

وَصَٰحِبَتِهِۦ وَأَخِيهِ ۝

the kinsfolk who gave him shelter, (13)

وَفَصِيلَتِهِ ٱلَّتِي تُـٔۡوِيهِ ۝

and all those on earth, if it could save him. (14)

وَمَن فِي ٱلۡأَرۡضِ جَمِيعٗا ثُمَّ يُنجِيهِ ۝

But no! It is the raging fire (15)

كَلَّآ إِنَّهَا لَظَىٰ ۝

that tears the skin away. (16)

نَزَّاعَةٗ لِّلشَّوَىٰ ۝

It will claim all who turn their backs, and turn away from the truth, (17)

تَدۡعُواْ مَنۡ أَدۡبَرَ وَتَوَلَّىٰ ۝

amass riches and hoard them. (18)

وَجَمَعَ فَأَوۡعَىٰٓ ۝

Man is born with a restless disposition: (19)

إِنَّ ٱلۡإِنسَٰنَ خُلِقَ هَلُوعًا ۝

247

when misfortune befalls him, he is fretful; (20)

إِذَا مَسَّهُ ٱلشَّرُّ جَزُوعًا ۝

and when good fortune comes his way, he grows tight-fisted. (21)

وَإِذَا مَسَّهُ ٱلْخَيْرُ مَنُوعًا ۝

Not so those who pray, (22)

إِلَّا ٱلْمُصَلِّينَ ۝

and always attend to their prayers; (23)

ٱلَّذِينَ هُمْ عَلَىٰ صَلَاتِهِمْ دَآئِمُونَ ۝

who give a due share of their possessions (24)

وَٱلَّذِينَ فِىٓ أَمْوَٰلِهِمْ حَقٌّ مَّعْلُومٌ ۝

to the one who asks [for help] and the one who is deprived; (25)

لِّلسَّآئِلِ وَٱلْمَحْرُومِ ۝

who believe in the Day of Judgement; (26)

وَٱلَّذِينَ يُصَدِّقُونَ بِيَوْمِ ٱلدِّينِ ۝

who stand in fear of their Lord's punishment, (27)

وَٱلَّذِينَ هُم مِّنْ عَذَابِ رَبِّهِم مُّشْفِقُونَ ۝

for none may feel totally secure from their Lord's punishment; (28)

إِنَّ عَذَابَ رَبِّهِمْ غَيْرُ مَأْمُونٍ ۝

who guard their chastity (29)

وَٱلَّذِينَ هُمْ لِفُرُوجِهِمْ حَٰفِظُونَ ۝

except with those joined to them in marriage, or those whom they rightfully possess – for then, they are free of all blame, (30)

إِلَّا عَلَىٰٓ أَزْوَٰجِهِمْ أَوْ مَا مَلَكَتْ أَيْمَٰنُهُمْ فَإِنَّهُمْ غَيْرُ مَلُومِينَ ۝

whereas those who seek to go beyond that [limit] are indeed transgressors; (31)

فَمَنِ ٱبْتَغَىٰ وَرَآءَ ذَٰلِكَ فَأُوْلَـٰئِكَ هُمُ ٱلْعَادُونَ ۝

who are faithful to their trusts and to their pledges; (32)

وَٱلَّذِينَ هُمْ لِأَمَـٰنَـٰتِهِمْ وَعَهْدِهِمْ رَٰعُونَ ۝

who stand up for the truth when they bear witness; (33)

وَٱلَّذِينَ هُم بِشَهَـٰدَٰتِهِمْ قَآئِمُونَ ۝

and who attend to their prayers without fail. (34)

وَٱلَّذِينَ هُمْ عَلَىٰ صَلَاتِهِمْ يُحَافِظُونَ ۝

They are the ones to be honoured in the gardens of paradise. (35)

أُوْلَـٰئِكَ فِى جَنَّـٰتٍ مُّكْرَمُونَ ۝

What is wrong with the un-believers, that they run confusedly before you, (36)

فَمَالِ ٱلَّذِينَ كَفَرُواْ قِبَلَكَ مُهْطِعِينَ ۝

from the right and the left, in crowds? (37)

عَنِ ٱلْيَمِينِ وَعَنِ ٱلشِّمَالِ عِزِينَ ۝

Does every one of them hope to enter a garden of bliss? (38)

أَيَطْمَعُ كُلُّ ٱمْرِئٍ مِّنْهُمْ أَن يُدْخَلَ جَنَّةَ نَعِيمٍ ۝

No! We have created them from the substance they know. (39)

كَلَّآ إِنَّا خَلَقْنَـٰهُم مِّمَّا يَعْلَمُونَ ۝

By the Lord of all star risings and settings, We certainly have the power (40)

فَلَآ أُقْسِمُ بِرَبِّ ٱلْمَشَـٰرِقِ وَٱلْمَغَـٰرِبِ إِنَّا لَقَـٰدِرُونَ ۝

to replace them with better people. There is nothing to prevent Us from doing so. (41)

عَلَىٰٓ أَن نُّبَدِّلَ خَيْرًا مِّنْهُمْ وَمَا نَحْنُ بِمَسْبُوقِينَ ﴿٤١﴾

Leave them to indulge in idle talk and play until they face the day they have been promised, (42)

فَذَرْهُمْ يَخُوضُوا۟ وَيَلْعَبُوا۟ حَتَّىٰ يُلَٰقُوا۟ يَوْمَهُمُ ٱلَّذِى يُوعَدُونَ ﴿٤٢﴾

the day when they shall come in haste from their graves, as if rallying to a flag, (43)

يَوْمَ يَخْرُجُونَ مِنَ ٱلْأَجْدَاثِ سِرَاعًا كَأَنَّهُمْ إِلَىٰ نُصُبٍ يُوفِضُونَ ﴿٤٣﴾

with eyes downcast, with ignominy overwhelming them. Such is the day they have been promised. (44)

خَٰشِعَةً أَبْصَٰرُهُمْ تَرْهَقُهُمْ ذِلَّةٌ ذَٰلِكَ ٱلْيَوْمُ ٱلَّذِى كَانُوا۟ يُوعَدُونَ ﴿٤٤﴾

The Truth of the Hereafter

An inquirer has asked about a suffering which is bound to befall the unbelievers. Nothing can ward it off, as it comes from God, the Lord of the Ways of Ascent. (Verses 1–3)

The very concept of the hereafter was very difficult for the Arab polytheists to understand. They strongly resisted it. In fact they received it with so much amazement that they denied it outright. They further challenged the Prophet, in various ways, to bring it about or to define its timing. A report attributed to Ibn ʿAbbās mentions that the man who asked the question quoted in the first verse of the *sūrah* was al-Naḍr ibn al-Ḥārith. Another report quotes him as saying that the reference is to "the unbelievers' question about God's punishment, which is certain to engulf them."

Regardless of who the specific individual was the *sūrah* reports that someone asked about this punishment, indeed, sought to hasten it, and further confirms that it is inevitable because it has been determined by God and that it will soon come. It states that no one can prevent its happening or ward it off. Therefore, to question or hasten it is ill-advised. Moreover, this punishment is to befall the unbelievers, in total, which means that those who question it are included like every other unbeliever. It is administered by God, '*the Lord of the Ways of Ascent*'. This is an expression of highness, which is one of God's attributes mentioned in different ways in the Qur'ān, such as: "*High above all orders [of being] is He, the Lord of the Throne.*" (40: 15)

Having absolutely confirmed the inevitability of such punishment, the *sūrah* describes the day when it will take place, affirming that it will soon arrive. However, God's measure is different from mankind's:

> *All the angels and the Spirit will ascend to Him, on a day the length of which is fifty thousand years. Therefore, endure all adversity with goodly patience. People think it to be far away, but We see it near at hand.* (Verses 4–7)

Most probably the day to which these verses refer is the Day of Resurrection, as the *sūrah* almost defines it as so. On that day, the angels and the Spirit will ascend to God. The Spirit refers, in all probability, to the Angel Gabriel, since he is given this name elsewhere in the Qur'ān. He is specifically mentioned here, after the reference to all angels, because of his special status. Likewise, the angels' ascension on that day is highlighted so as to give it special importance; they will do so to fulfil what is assigned to them on that day. We do not know, nor are we required to know, the nature of their assignments, or how the angels ascend, or to where. All these are details that belong to the realm beyond the reach of our perception. To know them does not add to the statement's import. We have nothing to point to such information. Therefore, we do not attempt any further explanation. It is enough for us to reflect on the image to appreciate the great importance of that day when the angels and the Spirit are busy conducting their assigned tasks.

The statement that the length of that day is *fifty thousand years* may be an expression of very long duration as is customary in Arabic idiom, or it may express a true fact meaning that the day in question is equal to fifty thousand of our years despite its being just a single day. We can easily imagine this considering that our earth days represent the length of time the earth takes to revolve once in position. There are stars, however, which take thousands of our days to revolve once. This is not to say that this is what is meant here; we only state this to make it clear that the length of days can differ greatly.

If one of God's days is equal to fifty thousand of our years, then the punishment of the Day of Judgement is certainly close, according to God's measure, even though people may think it far away. Therefore, God tells His Messenger to be patient with them: "*People think it to be far away, but We see it near at hand.*" (Verses 6–7) The order to remain patient is part of the divine message's essence; it is required of every messenger and every believer. This is fundamentally necessary because the burden is heavy and the task hard. It is vitally important to keep the believers united and content, looking to their ultimate goal.

Goodly or 'beautiful' patience, to use a literal translation of the Qur'ānic term, is that type of patience coupled with a feeling of contentment and reassurance. It is undisturbed by displeasure, worry or doubt in the true promise. It is the type of patience shown by one who is certain of the outcome, content with God's will, appreciating His wisdom in the trying times he goes through, looking to Him in all situations. It is this type of goodly patience that is worthy of one who advocates the divine message. It is after all God's message calling on people to believe in Him. Its advocates have no personal interest in it; they seek no gain out of it. Whatever they suffer as a result is for God's sake, and whatever happens to it is by His will. Goodly patience, therefore, is the only attitude that fits properly with this truth.

God, who has bestowed this message from on high and has made this promise which the unbelievers hasten, determines events and their timings as He pleases, according to His overall plan for the universe. Human beings remain unaware of His will and plan; therefore, they hasten things. When time goes by without fulfilment of the promise, they begin to doubt. Worry may also be experienced by advocates of the divine message themselves. They too may entertain thoughts and desires that the promise be fulfilled soon. Therefore, they are given the following instruction so that they may remain firm: "*Therefore, endure all adversity with goodly patience.*" (Verse 5) The address here is delivered to the Prophet so as to give him reassurance in the face of the opposition and rejection he faced. It also adds another truth here, highlighting the fact that God sees matters in a different way. He does not measure things by means of our small measures: "*People think it to be far away, but We see it near at hand.*" (Verses 6–7)

Celestial Events

> *On the day when the sky will be like molten lead, and the mountains like tufts of wool.* (Verses 8–9)

The Qurʾān mentions in several places that great celestial events will take place on that promised day, and as a result change will affect different celestial bodies in their positions and characteristics, as well as their inter-relations. One of these events changes the sky making it like molten lead, or molten metals generally as signified by the Arabic word used here, *al-muhl.* These statements should be reflected upon by physicists and astronomers. They suggest that most probably celestial bodies are composed of metals that have melted and taken gas form, which is a stage far beyond that of melting by excessive heat. It is possible that they will lose their heat on the Day of Judgement and cool down to a fluid stage, changing their present status. Elsewhere in the Qurʾān we have the following statement as a mark of the Day of Judgement: "*When the stars fall and disperse.*" (81: 2)

At any rate, this is only one possible explanation, which may or may not be worth further study by scientific researchers. As for us, we read the text and look at the awesome image painted, with the sky becoming like molten metal and the mountains like tufts of wool. We also contemplate what is beyond this image of frightening events that leave their marks on people in an unusual way which the Qurʾān accurately describes:

> *On the day when the sky will be like molten lead, and the mountains like tufts of wool, when no friend will ask about his friend, though*

they may be within sight of one another. The guilty one will wish he could ransom himself from the suffering on that day by sacrificing his own children, his wife, his brother, the kinsfolk who gave him shelter, and all those on earth, if it could save him. (Verses 8–14)

People will be totally preoccupied in a way that does not allow anyone to look at anything other than his own situation. No thought will they give to anyone but themselves: *"When no friend will ask about his friend."* The frightening event severs all bonds, locking everyone within their own problems. Yet they are made to see one another: *"though they may be within sight of one another,"* as if deliberately brought so. However, each will be totally absorbed with their own impending fate so that none will even think of enquiring about a friend or even asking a friend for help.

What about the guilty one? The terror he feels is so overwhelming that he wishes he could offer anything as a ransom so as to be spared the punishment awaiting him. He is ready to sacrifice his nearest and dearest, the very ones whom he so cared for that he would render any sacrifice for their sake. He is willing to sacrifice his own children, wife, brothers and all his kinsfolk who used to afford him shelter and protection. Indeed his eagerness to escape the approaching torment is so strong that he loses all feeling for anyone else. Indeed he would sacrifice everyone on earth if only he could be spared. What a frightening image of distress and panic!

In the midst of this situation, the guilty hears something that closes the door to any fleeting hope. Indeed, all will listen to what makes the situation abundantly clear:

But no! It is the raging fire that tears the skin away. It will claim all who turn their backs, and turn away from the truth, amass riches and hoard them. (Verses 15–18)

There is absolutely no place for such impossible notions of escape, even though one would offer one's children, spouse, brothers, kinsfolk and everyone else in ransom. *"But no! It is the raging fire."* (Verse 15) It rages on ready to burn, but it also *"tears the skin away."* (Verse 16) It tears the skin off both the face and head. Here, the fire is described as if it has a will of its own, deliberately taking part in inflicting punishment on the guilty. "*It will claim all who turn their backs, and turn away from the truth.*" (Verse 17) Those people who turned away when they were called upon to follow the truth embodied in the divine message are now called again. This time the caller is the raging fire, and this time they cannot turn away. In the past, they were busy amassing riches and hoarding them. Now their attentions cannot be diverted from responding to this call by the raging fire. Nor can they divert it from themselves, no matter what they offer in ransom.

Special emphasis is placed in this *surah*, as in the previous two *surahs*, on hindering good actions, discouraging the feeding of the needy and hoarding amassed riches. All these are placed side by side with disbelief and denying the divine message. Such repeated emphasis suggests that there were in that early period in Makkah people who combined greed and stinginess with disbelief and rejection. Everyone is warned against this and told of its consequences as a primary cause of punishment, second to disbelief in God and associating partners with Him.

The *surah* includes other references confirming this and showing some features of the prevailing environment Islam faced in Makkah. The whole social set up concentrated on amassing wealth through trade and usury. The Quraysh elders were the ones so engaged in such trade. They used to organize trade caravans in winter and summer. Their preoccupation with wealth meant that many were poor and deprived. Hence, the need for such repeated reminders and warnings. The Qur'ān continued to address these social ills, fighting greed and stinginess within people's souls, both before and after the conquest of Makkah. Anyone who follows the Qur'ānic verses addressing such social ills will appreciate this. These verses give clear warnings against usury, the wrongful taking of other people's money, devouring the wealth of orphans when they are still young, the oppression of orphan girls and forcibly marrying them to obtain their money, the ill-treatment of beggars, orphans and the needy generally. In all this, the Qur'ān launches a strong campaign against unfair practices, giving us at the same time a fair idea of the prevailing social environment. Moreover, these verses provide directives on how to rid the human soul, in all situations, of its gripping obsession with amassing wealth.

Between Good and Evil

The *sūrah* now depicts how man faces good and evil, in both situations of faith and unfaith. It also outlines the qualities of the believers and states their ultimate end in contrast to the fate of those who are guilty:

> *Man is born with a restless disposition: when misfortune befalls him, he is fretful; and when good fortune comes his way, he grows tight-fisted. Not so those who pray, and always attend to their prayers; who give a due share of their possessions to the one who asks [for help] and the one who is deprived; who believe in the Day of Judgement; who stand in fear of their Lord's punishment, for none may feel totally secure from their Lord's punishment; who guard their chastity except with those joined to them in marriage, or those whom they rightfully possess – for then, they are free of all blame, whereas those who seek to go beyond that [limit] are indeed transgressors; who are faithful to their trusts and to their pledges; who stand up for the truth when they bear witness; and who attend to their prayers without fail. They are the ones to be honoured in the gardens of paradise.* (Verses 19–35)

The picture the Qur'ān draws of a man devoid of faith is remarkably accurate and expressive. Only faith can elevate him above such qualities. It is faith that gives him the bond of reassurance so that he does not panic when confronted with evil and is not stingy when his fortunes turn good: "*Man is born with a restless disposition: when misfortune befalls him, he is fretful; and when good fortune comes his way, he grows tight-fisted.*" (Verses 19–21)

Like the brushstrokes of a talented painter, every word in these verses draws a line delineating a human feature. Yet we have here only three very short verses, and these composed of only a small number of words. However, by the time they are finished, the picture drawn comes alive and man, with his distinctive and permanent features, is revealed. He has a restless disposition. He is fretful, feeling the pain of misfortune when it occurs. He panics, lest this should be permanent. He thinks the present moment will last forever. His worry soon imprisons him behind

AL-MAʿĀRIJ (Ways of Ascent) 70

the bars of the present moment and its misfortune so that he despairs of any change. Fear and worry tear him apart. How can he be otherwise when he does not have the steadying influence of faith and the hope it generates? When his fortunes turn good, he is stingy. He thinks that what he receives has been hard earned by his own efforts. Hence, he does not want others to take anything of it. He wants it all for himself. He becomes the prisoner of his own wealth. The truth is that he does not understand his actual role in getting whatever he earns. He does not look to receive from God what is better than all he has. How can he when his heart is devoid of faith? Thus, he is restless and worried in both situations. This is a very miserable picture of man when faith has no place in his heart.

Thus we see that faith is a very serious issue in man's life. It is not merely a word we utter, or worship rituals we offer. It is a state of mind and a code of living based on a complete value system with which to judge events and situations. Should a person lack such a steadying influence, he is likely to sway with the trend; he is in a permanent state of worry whatever fortune befalls him. By contrast, when his heart is enlightened by faith, he is content and reassured because he feels his bond with the One who conducts events and changes situations. He trusts to His will, feels His mercy, accepts His test, always looks to the relief of his hardship, ready to do good and be charitable knowing that whatever he gives away comes from Him, and whatever is spent for His sake will be rewarded both in this life and in the life to come. Faith is indeed a real gain, which believers receive in this present life before they are rewarded for it in the life to come. This gain is reflected in their state of comfort and reassurance throughout their life on earth.

The Exceptions

The *sūrah* now gives a detailed account of the believers who do not share the common human feature of restlessness and worry. "*Not so those who pray, and always attend to their prayers.*" (Verses 22–23) It is true that prayer is an essential Islamic duty providing the mark of faith. Yet it is much more than this: it is rather the means of contact with God Almighty and the sign of true servitude to Him. In prayer, the relative positions of God and servant are clearly and specifically outlined. The *sūrah* adds here that believers attend to their prayers all the time and in all situations. It thus gives an image of permanence and stability. Their prayer is disrupted through negligence or laziness. It is a permanent bond. When the Prophet performed voluntary worship, he used to do so regularly. He also said: "The actions that please God most are the ones offered regularly, even though they may be small." [Related in all six anthologies of authentic *aḥādīth*.]

"*Who give a due share of their possessions to the one who asks [for help] and the one who is deprived.*" (Verses 24–25) This due share is *zakāt* in particular and other charitable donations of specified amounts. These are due, by right, from all believers. Perhaps this statement has a broader meaning too, signifying that believers assign a share of their wealth considering it to be due for such needy people. To do so is to rid oneself of stinginess and to rise above the desire to amass wealth. It also implies a recognition by the one who is well off within the community of believers of his duty towards the one who is deprived. When a believer accepts that the needy and the deprived have a rightful claim to a portion of his wealth, he acknowledges the grace God has bestowed on him and the bond he has with fellow human beings. It signifies freedom from greed and stinginess. Moreover, it guarantees mutual cooperation and care within the Muslim community. Thus, *zakāt* appears a duty with far-reaching significance on several levels, within oneself and in the life of the community.

"*Who believe in the Day of Judgement.*" (Verse 26) Drawing an essential but general outline of a believer's character, this quality is directly related to the *sūrah*'s main theme. To believe in the Day of Judgement is half of faith, having as it does a marked influence on one's life, with respect to both emotions and actions. The standard by which a believer in the Day of Judgement weighs up things, events, actions and life altogether is different from that of one who does not believe. Such a believer approaches matters and takes action looking up to heaven and thinking of the hereafter. He treats all events, good or bad, as preludes, while the results come later, in the life to come. Therefore, he looks at these with their expected results and evaluates them on that basis. By contrast, the one who does not believe in the Day of Judgement looks at everything in the light of what he stands to gain from it in this present, short and limited life. Whatever action he takes is considered within the scope of life on earth. Hence, he weighs things, events and actions differently, arriving at very different conclusions. He is always worried and miserable because what he goes through in this his first life may not be reassuring, comfortable, fair or reasonable unless he adds to it what happens in the next stage, which is longer and broader. Hence, the one who does not take the hereafter into account will be unhappy or will cause unhappiness to those who are close to him. He cannot conceive of a higher level of life bringing him its clear rewards. Hence, believing in the Day of Judgement is half of faith, and it is on this belief that the Islamic code of living is based.

"Who stand in fear of their Lord's punishment, for none may feel totally secure from their Lord's punishment." (Verses 27–28) This takes us a step further than the mere belief in the Day of Judgement. It adds clear sensitivity and alertness, as well as a feeling that despite one's worship one is falling short in the fulfilment of one's duty towards God. One fears to slip at any time and, as a result, deserve punishment. Therefore, one looks for God's help and protection. In his position as a Messenger of God, the Prophet was always on the alert, and in fear of God's punishment. He was convinced that his actions would not ensure his admittance into heaven unless God bestowed His grace on him. He said to his Companions in this respect: 'No one's actions will be enough to ensure their admittance into heaven.' They asked: 'Not even you, Messenger of God?' He said: 'Not even me, unless God bestows His grace on me.' [Related by al-Bukhārī, Muslim and al-Nasā'ī.]

"None may feel totally secure from their Lord's punishment." (Verse 28) This statement suggests permanent awareness of God's punishment, because what incurs such punishment may occur at any moment. God does not require anything more than such awareness from people. Should they slip or succumb to weaknesses, His forgiveness and mercy are always available, and the door to repentance is always open. This is the middle course Islam charts between a total lack of awareness on the

one hand and excessive worry on the other. A believer's heart counters worry with hope, reassured of God's grace in all situations.

"Who guard their chastity except with those joined to them in marriage, or those whom they rightfully possess – for then, they are free of all blame, whereas those who seek to go beyond that [limit] are indeed transgressors." (Verses 29–31) This ensures purity for oneself and the community. Islam builds a community based on purity but with a clear and open approach. It ensures that all important functions are fulfilled and all natural desires are met but without chaos or perversion. A legitimate family, living openly in its home is the unit of Islamic society where every child knows his father and none is ashamed of its birth. In this way, sexual relations are based on a proper, clean, legitimate and long-lasting bond with clear objectives. They seek to fulfil human and social duties other than the satisfaction of a mere physical urge. Hence, the Qur'ān states this quality of believers here, making it clear that sex is permitted only with spouses or with women who are rightfully possessed.

A word needs to be said here concerning this second category, which refers to slave women, if they happen to lawfully exist in a Muslim society. The only lawful reason for their existence is their having been taken prisoner during a war fought for God's cause, which is the only legitimate war from an Islamic point of view. Islam lays down a ruling concerning prisoners of war, which is outlined in a verse of *Sūrah* 47, Muḥammad: *"Now when you meet the unbelievers in battle, smite their necks. Then when you have thoroughly subdued them, bind them firmly. Thereafter, set them free either by an act of grace or against ransom, until war shall lay down its burden."* (47: 4) Thus, the final ruling on prisoners of war is to set them free, either by an act of grace or against ransom. However, in some situations there may remain prisoners of war who are not set free. When such women slaves exist, sexual relations with them is permitted but only with their master. All the while, however, different ways of regaining their freedom are available to them. In fact, Islam provides many ways to ensure that slavery is abolished altogether. In all this, Islam is open, ensuring clean sexual relations in society. It does not leave such women prisoners of war to be the victims of rape and filthy and exploitative relations, as often happens elsewhere in war situations. Nor does it put a false tag on the situation, calling such women free when they are in fact slaves.

"*Those who seek to go beyond that [limit] are indeed transgressors.*" (Verse 31) Thus Islam closes the door on all dirty sexual relations, keeping only these two open forms as legitimate. According to Islam, sex is a legitimate and clean function to which dirt may attach when it is practised in an illegitimate or deviant way.[1]

"*Who are faithful to their trusts and to their pledges.*" (Verse 32) This is one of the basic moral qualities on which Islamic society is founded. The honouring of trust and pledges begins, according to Islam, with honouring the great trust that God offered to the heavens, the earth and the mountains but they refused to accept it, fearing that they would not be able to fulfil its commitments. Man however accepted it. This is the trust of faith and the fulfilment of its requirements out of choice but without compulsion. It also involves honouring the first pledge taken from man's nature, before birth, when this nature testifies to the truth of God's oneness. Faithfulness to all trusts and pledges in worldly transactions is founded on honouring this first trust and this first pledge. Islam repeatedly emphasizes the importance of such faithfulness, to trust, confirming its role in building its society on solid foundations. It considers such faithfulness a distinctive feature of a believer, whereas the opposite quality distinguishes unbelievers. This is often repeated in the Qur'ān and the *Sunnah*, leaving no room for doubt as to the importance Islam attaches to faithfulness.

"*Who stand up for the truth when they bear witness.*" (Verse 33) To bear witness and give testimony is, according to Islam, the basis of the fulfilment of many rights. Indeed, preventing any transgression of the bounds set by God can only be ensured on such a basis. Hence, God has rightly placed strong emphasis on bearing witness, without hesitation, and testifying when a dispute needs to be adjudged. When bearing witness, the truth must be stated without distortion or twisting. Indeed, God has

---

1. For further treatment please refer to comments on *Sūrah* 23, in Volume XII, pp. 193–195, and on *Sūrah* 47, in Volume XV, pp. 393–401

made bearing witness an act done for Him so as to link it to obedience of Him. He gives us the instruction: *"Bear witness before God."* (65: 2) Here, it is made a feature of believers. It is indeed one of the trusts that need to be fulfilled. It is given special mention in order to further emphasize its importance.

This list of believers' qualities started with attendance to prayers, and it now concludes with that same quality: *"And who attend to their prayers without fail."* (Verse 34) The earlier reference to prayer mentioned that it is always attended to. Now, the point at issue is that it is done *'without fail'*. The two points are not the same. Here, the emphasis is on offering prayers on time, performing the obligatory part and adding the voluntary one, adhering to its form and spirit. Believers are neither negligent of this, nor are they careless. Needless to say, mentioning prayer as the first and the last of believers' distinctive qualities confirms the importance attached to it.

At this point, the fate of this group is stated: *"They are the ones to be honoured in the gardens of paradise."* (Verse 35) This short verse combines an aspect of material enjoyment with a spiritual one. They are in gardens of paradise, but they are also honoured there. Thus, when they enjoy what is provided for them in paradise, they also enjoy being honoured for maintaining heir high moral standard.

The Unbelievers' Attitude

The *sūrah* then depicts a Makkan scene in which we see the unbelievers going hurriedly to where the Prophet was reading the Qur'ān. Once there, they would split into groups around him. The *sūrah* criticizes their hurrying and grouping when they had no intention of listening to or of heeding his advice:

What is wrong with the unbelievers, that they run confusedly before you, from the right and the left, in crowds? (Verses 36–37)

There is implied sarcasm in the question. It describes their confused movement, with the Arabic expression adding a connotation of their being led. The question wonders at their confusion: they move hurriedly, but without any intention of receiving guidance. They only want to learn what the Prophet says before splitting into small groups discussing how to resist what they have heard. What is wrong with them, then? *"Does every one of them hope to enter a garden of bliss?"* (Verse 38) How can they entertain such hopes when their behaviour leads only to hell, and not to heaven and its gardens of bliss? Do they think that they have a high position with God to ensure that they will enter heaven despite the fact that they disbelieve in Him, oppose the Prophet, scheme against Islam? They must imagine that they command very high value with God to achieve such elevation.

The answer is swift and decisive: *"No!"* It is delivered in the negative, implying contempt. *"We have created them from the substance they know."* (Verse 39) They are aware that they have been created from a humble fluid they know well enough. There is an implicit, yet profound touch here, destroying all their pride and arrogance without using a single objectionable word. Yet the verse is so expressed that it depicts a state of utter humiliation and ignominy. How can they hope to be in heaven when they disbelieve and commit evil deeds, knowing from what substance they are created? In God's measure, they are too lowly to hold favour with Him. Why would He waive His law of administering justice to all according to their deeds just for them?

Confirming their unimportance and lowly status, the *sūrah* states that God is able to replace them with better creatures. Furthermore, they cannot escape the punishment their actions deserve:

> *By the Lord of all star risings and settings, We certainly have the power to replace them with better people. There is nothing to prevent Us from doing so.* (Verses 40–41)

The point at issue needs no oath, but the mention of risings and settings reflects God's greatness. These movements may refer to the rise risings and settings of the millions upon millions of stars in the universe. On the other hand, this may be a reference to sunrise and sunset over every point on our planet. At every moment, there is a sunrise and a sunset, as the earth continues to revolve. Whichever the meaning intended, the mention of these risings and settings gives us a feeling of the greatness of the universe and the Almightiness of God who created the universe. Do those people, created from humble fluid, need an oath by the Lord of all star risings and settings to realize that He is able to create better people? Do they need an oath confirming that they cannot escape from Him?

The *sūrah* concludes with an address to the Prophet telling him to leave them to face their fate on that promised day. It shows their status then when they utterly distressed:

> *Leave them to indulge in idle talk and play until they face the day they have been promised, the day when they shall come in haste from their graves, as if rallying to a flag, with eyes downcast, with ignominy overwhelming them. Such is the day they have been promised.* (Verses 42–44)

This address implies a definite warning that should fill them with worry and anticipation. Indeed, the image describing them and their movements on that day should add intense fear. Moreover, it carries a clear element of sarcasm to parallel their pride and conceit. We see them coming out of their graves, hurrying on like people rallying to a flag or to a statue they worship. This is consistent with what they do in this life when they rally to flags and statues on festive days. Now they do the same, but there is no festivity on that day. Their description is completed by the statement, '*with ignominy overwhelming them.*' We can almost see their faces clearly through these words. We see them humiliated, overwhelmed by ignominy. They used to play and indulge in idle talk, but now they are exhausted, broken: "*Such is the day they have been promised.*" (Verse 44) That is the day they doubted would ever happen. Yet in their denial, they tried to hasten its arrival.

Thus the *sūrah* ends, with perfect harmony between its opening and end. It represents an episode in the long discussion of the major issue of resurrection, reckoning and requital, setting the Islamic concept of life in contrast with un-Islamic concepts.

SŪRAH 71

Nūḥ
(Noah)

Prologue

This *sūrah*, devoted to the story of Noah and his people, describes an important experience of advocacy of the divine message on earth. It represents a cycle in the consistent and permanent treatment of mankind, and of the ever-raging battle between good and evil, guidance and error, truth and falsehood. This episode depicts a humanity that is stubborn, hard, established in its ways, toeing the line drawn by arrogant leadership, unwilling to consider the guidance provided or to look at the pointers to faith. These are available everywhere in the universe and within people's own selves, recorded in the open book of the universe and in man's inner soul. At the same time, the *sūrah* shows an aspect of divine mercy represented in the fact that God sent messengers to rescue mankind from their stubborn rejection of guidance, and their blind following of arrogant and erroneous leadership.

The *sūrah* also paints a picture of the tireless efforts of God's messengers to provide erring humanity with guidance. They showed unparalleled patience despite all the adversity they had to contend with and when they had no personal interest in the matter: they did not expect any reward from those who benefited by their guidance, nor did they hope for any personal favour from those who attained faith as a result of their efforts. They received nothing like the fees charged by universities and educational institutes for the services they provide.

In this *sūrah*, Noah presents to God the final outcome of the 950 years he spent exerting such tireless efforts in advocating the divine faith among his people. Essentially, they had continued to arrogantly and stubbornly follow their leaders who, in turn, possessed wealth and power. His report, as outlined in the *sūrah* states: "*My Lord! I have been pleading with my people night and day, but the more I call them, the further they run away. Whenever I call on them, so that You may forgive them, they thrust their fingers into their ears, draw their garments over their heads, grow obstinate and become even more arrogant and insolent. I have called them openly; I have preached to them in public, and I spoke to them secretly, in private. I said: "Ask your Lord for forgiveness: He is ever forgiving. He will let loose the sky over you with abundance, and will give you wealth and children; and will provide you with gardens and rivers. What is the matter with you? Why do you behave with such insolence towards your Lord, when it is He who has created you in successive stages? Do you not see how God has created seven heavens in layers, placing in them the moon for a light and the sun for a lantern? God has made you spring from the earth like a plant, and He will return you into it and then bring you out again. God has made the earth a vast expanse for you, so that you may walk along its spacious paths.*" (Verses 5–20) Having thus outlined the efforts he made and the varied methods he employed in advocating the divine message among his people, Noah says: "*My Lord! They have disobeyed me and followed those whose wealth and children lead them increasingly into ruin. They have devised a mighty plot, and said to each other: "Do not ever renounce your gods! Do not abandon Wadd, Suwā', Yaghūth, Ya'ūq or Nasr. They have led many astray.*" (Verses 21–24)

The result is very negative. Yet a messenger's task remains the same: to advocate God's message.

This extremely difficult experience is shown to the Prophet Muḥammad (peace be upon him), who inherited the trust of advocating the divine message throughout the earth until the end of time and who shouldered the heaviest burden assigned to any prophet. He is shown how a former brother of his sought to establish the truth of faith on earth. He is, thus, able to see just how stubborn man can be in resisting the message of truth, and how corrupt deviant leadership can be and how it can overpower guided leadership. He learns of God's will to send messenger after messenger to provide mankind with guidance, and this despite all the stubborn and continuous rejection from as early as the days of Noah (peace be upon him).

This experience is shown to the Muslim community in Makkah, and to the Muslim community generally, because it is the heir to God's message to mankind. It is charged with implementing the code of life based on the divine message, even in the midst of the *jāhiliyyah* prevalent at the time, and in the midst of every subsequent *jāhiliyyah*. The Muslim community thus sees the picture of firm resolve represented by Noah, the second father of mankind, who struggled over such a long period of time, to present God's message. It sees the care God took of the small number of believers who accepted Noah's message and who were saved from the total destruction that engulfed their unbelieving fellows.

Noah's experience is also presented to the Makkan unbelievers, showing them the fate suffered by their unbelieving predecessors. They may thus realize that God has bestowed a great favour on them, sending them a kind Messenger who cares greatly for them. This Messenger does not appeal to God to destroy them as Noah did. It is God's grace that has determined that they will be given respite. Noah prayed to God to take away all unbelievers after he had exhausted all means, efforts and methods in calling on them to follow divine guidance. It was only at that juncture that he made his heartfelt appeal: "*And Noah said: 'Lord! Do not leave a single unbeliever on earth. If you spare them, they will lead Your servants astray and beget none but sinners and hardened unbelievers.*" (Verses 26–27)

In presenting this episode in the advocacy of God's message, the *sūrah* clearly shows the unity of the divine faith and its firm, unchanging roots, as well as its close link with the universe, God's will and life's events as they take place according to what God has determined. We see all this through what Noah says to his people by way of warning and instruction: "*He said: 'My people, I am here to warn you plainly. Worship God alone and fear Him, and obey me. He will forgive you your sins and grant you respite for an appointed term. When God's appointed*

term comes, it can never be put back, if you but knew it." (Verses 2–4)
We also see it as the *sūrah* quotes Noah saying to his people: "*What is
the matter with you? Why do you behave with such insolence towards your
Lord, when it is He who has created you in successive stages? Do you not see
how God has created seven heavens in layers, placing in them the moon for
a light and the sun for a lantern? God has made you spring from the earth
like a plant, and He will return you into it and then bring you out again.
God has made the earth a vast expanse for you, so that you may walk along
its spacious paths.*" (Verses 13–20)

Establishing this truth about the unity of God's message in the hearts
of the Muslim community is particularly important. It helps Muslims
to understand the truth of their message and that they descend from a
long line of believers starting from the very early days of humanity. It
also tells them of their role in advocating this message, which embodies
the code God has laid down for human life.

Why the Effort?

When we look at the great efforts exerted by God's messengers (peace
be upon them all) in presenting guidance to a stubbornly erroneous
humanity, and consider that it has been God's will to send them,
one after another, for this purpose, we should be nothing less than
overwhelmed.

One may well ask whether the results have justified such long efforts
and noble sacrifices, from Noah's early time through to Muhammad's
own time, as well as the intervening and subsequent efforts and sacrifices
made by believers in God's message. Nonetheless such efforts and
sacrifices have continuously been made and this in the face of ridicule
and abuse. Indeed some messengers faced burning in the fire or were cut
in halves with a saw, or had to flee their homeland and abandon their
families. When the final message was given, the Prophet Muhammad and
those who followed him made strenuous efforts to establish it. Further
efforts and sacrifices have been made by believers ever since. The question
is, then whether the results justify such efforts and sacrifices? Should
this struggle be maintained? Does humanity deserve such divine care?
Does this insignificant creature called man, so arrogant and stubborn

that he still resists the truth, deserve such care from God manifested in sending messenger after messenger?

The answer based on much thought and reflection is unarguably 'Yes, indeed.' To establish the truth of faith on earth merits all these efforts, struggles and sacrifices made by God's messengers and their followers throughout every generation. Perhaps the establishment of this truth is greater than man's existence, and greater than the earth and all who live on it. It is indeed greater than the universe in which the earth is no more than a little, hardly visible particle.

God has willed to create man with special qualities that make the establishment of this truth in his conscience and way of life dependent on his own human effort, with God's help and guidance. We do not know why God created man such, why He let his acquisition of faith be dependent on his own efforts, or why He made him neither a naturally obedient believer like the angels nor a completely evil, disobedient creature like Satan. We believe, however, that creating man with such a nature and qualities serves a divine purpose related to the creation of the universe and its operative system.

This means that human efforts are needed to establish the truth of faith in man's world. God has chosen some of the best of His servants to make such efforts. These are the prophets and the messengers, as well as select groups of true followers. These are the ones assigned the task of establishing this truth on earth; it deserves such strenuous efforts and great sacrifices. When this truth is firmly rooted in a human heart, then that heart enjoys a ray of God's light. It harbours one of His secrets and becomes a means for the fulfilment of His will, a will that will inevitably be done. All this is fact, not just a figure of speech. It is a truth that is greater than man and his world, and even the whole universe.

Moreover, the establishment of this truth in the life of humanity, or a section of it, provides a link between this earthly life of ours and eternal life. Thus, human life is elevated to maintain the link between what ends in death and what is eternal, between the part and the whole, between the defective and the absolutely perfect. Such a result is greater than all efforts and sacrifices, even though it may last for a day or part of one day during human life on earth. When this truth is thus established, it provides all generations of humanity with a lantern of true light. This lantern then takes practical form which it will strive to maintain.

History has repeatedly shown that humanity only attained the heights it is able to reach when the truth of God was established. No other means enabled mankind to reach such summits. Those periods in history when truth was so established, and its advocates were in leadership, were indeed the highest summits reached in human life. This was greater than man's ultimate dreams, yet it was a living reality. It is simply not possible for humanity to rise with the help of any philosophy, science, art, creed or system to the level it attained and can always attain through the establishment of faith in people's hearts, lives, morality, values and standards. This truth of faith provides the basis of a complete way of life, whether it is given in a general form as in the early messages, or in a very detailed one as is the case in its final version.

When humanity lost the leadership of true believers, it suffered depression, intellectual confusion and nervous ailments, despite its progress in all spheres of civilization. It might have had abundance of the means of physical comfort, intellectual enjoyment and material affluence, but it could not achieve true happiness.

Without doubt, then, the effort is worth it. We should strive with whatever we have and make what sacrifices are necessary to establish this truth of faith on earth. Mankind, however, will continue to turn away, as they did when they were addressed by Noah, Abraham, Moses, Jesus, Muḥammad and others of God's noble messengers. They will continue to follow those who lead them far astray. Their leadership will continue to persecute the advocates of faith, inflicting on them whatever brutal treatment they can. Yet despite all this, the divine message will continue along its way, as God wants it to be, because the outcome deserves it all, even though it is no more than a single heart receiving God's light.

The fact that messengers continued to be sent by God, from the time of Noah to the time of Muḥammad, (peace be upon both of them), confirms that it is God's will that advocacy of the divine faith should continue so that it produces its extraordinary results. The minimum result is that the truth of faith becomes well settled in the hearts of its advocates so that they hold firmly to it even though they may be exposed to death or what is worse than death. In this way, they will rise above all the lure of this life, and this by itself is a great gain for those advocates in person and for humanity as a whole. Indeed, humanity gains in honour through the presence of such people. It becomes worthy of the honour God gave it when He commanded the angels to prostrate themselves before Adam, the creature who corrupts the earth and sheds blood but who can, nevertheless, through his own efforts and sacrifices, become worthy of receiving a ray of God's light.

Nūḥ (Noah)

In the Name of God, the Lord of Grace, the Ever Merciful

We sent Noah to his people: 'Warn your people, before grievous suffering befalls them.' (1)

He said: 'My people, I am here to warn you plainly. (2)

Worship God alone and fear Him, and obey me. (3)

He will forgive you your sins and grant you respite for an appointed term. When God's appointed term comes, it can never be put back, if you but knew it.' (4)

He said: 'My Lord! I have been pleading with my people night and day, (5)

but the more I call them, the further they run away. (6)

Whenever I call on them, so that You may forgive them, they thrust their fingers into their ears, draw their garments over their heads, grow obstinate and become even more arrogant and insolent. (7)

بِسْمِ اللَّهِ الرَّحْمَٰنِ الرَّحِيمِ

إِنَّا أَرْسَلْنَا نُوحًا إِلَىٰ قَوْمِهِ أَنْ أَنذِرْ قَوْمَكَ مِن قَبْلِ أَن يَأْتِيَهُمْ عَذَابٌ أَلِيمٌ ۝١

قَالَ يَٰقَوْمِ إِنِّي لَكُمْ نَذِيرٌ مُّبِينٌ ۝٢

أَنِ اعْبُدُوا اللَّهَ وَاتَّقُوهُ وَأَطِيعُونِ ۝٣

يَغْفِرْ لَكُم مِّن ذُنُوبِكُمْ وَيُؤَخِّرْكُمْ إِلَىٰ أَجَلٍ مُّسَمًّى إِنَّ أَجَلَ اللَّهِ إِذَا جَاءَ لَا يُؤَخَّرُ لَوْ كُنتُمْ تَعْلَمُونَ ۝٤

قَالَ رَبِّ إِنِّي دَعَوْتُ قَوْمِي لَيْلًا وَنَهَارًا ۝٥

فَلَمْ يَزِدْهُمْ دُعَائِي إِلَّا فِرَارًا ۝٦

وَإِنِّي كُلَّمَا دَعَوْتُهُمْ لِتَغْفِرَ لَهُمْ جَعَلُوا أَصَٰبِعَهُمْ فِي آذَانِهِمْ وَاسْتَغْشَوْا ثِيَابَهُمْ وَأَصَرُّوا وَاسْتَكْبَرُوا اسْتِكْبَارًا ۝٧

In the Shade of the Qur'ān

I have called them openly; (8)

ثُمَّ إِنِّي دَعَوْتُهُمْ جِهَارًا ۝

I have preached to them in public, and I spoke to them secretly, in private. (9)

ثُمَّ إِنِّي أَعْلَنتُ لَهُمْ وَأَسْرَرْتُ لَهُمْ إِسْرَارًا ۝

I said: "Ask your Lord for forgiveness: He is ever forgiving. (10)

فَقُلْتُ اسْتَغْفِرُوا رَبَّكُمْ إِنَّهُ كَانَ غَفَّارًا ۝

He will let loose the sky over you with abundance, (11)

يُرْسِلِ السَّمَاءَ عَلَيْكُم مِّدْرَارًا ۝

and will give you wealth and children; and will provide you with gardens and rivers. (12)

وَيُمْدِدْكُم بِأَمْوَالٍ وَبَنِينَ وَيَجْعَل لَّكُمْ جَنَّاتٍ وَيَجْعَل لَّكُمْ أَنْهَارًا ۝

What is the matter with you? Why do you behave with such insolence towards your Lord, (13)

مَّا لَكُمْ لَا تَرْجُونَ لِلَّهِ وَقَارًا ۝

when it is He who has created you in successive stages? (14)

وَقَدْ خَلَقَكُمْ أَطْوَارًا ۝

Do you not see how God has created seven heavens in layers, (15)

أَلَمْ تَرَوْا كَيْفَ خَلَقَ اللَّهُ سَبْعَ سَمَاوَاتٍ طِبَاقًا ۝

placing in them the moon for a light and the sun for a lantern? (16)

وَجَعَلَ الْقَمَرَ فِيهِنَّ نُورًا وَجَعَلَ الشَّمْسَ سِرَاجًا ۝

God has made you spring from the earth like a plant, (17)

وَاللَّهُ أَنبَتَكُم مِّنَ الْأَرْضِ نَبَاتًا ۝

and He will return you into it and then bring you out again. (18)

ثُمَّ يُعِيدُكُمْ فِيهَا وَيُخْرِجُكُمْ إِخْرَاجًا ﴿١٨﴾

God has made the earth a vast expanse for you, (19)

وَٱللَّهُ جَعَلَ لَكُمُ ٱلْأَرْضَ بِسَاطًا ﴿١٩﴾

so that you may walk along its spacious paths."' (20)

لِتَسْلُكُوا مِنْهَا سُبُلًا فِجَاجًا ﴿٢٠﴾

Noah said: 'My Lord! They have disobeyed me and followed those whose wealth and children lead them increasingly into ruin. (21)

قَالَ نُوحٌ رَّبِّ إِنَّهُمْ عَصَوْنِي وَٱتَّبَعُوا مَن لَّمْ يَزِدْهُ مَالُهُ وَوَلَدُهُ إِلَّا خَسَارًا ﴿٢١﴾

They have devised a mighty plot, (22)

وَمَكَرُوا مَكْرًا كُبَّارًا ﴿٢٢﴾

and said to each other: "Do not ever renounce your gods! Do not abandon Wadd, Suwāʿ, Yaghūth, Yaʿūq or Nasr." (23)

وَقَالُوا لَا تَذَرُنَّ ءَالِهَتَكُمْ وَلَا تَذَرُنَّ وَدًّا وَلَا سُوَاعًا وَلَا يَغُوثَ وَيَعُوقَ وَنَسْرًا ﴿٢٣﴾

They have led many astray. Lord, grant the wrongdoers increase in nothing but error.' (24)

وَقَدْ أَضَلُّوا كَثِيرًا وَلَا تَزِدِ ٱلظَّالِمِينَ إِلَّا ضَلَالًا ﴿٢٤﴾

Because of their sins, they were drowned, and were made to enter the fire. They found none besides God to support them. (25)

مِّمَّا خَطِيٓـَٔاتِهِمْ أُغْرِقُوا فَأُدْخِلُوا نَارًا فَلَمْ يَجِدُوا لَهُم مِّن دُونِ ٱللَّهِ أَنصَارًا ﴿٢٥﴾

And Noah said: 'Lord! Do not leave a single unbeliever on earth. (26)

وَقَالَ نُوحٌ رَّبِّ لَا تَذَرْ عَلَى ٱلْأَرْضِ مِنَ ٱلْكَافِرِينَ دَيَّارًا ﴿٢٦﴾

| If You spare them, they will lead Your servants astray and beget none but sinners and hardened unbelievers. (27) | إِنَّكَ إِن تَذَرْهُمْ يُضِلُّوا۟ عِبَادَكَ وَلَا يَلِدُوٓا۟ إِلَّا فَاجِرًۭا كَفَّارًۭا ۝ |
| My Lord! Forgive me, my parents and everyone who enters my house as a believer. Forgive all believing men and women. To the wrongdoers grant You no increase except in perdition.' (28) | رَّبِّ ٱغْفِرْ لِى وَلِوَٰلِدَىَّ وَلِمَن دَخَلَ بَيْتِىَ مُؤْمِنًۭا وَلِلْمُؤْمِنِينَ وَٱلْمُؤْمِنَـٰتِ وَلَا تَزِدِ ٱلظَّـٰلِمِينَ إِلَّا تَبَارًۢا ۝ |

The Message in Brief

The *sūrah* begins with a statement defining the source of this message of divine faith: "*We sent Noah to his people.*" (Verse 1) This is the source that assigns tasks to God's messengers and from whom they learn the truth of faith. It is the source of all existence and all life. It is He who created mankind, giving their nature the ability to know and worship Him. When they deviated from this straight path, He sent them messengers to bring them back to Him. Noah was the first of these messengers after Adam. The Qur'ān does not mention a message given to Adam after his fall to earth and life thereon. Perhaps he was a teacher who taught his children and grandchildren. With the passage of time, they went astray and adopted idols as deities. These were at first symbols of certain forces they considered holy. Then, they forgot what the symbols signified and worshipped the idols themselves. The most important of those idols were the five mentioned in this *sūrah*. God sent them Noah to bring them back to believing in His oneness and give them the right concept of God, life and existence. Earlier scriptures mention Idrīs as a messenger of God prior to Noah. However, what such scriptures mention is not part of the Islamic faith, because they were subject to distortion, addition and omission.

When we read the stories of earlier prophets given in the Qur'ān, we tend to believe that Noah lived when humanity was still in its dawn period. He spent 950 years of his life advocating God's message to his people who must have lived a similarly long life. This suggests that humans were still few in number. In saying this we draw on the observation that species that are small in number live long, and that the reverse is true. Perhaps this is a rule of balance. This is merely a personal point of view, but God knows best.

Having established the source of the message, the *surah* sums it up in a few words, and we learn that Noah was instructed to deliver a warning: "*Warn your people, before grievous suffering befalls them.*" (Verse 1) The report Noah presents to his Lord, as stated in the *surah*, shows that the state in which he found his people, heedless and arrogant, makes warning the sum of his message. In fact, the first thing he does by means of advocacy is to warn them of severe punishment, in either this world or the next, or in both.

The *surah* moves straight from assigning the task to its fulfilment, in which the delivery of the warning is prominent. However, this is coupled with a note that raises the hope of the forgiveness of past sins and the deferment of reckoning until the Day of Resurrection. Moreover, the *surah* gives a brief outline of the message Noah delivered to his people:

> He said: 'My people, I am here to warn you plainly. Worship God alone and fear Him, and obey me. He will forgive you your sins and grant you respite for an appointed term. When God's appointed term comes, it can never be put back, if you but knew it. (Verses 2–4)

"*My people, I am here to warn you plainly.*" (Verse 2) He immediately states his role as a warner, clearly explaining his argument. He does not hesitate or wrap his words in a false cover. He leaves no one in confusion as to what he has to say, or what those who reject his message can expect. What he calls for is plain and simple: "*Worship God alone and fear Him, and obey me.*" (Verse 3) All worship must be addressed to God alone, without partners. Fearing God should be the quality that is clearly reflected in feeling and behaviour. Obeying the messenger God sends to a people is the attitude that makes His orders the basis on which they build their way of life and how they determine their rules of behaviour.

These are the broad lines of divine faith in general, but messages may differ in points of detail as also in the concepts they outline, their relative scopes and how profound and comprehensive these are. To worship God alone provides a complete system of life that includes how man visualizes the nature of the Godhead and the nature of servitude to Him, the bond between the Creator and His creatures, as well as the nature of forces and values that operate in the universe and affect human life. Hence, a system for human life is developed on the basis of this concept, giving a special code of living. This code is based on the bond between God and His servants, and on the values He assigns to all things.

To be God-fearing is the true guarantee that people will follow this code of living, abide by it and never try to circumvent it or slacken in its implementation. Moreover, it is the quality that ensures sound moral behaviour that seeks no reward other than being acceptable to God. Moreover, obeying God's messenger is the means that ensures remaining consistent, receiving guidance from its original source. It maintains the link with heaven through the messenger who receives instructions from on high.

These were the broad lines that constituted what Noah called on his people to believe in. They remain the essence of the divine faith for every generation. God promised them in reward what He promises those who turn to Him in repentance: *"He will forgive you your sins and grant you respite for an appointed term."* (Verse 4) This verse states the reward promised for those who respond to the call to worship God alone, fear Him and obey His messenger. The reward is forgiveness of past sins, a respite lasting until the time appointed for reckoning, which means until the Day of Judgement, so that they will not be punished in this life like other communities that were totally destroyed. Later in the *sūrah*, we see that Noah promised his people certain other things to be granted in this life.

Noah also confirms that this appointed time is inevitable: it comes at the moment determined for it. It will not be postponed like the delayed punishment in this world: *"When God's appointed term comes, it can never be put back, if you but knew it."* (Verse 4) This statement may be understood to apply to every time appointed by God, so as to make this fact clear in their minds. It occurs at the appropriate place here, within the context of the promise that the reckoning will be deferred to the Day of Judgement if they heeded Noah's advice.

Untiring Efforts

Noah began his noble efforts to present guidance to his people. He had no personal interest in the matter, and stood to make no gain to compensate for all the arrogance and ridicule he had to put up with. He continued to do this for a thousand years minus fifty, with the number of those who responded positively hardly increasing. On the other hand, however, the level of rejection and insistence on following old erring ways did increase. At the end, Noah presented his account to God, who had assigned him this arduous task. He described his efforts even though he knew that God was fully aware of all that he had done. He is, therefore, simply making his heart-felt complaint to God, the only One to whom prophets, messengers and true believers ever complain:

> *My Lord! I have been pleading with my people night and day, but the more I call them, the further they run away. Whenever I call on them, so that You may forgive them, they thrust their fingers into their ears, draw their garments over their heads, grow obstinate and become even more arrogant and insolent. I have called them openly; I have preached to them in public, and I spoke to them secretly, in private. I said: 'Ask your Lord for forgiveness: He is ever forgiving. He will let loose the sky over you with abundance, and will give you wealth and children; and will provide you with gardens and rivers. What is the matter with you? Why do you behave with such insolence towards your Lord, when it is He who has created you in successive stages? Do you not see how God has created seven heavens in layers, placing in them the moon for a light and the sun for a lantern? God has made you spring from the earth like a plant, and He will return you into it and then bring you out again. God has made the earth a vast expanse for you, so that you may walk along its spacious paths.'* (Verses 5–20)

Thus, Noah describes his untiring efforts at the end of his long, long journey: *"My Lord! I have been pleading with my people night and day."*

(Verse 5) He never slackened or showed any sign of boredom or despair in the face of determined and increasing opposition: *"but the more I call them, the further they run away."* (Verse 6) They ran away from the messenger who called on them to believe in God, the Giver of life, the Provider of everything they had and the Source of every light and guidance. Yet this messenger from whom they ran away never asked for anything in return for what he presented or taught them. He only called on them to believe so that they might be forgiven their sins.

When they could not physically run away, because he addressed them face to face, taking every opportunity to make his address heard, they loathed listening to him or even looking at him. They turned away in arrogance, intent on following their erring ways. *"Whenever I call on them, so that You may forgive them, they thrust their fingers into their ears, draw their garments over their heads, grow obstinate and become even more arrogant and insolent."* (Verse 7) In this scene the advocate of the divine faith is seen using every opportunity to deliver his message, while they remain adamant, unwilling to hear. We see humanity here in its early stages, stubborn like a headstrong child, putting its fingers in its ears so that it does not hear, and covering its head and face. It is an image of childish resistance. The *sūrah* says they '*thrust their fingers into their ears*', yet people can only put the tips of their fingers into their ears. The statement, thus, imparts an impression of violent reaction, as if they wanted to put their whole fingers into their ears to ensure that nothing of Noah's words could be heard. How childish!

Provisions in Abundance

In his strenuous efforts to fulfil his mission, Noah used every method, addressing them openly at times, and speaking to them in private on others: *"I have called them openly; I have preached to them in public, and I spoke to them secretly, in private."* (Verses 8–9) In all this, he put before them immeasurable gains both in this life and in the life to come. The first prospect he put before them was forgiveness of their sins: *"I said: Ask your Lord for forgiveness: He is ever forgiving."* (Verse 10) He also put before them the prospect of abundant provisions to be granted through rain pouring down in plenty, so that plants can grow and rivers run. He also added other types of God's grace, ones they loved dearly: children and wealth: *"He will let loose the sky over you with abundance, and will give you wealth and children; and will provide you with gardens and rivers."* (Verses 11–12)

Noah linked granting such provisions to seeking God's forgiveness of sins and misdeeds. This correlation between following God's guidance and attaining purity of heart on the one hand and a life of plenty and prosperity on the other is stated in several places in the Qur'ān: *"had the people of those cities believed and been God-fearing, We would indeed have opened up for them blessings out of heaven and earth. But they disbelieved, so We smote them on account of what they had been doing."* (7: 96) *"If only the people of earlier revelations would believe and be God-fearing, We should indeed efface their [past] bad deeds, and bring them into gardens of bliss. If they would observe the Torah and the Gospel and all that has been revealed to them by their Lord, they would indeed be given abundance from above and from beneath."* (5: 65–66) *"Worship none but God. I come to you from Him as a warner and a bearer of glad tidings. Seek forgiveness of your Lord, and then turn towards Him in repentance, and He will grant you a goodly enjoyment of life for an appointed term. He will grant everyone with merit a full reward for his merit."* (11: 2–3)

This is, then, a true rule repeatedly stated in the Qur'ān. It is based on certain conditions involving a promise by God and the rules He set for human life. History confirms its fulfilment during different generations. The rule applies to communities and nations, not to individuals. Every community that implemented God's law, truly looking up to Him, doing good and beneficial deeds and seeking His forgiveness in a way that reflected fearing Him, benefited by this promise. Every community that worshipped God and feared Him, implementing His law and establishing justice and security for all people, was given provisions in plenty and a life of strength and affluence.

Having said this, we realize that some communities are left to enjoy a life of power and prosperity, despite the fact that they are far from being God-fearing or following His guidance. This is merely a test: *"We test you all with evil and good by way of trial."* (21: 35) Moreover, such prosperity is often accompanied by different ills such as the lack of social cohesion, loose morality, injustice, disregard for human dignity, etc. We see today two superpowers,[1] seemingly enjoying power and plentiful provisions: one of them is capitalist while the other communist. In the first, morality has sunk to the lowest level. The prevailing vision of life has become so low that all life has become materialistic, measured by the dollar. In the other, the value of man has gone below the level of slavery. Intelligence agencies have become too powerful and people live in constant fear, threatened in their own homes. Several massacres have taken place, and no one is assured that by the morning his head will remain in place. A false allegation can easily find it chopped off. Neither condition can be described as a truly prosperous human life.

We continue with Noah and his untiring efforts. We see him trying to turn people's attentions to the signs pointing to God, be these from within themselves or in the world around them. He wonders at their carelessness and rudeness: *"What is the matter with you? Why do you behave with such insolence towards your Lord, when it is He who has created you in successive stages?"* (Verses 13–14)

These stages of creation to which Noah refers must have been something which people either knew about or could understand at that time. He is obviously reminding them of something they know and hopes will have the desired effect of leading them to a positive response. Most commentators on the Qur'ān say that the expression refers to the different stages the embryo goes through, starting with a gamete, then becoming a clinging cell mass, before it becomes a human embryo, and acquires a skeleton and is subsequently given its full shape and form. Noah's people could understand this because pregnant women suffered abortions at different stages of pregnancy, thus giving man a clear idea of how the human grows. This is one interpretation of the statement. It could also be a reference to what embryology says about the creation of man. It starts like a one-celled creature, then becomes like a multi-celled creature before acquiring the form of a water animal, then it becomes like a mammal, before it acquires human shape. This was however far from comprehensible to Noah's people, being only a very recent discovery. This interpretation may be the meaning of another Qur'ānic statement that mentions the stages of the embryo before saying: *"We then bring this*

---

1. This is a reference to the USA and the Soviet Union. – Editor's note.

into being as another creation." (23: 14) Both statements, however, may mean something else that remains beyond our present knowledge. Be that as it may, Noah draws the attention of his people to look at their creation and how it is done in stages. He reproaches them for knowing this and yet remaining insolent in their attitude towards their Lord. This is all very singular.

Signs in Plenty

Noah directs his people's attention to the open book of the universe: *"Do you not see how God has created seven heavens in layers, placing in them the moon for a light and the sun for a lantern?"* (Verses 15–16) We cannot specify a meaning for the *'seven heavens'* on the basis of scientific theories about the universe, for these are only theories. Noah simply draws their attention to the skies. He tells them, as God taught him, that there are seven heavens in layers, and that they include the sun and the moon, which they could obviously see, just as they saw what they called the sky, which is that familiar blue coloured space. To know what it is exactly is not necessary. Nor has it been properly proven even today. The invitation to look though is enough to reflect on the supreme power that has brought such great creatures into existence. This is what Noah wanted his people to do. He then invites them to look at their own creation, starting from dust and returning to it after death, and emphasizing the truth of resurrection: *"God has made you spring from the earth like a plant, and He will return you into it and then bring you out again."* (Verses 17–18)

The reference to man originating from the earth like a plant is both amazing and inspiring. It is repeated in the Qur'ān in various forms: *"Good land brings forth its vegetation in abundance, by its Lord's leave, but from the bad land only poor and scant vegetation comes forth."* (7: 58) This verse refers to the similarity of the origin of both man and vegetation. Both are referred to in the same verse stressing the truth of resurrection: *"Mankind! If you are in doubt as to the resurrection, remember that We have created you out of dust, then out of a gamete, then out of a clinging cell mass, then out of an organized and unorganized embryo, so that We might make things clear to you. We cause to rest in the [mothers'] wombs whatever*

We please for an appointed term, and then We bring you forth as infants, that you may grow up and attain your prime. Some of you die young, and some live on to abject old age when all that they once knew they know no more. You can see the earth dry and barren; and [suddenly,] when We send down water upon it, it stirs and swells and puts forth every kind of radiant bloom." (22: 5) In the following *sūrah*,[2] the stages of the embryo are outlined in similar terms to the verse above. It is then followed by this statement: *"And by means of this water We bring forth for you gardens of date-palms and vines."* (23: 19)

This is certainly worth studying. It suggests that the origins of life on earth are the same, and that the making of man is the same as the making of plants. Man is made of the earth's simple elements and feeds on such elements to grow. Thus, he is a plant like the rest of earth's plants. He is given a form of life different from that of plants, but both originate from mother earth, which suckles them both. We see how faith gives a believer a complete and true concept of his relation to the earth and to other living things. This concept combines scientific accuracy with warm feelings, which is the distinctive mark of true Qur'ānic knowledge.

Those people who came out of the earth will go back into it, because God determines so, just like He brought them into being out of it. Their ashes become mixed with its dust and they become part of it again, just as they were before. Then again, God will bring them out like He did the first time. It is a simple matter that does not require a moment's hesitation if we only look at it from this Qur'ānic angle. Noah points out this truth to his people so that they feel how God's hand lets them grow out of the earth like plants do, and then returns them there. Once they do this, they can easily expect the second life and take it into account. It is so simple and easy, needing no further argument.

Finally, Noah directs his people's hearts to reflect on God's blessing as He enabled them to live easily on earth, conducting their various activities with ease and comfort: *"God has made the earth a vast expanse for you, so that you may walk along its spacious paths."* (Verses 19–20) This reality is so close to them and they see it all the time in full view. They cannot escape it like they tried to escape from Noah and his warnings.

---

2. In verse 14 of *Sūrah* 23, The Believers.

In relation to them, the earth is stretched out like a vast expanse. Even in its mountains, God placed paths that are easy for them to traverse. They walk and travel even more easily on the plains. They can thus move about seeking God's bounty, and exchanging goods and benefits. They did not need scientific studies that sought to understand the natural laws that govern and facilitate their life on earth in order to appreciate all this. Indeed, the greater human knowledge gets the more evident the truth of this statement is.

Varied Methods

We see how Noah tried to address his people in various ways, employing a wide range of methods. We also see his patience, perseverance and conscientiousness. He continued to exert these efforts over 950 years before giving this report to his Lord, complaining of the response he had had to contend with. From his succinct and accurate account we see a splendid image of the great efforts he made. Yet all this is merely one ring in the chain of divine messages to mankind. So, what happens next?

> Noah said: 'My Lord! They have disobeyed me and followed those whose wealth and children lead them increasingly into ruin. They have devised a mighty plot, and said to each other: "Do not ever renounce your gods! Do not abandon Wadd, Suwāʿ, Yaghūth, Yaʿūq or Nasr." They have led many astray. Lord, grant the wrongdoers increase in nothing but error.' (Verses 21–24)

It is a heart-felt complaint. After all Noah's endeavours, guidance and sound advice and the promise of an easy, plentiful life, they chose to disobey and follow the lead of those who had gone far astray, only because the latter enjoyed wealth, children and power. Yet such leaders benefit nothing by all these blessings. Indeed, their *"wealth and children lead them increasingly into ruin."* (Verse 21) What they possessed of wealth and children tempted them to go further astray, a scenario that could only end in misery and ruin. Yet these leaders did not stop at just going astray. Instead: *"They have devised a mighty plot."* (Verse 22)

285

Their plot was on a grand scale, and its aim was to foil Noah's efforts, to suppress his message and to prevent it from addressing people's hearts. They schemed to give their disbelief and ignorance an attractive colour. Therefore, they urged people to adhere to their false beliefs and to continue to worship those idols whom they called gods. They "*said to each other: 'Do not ever renounce your gods!'*" They sought to arouse people's personal emotions, making them feel that these idols were 'their own' gods. They mentioned the names of the most important ones, so as to stir people's false pride in them: "*Do not abandon Wadd, Suwā', Yaghūth, Ya'ūq or Nasr.*" (Verse 23) These were indeed the largest and the most important of their idols. Indeed, they continued to be worshipped in other ignorant communities until the time of the Islamic message.

This remains the practice of erring leaderships. They create idols that may differ in name and form, according to the going trends in different *jāhiliyyah* societies. They seek to rally the masses around such idols and stir their emotions to defend them so that they can lead them wherever they want to, ensuring that they remain in error. This is how they manage to lead people astray: "*They have led many astray.*" (Verse 24) Indeed every type of erring leadership tries to rally the people around idols, which may be in the form of statues, or humans or ideas. They are all the same, manipulated to turn people away from the divine message, creating a schism between them and its advocates. It is all part of a grand scheme, a mighty plot with a selfish end.

Noah's Prayer

A passionate prayer is then voiced by Noah against the oppressors, the wrongdoers who lead people astray through plots and schemes of their own devising: "*Lord, grant the wrongdoers increase in nothing but error.*" (Verse 24) It is the prayer of one who has tried for a long time, making every effort and using every method. Eventually, however, he came to the conclusion that those erring, wrongdoing hearts were altogether devoid of goodness, undeserving of divine guidance.

Before completing Noah's prayer, the *sūrah* gives us an image of the end suffered by those wrongdoers in this life and in the life to come.

Both situations are present in God's knowledge. They are events that admit no change:

Because of their sins, they were drowned, and were made to enter the fire. They found none besides God to support them. (Verse 25)

It is because of their sins and disobedience that they were made to drown and enter the fire. The two events are intentionally joined in succession, because their entry into the fire is connected to their drowning. The time gap between the two is so short that it is almost non-existent; according to God's measures it is negligible. The sequence is there: they were drowned in this life and they are made to enter the fire in the life to come. What is in between is perhaps the torment in the grave during the short gap between the two lives. "*They found none besides God to support them.*" (Verse 25) None whatsoever! No children, no wealth, no power and no patron from among their alleged deities.

In a single short verse, these mighty ones are swept away and no mention is left of them in human memory. No details are given here of their drowning or the floods that swept them away. This because the *sūrah* wants to leave us with the impression of swift punishment. Indeed, it covers the gap between their drowning and their entry into hell with the conjunction *fa*, rendered in translation as 'and'. This is a common feature of the inimitable Qur'ānic style. Therefore, we do not go into any further details of this event here.

The *sūrah* then gives the remainder of Noah's passionate prayer:

And Noah said: 'Lord! Do not leave a single unbeliever on earth. If You spare them, they will lead Your servants astray and beget none but sinners and hardened unbelievers. My Lord! Forgive me, my parents and everyone who enters my house as a believer. Forgive all believing men and women. To the wrongdoers grant You no increase except in perdition.' (Verses 26–28)

In his heart of hearts, Noah felt that the earth needed to have a complete change, a change that would eradicate the evil that had become so deeply entrenched among his people. Sometimes, only such eradication of the wrongdoers from the face of the earth will suffice. Their continued presence may put the divine message under siege, preventing it from touching people's hearts. This is exactly the scenario Noah states in his appeal to God to destroy these tyrannical oppressors, leaving none of them to walk the earth. He says: "*If You spare them, they will lead Your servants astray.*" (Verse 27) Describing those people forced to go astray as '*Your servants*' suggests that they are the believers. This is a reference to how such wrongdoers will always use brute force to turn people away from divine faith. He may also mean that they lead others astray when people see them enjoying power and authority, without being punished for their wrongdoing.

Moreover, they create an environment in which unbelievers are born and reared. This whole environment of unbelief and its determined rejection of God's message leaves no way for the young to see the light. It overwhelms them with its erroneous beliefs and practices. It is to this fact that Noah, God's noble messenger, refers when he says that these wrongdoers will, "*beget none but sinners and hardened unbelievers.*" (Verse 27) They create within the community an atmosphere based on falsehood and establish systems, traditions and situations that only help to lead the young into sin and disbelief. Thus, the new generation will always be composed of '*sinners and hardened unbelievers*', as Noah said.

It is for this reason that Noah made his sweeping appeal to God, and God answered his prayer, washing that evil off the face of the earth. Noah ended his appeal against the unbelievers by a request to God to increase their ruin: "*To the wrongdoers grant You no increase except in perdition.*" (Verse 28)

Noah also made a different sort of passionate and humble appeal to God: "*My Lord! Forgive me, my parents and everyone who enters my house as a believer. Forgive all believing men and women.*" (Verse 28) His prayer that God forgives him his sins is an aspect of the good manners all prophets maintain when addressing God. Noah knows that he is only a human being appealing to God. He knows that no matter how diligent he is in his obedience and worship, he makes mistakes and remains short of the high standard believers should try to attain. He also realizes the truth the Prophet Muḥammad (peace be upon him) later expressed when he said that no human being, not even a prophet, is admitted into heaven on the basis of his actions only, unless God bestows His grace on him. This appeal for forgiveness is exactly what he called upon his people to do, but they were too arrogant to take heed. Yet Noah, God's noble messenger who has untiringly sought to advocate God's message, seeks God's forgiveness at the moment he presents his account.

His prayer for his parents is an aspect of dutifulness towards parents who are believers. This is what we understand from the fact that he prayed for them. Had they been unbelievers, he would have been told not to pray for their forgiveness, as he was told that his son, an unbeliever, met his merited fate when he was drowned with the rest of the unbelievers. This is clearly mentioned in *Sūrah* 11, Hūd.

His special prayer for everyone who entered his home as a believer marks the mutual love between believers. Everyone loves for others to receive the same grace as he receives. This special mention of those who enter his home refers to the fact that they were the ones to be saved from the floods; they were the ones on the Ark with him.

Noah's final prayer is for the forgiveness of all believing men and women throughout all generations and localities. It emphasizes the close bond that unites them all, different as their communities and times may be. This is a remarkable quality of the divine faith, establishing this strong bond of genuine love between all believers across the centuries. It tells of the hidden secret God has incorporated into the divine faith and placed in believers' hearts.

Contrasted with this love among believers is the genuine aversion expressed towards unbelievers: "*To the wrongdoers grant You no increase except in perdition.*" (Verse 28)

In this way does the *sūrah* conclude after having given us a bright picture of Noah's struggle, as contrasted with the unbelievers' stubborn rejection. It leaves us with feelings of love towards this great prophet, and admiration for his hard struggle. It strengthens our resolve to follow the same route no matter what hardship we have to endure and no matter what sacrifices we are called upon to make. It is the only route that ensures mankind attains the highest standard possible in their life on earth.

SŪRAH 72

Al-Jinn
(The Jinn)

Prologue

This *sūrah* presents us with something very clear even before we look at any of the specific ideas it tackles. It is a symphony ringing out clear, strong beats coupled with an air of calm sadness and reflective sorrow. Consistent with this phenomenon are the images and scenes the *sūrah* portrays and the inspiring statements it includes, particularly in its last passage after the *jinn* concluded their discourse. In this last part, the *sūrah* addresses the Prophet in a way that fills the listener with much sympathy. He is commanded to declare that he looks for nothing in respect of his message other than delivering it, and that he is closely watched by God as he goes about this task: "*Say: 'I invoke my Lord alone, and I associate no partners with Him.' Say: 'It is not in my power to cause you harm or to set you on the right course.' Say: 'No one can ever protect me from God, nor can I ever find a place to hide from Him. My task is only to deliver what I receive from God and His messages.' Whoever disobeys God and His Messenger will have the fire of hell, where they will abide for ever. When they see what they have been promised, they will realize who has the lesser help and is smaller in number. Say: 'I do not know whether that which you have been promised is imminent, or whether my Lord has set for it a distant term. He alone knows that which is beyond the reach of human perception, and He does not disclose His secrets to anyone except to a messenger whom He has been pleased to choose. He then sends watchers to walk before and behind him, to know that they have delivered their Lord's messages. He has full knowledge of all they have. He takes count of everything.'* (Verses 20–28)

In addition, the *sūrah* delivers a special and psychological effect in its lucid presentation of what the *jinn* said and the truth included in their account. This truth is of great significance, inviting much reflection and contemplation. It also suits the sad overtone evident in the *sūrah's* rhythm. It only needs to be read rather slowly to impart the feeling we have just outlined.

Support from Another World

The *sūrah* presents a testimony to the truth of many aspects of the divine faith from a different world, a world beyond that of man. These aspects were the subject of much argument by the unbelievers who either denied them or who arrived at assumptions lacking any supporting evidence. The unbelievers in Makkah sometimes alleged that Muḥammad (peace be upon him) was in contact with the *jinn* who taught him what to say about faith. Now, a group of the *jinn* give their testimony, stating that they did not know anything about the Qur'ān until they listened to Muḥammad (peace be upon him) reciting it, and that they were then overwhelmed by its powerful truth. In fact, its effect on them was so profound that they could not remain silent. They had to speak in detail about what they had heard and felt. Their discourse reflects their total amazement at this great event with its lasting effects on the heavens, the earth, humans, *jinn*, angels and stars. Indeed, its effects cover the entire universe. Their testimony undoubtedly has a strong effect on man too.

Moreover, the *jinn's* statement corrects many aspects of superstition upheld by those addressed by the *sūrah* for the first time, and by many other people across successive generations. It presents clear facts about this type of God's creatures, without any exaggeration. The Arabs who were the first to be addressed by the Qur'ān believed that the *jinn* exercised much power on earth. When an Arab found himself at night in a valley or an open plain, he would seek shelter with the *jinnee* of that place, saying: "I seek shelter with the master of this valley against the designs of the wicked elements among his people." When he had said so, he could then sleep in peace. They also believed that the *jinn* had knowledge of *ghayb*, or what lies beyond the reach of human perception. They would give information to soothsayers who would then make predictions. Some Arabs worshipped the *jinn*, alleging that they were related to God. Some suggested that God had a wife from among the *jinn* and that she gave birth to angels.

Belief in the *jinn* on lines similar to these is widespread in all *jāhiliyyah* societies. Indeed, some legends and superstitions about them continue to be spread in different environments, even in the present day.

While such superstitions used to circulate widely, giving people different ideas and concepts about them, there were also other people who denied their existence altogether. They described any talk about the *jinn* as superstitious. Therefore, Islam sets the record straight. It confirms their existence and corrects wrong ideas about them, freeing people from the shackles of fear about the *jinn* and submission to their alleged authority.

The *jinn* do exist. They describe themselves in this *sūrah* in the following words: "*Some among us are righteous and others less so: we follow widely divergent paths.*" (Verse 11) Some go astray and lead people astray, while others are naïve and can easily be deceived: "*Some foolish ones among us have been saying some outrageous things about God. Yet we had thought that no man or* jinn *would ever utter a lie about God.*" (Verses 4–5) They are susceptible to divine guidance, able to listen to the Qur'ān, understand it and be affected by it: "*Say: It has been revealed to me that a group of the* jinn *listened in and then said: 'We have heard a wondrous discourse, giving guidance to what is sagacious, and we have come to believe in it. We shall never associate partners with our Lord.*" (Verses 1–2) By their nature, they can be punished, and the results of belief and unbelief can affect them: "*When we heard the guidance, we came to believe in it. Whoever believes in his Lord need never fear loss or injustice. Some of us submit to Him and others are unfair. Those who submit to God are the ones who have endeavoured to attain what is right. But those who are unfair will be the fuel of hellfire.*" (Verses 13–15) When humans appeal to them, they cannot benefit them; on the contrary,

293

they increase their affliction: "*True, in the past some among mankind sought refuge with some of the* jinn, *but they caused them further trouble.*" (Verse 6) They have no knowledge of the realm beyond their perception, and they no longer have any contact with heaven: "*We tried to reach heaven, but found it full of mighty guards and shooting stars. We used to take up positions there to listen, but whoever tries to listen now will find a shooting star in wait for him. We do not know if this bodes evil for those who live on earth, or if their Lord intends to guide them to what is right.*" (Verses 8–10) They have no relation to God Almighty: "*Sublimely exalted is the glory of our Lord! He has taken to Himself neither consort nor son.*" (Verse 3) They have no power to resist God's will: "*We know that we can never elude God on earth, and we can never elude Him by flight.*" (Verse 12)

We learn all this about the *jinn* from what is mentioned in this *sūrah*. Some of their other characteristics are mentioned elsewhere in the Qur'ān. For example, there is the reference to those of them who were made subservient to the Prophet Solomon. They did not know of his death until sometime after it occurred, which confirms that they have no knowledge of what is beyond their faculties of perception: "*When We decreed his death, nothing showed them that he was dead except an earthworm that gnawed away at his staff. And when he fell to the ground, the* jinn *saw clearly that, had they understood the reality which was beyond [their] perception, they would not have remained in humiliating servitude.*" (34: 14) The Qur'ān also refers to a quality of *Iblīs* and his folk. *Iblīs*, or Satan, belonged to the *jinn*, but he is devoted totally to evil, corruption and tempting others to do evil: "*Surely, he and his tribe watch you from where you cannot perceive them.*" (7: 27) This implies that the *jinn* have a form that humans cannot see, while they can see us. In addition, *Sūrah* 55, The Lord of Grace, states from which substances the *jinn* and human beings are created: "*He created man from dried clay, like pottery, and created the* jinn *from raging flames of fire.*" (55: 14–15) All this gives us a clear picture of this species that is concealed from us. It confirms its existence and gives us many of its characteristics. At the same time, it shows as false many of the ideas and superstitions people held about these creatures. It gives us a clear and accurate picture of them, one that is free of wild conjecture.

The *sūrah* corrects what the Arab unbelievers and other people used to say about the *jinn*, believing that they had exceptional powers and a large role to play in the universe. Others who have denied the existence of these creatures outright, mocking anyone who so believes, do not tell us the basis of their denial. Do they claim that they know every type of creature in the universe and cannot find the *jinn* among them? No scientist has ever made such a claim. The earth contains many species of creation which are discovered from time to time. No one claims that there will ever be an end to the discovery of new species.

Do they believe that they know all the powers at play in the universe and cannot find the *jinn* among them? No one can make such a claim. Every day, new powers are discovered, after having previously been unknown to man. Scientists try hard to know more of the powers and forces in the universe. They declare, in an attitude of humility, which their scientific discoveries have taught them, that they still stand at the edge of the unknown in the universe, and that they have hardly scraped the surface of it all.

Have they seen all the powers man utilizes and yet still cannot see the *jinn* among these? Not so. Since they managed to produce nuclear fission, scientists speak of the electron as scientific truth, yet none of them has seen an electron. They do not have in their laboratories a machine that can isolate an electron!

Why, then, are they so insistent on negating the very existence of this species of creature when man's information about the universe, its forces and dwellers is so scanty? Is it because so many superstitions have been weaved around the *jinn*? If so, the proper course of action is to show how such superstitions are false, just as the Qur'ān does. It is certainly not right to counteract it by denying their existence without having any proper evidence to support such a claim. Since this belongs to the realm that lies beyond the reach of our own perceptive faculties, we should refer to the only source from which we have accurate and confirmed information. This source cannot be contradicted by preconceived ideas. What this source tells us is final.

The *Jinn's* Account

This *sūrah* contributes significantly to the formulation of the Islamic concept of the truth of the Godhead and servitude to Him, as well as the truth of the universe, the creatures living in it and their interrelations.

In the *jinn's* account we have confirmation of God's oneness, a negation of His having a spouse or a son, affirmation of reckoning and requital in the life to come, and the fact that no creature can ever escape God anywhere in the universe. All will receive their fair dues. Some of the facts clearly stated by the *jinn* are then repeated in the part of the *sūrah* that addresses the Prophet: "*Say: 'I invoke my Lord alone, and I associate no partners with Him.'*" (Verse 20) "*Say: No one can ever protect me from God, nor can I ever find a place to hide from Him.*" (Verse 22)

The *jinn's* account asserts that Godhead belongs only to God, and that servitude to Him is the highest status people can attain: "*Yet when God's servant stood up to pray to Him, they pressed in on him in multitude.*" (Verse 19) The *sūrah* confirms this truth in its address to the Prophet: "*Say: It is not in my power to cause you harm or to set you on the right course.*" (Verse 21) The world beyond our perception belongs totally to God alone, and the *jinn* know nothing about it: "*We do not know if this bodes evil for those who live on earth, or if their Lord intends to guide them to what is right.*" (Verse 10) It is also unknown to God's messengers, apart from what God, in His infinite wisdom, chooses to inform them of: "*Say: I do not know whether that which you have been promised is imminent, or whether my Lord has set for it a distant term. He alone knows that which is beyond the reach of human perception, and He does not disclose His secrets to anyone except to a messenger whom He has been pleased to choose. He then sends watchers to walk before and behind him.*" (Verses 25–27)

We learn from this *sūrah* that some interaction may take place between different types of creatures even though they may have totally different natures and constitutions. An example of such interaction is what happens between man and the *jinn*, as mentioned in this *sūrah* as elsewhere in the Qur'ān. Even in his abode on earth, man is not isolated from other creation. He may have some interaction with them. The isolation man feels, as a species or a community or an individual, does not apply to the nature of the universe. This idea should broaden man's feelings towards the universe and the creatures, forces and secrets it contains. Man may not be aware of these, but they exist in the world around him. He is not the only dweller in the universe as he sometimes imagines.

Moreover, there is a definite causal relation between people's following the right way and the operation of some forces in the universe, according to God's will and its effect on His creatures: *"Had they established themselves on the right way, We would have given them abundant water to drink, so as to test them by this means. Anyone who turns away from his Lord's revelation will be made to endure uphill suffering."* (Verses 16–17) This is a truth that forms part of the Islamic concept of the interrelation between man, the universe and God's will.

As we see, the *sūrah* stretches with its inspiration over great areas and wide horizons, even though it consists of no more than 28 verses. Furthermore, it was revealed on a particular occasion to report on a certain event.

Reports of the Event

There are a number of different reports about the *jinn* listening to the Qur'ān. One quotes ʿAbdullāh ibn ʿAbbās as saying: "God's Messenger did not read the Qur'ān to the *jinn*, nor did he see them. What took place was that the Prophet and a group of his Companions once went to the ʿUkāz market place. The *jinn* had previously been barred from trying to reach heaven to eavesdrop and were struck by shooting stars. They went back to their people and told them what happened. They said: 'Something must have happened to prevent you from learning anything from heaven. Go in pursuit of information throughout the earth to find out what has happened. They went in groups, travelling east and west throughout the earth. The group that went to Tihamah drew close to the Prophet when he was in the Nakhlah Valley, going to ʿUkāz. He was leading his Companions in the *Fajr*, or Dawn, Prayer. They listened to him reciting the Qur'ān. When he finished his recitation, they said to each other: 'This is indeed what happened to cause you to be barred from learning news from on high.' They went back to their people and told them: '*We have heard a wondrous discourse, giving guidance to what is sagacious, and we have come to believe in it. We shall never associate partners with our Lord.*' God then revealed the *sūrah*, The *Jinn*, to the Prophet speaking of this event." [Related by al-Bukhārī and Muslim.]

Another report mentions that 'Abdullāh ibn Mas'ūd gave the following answer to the question about whether any of the Prophet's Companions were present with him when he met the *jinn*: "None of us were present. However, we were with him one night when he went missing. We looked for him everywhere, in valleys and on the paths, but could not find him. Some of us thought that he might have been taken or even killed. That was our worst night. In the morning, we saw him coming to us from the direction of Ḥirā'. We said: 'Messenger of God! We missed you and looked for you everywhere but could not find you. We had such a bad night.' He said: 'A caller from the *jinn* came to me and so I went and read the Qur'ān to them.' He took us to the place and showed us their traces and the remains of the fires they lit. They asked him for food. He said: 'Every bone of an animal slaughtered under God's name will be in your hands full of meat; and all animal droppings will be wholesome feed for your animals.' The Prophet then said to us: 'Do not use these to wipe off your personal dirt, because they are food for your brethren'." [Related by Muslim.]

There is a third report also attributed to Ibn Mas'ūd, but the chain of transmission of the one we have quoted makes it more reliable. We will, therefore, leave this and similar reports aside. The two authentic reports we have quoted seem to be mutually contradictory. Ibn 'Abbās says that the Prophet did not know of the *jinn*'s presence when they listened to him reading the Qur'ān, while Ibn Mas'ūd says that they called upon the Prophet and he went with them. Al-Bayhaqī resolves this apparent contradiction by saying that the two reports speak of two different occasions, not just one.

A different report is given by Ibn Isḥāq in his biography of the Prophet. He says that after the death of Abū Ṭālib, the Prophet's uncle, the Quraysh were able to inflict more harm on him than they could ever do during his uncle's lifetime. Therefore, the Prophet went to Taif, seeking support from the Thaqīf, the major tribe living there. He went there alone, hoping to gain a positive response:

Once at Ṭā'if, the Prophet approached its leading personalities, explaining his message… For ten days the Prophet spoke to one of their chiefs after another. None gave him a word of encouragement. The worst response came from three brothers, the sons of 'Amr ibn 'Umayr. These three brothers, 'Abd Yalīl, Mas'ūd and Ḥabīb, were the recognized leaders of Ṭā'if. One of them was married to a Qurayshi woman and the Prophet hoped that this relationship would work in his favour. In the event the three men were extremely rude in their rejection of the Prophet's approach.

The first one said: "I would tear the robes off the Ka'bah if it was true that God has chosen you as His Messenger." The second said: "Has God found no one other than you to be His Messenger?" The third said: "By God, I will never speak to you. If it is true that you are God's Messenger, you are too great for me to speak to you. If, on the other hand, you are lying, you are not worth answering."

Fearing that the news of their rejection would serve to intensify the Quraysh's hostility to Islam, the Prophet requested the Thaqīf notables not to publicize his mission. They refused him even that. Instead they set on him a crowd of their teenagers and servants, who chased and stoned him. His feet were soon bleeding and he was in a very sorry state. Zayd tried hard to defend him and protect him from the stones. The Prophet then sought refuge in an orchard which belonged to two brothers from Makkah. They were in their orchard, and they saw Muhammad when he entered. At first they watched him quietly, but he did not see them.

As the Prophet sat down, he said this highly emotional and touching prayer:

> To You, My Lord, I complain of my weakness, lack of support and the humiliation I am made to receive.
>
> Most compassionate and merciful! You are the Lord of the weak, and You are my Lord. To whom do You leave me? To a distant person who receives me with hostility? Or to an enemy to whom You have given power over me?
>
> If You are not displeased with me, I do not care what I face. I would, however, be much happier with Your mercy.

I seek refuge in the light of Your face by which all darkness
is dispelled and both this life and the life to come are put
on their right courses against incurring Your wrath or being
the subject of Your anger. To You I submit, until I earn Your
pleasure. Everything is powerless without Your support.

The owners of the orchard were none other than 'Utbah and
Shaybah, the two sons of Rabī'ah, who commanded positions
of high esteem in the Quraysh. Although the two brothers were
opposed to Islam and to Muḥammad, they felt sorry for him in
his unenviable plight. Therefore, they called a servant of theirs,
named 'Addās, and told him to take a bunch of grapes on a plate
to Muḥammad. 'Addās, who was a Christian from the Iraqi town
of Nineveh, complied.

As the Prophet took the grapes he said, as Muslims do before
eating: 'In the name of God.' Surprised, 'Addās said: 'This is
something no one in these areas says.' When 'Addās answered
the Prophet's question about his religion and place of origin, the
Prophet commented: 'Then you come from the same place as the
noble, divine Jonah.' Even more surprised, 'Addās asked: 'How did
you know about Jonah? When I left Nineveh, not even ten people
knew anything about him.' The Prophet said: 'He was my brother.
Like me, he was a prophet.' 'Addās then kissed the Prophet's head,
hands and feet in a gesture of genuine love and respect. As they
watched, one of the two owners of the orchard said to his brother:
'That man has certainly spoilt your slave.'

When 'Addās joined them they asked him the reason for his
very respectful attitude to Muḥammad. He said: 'There can be no
one on earth better than him. He has indeed told me something
which no one but a Prophet would know.' They said: 'You should
be careful, 'Addās. He may try to convert you while your religion
is better than his.'[1]

---

1. Ibn Hishām, *Al-Sīrah al-Nabawiyyah*, Vol. II, pp. 60–63. Also, Ibn Sayyid al-Nās,
'Uyūn al-Athar, pp. 231–233. Also, Adil Salahi (2002), *Muhammad: Man and Prophet*,
Leicester: The Islamic Foundation, pp. 179–180.

Continuing this report, Ibn Isḥāq says: "When the Prophet despaired of receiving any good response in Ṭā'if, he returned to Makkah. When he was at Nakhlah, he stood up praying in the middle of the night. It was at this time that a group of the *jinn* – seven in number from the town of Naṣībīn [in northern Syria] as I was told – passed by and listened to him reading the Qur'ān. When he finished his prayer, they left hurriedly to warn their people. They believed in Islam and God told the Prophet of what happened: "*We sent to you a group of* jinn *to listen to the Qur'ān. When they heard it, they said to one another, 'Listen in silence!' When the recitation ended, they returned to their people to warn them. 'Our people,' they said, 'we have been listening to revelation bestowed from on high after Moses, confirming what came before it. It guides to the truth and to a straight path. Our people! Respond to God's call and have faith in Him. He will forgive you your sins and deliver you from grievous suffering.*" (46: 29–31) He also revealed *Sūrah* 72, The Jinn."

Ibn Kathīr has the following comment to make on this last report: "The event itself is true, but to say that it took place on that night is questionable. The *jinn*'s listening to the Qur'ān occurred during the early days of prophethood, as clearly indicated in the above-quoted *ḥadīth* of Ibn 'Abbās. On the other hand, the Prophet's trip to Ṭā'if occurred after his uncle's death, one or two years before his migration to Madīnah, as confirmed by Ibn Isḥāq and others."

If Ibn Isḥāq's report is true and this incident took place when the Prophet was on his way back from Ṭā'if, hurt by the arrogant response of the Thaqīf elders, and after he had expressed his passionate prayer appealing to God, his Lord and Protector, then it is most remarkable that God should have sent him those *jinn* and told him about what they said to their people. Moreover, it gives fine impressions of God's care.

At whichever time and place this event took place, it is certainly very significant in itself and in what the *jinn* had to say about the Qur'ān and Islam. We will now discuss its presentation in the *sūrah*.

Al-Jinn (The Jinn)

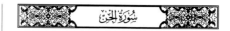

In the Name of God, the Lord of Grace, the Ever Merciful

Say: It has been revealed to me that a group of the *jinn* listened in and then said: 'We have heard a wondrous discourse, (1)

giving guidance to what is sagacious, and we have come to believe in it. We shall never associate partners with our Lord. (2)

Sublimely exalted is the glory of our Lord! He has taken to Himself neither consort nor son. (3)

Some foolish ones among us have been saying some outrageous things about God. (4)

Yet we had thought that no man or *jinn* would ever utter a lie about God. (5)

True, in the past some among mankind sought refuge with some of the *jinn*, but they caused them further trouble. (6)

303

They thus came to think, just like you thought, that God will not raise anyone. (7)

وَأَنَّهُمْ ظَنُّوا۟ كَمَا ظَنَنتُمْ أَن لَّن يَبْعَثَ ٱللَّهُ أَحَدًا ۝

We tried to reach heaven, but found it full of mighty guards and shooting stars. (8)

وَأَنَّا لَمَسْنَا ٱلسَّمَآءَ فَوَجَدْنَٰهَا مُلِئَتْ حَرَسًا شَدِيدًا وَشُهُبًا ۝

We used to take up positions there to listen, but whoever tries to listen now will find a shooting star in wait for him. (9)

وَأَنَّا كُنَّا نَقْعُدُ مِنْهَا مَقَٰعِدَ لِلسَّمْعِ فَمَن يَسْتَمِعِ ٱلْءَانَ يَجِدْ لَهُۥ شِهَابًا رَّصَدًا ۝

We do not know if this bodes evil for those who live on earth, or if their Lord intends to guide them to what is right. (10)

وَأَنَّا لَا نَدْرِىٓ أَشَرٌّ أُرِيدَ بِمَن فِى ٱلْأَرْضِ أَمْ أَرَادَ بِهِمْ رَبُّهُمْ رَشَدًا ۝

Some among us are righteous and others less so: we follow widely divergent paths. (11)

وَأَنَّا مِنَّا ٱلصَّٰلِحُونَ وَمِنَّا دُونَ ذَٰلِكَ كُنَّا طَرَآئِقَ قِدَدًا ۝

We know that we can never elude God on earth, and we can never elude Him by flight. (12)

وَأَنَّا ظَنَنَّآ أَن لَّن نُّعْجِزَ ٱللَّهَ فِى ٱلْأَرْضِ وَلَن نُّعْجِزَهُۥ هَرَبًا ۝

When we heard the guidance, we came to believe in it. Whoever believes in his Lord need never fear loss or injustice. (13)

وَأَنَّا لَمَّا سَمِعْنَا ٱلْهُدَىٰٓ ءَامَنَّا بِهِۦ فَمَن يُؤْمِنۢ بِرَبِّهِۦ فَلَا يَخَافُ بَخْسًا وَلَا رَهَقًا ۝

Some of us submit to Him and others are unfair. Those who submit to God are the ones who have endeavoured to attain what is right. (14)

وَأَنَّا مِنَّا ٱلْمُسْلِمُونَ وَمِنَّا ٱلْقَٰسِطُونَ فَمَنْ أَسْلَمَ فَأُو۟لَٰٓئِكَ تَحَرَّوْا۟ رَشَدًا ۝

But those who are unfair will be the fuel of hellfire. (15)

وَأَمَّا ٱلْقَٰسِطُونَ فَكَانُوا۟ لِجَهَنَّمَ حَطَبًا ۝

Had they established themselves on the right way, We would have given them abundant water to drink, (16)

وَأَلَّوِ ٱسْتَقَٰمُوا۟ عَلَى ٱلطَّرِيقَةِ لَأَسْقَيْنَٰهُم مَّآءً غَدَقًا ۝

so as to test them by this means. Anyone who turns away from his Lord's revelation will be made to endure uphill suffering. (17)

لِنَفْتِنَهُمْ فِيهِ وَمَن يُعْرِضْ عَن ذِكْرِ رَبِّهِۦ يَسْلُكْهُ عَذَابًا صَعَدًا ۝

Places of worship are for God alone; therefore, do not invoke anyone other than God. (18)

وَأَنَّ ٱلْمَسَٰجِدَ لِلَّهِ فَلَا تَدْعُوا۟ مَعَ ٱللَّهِ أَحَدًا ۝

Yet when God's servant stood up to pray to Him, they pressed in on him in multitude. (19)

وَأَنَّهُۥ لَمَّا قَامَ عَبْدُ ٱللَّهِ يَدْعُوهُ كَادُوا۟ يَكُونُونَ عَلَيْهِ لِبَدًا ۝

Say: 'I invoke my Lord alone, and I associate no partners with Him.' (20)

قُلْ إِنَّمَآ أَدْعُوا۟ رَبِّى وَلَآ أُشْرِكُ بِهِۦٓ أَحَدًا ۝

Say: 'It is not in my power to cause you harm or to set you on the right course.' (21)

قُلْ إِنِّى لَآ أَمْلِكُ لَكُمْ ضَرًّا وَلَا رَشَدًا ۝

Say: 'No one can ever protect me from God, nor can I ever find a place to hide from Him. (22)

قُلْ إِنِّى لَن يُجِيرَنِى مِنَ ٱللَّهِ أَحَدٌ وَلَنْ أَجِدَ مِن دُونِهِۦ مُلْتَحَدًا ۝

My task is only to deliver what I receive from God and His messages.' Whoever disobeys God and His Messenger will have the fire of hell, where they will abide for ever. (23)

إِلَّا بَلَٰغًا مِّنَ ٱللَّهِ وَرِسَٰلَٰتِهِۦۚ وَمَن يَعْصِ ٱللَّهَ وَرَسُولَهُۥ فَإِنَّ لَهُۥ نَارَ جَهَنَّمَ خَٰلِدِينَ فِيهَآ أَبَدًا ۝

When they see what they have been promised, they will realize who has the lesser help and is smaller in number. (24)

حَتَّىٰٓ إِذَا رَأَوْا۟ مَا يُوعَدُونَ فَسَيَعْلَمُونَ مَنْ أَضْعَفُ نَاصِرًا وَأَقَلُّ عَدَدًا ۝

Say: 'I do not know whether that which you have been promised is imminent, or whether my Lord has set for it a distant term. (25)

قُلْ إِنْ أَدْرِىٓ أَقَرِيبٌ مَّا تُوعَدُونَ أَمْ يَجْعَلُ لَهُۥ رَبِّىٓ أَمَدًا ۝

He alone knows that which is beyond the reach of human perception, and He does not disclose His secrets to anyone (26)

عَٰلِمُ ٱلْغَيْبِ فَلَا يُظْهِرُ عَلَىٰ غَيْبِهِۦٓ أَحَدًا ۝

except to a messenger whom He has been pleased to choose. He then sends watchers to walk before and behind him, (27)

إِلَّا مَنِ ٱرْتَضَىٰ مِن رَّسُولٍ فَإِنَّهُۥ يَسْلُكُ مِنۢ بَيْنِ يَدَيْهِ وَمِنْ خَلْفِهِۦ رَصَدًا ۝

to know that they have delivered their Lord's messages. He has full knowledge of all they have. He takes count of everything.' (28)

لِّيَعْلَمَ أَن قَدْ أَبْلَغُوا۟ رِسَٰلَٰتِ رَبِّهِمْ وَأَحَاطَ بِمَا لَدَيْهِمْ وَأَحْصَىٰ كُلَّ شَىْءٍ عَدَدًا ۝

A Surprise for the *Jinn*

> *Say: It has been revealed to me that a group of the* jinn *listened in and then said: 'We have heard a wondrous discourse, giving guidance to what is sagacious, and we have come to believe in it. We shall never associate partners with our Lord. Sublimely exalted is the glory of our Lord! He has taken to Himself neither consort nor son. Some foolish ones among us have been saying some outrageous things about God. Yet we had thought that no man or* jinn *would ever utter a lie about God. True, in the past some among mankind sought refuge with some of the* jinn, *but they caused them further trouble. They thus came to think, just like you thought, that God will not raise anyone.' (Verses 1–7)*

The Arabic word *nafar*, used in the opening verse and translated here as 'a group', signifies a group of people between three and nine in number. Some reports suggest that they were seven.

This opening suggests that the Prophet learnt of the *jinn*'s listening to his recitation and what they did afterwards through revelation from on high. It is God who told him about that of which he had no knowledge. This might have been the first time, and there might have been one or more other occasions when the Prophet read out the Qur'ān to the *jinn*, as reported by Jābir in a *ḥadīth* that says: "God's Messenger read out *Sūrah* 55, The Lord of Grace, in full to his Companions. When he finished, they were silent. He said: 'I read this *sūrah* to the *jinn* and they gave a better response than you. Every time I read the repeated verse, '*Which, then, of your Lord's blessings do you both deny?*' they said: 'None of Your blessings, our Lord, do we deny. All thanks are due to You'." [Related by al-Tirmidhī.] This report confirms the one by Ibn Masʿūd mentioned in the Prologue.

The event mentioned in the present *sūrah* must be the same referred to in *Sūrah* 46, The Sand Dunes, which says: "*We sent to you a group of* jinn *to listen to the Qur'ān. When they heard it, they said to one another, 'Listen in silence!' When the recitation ended, they returned to their people to warn them. 'Our people,' they said, 'we have been listening to revelation bestowed from on high after Moses, confirming what came before it. It guides to the truth and to a straight path. 'Our people! Respond to God's call and have faith in Him. He will forgive you your sins and deliver you from grievous suffering. He who does not respond to God's call cannot elude Him on earth, nor will they have any protector against Him. They are indeed in manifest error.*" (Verses 29–32) These verses speak, as does the present *sūrah*, of the great surprise felt by the *jinn* when they first listened to the Qur'ān. It had such a great effect on their minds, hearts and feelings. They were filled with emotion, resulting in their travel in great haste to tell their people. Their report expresses such overflowing emotions. Indeed, it is stated in an exceptionally fluent, warm, charged and very happy style. The surprise for them was great and their reaction was only natural.

"We have heard a wondrous discourse." (Verse 1) The first thing they realize about the Qur'ānic discourse is that it is unfamiliar, and that it makes the listener wonder. This is how the Qur'ān is received by anyone who listens with an open and positive mind. He will find that the Qur'ān contains intrinsic power, strong appeal and beautiful music that touch hearts and feelings. It is '*wondrous*' indeed, which tells us that the group of *jinn* listening to it had refined literary tastes.

"Giving guidance to what is sagacious." (Verse 2) This is the second prominent feature of the Qur'ān which the *jinn* immediately felt within their hearts. That they use the word 'sagacious' to describe it is particularly significant. It is true that the Qur'ān guides to what is right and sensible, but the term 'sagacious' also connotes maturity and wisdom that distinguishes right from wrong. It adds an element of awareness that naturally guides to the truth and to what is right and good. It establishes a bond with the source of light and guidance, as well as harmony with major universal laws. In doing so, the Qur'ān guides to what is sagacious, as indeed it does by providing a code of living the like of which has never been experienced by any other human community. Yet this system enabled individuals and communities to attain sublime standards in personal morality and values as well as in social relations and interactions.

"And we have come to believe in it." (Verse 2) This is the natural and sound reaction to listening to the Qur'ān and understanding its nature. The *sūrah* puts this response to the unbelievers in Makkah who used to listen to the Qur'ān but who would not believe in it. They even attributed it to the *jinn*, alleging that the Prophet was a soothsayer, a poet or a

madman, influenced by the *jinn*. Here, we see the *jinn* wondering at the Qur'ān, profoundly influenced by its discourse, unable to resist it. We see them able to discern the truth and submit to it: "*We have come to believe in it.*" They could not turn away from the truth they clearly felt.

"*We shall never associate partners with our Lord.*" (Verse 2) Theirs, then, is a case of complete faith, untainted by delusions, superstitions or any element of polytheism. It is faith based on understanding the truth presented by the Qur'ān, i.e. the truth of God's absolute oneness.

"*Sublimely exalted is the glory of our Lord! He has taken to Himself neither consort nor son.*" (Verse 3) The *sūrah* uses here the Arabic word *jadd*, attributing it to God. This word connotes share, position, authority and greatness. All these connotations are meant here. Hence the translation of the first sentence in the verse. What is intended here is to impart a clear feeling of God's greatness and His being far above taking a wife or child for Himself. The Arabs used to allege that the angels were God's daughters through a marriage to the *jinn*. Now the *jinn* deny such a superstition in a most expressive way. They glorify God and deny that such a notion could ever have happened. The *jinn* would have proudly proclaimed such a connection had there been any possibility of it ever having taken place. Their denial delivers a massive blow at the unbelievers' baseless claims, and indeed at every similar claim alleging that God has taken a son to Himself in any way, shape or form.

"*Some foolish ones among us have been saying some outrageous things about God. Yet we had thought that no man or* jinn *would ever utter a lie about God.*" (Verses 4–5) This is a critical examination of what the *jinn* used to hear some of the foolish among them say. Those are the ones who did not believe in God's oneness and who alleged that He had a wife, a son and partners. Now that they have heard the Qur'ān, they realize this is all absolutely false. Those who promote such ideas are, therefore, foolish, lacking sound mind. They explain their own earlier belief of what those foolish ones said by the fact that they could not imagine that any creature, human or *jinn*, would ever perpetrate a lie about God. To them, that was an absolute enormity. Therefore, when those foolish people told them that God had a wife, a son and partners, they believed them because they could not conceive of how anyone would knowingly utter an untruth about God. Indeed, their perception of the enormity of lying about God is what qualified this group of *jinn* to immediately declare their belief when they listened to the Qur'ān. It shows that their hearts and minds were free of deviation. They had only fallen into error as a result of the trust they assumed in other people. When they heard the truth, they immediately realized it. They recognized it and submitted to it. They made their declaration definitive: "*We have heard a wondrous discourse, giving guidance to what is sagacious, and we have come to believe in it. We shall never associate partners with our Lord. Sublimely exalted is the glory of our Lord! He has taken to Himself neither consort nor son.*" (Verses 1–3)

This immediate and instinctive reaction to the truth should have been enough to awaken many of those who were deluded by the Quraysh elders and their claims that God had partners, or a wife and son. It should have made them more cautious about what they heard and alerted them to the need to examine what the Prophet Muḥammad said in a meaningful attempt to arrive at the truth. This should have been enough to shake the blind trust they placed in what those foolish Quraysh elders said to the contrary. This is what the *sūrah* intends by virtue of its effects. It is all intended as part of its long treatment of the lingering traces of *jāhiliyyah* in people's minds and thoughts, many of whom were simple but deluded by false claims and superstitions.

Between Humans and *Jinn*

"*True, in the past some among mankind sought refuge with some of the* jinn*, but they caused them further trouble.*" (Verse 6) Here, the *jinn* refer to what was widely accepted in pre-Islamic days in Arabian society, and which remains accepted in many other communities, claiming that the *jinn*, exercized power on the earth and against humans. Indeed, it was thought that they were able to bring about benefit and cause harm to people, and that they were in full control of certain areas of land, sea and air. Satan is given access to people's minds and hearts. Only those who seek protection with God are saved from him. Whoever listens to him is listening to his own worst enemy who will not bring him any benefit. On the contrary, he will increase his problems. This group of *jinn* report on what used to happen: "*True, in the past some among mankind*

sought refuge with some of the jinn, *but they caused them further trouble."*
(Verse 6) Perhaps this misguidance refers to the worry and loss that are
experienced by those who seek help from their enemy, Satan, and who
do not seek refuge with God against his scheming and plotting. Their
action is the opposite of what they have been commanded to do ever
since their first father, Adam, and what took place between him and
Iblīs, or Satan, leading to permanent hostility between them. It is a
confirmed truth that when man turns to any other than God, hoping
to gain benefit or to ward off harm, he ends up with nothing other
than increased worry, loss and instability. This combination is the worst
trouble people can experience. It is the type of trouble that leaves no
room for comfort or security.

Everyone and everything other than God is temporary, changing
and unstable. When a man's heart clings to any such thing or person,
it is bound to shake and have worries and forebodings. Such a person
will continue to change direction with every change of mood by the
one to whom he is attached. Only God is the Eternal who neither dies
nor changes. Whoever places his trust in Him relies on the One who
never changes.

*"They thus came to think, just like you thought, that God will not raise
anyone."* (Verse 7) The group of *jinn* are still talking to their own people
about those humans who sought refuge with some of the *jinn*, telling
them that those humans thought like the *jinn* that God would not be
sending any messenger. Now, He has sent a Messenger and has given
him this Qur'ān which guides to wisdom and sagacity. Alternatively, the
verse may mean that they all thought there would be no resurrection,
reckoning or requital.² Therefore, they did not prepare for their future
lives. They denied what God's Messenger told them about it because
they did not believe that it would ever happen.

Both thoughts are erroneous, betraying ignorance of God's wisdom
in creating mankind with the dual tendency toward good or evil and

---

2. The Arabic word *yab'ath*, which is used in this verse, has the dual meaning of 'to
send' and 'to bring up or resurrect'. Hence, the author explains the verse on the basis of both
meanings. – Editor's note.

to following guidance or error.[3] Hence, it is an aspect of God's grace that He has willed to help mankind by sending them messengers to promote goodness in their natures and to enhance their tendency to follow guidance. There are no grounds, then, for thinking that God would not be sending any messengers.

This is true when we take the verse to refer to sending God's messengers. If we take the reference to mean resurrection on the Day of Judgement, we say again that it is necessary for humans, since they do not finish their life's account in this present world. This is to fulfil a certain purpose of God's. It relates to the design He has chosen for the universe, yet we know nothing about this design. He has decreed that all will be resurrected to receive their accounts and resume life along the path their first life qualifies them for. Again, this leaves no room to suggest that God will not resurrect anyone. Such a suggestion is contrary to believing in God's wisdom and perfection.

This group of *jinn* presents the right belief directly to their people. Furthermore, the Qur'ān reports it to show the falsehood in the unbelievers' way of thinking.

Shooting Stars

Continuing to report on what they learnt about the last divine message and its echoes throughout the universe, the *jinn* disclaim any knowledge of the realm that lies beyond the reach of theirs and human perception. They disclaim having any role in it:

> *We tried to reach heaven, but found it full of mighty guards and shooting stars. We used to take up positions there to listen, but whoever tries to listen now will find a shooting star in wait for him. We do not know if this bodes evil for those who live on earth, or if their Lord intends to guide them to what is right. (Verses 8–10)*

---

3. We also learn from this *sūrah* that the *jinn* also have a dual nature, except for *Iblīs* or Satan who belonged to them but dedicated himself totally to evil. He was expelled from God's mercy and became totally evil with no room for goodness in him.

This suggests that in the period that preceded the revelation of God's final message, perhaps in between it and Jesus' message, the *jinn* used to try to reach up to heaven to eavesdrop on the angels and their discussion of their assignments with respect to the affairs of God's creatures on earth. They would impart such information to their human friends, the soothsayers and astrologers, to enable them to delude people. In accordance with Satan's plot, these soothsayers and astrologers would then use a small portion of the truth they so received and mix it with much falsehood, circulating it among people. This might have been the case when there was no messenger preaching the divine message on earth, in the intervening period between Jesus and Muḥammad (peace be upon them both). What form this took we do not know, because the Qur'ān has not given us any information about it. In any case, there is no need to explore it further because we accept it as the sum of this fact.

This group of *jinn* say that such eavesdropping, to which they refer by '*reaching up to heaven*', was no longer possible. When they tried it, they found the way blocked by mighty guards and shooting stars aimed at them, indeed killing them. They declare that they know nothing about the prospect determined for mankind: "*We do not know if this bodes evil for those who live on earth, or if their Lord intends to guide them to what is right.*" (Verse 10) They, thus, clearly declare that they have no access to such information because it is part of God's own knowledge. When the very source the soothsayers claim to receive their very special information from declares that it has no such knowledge, then nothing more can be said. All soothsaying and astrology are thus shown to be false. The world beyond belongs to God who alone knows it all. No one can dare claim any special knowledge of it or predict it. The Qur'ān declares that the human mind must remain free of any such delusion. It rids mankind of all such superstitions.

Who or what are those mighty guards? Where do they stand? How do they aim the shooting stars at the devils trying to eavesdrop? Neither the Qur'ān nor the *Ḥadīth* tells us anything of these questions. We do not have any other source to rely on. Had it been useful for us to learn any details of this, God would have given us them. Since He has chosen not to do so, it is futile for us to try anything in this regard. It does not add anything to our lives or to our useful knowledge.

Nor is there any use objecting to this information, or arguing that shooting stars function according to a particular celestial order that remained in operation before and after the Prophet's message, or by adding that astronomers are still trying to explain how this system works. Whatever theories astronomers and scientists come up with, and whether these are correct or not, are outside our discussion here. The system does not preclude that these shooting stars aim at devils as they try to eavesdrop, or that they move in accordance with God's will that gave them their operational system, whether they are meant to hit anyone or not.

Others view all this discussion as figurative, giving us an abstraction of how God preserves His message from being mixed up with falsehood. They maintain that such statements should not be taken at face value. The reason they take this line is that they approach the Qur'ān with preconceived ideas that they acquire from other sources and try to give the Qur'ān an interpretation that fits such preconceptions. Thus, they view the angels as a symbol of goodness and obedience to God, Satan and his group as a symbol of evil and disobedience, and the shooting stars as a symbol of the power of preservation and protection. This is because their notions, which they conceive before they look at the Qur'ān, tell them that neither the angels, devils nor *jinn* could have any physical existence, or take any tangible action, or leave any practical effect. Where do they get all this from? How do they arrive at such preconceptions to which they subject Qur'ānic and *Ḥadīth* statements?

The proper approach to understanding the Qur'ān is to abandon all preconceptions, whether emotional, intellectual or logical, and to formulate our concepts on the basis of the Qur'ān's presentation of the truth about the universe. In other words, the Qur'ān and *Ḥadīth* must be taken only in light of the Qur'ān. We must not try to negate or interpret anything stated in the Qur'ān, or to prove anything the Qur'ān negates or considers invalid. On anything else the Qur'ān neither proves nor negates, we may judge according to logic and experience.

We naturally say this to people who believe in the Qur'ān, yet try to interpret its statements according to their own preconceived ideas of how things in the universe must be.[4] Those, on the other hand, who do not believe in the Qur'ān, yet arbitrarily try to negate certain facts because science has not proven them, make laughable claims. Science has not yet fathomed the secrets of things that are available to scientists who use them in their research. This lack of knowledge does not negate their existence. Moreover, large numbers of scientists began to believe in the unknown on the same lines as the advocates of religion, or at least these scientists do not deny what they do not know. Pursuing their scientific work, they have found themselves facing some unknowns, when they had thought these to be totally known to man. Hence, they have become humble, unprepared to make wild claims about that which they do not know. They do not disregard the unknown as some of those who deny religion altogether do, claiming that they monopolize scientific thinking.

To Tread the Unknown

The universe around us is full of secrets, spirits and forces. This *sūrah*, like many others, gives us a glimpse of some truths in the universe to help us formulate a proper concept of it and what it contains of forces and lives that carry on around us as also interact with us and with human life in general. This is the concept that distinguishes us, Muslims, putting us in the right position, leaning neither to delusion and superstition, nor to arrogance and insupportable claims. It is a concept based on the Qur'ān and *Ḥadīth*. It is to these two that a Muslim refers all theories and interpretations.

The human mind is given a certain area where man can explore the unknown; indeed Islam directs man to do so, pressurizing him into such action. However, beyond this scope lies a wide area that the human mind cannot access, and to which it does not need such access. It is of

---

4.   I do not absolve myself of falling into this trap in my previous works and in the early volumes of this work. I hope to rectify this in the second edition of this book. What I am stating here is what I believe to be the truth in the light of God's guidance.

Needless to say, the author is here referring to the first Arabic edition of these volumes, which was much shorter and less detailed than the second. This English translation is based on the second edition. – Editor's note.

no use to us in the fulfilment of the task assigned to us, namely, building human life on earth. Hence, man has not been given such access; it is outside of his remit. Whatever he needs to know of this unknown realm in order to understand his own position in relation to the universe and what is around him has been explained to him by God, in terms that he can understand. Aspects of this area that we have been given information about include the angels, the devils, the spirit, our origin and our ultimate destination.

Those who follow divine guidance accept what God has revealed to them of these aspects in His book and through His messengers. They benefit by this feeling of God's majesty and His wisdom with regard to creation. They also learn man's position in relation to such forces and spirits. They dedicate themselves to making whatever scientific discoveries they can manage within the area of the universe made available to man. They utilize their discoveries in the all important task assigned to them, which is building sound human life on the basis of divine guidance, seeking God's acceptance and endeavouring to rise to the sublime level man can achieve.

Others who turn their backs on divine guidance are split into two large groups. One continues to strive, with their own finite minds, to understand the infinite, and to learn the hidden truth from sources other than God's revelations. Among these have been some philosophers who tried to explain the universe and the mutual bonds between its different parts. They made fatal errors, just like children who try to climb a very high mountain with no known summit. They are trying to solve the essential secret of the universe when they have not yet learnt the alphabet! Prominent philosophers among them even arrived at ludicrous concepts. When these are compared to the consistent and lucid concept Islam presents, they appear absurd, full of errors and ironies. They are too naïve to explain the universe, great as it certainly is. I make no exception here in respect of the great Greek philosophers of old, or the Muslim philosophers who toed their line, or of contemporary philosophers.

The other large group recognizes the futility of such attempts and limits itself and its efforts to experimental and applied scientific research. It makes no attempt to penetrate into the unknown, where it knows it cannot go. Scientists in this group refuse to accept God's guidance on this because they do not recognize God. This group was at its most extreme during the eighteenth and nineteenth centuries, but began in the early years of the twentieth century to wake up and reconsider its extremism. What produced its wake-up call was the transformation of matter in the hands of scientists to radiation, which is of 'unknown nature' and subject to almost unknown law.

By contrast, Islam remained at its vantage point of certainty, giving mankind a measure of the unknown that is good and beneficial for them, allowing them to dedicate themselves to work for the elevation of human life. It gives them the scope in which their minds can work in safety and security. It guides them to what is best in respect of what is known and what remains unknown.

The *Jinn* Community

The *jinn* then describe their own situation and their attitude towards divine guidance. We understand from this that they have a similar nature to mankind, with the dual propensity to either believe or go astray. This group who believed now speak of their faith and what fate awaits the follower of either course:

> *Some among us are righteous and others less so: we follow widely divergent paths. We know that we can never elude God on earth, and we can never elude Him by flight. When we heard the guidance, we came to believe in it. Whoever believes in his Lord need never fear loss or injustice. Some of us submit to Him and others are unfair. Those who submit to God are the ones who have endeavoured to attain what is right. But those who are unfair will be the fuel of hellfire.* (Verses 11–15)

The statement that some of them are righteous and some less so, that some submit to God and others refuse to do so, clearly indicates their dual capacity, except that is for those of them who were determined to be unfair permanently, i.e. Satan and his group. This is a very important statement as it corrects our general perception of these creatures. Many of us, including scholars, tend to think that the *jinn* represent evil, that their nature is decidedly bad, while man is the only creature capable of good or evil. It is time we corrected this ill-founded idea.

This group of *jinn* says: "*Some among us are righteous and others less so.*" (Verse 11) They describe their general situation: "*We follow widely divergent paths.*" (Verse 11) This means that each group takes a totally different course from the other, and the two paths do not meet. They go on to explain their own beliefs after they have accepted the divine faith: "*We know that we can never elude God on earth, and we can never elude Him by flight.*" (Verse 12) They know God's power. They know they can never escape from Him or what He wills for them. They cannot elude Him on earth nor can they elude Him by running away from earth. They thus acknowledge their weakness before the Creator. They know that everything in the universe is subject to His absolute power.

It is these very creatures, the *jinn*, to whom some humans appeal for support and protection, and who they call upon for help. They are the ones whom the unbelievers claimed to have a marriage relation with God. Yet here they acknowledge their own weakness and God's might. They, thus, correct their own people's and the unbelievers' notion about the only power to which no other can stand.

Although they had already stated their belief, they repeat this here in the context of the *jinn*'s differing attitudes to divine guidance: "*When we heard the guidance, we came to believe in it.*" (Verse 13) This is what everyone who hears divine guidance should do. What they heard was the Qur'ān, but here they call it '*the guidance*', confirming its nature and outcome. They follow this by a statement confirming their absolute trust in God: "*Whoever believes in his Lord need never fear loss or injustice.*" (Verse 13) They have complete trust in God's justice and power. They know the nature of faith. God is fair and He will never fail to give a believer his fair reward. He never burdens him with what he cannot bear. He will protect believers against loss and injustice. Who can inflict loss on a believer or overburden him when he is under God's care, enjoying His protection? Some believers may be deprived of some of life's riches, but this is not what is meant by '*loss*'. Such losses are easily compensated for to ensure fairness. A believer may also suffer harm caused him by some earthly forces, but this is not the '*injustice*' the Qur'ānic verse refers to. God will always give the believer an increase of energy to be able to tolerate the pain and channel it in a positive way so as to strengthen him. His ties with his Lord will ease the hardship, turning it to what is good for him both in this life and in the life to come.

A believer is thus reassured that he will suffer neither loss nor injustice. This reassurance gives him great confidence throughout times of ease. He is free of worry and fear. When things change and he suffers adversity, he neither panics nor feels overwhelmed. He considers such hardship and misfortune to be a trial God wants him to go through. He bears such adversity with patience. Indeed, he is rewarded for his patience. Furthermore, he hopes that God will relieve this adversity and that again he will be rewarded. Hence, whether the situation be one of ease or adversity, he does not fear or experience either loss or unfairness. This group of *jinn* give a true description of this truth.

The *jinn* now refer to their views about guidance and error and the requital for each: *"Some of us submit to Him and others are unfair. Those who submit to God are the ones who have endeavoured to attain what is right. But those who are unfair will be the fuel of hellfire."* (Verses 14–15) The *jinn* thus contrast those who are unfair with those who submit themselves to God, or are Muslims. This is a fine touch. A Muslim who submits himself to God is always fair and righteous.

"Those who submit to God are the ones who have endeavoured to attain what is right." (Verse 14) The way this sentence is phrased suggests that to be guided to Islam a person needs to be very careful and meticulous in seeking proper guidance. It also implies a conscious choice of what is right, based on careful study and clear vision. This does not, however, come about by coincidence, or by following the crowd, as it were! It means that these people arrived at what is right when they chose Islam and submitted themselves to God. *"But those who are unfair will be the fuel of hellfire."* (Verse 15) Their fate is settled. They will become the fuel of hell, and it will rage even more fiercely when they are cast into it.

This confirms that the *jinn* are also punished in hell. It similarly implies that the good among them are destined for heaven. The Qur'ānic text also bears this out and it is from the Qur'ān that we derive our beliefs. No one, then, can say anything that is not based on the Qur'ān, particularly about the nature of the *jinn*, hell and heaven. Whatever else is said in this regard is futile.

What applies to the *jinn*, as they explained it to their people, also applies to humans. They have been informed of this through revelation recited to them by the Prophet.

Different Types of Trial

Up to this point, the *sūrah* has quoted what the *jinn* said about themselves. Now, it summarizes what they said about what God does with those who follow the right course, obeying His commands. In doing so, the Qur'ān reports their ideas without actually quoting their precise words:

> *Had they established themselves on the right way, We would have given them abundant water to drink, so as to test them by this means. Anyone who turns away from his Lord's revelation will be made to endure uphill suffering.* (Verses 16–17)

God Almighty confirms what the *jinn* said to the effect that had people maintained following the right way, or had those who were unfair followed the right way, He would have given them water in plenty, which would have ensured their prosperity. All this would be *"so as to test them by this means."* (Verse 17) Such a trial establishes whether they are grateful or not.

This change of style, from quoting direct speech to reporting it, enhances the effect because it attributes the message and the promise it gives to God Almighty. Such changes are frequent in the Qur'ān. It reinforces the meaning and draws attention to it.

These two verses include several facts related to Islamic beliefs, how we look at events and how they interrelate. The first of these is the direct relation between following the straight path leading to God, by nations and communities, and their enjoying prosperity and provisions in plenty. The most essential requirement of such prosperity is abundant water. All life depends on water. This is true even in our own times when industry has acquired much greater importance, and agriculture is no longer the only source of plentiful provisions and prosperity. Water still remains as important as ever for a flourishing civilization.

That prosperity and security depend on following the right way and maintaining it with resolve is certainly true. The Arabs were desert people living in total poverty. When they followed the right way with strong resolve, the world opened up to them providing plentiful water and provisions. Then they deviated from that way, and all the good things in life were taken away from them. They will continue to live a life of stress and poverty until they regain the right way and follow it.[5] Only then will God's promise be fulfilled to them.

There are certainly communities that turn away from the line God wants people to follow in this life, yet they enjoy affluence. However, when we look at the life they lead we find that they suffer from other ills that detract from their humanity, security or man's dignity and freedom. Thus their riches do not provide them with real prosperity. On the contrary, life in such societies becomes a curse for man depriving him of dignity, security and proper morality.

The second fact that the verses above establish is that prosperity is a means of trial God sets for His creatures: *"We test you all with evil and good by way of trial."* (21: 35) Indeed, maintaining the right way in times of plenty and prosperity, giving due thanks for God's favours and using them for good purposes is, contrary to what appears at first sight, more difficult than patience in adversity. Many are those who show courage and perseverance when things go against them. They rally and put in sustained efforts to overcome such adversity. They more readily remember God, pray to Him and seek His help, realizing that only He can bring them through their troubles. When people are prosperous, enjoying a life of plenty, however, they tend to forget God and be distracted. The element of resistance is no longer needed. There is every opportunity for arrogance, treating God's blessings as merited dues. This then opens the way for Satan and his machinations.

A trial with prosperity requires constant alertness to resist such temptation, because the blessings of affluence often lead to transgression,

---

5. It may be suggested that oil has given Arabs, or many of them at least, wealth and comfortable living. Oil provides only temporary means of affluence. Besides, it brought the Arabs much stress and misery, with the mighty powers of the world imposing a state of almost total powerlessness on Arab countries. Today, for the Arabs to regain control of their own destiny seems an extremely remote possibility for most educated Arabs. – Editor's note.

ingratitude, arrogance, injustice, depriving other people of their rights and also disrespecting sanctities. God may favour some people with beauty, but this blessing often leads to arrogance and sin. He may give them intelligence, yet again this blessing may lead to conceit, disrespect of others and disregard for values and standards. Almost every blessing and favour God grants us involves some temptation that takes the person away from the right path. Only those who always remember God and, who as a result, enjoy His protection are excepted.

When a trial of prosperity leads to moving away from God's path, this makes God's punishment inevitable. The Qur'ānic verse mentions a particular quality of such punishment: *"Anyone who turns away from his Lord's revelation will be made to endure uphill suffering."* (Verse 17) This gives a sense of increased difficulty, because whoever goes uphill finds the going harder as he climbs higher. The Qur'ān often refers to such hardship as going uphill. Other examples include: *"Whomever God wills to guide, He makes his bosom open wide with willingness towards self-surrender (to Him); and whomever He wills to let go astray, He causes his bosom to be tight and constricted, as if he were climbing up into the skies."* (6: 125) *"I will constrain him to endure a painful uphill climb."* (74: 17) This is a well-known fact. The contrast between a trial of affluence and hard punishment in requital is, thus, abundantly clear.

None Other Than God

The next verse may represent another quotation from the *jinn*, or it may be a direct statement made by God:

Places of worship are for God alone; therefore, do not invoke anyone other than God. (Verse 18)

In both cases it makes clear that worship, and places of worship, which is expressed in the Arabic text in the form of prostration, must be devoted to God alone. That is where God's oneness is strictly observed, leaving no room whatsoever for anyone else, be that a person, a value or an idea. The whole atmosphere must be dedicated to the pure worship of God alone. Invoking someone other than God may take the form of worshipping that someone, appealing to him, or even directing one's thoughts and feelings towards him instead of God.

If we take the verse to be a statement made by the *jinn*, it serves as a reconfirmation of their earlier pledge: "*We shall never associate partners with our Lord.*" (Verse 2) This is repeated at the mention of places of worship and prostration before God. If we take it as a statement by God, it serves as a directive that fits with what the *jinn* said about their belief in God's oneness. The same applies to the verse that follows:

> *Yet when God's servant stood up to pray to Him, they pressed in on him in multitude.* (Verse 19)

The verse describes how the unbelievers pressed upon this servant of God when he stood to invoke and pray to Him. If we treat this verse as quoting the *jinn*'s statement, then they are telling us about what the Arab unbelievers did when they gathered in groups around the Prophet as he stood up to pray or as he recited the Qur'ān. This is referred to in an earlier *sūrah* in this volume: "*What is wrong with the unbelievers, that they run confusedly before you, from the right and the left, in crowds?*" (70: 36–37) They listen with amazement, yet they do not respond. Alternatively, the expression, '*they pressed on him in multitude,*' means that they tried to inflict harm on him but God protected him, as repeatedly happened. In this case, the *jinn* are reporting this event to their people, describing how singular the Arab unbelievers' attitude was.

If we take the verse as a statement made by God, then it tells us about this group of *jinn*'s reaction when they listened to the Qur'ān. They were totally amazed, pressing on the Prophet, close to each other. This is perhaps more probable as it fits with the feelings of surprise, amazement and alarm that are clearly apparent in the *jinn*'s account.

Both *Jinn* and Human

Having completed its account of what the *jinn* said about the Qur'ān, and their total amazement at its discourse, the *sūrah* now addresses the Prophet in a decisive tone, requiring him to deliver his message and to make it clear that once he has done so, he has no say in what happens afterwards. He is to make clear that he has no knowledge whatsoever of the world beyond, or of how people fare. This address carries an overtone of sorrow and sadness that particularly suits its seriousness and decisive manner:

> Say: 'I invoke my Lord alone, and I associate no partners with Him.' Say: 'It is not in my power to cause you harm or to set you on the right course.' Say: 'No one can ever protect me from God, nor can I ever find a place to hide from Him. My task is only to deliver what I receive from God and His messages.' Whoever disobeys God and His Messenger will have the fire of hell, where they will abide for ever. When they see what they have been promised, they will realize who has the lesser help and is smaller in number. Say: 'I do not know whether that which you have been promised is imminent, or whether my Lord has set for it a distant term. He alone knows that which is beyond the reach of human perception, and He does not disclose His secrets to anyone except to a messenger whom He has been pleased to choose. He then sends watchers to walk before and behind him, to know that they have delivered their Lord's messages. He has full knowledge of all they have. He takes count of everything.' (Verses 20–28)

You, Muḥammad! Say it to all people: *"I invoke my Lord alone, and I associate no partners with Him."* (Verse 20) Coming after the *jinn's* statement, *"We shall never associate partners with our Lord,"* this declaration acquires special effect. It is the same words, declared by *jinn* and humans. These unbelievers who do not share in it break away from all worlds.

No Help from Anyone

"Say: It is not in my power to cause you harm or to set you on the right course." (Verse 21) The Prophet is commanded to disclaim any of God's qualities and attributes. It is God alone who must be worshipped, without partners, and He alone who can cause harm and bring benefit. The verse contrasts harm with being *'on the right course,'* which means following divine guidance. This was clearly expressed by the *jinn* earlier:

"*We do not know if this bodes evil for those who live on earth, or if their Lord intends to guide them to what is right.*" (Verse 10) Thus, the two statements have the same drift and are almost identical in their wording. This is deliberate. It is also a frequently used structure in the Qur'ān where we always see such complementarity between a story and the Qur'ānic comments on events.

Thus the *jinn*, who are often thought to be able to cause harm and bring about benefit, and the Prophet disclaim any such ability. It all belongs to God alone. The divine faith makes this absolutely clear, with no possibility for confusion.

"*Say: No one can ever protect me from God, nor can I ever find a place to hide from Him. My task is only to deliver what I receive from God and His messages.*" (Verses 22–23) This is indeed frightening. It fills our hearts with the seriousness of advocating the divine message. The Prophet is commanded to declare this great truth stating that he himself has neither protection nor hiding place unless he discharges his task, fulfils his trust and delivers his message. This is his only safe resort. The message itself does not belong to him; his only task is to deliver it, which he must fulfil. It is required of him by God Himself, and unless he meets this requirement, he will have nowhere to go and no help from anyone.

How serious! How frightening! Advocating God's message is not something one volunteers to do; it is a serious assignment that must be fulfilled, because it is given by God Almighty. Its motive is not the pleasure one finds in presenting guidance and goodness to people; it is a command given from on high which cannot be shirked. Nor can one show any hesitation in the matter.

"*Whoever disobeys God and His Messenger will have the fire of hell, where they will abide for ever. When they see what they have been promised, they will realize who has the lesser help and is smaller in number.*" (Verses 23–24) There is a warning here, both implicit and explicit, given to everyone who receives this order and disobeys it. If the unbelievers are content with their power and numbers, comparing their strength to that of Muḥammad and his few followers, they will come to know when they see what they have been promised, either in this life or in the life to come, which of the two parties is weaker and will end up the loser. Again, we note how this comment echoes the earlier one made by the *jinn*: "*We do not know if this bodes evil for those who live on earth, or if their Lord intends to guide them to what is right.*" (Verse 10)

Limited Knowledge

The Prophet is also commanded to disclaim any knowledge of the world beyond human perception: "*Say: I do not know whether that which you have been promised is imminent, or whether my Lord has set for it a distant term.*" (Verse 25)

In summary, then, this message does not belong to the Prophet; he has no say in it other than to deliver it as he is commanded. Only this will bring him safety. Likewise, the punishment the unbelievers are threatened with also belongs to God and the Prophet has no say in it, nor does he know when it will take place. It may be close at hand or it may be deferred by God to a time of His own choosing. This applies to punishment both in this life and in the life to come. All this is known only to God. The Prophet has no say here whatsoever, not even knowing its timing. It is to God that such knowledge of the world beyond belongs: "*He alone knows that which is beyond the reach of human perception, and He does not disclose His secrets to anyone.*" (Verse 26) The Prophet has neither title nor position, other than that of being God's servant. This is his title and his highest position. The Islamic concept is thus stated in all clarity, free of any confusion. The Prophet is given the order to state his position and he does so without hesitation: "*Say: I do not know whether that which you have been promised is imminent, or whether my Lord has set for it a distant term. He alone knows that which is beyond the reach of human perception, and He does not disclose His secrets to anyone.*" (Verses 25–26)

There is only one exception. God may inform His messengers of something that belongs to this world beyond, within the limits that help them to deliver His message to people. Indeed, all that He reveals to them is part of His knowledge which He imparts to them at a certain point in time and within certain limits. He observes them and looks after them as they deliver His messages. The Prophet is commanded here to declare this exception in a very serious way: "*except to a messenger whom He has been pleased to choose. He then sends watchers to walk before and behind him, to know that they have delivered their Lord's messages. He has full knowledge of all they have. He takes count of everything.*" (Verses 27–28) Those messengers whom God chooses to deliver His message are given some information that belongs to the world beyond human perception. They are, for example, given revelation, its subject matter, method, the angels imparting it, its source and its preservation in the guarded tablet, as well as all that is related to what their messages contain. Prior to giving them such information, it was all there, in the realm that lies beyond human perception.

At the same time, these messengers are surrounded by watchers and guards to protect them. They protect them from Satan's whispers and attempts to derail their efforts, from personal promptings and aspirations, from human weaknesses, forgetfulness, deviation and all other shortcomings that may affect a messenger and disrupt his work. The notion is also a frightening one, "*He then sends watchers to walk before and behind him.*" (Verse 27) This describes the careful, complete and permanent monitoring of the messenger as he goes about his great task, delivering his message. This monitoring has a purpose: "*to know that they have delivered their Lord's messages.*" (Verse 28) God certainly knows this. What is meant here is that the messengers fulfil their assignments and that this brings about their fulfilment in the practical world.

"*He has full knowledge of all they have.*" (Verse 28) Everything in their hearts and lives, everything around them is known to Him; nothing escapes. "*He takes count of everything.*" (Verse 28) This is not though limited to just the messengers; it applies to all things: they are all counted up, which signifies the most accurate type of knowledge.

Just imagine this situation: God's Messenger is surrounded by guards and watchers, with God's knowledge already having counted all he has and all that is around him. He receives the command as a soldier who has no option but to comply. He goes about his task but he is not left to himself, to suffer from his own weaknesses or desires. What he likes or dislikes is not allowed to affect him. The whole matter is one of complete seriousness and careful monitoring. He knows all this and moves along his way, turning neither here nor there, because he knows that he is constantly watched by the most alert of guards. It is a situation that draws much sympathy for God's Messenger. It also fills us with awe when we consider the seriousness of it all.

This very awesome note brings the *sūrah* to its conclusion. It began with a feeling of awe and amazement that is clearly noticeable in the long discourse about the *jinn*. In no more than 28 verses, the *sūrah* outlines a large number of truths that are part of the Islamic faith. They are essential in the formulation of the clear and balanced vision a Muslim must have, leaning towards no extreme. It keeps all doors to knowledge open, leaving no room for delusion or superstition.

Especially true is the statement delivered by the group of *jinn* that listened to the Qur'ān: "*We have heard a wondrous discourse, giving guidance to what is sagacious, and we have come to believe in it.*" (Verses 1–2)

SŪRAH 73

Al-Muzzammil
(The Enfolded One)

Prologue

A report in connection with the revelation of this *sūrah* suggests that the Quraysh elders held a meeting in Dār al-Nadwah, a place where they normally gathered, in order to discuss any momentous event. This time they were discussing their strategy as regards the Prophet and the message he advocated. When the Prophet heard of this meeting, he was distressed. He wrapped himself in his clothes, covered himself and went to sleep. The Angel Gabriel then brought him the first passage of this *sūrah*, comprising 19 verses, with the command to stay up in worship at night. Its final part, consisting of Verse 20, was delayed for a full year, during which the Prophet and some of his Companions attended to their night worship until their legs were swollen from the effort. Only then was the *sūrah*'s second part revealed reducing their burden.

Another report also tells of the occasion of this *sūrah*'s revelation, but it also applies to the revelation of the next *sūrah*, Wrapped in Cloak, as we will mention in our discussion there, God willing. In summary, this report mentions that three years before the start of his message, the Prophet used to go to a cave in Mount Ḥirā', about two miles from Makkah, where he spent the month of Ramaḍān in worship. In this way, his family were not far from him, enabling him to stay in the cave for the whole month. Here, he would feed any poor person who happened to pass by, and spend the rest of his time in worship and contemplation. His thoughts would go to the universe and its amazing scenes, suggesting that it is the creation of a great power. He was unhappy with the flimsy beliefs of his people who were idolaters. Yet he had no clear vision or thoughts. No consistent line presented itself to him.

This seclusion was an aspect of how God guided him, indeed, prepared him, for the great task which was later to be assigned him. He was alone, away from the hassle of life and its preoccupations. He just wanted to broaden his scope, feel the beauty of the universe and try to understand what message it imparts to a clear mind. Whoever is chosen to carry out the task of influencing and changing the direction of humanity needs such seclusion where he is free from life's minor concerns and preoccupations. He certainly needs a period of contemplation when he can look at the open universe and try to understand the truth it signifies. When a person is attending to life's concerns, he finds himself in a familiar environment, which he will complacently accept. He does not think of changing it. It is only moving away from the immediate environment and its concerns that gives the soul its ability to discern what is not readily apparent. Seclusion provides the training ground to appreciate the world around us, without reference to prevailing concepts.

This is, then, what God designed for Muhammad as He prepared him to shoulder the greatest trust. It would be his task to change the direction of human life and thus the world. For three years before the start of his mission, God sent the Prophet into seclusion for one month every year.

When God willed to bestow this great aspect of His grace on the dwellers of the earth, the Angel Gabriel went to the Prophet Muhammad in the cave at Hirā'. The Prophet gives this report about what then took place:

> The Prophet said: "While I was asleep he came to me carrying a case of a very rich material in which there was a book. He said: 'Read.' I replied: 'I am not a reader.' He pressed me so hard that I felt that I was about to die. Then he released me and said, 'Read.' I asked: 'What shall I read?' (I said this only out of fear that he

might repeat what he had done to me before.) He said: 'Read: in the name of Your Lord Who created. It is He Who created man from a clinging cell mass . Read! Your Lord is the Most Bounteous, Who has taught the use of the pen. He has taught man what he did not know.' (96: 1–5) I read it. He stopped. Then he left me and went away. I woke up feeling that it was actually written in my heart."

The Prophet went on to say: "When I was halfway up the mountain, I heard a voice coming from the heavens saying: 'Muḥammad, you are the Messenger of God and I am Gabriel.' I raised my head up to the sky and I saw Gabriel in the image of a man with his feet next to one another up on the horizon. He said again: 'Muḥammad, you are the Messenger of God and I am Gabriel.' I stood in my place looking up at him; this distracted me from my intention. I was standing there unable to move. I tried to turn my face away from him and to look up at the sky, but wherever I looked I saw him in front of me. I stood still, moving neither forward nor backward. Khadījah sent her messengers looking for me and I remained standing in my place all the while until they went back to her. He then left me and I went back to my family. When I reached home I sat next to Khadījah, leaning on her. She said: 'Where have you been? I sent people after you and they went to the outskirts of Makkah looking for you.' I told her of what happened, and she said: 'Rejoice! By God, I was certain that God would bring you only what is good. I certainly hope that you are the Prophet of this nation.'[1]

The revelation stopped for a while, and then when the Prophet went again to the mountain, he looked up and saw the Angel Gabriel. He was overwhelmed with such a shudder that he fell to the ground. He then hurriedly went home, saying to his family: 'Cover me! Wrap me.' They did so. He continued to shiver, so great was his fear. Then Gabriel called him: "*You enfolded one!*" (Verse 1) It is also reported that Gabriel

---

1. Adil Salahi (2002), *Muḥammad: Man and Prophet*, Leicester, The Islamic Foundation, pp. 67–72.

called him: "*You wrapped in your cloak.*" (74: 1) God knows best which of these statements was expressed.

Regardless of whether the first or the second report about this *sūrah*'s revelation is correct, the Prophet learnt that from now on he would only have a little sleep. He had a heavy duty to shoulder, requiring a long struggle. He was always to be on the alert, ready to work hard with little or no rest. The Prophet was told to stay up, and he did, for more than 20 years. He never slackened, but devoted himself completely to his message, attending to its requirements. He shouldered his very heavy burden without complaint. It was the burden of the greatest trust of all, the divine faith and the hard struggle it required.

His first area of struggle was the human mind burdened as it was with a great heap of erroneous concepts, wrong ideas and shackled with personal desires and earthly attractions. When he had purged the minds of some of his Companions of this heavy burden, another battle in a different field beckoned. In fact, this was to culminate in a series of battles against the enemies of the divine message, who marshalled their forces to crush the new message and supplant its tree before it could establish roots and send out its branches. He had hardly finished with these battles in the Arabian Peninsula when the Byzantine Empire began to prepare itself to deal a heavy defeat against this fledgling Islamic state in Arabia.

Yet throughout this long struggle, the first battle for the human mind was not over. This is a permanent battle against Satan who does not stop even for a moment in his attempts to lure people. Regardless, the Prophet continued to nurture God's message, living in poverty when great riches were available to him, putting in strenuous efforts whilst his Companions enjoyed comfort and security. His was a continuous and hard struggle, one that required patience, perseverance, night worship, recitation of the Qur'ān and the permanent pursuit of God's pleasure. It was a full implementation of divine orders: "*You enfolded one! Stand in prayer at night, all but a small part of it, half of it, or a little less, or add to it. Recite the Qur'ān calmly and distinctly. We shall bestow on you a weighty message. The night hours are strongest of tread and most upright of speech. During the day you have a long chain of things to attend to. Therefore, remember your Lord's name and devote yourself wholeheartedly to Him. He is the Lord of the east and the west. There is no deity other than Him. Take Him for your guardian. Endure with patience what people may say, and leave their company with noble dignity."* (Verses 1–10) Thus did Muḥammad stand in prayer, and thus did he continue to fight a raging battle for over 20 years. He let nothing distract him from this. From the moment he heard the divine call assigning his duty to him he remained focused on his task. May God reward him with His best reward.

The first half of the *sūrah* maintains the same rhythm, and almost the same rhyme, with an 'l' followed by a long 'a', throughout. It gives the *sūrah* a relaxed but courtly beat, one that suits its majestic command, the seriousness of the duty and the successive and momentous images the *sūrah* portrays. These include the weighty message and the frightening warning: *"Leave to Me those who deny the truth and enjoy the comforts of this life. Bear with them for a little while. We have heavy fetters and a blazing fire, food that chokes and painful suffering."* (Verses 11–13) There are also the awesome images drawn from the great universe and from the depths of the human soul: *"on the day when the earth and the mountains will shake, and the mountains will crumble into heaps of shifting sand."* (Verse 14) *"How will you, if you continue to disbelieve, guard yourselves against a day that will turn children's hair grey? That is the day when the skies shall be rent asunder. God's promise will certainly be fulfilled."* (Verses 17–18)

The long verse that comes at the end of the *sūrah* was revealed a whole year later, during which time the Prophet and some of those who followed him maintained night worship for much of the night, every night. This was an aspect of their preparation for the role God wanted them to play. When this year had passed, the order of night worship was relaxed, but this relaxation was coupled with the reassurance that it was God's choice for them, according to His knowledge and wisdom, taking into account the duties He had assigned to them. This verse runs in a different style: it is long, with a varied, calm and steady lilt. The ending, with its 'm' preceded by a long 'e', perfectly suits this steady calmness.

In its two parts, the *sūrah* portrays a stage of the Islamic message, beginning with the address from on high outlining the heavy assignment. It describes the preparation for this heavy duty by night worship, constant prayer, recitation of the Qur'ān, and glorifying God, relying on Him alone, enduring hardship with forbearance, withdrawing with dignity from the unbelievers and leaving them to God Almighty, to whom the message belongs and who conducts the battle. The *sūrah* ends with a kindly touch, relieving some of the burden and lightening the duty, with a directive to attend to voluntary tasks that earn His reward. Finally, it holds out the prospect of God granting forgiveness and bestowing grace: "*God is Much Forgiving, Ever Merciful.*" (Verse 20) The *sūrah* as a whole represents a stage in the noble efforts made by that chosen community to return erring humanity to its Lord, enduring all the hardship involved and looking for no gain in this life.

334

Al-Muzzammil
(The Enfolded One)

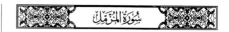

In the Name of God, the Lord of Grace, the Ever Merciful

يَـٰٓأَيُّهَا ٱلْمُزَّمِّلُ ﴿١﴾

You enfolded one! (1)

قُمِ ٱلَّيْلَ إِلَّا قَلِيلًا ﴿٢﴾

Stand in prayer at night, all but a small part of it, (2)

نِّصْفَهُۥ أَوِ ٱنقُصْ مِنْهُ قَلِيلًا ﴿٣﴾

half of it, or a little less, (3)

أَوْ زِدْ عَلَيْهِ وَرَتِّلِ ٱلْقُرْءَانَ تَرْتِيلًا ﴿٤﴾

or add to it. Recite the Qur'ān calmly and distinctly. (4)

إِنَّا سَنُلْقِى عَلَيْكَ قَوْلًا ثَقِيلًا ﴿٥﴾

We shall bestow on you a weighty message. (5)

إِنَّ نَاشِئَةَ ٱلَّيْلِ هِىَ أَشَدُّ وَطْـًٔا وَأَقْوَمُ قِيلًا ﴿٦﴾

The night hours are strongest of tread and most upright of speech. (6)

إِنَّ لَكَ فِى ٱلنَّهَارِ سَبْحًا طَوِيلًا ﴿٧﴾

During the day you have a long chain of things to attend to. (7)

وَٱذْكُرِ ٱسْمَ رَبِّكَ وَتَبَتَّلْ إِلَيْهِ تَبْتِيلًا ﴿٨﴾

Therefore, remember your Lord's name and devote yourself wholeheartedly to Him. (8)

He is the Lord of the east and the west. There is no deity other than Him. Take Him for your guardian. (9)

رَبُّ ٱلْمَشْرِقِ وَٱلْمَغْرِبِ لَآ إِلَٰهَ إِلَّا هُوَ فَٱتَّخِذْهُ وَكِيلًا ۞

Endure with patience what people may say, and leave their company with noble dignity. (10)

وَٱصْبِرْ عَلَىٰ مَا يَقُولُونَ وَٱهْجُرْهُمْ هَجْرًا جَمِيلًا ۞

Leave to Me those who deny the truth and enjoy the comforts of this life. Bear with them for a little while. (11)

وَذَرْنِي وَٱلْمُكَذِّبِينَ أُوْلِي ٱلنَّعْمَةِ وَمَهِّلْهُمْ قَلِيلًا ۞

We have heavy fetters and a blazing fire, (12)

إِنَّ لَدَيْنَآ أَنكَالًا وَجَحِيمًا ۞

food that chokes and painful suffering (13)

وَطَعَامًا ذَا غُصَّةٍ وَعَذَابًا أَلِيمًا ۞

on the day when the earth and the mountains will shake, and the mountains will crumble into heaps of shifting sand. (14)

يَوْمَ تَرْجُفُ ٱلْأَرْضُ وَٱلْجِبَالُ وَكَانَتِ ٱلْجِبَالُ كَثِيبًا مَّهِيلًا ۞

We have sent you a Messenger to be your witness, just as We sent a messenger to Pharaoh. (15)

إِنَّآ أَرْسَلْنَآ إِلَيْكُمْ رَسُولًا شَٰهِدًا عَلَيْكُمْ كَمَآ أَرْسَلْنَآ إِلَىٰ فِرْعَوْنَ رَسُولًا ۞

Pharaoh disobeyed the messenger, and so We inflicted on him a severe punishment. (16)

فَعَصَىٰ فِرْعَوْنُ ٱلرَّسُولَ فَأَخَذْنَٰهُ أَخْذًا وَبِيلًا ۞

How will you, if you continue to disbelieve, guard yourselves against a day that will turn children's hair grey? (17)

فَكَيْفَ تَتَّقُونَ إِن كَفَرْتُمْ يَوْمًا يَجْعَلُ ٱلْوِلْدَٰنَ شِيبًا ۝

That is the day when the skies shall be rent asunder. God's promise will certainly be fulfilled. (18)

ٱلسَّمَآءُ مُنفَطِرٌۢ بِهِۦ كَانَ وَعْدُهُۥ مَفْعُولًا ۝

This is but a reminder. Let him who will, take the way to his Lord. (19)

إِنَّ هَٰذِهِۦ تَذْكِرَةٌ فَمَن شَآءَ ٱتَّخَذَ إِلَىٰ رَبِّهِۦ سَبِيلًا ۝

Your Lord knows that you stand in prayer nearly two-thirds of the night, or one-half or a third of it, as do some of your followers. It is God who determines the measure of night and day. He is aware that you will not be able to keep a measure of it, and therefore He turns towards you in His grace. Recite of the Qur'ān as much as may be easy for you. He knows that some of you will be sick, others will go about in the land seeking God's bounty, and others will be fighting for God's cause. Therefore, recite whatever you may do with ease. Attend regularly to prayer, pay your obligatory charity [i.e. zakāt], and give God a goodly loan. Whatever good

إِنَّ رَبَّكَ يَعْلَمُ أَنَّكَ تَقُومُ أَدْنَىٰ مِن ثُلُثَيِ ٱلَّيْلِ وَنِصْفَهُۥ وَثُلُثَهُۥ وَطَآئِفَةٌ مِّنَ ٱلَّذِينَ مَعَكَ وَٱللَّهُ يُقَدِّرُ ٱلَّيْلَ وَٱلنَّهَارَ عَلِمَ أَن لَّن تُحْصُوهُ فَتَابَ عَلَيْكُمْ فَٱقْرَءُوا۟ مَا تَيَسَّرَ مِنَ ٱلْقُرْءَانِ عَلِمَ أَن سَيَكُونُ مِنكُم مَّرْضَىٰ وَءَاخَرُونَ يَضْرِبُونَ فِي ٱلْأَرْضِ يَبْتَغُونَ مِن فَضْلِ ٱللَّهِ وَءَاخَرُونَ يُقَٰتِلُونَ فِي سَبِيلِ ٱللَّهِ فَٱقْرَءُوا۟ مَا تَيَسَّرَ مِنْهُ وَأَقِيمُوا۟ ٱلصَّلَوٰةَ وَءَاتُوا۟ ٱلزَّكَوٰةَ وَأَقْرِضُوا۟ ٱللَّهَ قَرْضًا حَسَنًا وَمَا تُقَدِّمُوا۟

you may offer on your own behalf, you shall find it with God to be better and richer in reward. Seek God's forgiveness, for God is Much-Forgiving, Ever Merciful. (20)

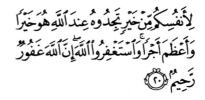

The One Enfolded

You enfolded one! Stand in prayer at night, all but a small part of it, half of it, or a little less, or add to it. Recite the Qur'ān calmly and distinctly. We shall bestow on you a weighty message. The night hours are strongest of tread and most upright of speech. During the day you have a long chain of things to attend to. Therefore, remember your Lord's name and devote yourself wholeheartedly to Him. He is the Lord of the east and the west. There is no deity other than Him. Take Him for your guardian. (Verses 1–9)

"*You enfolded one! Stand...*" This is a call from on high, given by God Almighty. Stand, for you have a great mission and a heavy burden. Stand, for you need to put in sustained efforts. Stand, for the time of sleep and comfort is over. You need to prepare for the task ahead of you.

This is an awesome command requiring the Prophet to pull himself out from the warmth of his bed in a comfortable home and with a happy family life so as to place himself in the midst of a hard struggle, with different forces pulling him here and there. A man who lives for himself may find comfort and ease, but he lives small and dies small. The noble soul who shoulders such a heavy burden has a different perspective: what has he got to do with sleep, comfort, a warm bed and an easy life? The Prophet realized and accepted this. When his wife, Khadījah, once told him to go to bed and relax, he said to her: "The time for sleep has passed." Yes, indeed. He had nothing more than long nights and a long struggle ahead of him.

"*You enfolded one! Stand in prayer at night, all but a small part of it, half of it, or a little less, or add to it. Recite the Qur'ān calmly and distinctly.*" (Verses 1–4) Such is the preparation for the great task. It uses divine methods, which are guaranteed to succeed. The method is night worship, which on the higher level of remembrance of God takes up more than half the night but less than two-thirds, and on the lower level, but still in complete remembrance of Him, takes one-third of the night. This long time should be spent in prayer and recitation of the Qur'ān, aloud but with calmness and without singing. It is authentically reported that the Prophet prayed his *Witr* in no more than 11 *rak'ahs*, but these took up nearly two-thirds of the night, and he read at length from the Qur'ān.

"Sa'īd ibn Hishām reports that he asked Ibn 'Abbās how the Prophet prayed *Witr*. He said: 'Shall I tell you who of all people knows this best?' He said: 'Yes.' Ibn 'Abbās said: 'Go and ask 'Ā'ishah and then come back and tell me her answer'." Sa'īd continues: "I said to her: 'Mother of the believers, tell me what was the Prophet like in his manners?' She said: 'Do you not read the Qur'ān?' I said I did. She said: 'His manners were as the Qur'ān says.' I was about to leave, but then I thought of the Prophet's night worship, so I said: 'Mother of the believers, tell me how the Prophet offered his night worship.' She said: 'Do you not read the *sūrah* starting with, *You enfolded one!*' I said I did. She said: 'God made night worship obligatory at the opening of the *sūrah*, and the Prophet and his Companions offered night worship until their feet were swollen. God retained the end of that *sūrah* with Himself for 12 months, then the relaxation was given. Thus, night worship became voluntary after it had been obligatory.' I was about to rise, but then I remembered *Witr*, and I said to her: 'Mother of the believers, tell me how the Prophet offered *Witr*.' She said: 'We used to prepare for him his tooth stick and the water for his ablutions. He would rise at night, as God wished, and he would use his tooth stick to brush his teeth, then would perform his ablution. He would offer eight *rak'ahs* without sitting in between until he had completed the eighth *rak'ah*. He would then sit down and glorify God and supplicate, then he would stand before ending his prayer, to offer his ninth *rak'ah*. He would sit glorifying God alone, then supplicating. He would then finish his prayer with *Salām*. He said it aloud so that we would hear it. He then prayed two *rak'ahs* sitting down. Thus he would complete 11 *rak'ahs*. When he was older and put on some weight, he would pray *Witr* in seven *rak'ahs* and do two *rak'ahs* seated to complete nine. When the Prophet offered some voluntary prayers he liked to keep this up. If something distracted him from night worship, such as sleep or illness, he would offer 12 *rak'ahs* during the day. I know that the Prophet never read the whole of the Qur'ān in one night up to the morning, and I know that he never fasted a complete month other than Ramaḍān'." [Related by Aḥmad and Muslim.][2]

A Heavy Weight to Carry

All these preparations were made so that the Prophet could receive the weighty discourse: "*We shall bestow on you a weighty message.*" (Verse 5) This is a reference to the Qur'ān and the assignment it gives the Prophet. The Qur'ān is not weighty in its phraseology; on the contrary, it is both easy to bear in mind and recite. However, it is weighty in the scales of truth, and profound in its effect on people's hearts: "*Had We brought down this Qur'ān upon a mountain, you would have seen it humble itself and break asunder for fear of God.*" (59: 21) Instead, God sent down the Qur'ān to a man's heart, which received it and was steadier than a mountain.

Receiving such an overflow of light and knowledge and understanding it is certainly a weighty task. Dealing with great universal truths as they are is weighty indeed. Likewise, to be in contact with those on high and with the spirits of animate and inanimate creatures in the manner the Prophet was is also weighty. Moreover, to undertake this mission without hesitation and not to turn away here or there in response to temptation is mightily weighty. All this certainly requires long preparation.

Standing up in night worship when others are asleep, leaving aside the distractions of daily life, being in contact with God, receiving His light and bounty, seeking the pleasure of being alone with Him, reciting the Qur'ān in the deep silence of the night as if it is being bestowed now from on high so as to be echoed by the whole universe, and receiving

---

2. There are many *aḥādīth* and reports describing the Prophet's night prayer and his *Witr*, which show that the Prophet varied these prayers. For a full discussion, refer to *Zād al-Ma'ād* by Ibn al-Qayyim, in which a chapter is devoted to describing the Prophet's night worship.

inspiration from the Qur'ān and its melody in the quiet of the night...
is all part of the preparation. It provides the necessary preparedness to
shoulder the weighty task and undertake the sustained and strenuous
efforts required of the Prophet and anyone who advocates the message
of Islam. It enlightens advocates' hearts along their hard way, protecting
them from Satan's whispering and temptations, and guiding their
footsteps so that they do not fall into the dark maze that stands adjacent
to this shining road.

"*The night hours that are strongest of tread and most upright of speech.*"
(Verse 6) The night hours referred to here are those that follow the *Isha*
Prayer. This verse describes these hours as '*strongest of tread*', which means
more physically exhausting, and '*most upright of speech*', which means
better rewarding, [according to Mujāhid]. To overcome the appeal of bed
after a long day is exhausting, but it declares the triumph of the spirit in
response to God's instructions. Since the person spending these hours in
worship prefers to be in contact with God, these hours are most upright
of speech, because they give a special taste to God's glorification. They
make prayer more enlightening, and supplication more transparent.
They fill the heart with light and happiness that may not be felt in day
prayers. God, who created man and his heart, knows how it responds,
what it takes in, how it opens to callers, and at which times it is more
responsive and better prepared.

When God wanted to prepare His servant and Messenger, Muḥammad
(peace be upon him), for his weighty message, He chose for him night
worship because the night hours are the ones that are strongest of tread,
producing the most profound impression, and most upright of speech.
God knows that during the day he had to attend to different tasks that
took up much of his energy. "*During the day you have a long chain of
things to attend to.*" (Verse 7) Let him, then, do whatever he needs to
do during the day, putting in whatever effort was necessary. When the
night comes, however, he should devote himself to his Lord, offering
prayer and glorifying Him: "*Therefore, remember your Lord's name and
devote yourself wholeheartedly to Him.*" (Verse 8)

Remembering God's name does not mean repeating His honoured
name verbally, counting with a bead of one hundred or a thousand pieces.
Rather, this is a heart-felt remembrance along with verbal mention, or

it means prayer and reading the Qur'ān while praying. Wholehearted devotion means concentrating all one's attention on God, addressing one's worship to Him, discarding all thoughts and feelings other than the bond with Him.

The *sūrah* follows this instruction by making it clear that there is none other than God to turn to: "*He is the Lord of the east and the west. There is no deity other than Him. Take Him for your guardian.*" (Verse 9) He is the Lord of all, the One God other than whom there is no deity. To devote oneself to Him is to be with the only truth in the universe, and to place one's trust in Him is to place it in the only power in the universe. Such reliance on Him is the natural result of believing in His oneness and His control of the east and the west, or in other words, His control of the entire universe. The Prophet, who is told to stand in order to carry his heavy burden, needs to devote himself wholeheartedly to God and to rely on Him only. It is from this that he derives the strength necessary to carry his heavy burden along his long way.

Flattened Mountains

God then directs His Messenger to remain content and patient in the face of all opposition and false accusation, telling him to leave those people who so behave to Him to deal with:

Endure with patience what people may say, and leave their company with noble dignity. Leave to Me those who deny the truth and enjoy the comforts of this life. Bear with them for a little while. We have heavy fetters and a blazing fire, food that chokes and painful suffering on the day when the earth and the mountains will shake, and the mountains will crumble into heaps of shifting sand. We have sent you a Messenger to be your witness, just as We sent a messenger to Pharaoh. Pharaoh disobeyed the messenger, and so We inflicted on him a severe punishment. How will you, if you continue to disbelieve, guard yourselves against a day that will turn children's hair grey? That is the day when the skies shall be rent asunder. God's promise will certainly be fulfilled. (Verses 10–18)

If the first report concerning the revelation of this *sūrah*'s opening is correct and that it took place during the early days of the Islamic message, this means that this second passage was revealed later, after the call to Islam went public and began to encounter opposition from those who denied it. Some of these were arrogant in their opposition, speaking ill of the Prophet and the believers. If, on the other hand, the second report is more accurate, then the first part of the *sūrah* was revealed in full when the Prophet was at the receiving end of the unbelievers' determined opposition to his message. Be that as it may, we see that the directive to remain patient comes after the one to attend to night worship and engage in glorifying God. These two instructions are often given together with the aim of reinforcing the advocates of the divine message with the help they need along their long journey. These advocates contend with difficulties both from within themselves and from outside by the opponents of Islam. Both types of difficulty are extremely hard to deal with. Hence, the first directive is to remain patient: "*Endure with patience what people may say*", which may be infuriating. Next comes a similarly magnanimous directive: "*And leave their company with noble dignity.*" (Verse 10) No need for any remonstration, showing anger, friction or hostility. Such was the policy of the Islamic message in Makkah, particularly in the early days. It was only an address to hearts and minds, putting the truth before people in a calm and dignified way.

This policy of leaving the company of arrogant opponents with noble dignity is not easy; it requires patience in addition to remembrance and glorification of God. Patience was enjoined by God on every one of His messengers, time after time, and enjoined on His servants who believed in His messengers. No one can dedicate himself to God's message unless he makes patience his main resort, equipment and armament. Advocacy of the divine message is a hard struggle. It requires striving against one's own weaknesses, distractions, desires, haste and despair, and striving against the opponents of the message, their schemes, plots as well as the harm they may directly seek to inflict on the message and its supporters. It also involves striving against general trends to abandon the divine message and its duties, and to disregard its values while paying lip-service to it. Facing such a struggle, an advocate of Islam can resort to nothing other than patience. Turning to God and glorifying Him goes hand in hand with patience in almost every situation.

So, the Prophet is instructed to endure with patience whatever is said against his message and to leave with noble dignity the company of those who are so hostile to it, leaving them to God to deal with: "*Leave to Me those who deny the truth and enjoy the comforts of this life. Bear with them for a little while.*" (Verse 11) This is said by none other than the Almighty, who has control of all forces. It is He who says: "*Leave to Me those who deny the truth.*" They are only ordinary people while this threat is issued by the One who originated them and created this vast universe needing for the purpose nothing more than to say, '*Be*'. God is saying here that the message is His own, so those who deny it should be left to Him, while the Prophet should carry on with his task of delivering the message. If they want to persist in their denial, then let them do so, but leave their company with noble dignity. It is God who will take care of them and foil their designs. The Prophet need not think further about them.

The warning is terrifying and stunning. It implies that the Almighty will deal with such petty people. They "*may enjoy the comforts of this life*", but they remain powerless in front of Him, no matter how despotic they may be in this world.

"*Bear with them for a little while.*" (Verse 11) If he were to bear with them for the length of life on earth, this would still only represent '*a little while*', because this life is in God's measure only a day or a part of a day. Indeed, it will seem thus to them when it is over. On the Day of Judgement, they will feel that it was no more than an hour of a day. So, it remains '*a little while*' no matter how long this may be; even if they depart this life in safety, without being punished in this world.

"*We have heavy fetters and a blazing fire, food that chokes and painful suffering.*" (Verses 12–13) All these are fitting requitals for those who enjoy a life of comfort in this world but who continue to deny the divine message. They do not appreciate what they are given; nor do they give due thanks for the comforts they enjoy. Therefore, you, Muḥammad, bear with patience what they say and do, and leave them to Me. We have what they deserve: heavy fetters, a blazing fire, food that is so hard to swallow and a painful suffering on a day that fills everyone with fear.

An image of that day and the fear it spreads is then drawn: "*On the day when the earth and the mountains will shake, and the mountains will crumble into heaps of shifting sand.*" (Verse 14) The feeling of fear transcends all people to spread over the whole earth: it thus shudders and crashes, with the great mountains crumbling into heaps of sand. How, then, will humans react?

Having given this scary image, the *sūrah* addresses those unbelievers who enjoy a life of luxury reminding them of a great tyrant, Pharaoh, and how God swept him away: "*We have sent you a Messenger to be your witness, just as We sent a messenger to Pharaoh. Pharaoh disobeyed the messenger, and so We inflicted on him a severe punishment.*" (Verses 15–16) The terrible end suffered by Pharaoh is given in such a brief word that it strikes even more fear into their hearts, and this after the scene depicting the earth shaking and the mountains flattened.

These are two images of punishment, one in this life and one in the hereafter. How do those unbelievers think they will be saved from such punishment? "*How will you, if you continue to disbelieve, guard yourselves against a day that will turn children's hair grey? That is the day when the skies shall be rent asunder.*" (Verses 17–18) This is an image of a fearful event that leaves the sky rent asunder, after the earth and the mountains have crumbled into sand. It turns children's hair grey. The images of this terrifying event are drawn from a silent landscape as well as a living humanity. The *sūrah* portrays these images before the addressees as if they are taking place now. It then confirms this most emphatically: "*God's promise will certainly be fulfilled.*" (Verse 18) It is happening, no doubt. Whatever God wills is certain to be done.

Now the *sūrah* gives their hearts a gentle touch so that they may remember and choose the road to safety: "*This is but a reminder. Let him who will, take the way to his Lord.*" (Verse 19) The way to God is safer and easier to traverse. It spares people such a terrible outcome.

The verses carrying these warnings strike the unbelievers hard. They shake them violently, leaving them in great fear. At the same time, they provide strengthening reassurance to the Prophet and his small group of followers. They feel that God is with them, punishing their enemies. It is only but a short while and the appointed time will arrive. The matter will then be settled. God will take His enemies, who are their enemies, and put them to the fate they deserve. God does not abandon the believers to His enemies, even though He may give His enemies respite for a while.

A Hard Duty is Relaxed

Then comes the second part of the *sūrah*, consisting of a single, long verse that was revealed one year after the first part, according to the more authentic reports:

> *Your Lord knows that you stand in prayer nearly two-thirds of the night, or one-half or a third of it, as do some of your followers. It is God who determines the measure of night and day. He is aware that you will not be able to keep a measure of it, and therefore He turns towards you in His grace. Recite of the Qur'ān as much as may be easy for you. He knows that some of you will be sick, others will go about in the land seeking God's bounty, and others will be fighting for God's cause. Therefore, recite whatever you may do with ease. Attend regularly to prayer, pay your obligatory charity [i.e. zakāt], and give God a goodly loan. Whatever good you may offer on your own behalf, you shall find it with God to be better and richer in reward. Seek God's forgiveness, for God is Much-Forgiving, Ever Merciful. (Verse 20)*

This is a compassionate touch, providing relief after much fatigue. It is a relaxation by God granted to the Prophet and the believers, when they have proved themselves to be dedicated totally to His divine message. They were exhausted after having stood up for long hours at night offering prayers in which very long passages of the Qur'ān were recited. God never wanted to afflict His Prophet with the Qur'ān, putting him to such hardship. Rather, He was only preparing him for the hard task that he was to undertake for the rest of his life. The believers who followed him would also have to share in this heavy burden.

The verse starts with friendly reassurance: "*Your Lord knows that you stand in prayer nearly two-thirds of the night, or one-half or a third of it, as do some of your followers.*" (Verse 20) He has seen you doing it, and what you and your Companions offered of night worship has been accepted and entered in God's records. He knows that you have abandoned your beds, warm as they are on a cold night, preferring to listen to His directives. He is Compassionate towards you and those who are with you. "*It is God who determines the measure of night and day.*" (Verse 20) He causes the one to be longer and the other to be shorter. Thus, the night may get longer or shorter, but you are all carrying on with the duty required of you, staying up close to two-thirds of the night, or half of it, or even a third. He is aware of your weakness. He does not want to afflict you or put you to unbearable hardship; all He wants is that you should have the necessary training. Now that you have been trained, you can relax and take things easier: "*Recite of the Qur'ān as much as may be easy for you,*" during your night worship, without putting yourselves to much difficulty. God knows that things will happen to you and drain your energy, making standing long into the night worshipping too hard: "*He knows that some of you will be sick,*" and these cannot offer night worship. "*Others will go about in the land seeking God's bounty.*" (Verse 20) These need to attend to their work and earn their living. This is essential. God does not want people to abandon their life's needs and lead the life of a monk who is totally devoted to worship. "*And others will be fighting for God's cause.*" (Verse 20) God will permit you to stand up and fight against those who wage aggression against you. He will permit you to fight so that Islam will have its safe and sovereign place. You may, then, relax and approach your duty in a comfortable way: "*Therefore, recite whatever you may do with ease.*" (Verse 20) Let there be no exhaustion or hardship. However, you must attend to all obligatory worship: "*Attend regularly to prayer, pay your obligatory charity [i.e. zakāt].*" (Verse 20) When you have done this you may wish to add voluntary charity, which will increase your reward: "*And give God a goodly loan. Whatever good you may offer on your own behalf, you shall find it with God to be better and richer in reward.*" (Verse 20) Turn to God, appealing for forgiveness of your shortcomings. Man remains short of what is needed, no matter how diligent he tries to be. "*Seek God's forgiveness, for God is Much-Forgiving, Ever Merciful.*" (Verse 20)

This is a compassionate touch, providing relaxation and reassurance after a whole year of night worship. God relaxed this duty for Muslims, making night worship voluntary, rather than an obligatory duty. The Prophet, however, continued on the same lines, offering night worship for no less than one-third of the night. He would appeal to his Lord in the depths of the night, and receive from Him what he needed for his struggle in life. Although his eyes might sleep, his heart would not. His heart was always busy with God's remembrance. It had no desire for anything else in this life.

SŪRAH 74

Al-Muddaththir
(Wrapped in Cloak)

Prologue

The information we expressed in the previous *sūrah*, The Enfolded One, about the occasion and timing of its revelation, also applies to this *sūrah*. Some reports suggest that it was the first to be revealed after *Sūrah* 96, The Germ Cell, while other reports suggest that it was revealed after the Islamic message went public, when the unbelievers began their persecution campaign against the believers in earnest.

Al-Bukhārī mentions a report by Yaḥyā ibn Abī Kathīr who says that he asked Abū Salamah ibn 'Abd al-Raḥmān about the first Qur'ānic revelation. He answered that it was *Sūrah Al-Muddaththir*. "I told him that people said that it was *Sūrah* 96, beginning with '*Read in the name of your Lord*.' Abū Salamah said that he asked Jābir ibn 'Abdullāh about this and when Jābir replied that it was *al-Muddaththir*, he said to him what you had just said. Jābir replied that he only gave me what the Prophet himself said to his Companions: 'I went in seclusion at Ḥirā', and when I finished my time there, I came down. I heard a call, and I looked to my right and left but could see nothing. I came to Khadījah, saying: "Wrap me in a cloak and pour some cold water on me." They did so. I then received the revelation: "*You, wrapped in your cloak, arise and give warning. Glorify your Lord's greatness.*"

349

Jābir reports that he heard the Prophet speaking about early revelations. He said: "While I was walking, I heard a voice coming from the sky. I lifted my eyes to the sky and I saw the angel who came to me when I was at Ḥirā' sitting on a chair in between the sky and the earth. I fell to the ground. Then I came hurriedly to my people, saying: 'Wrap me. Cover me.' I then received the revelation: *'You, wrapped in your cloak, arise and give warning. Glorify your Lord's greatness; clean your garments; stay away from all filth.'* Then more revelations came in succession.

Commenting on this *ḥadīth*, Ibn Kathīr says in his commentary on the Qur'ān: "This is the accepted report. It means that revelations started before this, because of the Prophet saying, 'I saw the angel who came to me when I was at Ḥirā'.' That angel was obviously Gabriel who visited the Prophet saying: *'Read in the name of your Lord who has created – created man out of a clinging cell mass.[1] Read – for your Lord is the most Bountiful One, who has taught the use of the pen, taught man what he did not know.'* (96: 1–5) A lull in revelation then took place, and thereafter the angel again came to him. To reconcile the different reports we say that the first revelation the Prophet received after the lull was this *sūrah*."

A different report is given by al-Ṭabarānī on the authority of Ibn 'Abbās: "Al-Walīd ibn al-Mughīrah prepared food for a number of people from the Quraysh, and when they had finished their meal, he asked them what they thought of Muḥammad. Some said that he was a sorcerer, but others said he was not. Some said he was a soothsayer, but others denied this. Others still said he was a poet, but yet others objected. Then some said that what he said was mere 'sorcery handed down from olden times'. They all agreed to this. When the Prophet was informed of this, he felt very sad. He covered his head and wrapped himself up. God revealed to him: *"You, wrapped in your cloak, arise and give warning. Glorify your Lord's greatness; clean your garments; stay away from all filth; do not hold up what you give away, showing it to be much; but to your Lord turn in patience."* (Verses 1–7)

---

1. This translation of this second verse of *Sūrah* 96 is more accurate than what I have given in Vol. XVIII, or what is variously given in other Qur'ānic translations. – Editor's note.

This report is almost identical to the one that refers to the preceding *sūrah*, The Enfolded One. Thus, we cannot be at all certain which of these two *sūrahs* preceded the other, or which was revealed on what occasion.

Yet a close look at the text of the *sūrah* suggests that its first seven verses were probably revealed in the very early days of the Islamic message. The same may be said of the first nine verses of *Sūrah* 73, The Enfolded One. Both openings aimed to prepare the Prophet for his great task, particularly when he needed to go public and address all the community with his message. He would then have to face strong opposition and compounded trouble that required such preparations. This would mean that the rest of the two *sūrahs* was revealed later, when the Prophet faced determined rejection and false accusations of fabricating his message.

Nevertheless, this does not exclude the other possibility that the openings of the two *sūrahs* were revealed together with what followed them. This so as to reply to the denial by the Quraysh and to comfort the Prophet who took their scheming to heart. Thus, the two *sūrahs* would be like *Sūrah* 68, The Pen, which is also discussed in this volume.

Be that as it may, the *sūrah* begins with an address from on high assigning a great mission to the Prophet, one that required he get out of bed and start striving: *"You, wrapped in your cloak, arise and give warning."* (Verses 1–2) He is directed to prepare himself for his great task, taking the measures outlined to him in the *sūrah*: *"Glorify your Lord's greatness; clean your garments; stay away from all filth; do not hold up what you give away, showing it to be much; but to your Lord turn in patience."* (Verses 3–7) Like the one in the preceding *sūrah*, this directive ends with the need to be patient.

The *sūrah* then includes a strong warning to those who deny the Day of Judgement, threatening them with a war directly waged by God, on the same lines as the warning given in the preceding *sūrah*: *"When the trumpet is sounded that will be a day of anguish, far from easy for the unbelievers. Leave to me the one I created alone, to whom I have granted vast wealth, and sons by his side, making life smooth and easy for him; yet he greedily desires that I give him more. No! He has set himself stubbornly against Our revelations. I will constrain him to endure a painful uphill climb."* (Verses 8–17)

The *sūrah* makes special mention of this person who was particularly hostile to the Islamic message, but without naming him. It paints an image of his scheming against Islam, in the same way as we have seen in *Sūrah* 68. It may be that both *sūrahs* talk of the same person, said to be al-Walīd ibn al-Mughīrah, but more of this later. The *sūrah* mentions the reason for God's warning to this person: "*He thought and he schemed. Damn him, how he schemed! Again, damn him, how he schemed! He looked around, then he frowned and glared, then he turned his back and gloried in his arrogance, and said, 'This is just sorcery handed down from olden times! This is nothing but the word of a mere mortal!'*" (Verses 18–25) The *sūrah* then specifies his destiny: "*I will cast him into the scorching fire. Would that you knew what the scorching fire is like! It leaves nothing, and spares nothing; it appears before mankind, guarded by nineteen.*" (Verses 26–30)

The mention of the '*scorching fire*' and the nineteen guards in charge of it invited much questioning from the unbelievers who also added to it ridicule and sarcastic remarks, and raised doubts among those who were not firm in faith. The *sūrah* outlines God's wisdom in mentioning this number, giving us a glimpse of the world beyond our perception and the fact that knowledge of this world is God's own preserve. This glimpse sheds light on some aspects of the Islamic concept of this world beyond: "*We have appointed none other than angels to guard the fire, and We have made their number a test for the unbelievers. Thus those who have been granted revelations in the past may be convinced and the believers may grow yet more firm in their faith; and so those who have been granted revelations and the believers will entertain no doubt; but the sick at heart and the unbelievers will ask, 'What could God mean by this image?' Thus God lets go astray whomever He wills, and guides whomever He wills. No one knows your Lord's forces except Him. This is all but a reminder for mankind.*" (Verse 31)

The whole question of hell and the life to come is then related to some scenes of the universe which all people see. Thus the *sūrah* combines the inspiration of these scenes with the feelings aroused by the earlier warnings: "*No! By the moon! By the night when it departs, and the shining dawn! It is indeed one of the mighty things, a warning to all mankind, to those of you who choose to go ahead or to lag behind.*" (Verses 32–37)

The *sūrah* shows the respective positions of the unbelievers and the righteous. The unbelievers will make a long confession explaining the reasons why they deserved their fate on that day of reckoning and requital. This is followed by a final word about them, when no word of intercession on their behalf will be of any use: "*Every soul is held in pledge for what it has wrought, except for those on the right hand. They will be in gardens, and will ask about the guilty ones: 'What brought you into the scorching fire?' They will answer: 'We were not among those who prayed, neither did we feed the needy; but we indulged with others in vain talk, and we denied the Day of Judgement until there came upon us that which is certain.' So, of no benefit to them could be the pleas of any intercessors.*" (Verses 38–48)

Having painted this image of their position of humiliation and shameful confession, the *sūrah* wonders at the unbelievers' attitude to the call that seeks to remind them of the way to save themselves. It paints a sarcastic picture that invites ridicule at their wild resistance: "*What is the matter with them that they turn away from all admonition like terrified asses fleeing from a lion?*" (Verses 49–51) It exposes their arrogance, which is the true reason for their obstinate rejection of every caring advice: "*Every one of them demands to be given revelations unfolded before him.*" (Verse 52) They are so envious of the Prophet, thinking that they were more deserving of being given the divine message. There is, however, another deep reason: "*No! They do not fear the life to come.*" (Verse 53)

Finally, the *sūrah* makes a categorical statement that leaves no room for favours for anyone: "*No! This is indeed an admonition. Let him who will, take heed.*" (Verses 54–55) All is left up to God's will: "*They, however, will not take heed unless God so wills. He is the Lord to be feared, the Lord of forgiveness.*" (Verse 56)

The *sūrah* represents a stage of the hard fought struggle in which the Qur'ān is in combat with *jāhiliyyah* and its ingrained notions and concepts. It was also combating headstrong and deliberate rejection using diverse methods. There are many similarities of approach between this *sūrah* and *Sūrahs* 73 and 68, which suggests that all three were revealed within the same period, dealing with similar situations. The only exception, of course, is the second part of *Sūrah* 73, which as we have seen deals with something different.

The present *sūrah* is characterized by short verses and a fast flow. Its verses have a variety of endings and rhymes. Its beat moves slowly at times, but is very fast at others, particularly when it describes the individual who comes in for criticism, or when it paints the image of hell's scorching fire. This variation of tone, beat, rhyme, images and scenery gives the *sūrah* a distinctive ambience, particularly as it picks up a rhyme that has already been used and changed, or when the rhyme changes in the same section to deliver an intended surprise. We will now look at the *sūrah* in detail.

Al-Muddaththir
(Wrapped in Cloak)

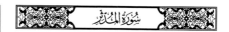

In the Name of God, the Lord of Grace, the Ever Merciful

You, wrapped in your cloak, (1)

يَٰٓأَيُّهَا ٱلْمُدَّثِّرُ ۝

arise and give warning. (2)

قُمْ فَأَنذِرْ ۝

Glorify your Lord's greatness; (3)

وَرَبَّكَ فَكَبِّرْ ۝

clean your garments; (4)

وَثِيَابَكَ فَطَهِّرْ ۝

stay away from all filth; (5)

وَٱلرُّجْزَ فَٱهْجُرْ ۝

do not hold up what you give away, showing it to be much; (6)

وَلَا تَمْنُن تَسْتَكْثِرُ ۝

but to your Lord turn in patience. (7)

وَلِرَبِّكَ فَٱصْبِرْ ۝

When the trumpet is sounded (8)

فَإِذَا نُقِرَ فِي ٱلنَّاقُورِ ۝

that will be a day of anguish, (9)

فَذَٰلِكَ يَوْمَئِذٍ يَوْمٌ عَسِيرٌ ۝

far from easy for the unbelievers. (10)

عَلَى ٱلْكَٰفِرِينَ غَيْرُ يَسِيرٍ ۝

Leave to me the one I created alone, (11)

ذَرْنِي وَمَنْ خَلَقْتُ وَحِيدًا ۝

to whom I have granted vast wealth, (12)

وَجَعَلْتُ لَهُۥ مَالًا مَّمْدُودًا ۝

and sons by his side, (13)

وَبَنِينَ شُهُودًا ۝

making life smooth and easy for him; (14)

وَمَهَّدتُّ لَهُۥ تَمْهِيدًا ۝

yet he greedily desires that I give him more. (15)

ثُمَّ يَطْمَعُ أَنْ أَزِيدَ ۝

No! He has set himself stubbornly against Our revelations. (16)

كَلَّآ إِنَّهُۥ كَانَ لِـَٔايَٰتِنَا عَنِيدًا ۝

I will constrain him to endure a painful uphill climb! (17)

سَأُرْهِقُهُۥ صَعُودًا ۝

He thought and he schemed. (18)

إِنَّهُۥ فَكَّرَ وَقَدَّرَ ۝

Damn him, how he schemed! (19)

فَقُتِلَ كَيْفَ قَدَّرَ ۝

Again, damn him, how he schemed! (20)

ثُمَّ قُتِلَ كَيْفَ قَدَّرَ ۝

He looked around, (21)

ثُمَّ نَظَرَ ﴿٢١﴾

then he frowned and glared, (22)

ثُمَّ عَبَسَ وَبَسَرَ ﴿٢٢﴾

then he turned his back and gloried in his arrogance, (23)

ثُمَّ أَدْبَرَ وَاسْتَكْبَرَ ﴿٢٣﴾

and said, 'This is just sorcery handed down from olden times! (24)

فَقَالَ إِنْ هَٰذَآ إِلَّا سِحْرٌ يُؤْثَرُ ﴿٢٤﴾

This is nothing but the word of a mere mortal!' (25)

إِنْ هَٰذَآ إِلَّا قَوْلُ الْبَشَرِ ﴿٢٥﴾

I will cast him into the scorching fire. (26)

سَأُصْلِيهِ سَقَرَ ﴿٢٦﴾

Would that you knew what the scorching fire is like! (27)

وَمَآ أَدْرَىٰكَ مَا سَقَرُ ﴿٢٧﴾

It leaves nothing, and spares nothing; (28)

لَا تُبْقِي وَلَا تَذَرُ ﴿٢٨﴾

it appears before mankind, (29)

لَوَّاحَةٌ لِّلْبَشَرِ ﴿٢٩﴾

guarded by nineteen. (30)

عَلَيْهَا تِسْعَةَ عَشَرَ ﴿٣٠﴾

We have appointed none other than angels to guard the fire, and We have made their number a test

وَمَا جَعَلْنَآ أَصْحَابَ النَّارِ إِلَّا مَلَـٰئِكَةً وَمَا جَعَلْنَا عِدَّتَهُمْ إِلَّا فِتْنَةً لِّلَّذِينَ

for the unbelievers. Thus those who have been granted revelations in the past may be convinced and the believers may grow yet more firm in their faith; and so those who have been granted revelations and the believers will entertain no doubt; but the sick at heart and the unbelievers will ask, 'What could God mean by this image?' Thus God lets go astray whomever He wills, and guides whomever He wills. No one knows your Lord's forces except Him. This is all but a reminder for mankind. (31)

كَفَرُوا۟ لِيَسْتَيْقِنَ ٱلَّذِينَ أُوتُوا۟ ٱلْكِتَٰبَ وَيَزْدَادَ ٱلَّذِينَ ءَامَنُوٓا۟ إِيمَٰنًا وَلَا يَرْتَابَ ٱلَّذِينَ أُوتُوا۟ ٱلْكِتَٰبَ وَٱلْمُؤْمِنُونَ وَلِيَقُولَ ٱلَّذِينَ فِى قُلُوبِهِم مَّرَضٌ وَٱلْكَٰفِرُونَ مَاذَآ أَرَادَ ٱللَّهُ بِهَٰذَا مَثَلًا كَذَٰلِكَ يُضِلُّ ٱللَّهُ مَن يَشَآءُ وَيَهْدِى مَن يَشَآءُ وَمَا يَعْلَمُ جُنُودَ رَبِّكَ إِلَّا هُوَ وَمَا هِىَ إِلَّا ذِكْرَىٰ لِلْبَشَرِ ۝٣١

No! By the moon! (32)

كَلَّا وَٱلْقَمَرِ ۝٣٢

By the night when it departs, (33)

وَٱلَّيْلِ إِذْ أَدْبَرَ ۝٣٣

and the shining dawn! (34)

وَٱلصُّبْحِ إِذَآ أَسْفَرَ ۝٣٤

It is indeed one of the mighty things, (35)

إِنَّهَا لَإِحْدَى ٱلْكُبَرِ ۝٣٥

a warning to all mankind, (36)

نَذِيرًا لِّلْبَشَرِ ۝٣٦

to those of you who choose to go ahead or to lag behind. (37)

لِمَن شَآءَ مِنكُمْ أَن يَتَقَدَّمَ أَوْ يَتَأَخَّرَ ۝٣٧

Every soul is held in pledge for what it has wrought, (38)

كُلُّ نَفْسِۭ بِمَا كَسَبَتْ رَهِينَةٌ ۞

except for those on the right hand. (39)

إِلَّآ أَصْحَٰبَ ٱلْيَمِينِ ۞

They will be in gardens, and will ask (40)

فِى جَنَّٰتٍ يَتَسَآءَلُونَ ۞

about the guilty ones: (41)

عَنِ ٱلْمُجْرِمِينَ ۞

'What brought you into the scorching fire?' (42)

مَا سَلَكَكُمْ فِى سَقَرَ ۞

They will answer: 'We were not among those who prayed, (43)

قَالُوا۟ لَمْ نَكُ مِنَ ٱلْمُصَلِّينَ ۞

neither did we feed the needy; (44)

وَلَمْ نَكُ نُطْعِمُ ٱلْمِسْكِينَ ۞

but we indulged with others in vain talk, (45)

وَكُنَّا نَخُوضُ مَعَ ٱلْخَآئِضِينَ ۞

and we denied the Day of Judgement (46)

وَكُنَّا نُكَذِّبُ بِيَوْمِ ٱلدِّينِ ۞

until there came upon us that which is certain.' (47)

حَتَّىٰٓ أَتَىٰنَا ٱلْيَقِينُ ۞

So, of no benefit to them could be the pleas of any intercessors. (48)

فَمَا تَنفَعُهُمْ شَفَٰعَةُ ٱلشَّٰفِعِينَ ۞

What is the matter with them that they turn away from all admonition (49)

فَمَا لَهُمْ عَنِ ٱلتَّذْكِرَةِ مُعْرِضِينَ ﴿٤٩﴾

like terrified asses (50)

كَأَنَّهُمْ حُمُرٌ مُّسْتَنفِرَةٌ ﴿٥٠﴾

fleeing from a lion? (51)

فَرَّتْ مِن قَسْوَرَةٍ ﴿٥١﴾

Every one of them demands to be given revelations unfolded before him. (52)

بَلْ يُرِيدُ كُلُّ ٱمْرِئٍ مِّنْهُمْ أَن يُؤْتَى صُحُفًا مُّنَشَّرَةً ﴿٥٢﴾

No! They do not fear the life to come. (53)

كَلَّا بَل لَّا يَخَافُونَ ٱلْآخِرَةَ ﴿٥٣﴾

No! This is indeed an admonition. (54)

كَلَّا إِنَّهُ تَذْكِرَةٌ ﴿٥٤﴾

Let him who will, take heed. (55)

فَمَن شَاءَ ذَكَرَهُ ﴿٥٥﴾

They, however, will not take heed unless God so wills. He is the Lord to be feared, the Lord of forgiveness. (56)

وَمَا يَذْكُرُونَ إِلَّا أَن يَشَاءَ ٱللَّهُ هُوَ أَهْلُ ٱلتَّقْوَىٰ وَأَهْلُ ٱلْمَغْفِرَةِ ﴿٥٦﴾

Essential Preparations

You, wrapped in your cloak, arise and give warning. Glorify your Lord's greatness; clean your garments; stay away from all filth; do not hold up what you give away, showing it to be much; but to your Lord turn in patience. (Verses 1–7)

This is an address from on high, calling on the Prophet to get ready for his great task. He is to warn mankind, wake them up and save them from evil in this life and from the fire in the life to come, setting them on the way to salvation before it is too late. This is a hard, momentous task when assigned to an individual human being, even though he may be God's Prophet and Messenger. Mankind had, however, gone so far astray and were too steeped in sin, rebellion, arrogance and persistence. All this made advocacy of the divine faith the most difficult task to be assigned to anyone.

"You, wrapped in your cloak, arise and give warning." (Verses 1–2) To give warning is the most obvious aspect of the divine message. It alerts people to the impending danger that threatens to engulf those who are oblivious of it, heading unaware into error. Such warning manifests God's grace which He bestows on people. They take away nothing of His kingdom when they go astray, and increase His kingdom by nothing when they follow His guidance. However, it is out of His grace that He gives them such care so as to save themselves from severe punishment in the life to come and to rid themselves of evil in this life. The fact that His messengers call on them to respond so as to earn His forgiveness and be admitted into His heaven is certainly a manifestation of His grace.

Having given His Messenger the instruction to warn others, He adds some directives for the Prophet to observe in his own life. The first of these is to *"Glorify your Lord's greatness."* (Verse 3) Only your Lord is great and only He deserves to be glorified. This directive lays down an aspect of the Islamic concept of God and His oneness. Every person, every creature, every value and everything is small, while God alone is great. All entities, sizes, forces, values, events, situations, concepts and shapes dwindle into insignificance, while God alone is supreme, perfect and majestic. The Prophet is instructed to warn mankind, bearing all the difficulties of such a task, with this vision in mind. He will then think little of any force or plot aiming to impede his work, as he realizes that his Lord alone is great. Advocates of the divine message need to always keep this principle in mind when they go about fulfilling their difficult task.

361

The Prophet is then directed to maintain purity and cleanliness: "*Clean your garments.*" (Verse 4) In Arabic usage, this expression of cleaning one's garments means maintaining purity of heart and high moral values together with clean action. It refers to the purity of self which is covered by those garments. Such purity and cleanliness signify the condition that is best suited for receiving instructions from on high. Moreover, it is the closest thing to the nature of the Islamic message. Furthermore, it is necessary for the task of warning and delivering the message, advocating it in the midst of a multitude of forces and trends that bring with them much filth, dirt and indecency. The advocate of the divine faith needs to be perfectly clean so that he can save those who are tainted while allowing nothing to taint him. This directive shows deep understanding of the needs of those who undertake advocacy of God's faith in all types of social environment and situations.

The next directive requires the Prophet to steer away from polytheism and all that exposes people to God's punishment: "*stay away from all filth.*" (Verse 5) The Prophet stayed away from all this long before he was endowed with prophethood. His was an upright nature that disliked all deviation from the truth, and disowned all erroneous beliefs and loose morality. He never indulged in any unbecoming practice. However, this directive is a declaration of separation between two different routes that can never cross. The Arabic word *rujz*, which is translated here as 'filth', originally meant suffering or torment. It then came to signify anything that leads to it. Hence, the directive to abandon all such filth that incurs punishment and torment.

The Prophet is also directed to be self-effacing so as not to hold up what he has to exert of effort, thinking it to be much: "*Do not hold up what you give away, showing it to be much.*" (Verse 6) He was to give much, sacrifice much and put up with much hardship. Yet God wants him not to think too highly of what he has to give, feeling that it is much. To be a true advocate of the divine faith, one must not think of what one has to give or sacrifice for it. The sacrifice required is so great that no one can give it willingly unless he also forgets it, or rather does not feel it in the first place because he is so preoccupied with his duty towards God. In essence, he feels that whatever he has to give for His sake is only part of His grace and favour. Thus, giving the sacrifice and exerting the effort are an aspect of grace God bestows on us. We should be grateful to Him for enabling us to give it in the first place, rather than holding it up, thinking we have done something great.

The last directive is to be patient: "But to your Lord turn in patience." (Verse 7) This is a directive that is given every time the Prophet is assigned a task or needs counselling. Patience is the most important prerequisite in this hard battle of advocating God's message. It is a battle against two enemies simultaneously: personal desires on the one hand, and external enemies motivated by their own desires on the other. The most effective weapon in this hard and long battle is patience for God's sake and with the aim to please Him.

When this divine directive has been given to the noble Prophet, the *sūrah* outlines the terms of the warning to be given. This is delivered in a way that alerts attention to the hard day they are warned about:

When the trumpet is sounded that will be a day of anguish, far from easy for the unbelievers. (Verses 8–10)

The sounding of the trumpet is here expressed in a stronger way than normally used in other *sūrahs*. In its Arabic expression, *nuqira fin-nāqūr*, it gives a feeling of a sound that is sharper to the ear, almost beating on it. Hence, the day will be hard for the unbelievers. Its hardship is emphasized by negating all traces of ease. It is hard from start to finish, without any respite. No details are given of this hardship; it is left in general terms to impart a feeling of distress and choking. It behoves those unbelievers, then, to heed the warning before the trumpet is sounded, ushering in this very hard day.

Singled Out

This general warning gives way to the case of a particular individual who seems to have played a leading role in rejecting the divine message and plotting against it. The *sūrah* issues a crushing warning, painting an ugly image of him that invites derision. This is particularly so when his unpleasant features appear lifelike before our eyes:

Leave to me the one I created alone, to whom I have granted vast wealth, and sons by his side, making life smooth and easy for him; yet he greedily desires that I give him more. No! He has set himself stubbornly against Our revelations. I will constrain him to endure a painful uphill climb! He thought and he schemed. Damn him, how he schemed! Again, damn him, how he schemed! He looked around, then he frowned and glared, then he turned his back and gloried in his arrogance, and said, 'This is just sorcery handed down from olden times! This is nothing but the word of a mere mortal!' I will cast him into the scorching fire. Would that you knew what the scorching fire is like! It leaves nothing, and spares nothing; it appears before mankind, guarded by nineteen. (Verses 11–30)

There are several reports suggesting that the person so referred to is al-Walīd ibn al-Mughīrah. 'Ikrimah reports: "Al-Walīd ibn al-Mughīrah met the Prophet who read to him a passage of the Qur'ān. It appeared as though al-Walīd softened a bit. Abū Jahl heard of this, so he went to al-Walīd and said to him: 'Uncle! Your people are raising some money for you.' He asked for what reason. Abū Jahl answered: 'They want to give it to you, because you went to Muḥammad to see what you might gain from him.' [Abū Jahl was thus playing on a most sensitive point, trying to arouse al-Walīd's pride.] Al-Walīd said: 'The Quraysh know that I am the richest among them.' Abū Jahl said: 'Then say about him something to make clear to your people that you are opposed to what he says.' Al-Walīd said: 'What shall I say. None of you has better knowledge of poetry than me. I know all about poetry including the poetry of the *jinn*. What Muḥammad says is nothing like that. What he says is indeed sweet; it towers over all speech; it rises high and nothing can top it.' Abū Jahl said: 'Your people will not be satisfied unless you say something negative about him.' Al-Walīd said: 'Then give me time to think.' When he thought it over, he said of the Qur'ān: 'This is sorcery taken from olden times.' The above passage was then revealed in reference to him.

In another report, it is said that some of the Quraysh said: 'If al-Walīd follows Muḥammad, the whole tribe will follow suit.' Abū Jahl said: 'I will take care of him.' He went to see him… The report then mentions the above conversation between the two, and that after long thinking al-Walīd said: 'It is sorcery handed down from olden times. Do you not see how it causes divisions between a man and his family, children and servants?'

Such was the event as reported. The Qur'ān, however, describes it in its own moving way. It so starts with a fearsome threat: "*Leave to me the one I created alone.*" (Verse 11) The address is made to the Prophet. He is told to leave this person to God. He created him alone, without anything in which he now takes pride, such as wealth, children, comforts and luxuries. Yet he still seeks to possess more. God says to the Prophet to leave him to Him, for He will battle with him. Here, we can only shudder as we imagine the overwhelming power of the Almighty moving to crush this powerless individual. This shuddering is experienced by the reader and the listener who are not meant by it. How, then, about the one facing this power?

The *sūrah* describes at length this creature and what God has given him of favours, before it mentions his headstrong rejection of the truth. God created him alone, deprived of everything, naked. Then He gave him plentiful wealth, and able sons who attend to his needs and give him authority and protection. He facilitated life for him. Yet, "*he greedily desires that I give him more.*" (Verse 15) He is neither content nor grateful. Or perhaps he hopes to receive revelations and a sacred book, as mentioned towards the end of the *sūrah*: "*Every one of them demands to be given revelations unfolded before him.*" (Verse 52) He did indeed envy the Prophet.

At this point he is strongly repudiated for his greed. He has not shown any gratitude to God for what He has given him.

"*No!*" The repudiating word is decisive. "*He has set himself stubbornly against Our revelations.*" (Verse 16) He deliberately set himself against all pointers to the truth and indicators of the way to true faith. He opposed the divine message and the Messenger preaching it, prevented others from listening to it and spread false rumours about it. This repudiation of the man and his attitude is followed by a threat to replace his ease with hardship: "*I will constrain him to endure a painful uphill climb.*" (Verse 17) This verse paints hardship in the movement. Going uphill is the most difficult and tiring way of walking. If the person set on such an uphill road has no intention of so going up, but is instead being pushed, the hardship is even greater and more exhausting. At the same time, the statement expresses a reality. A person who moves away from the easy, friendly and facilitated path of faith will find himself in a hard to traverse passage that leads nowhere. He goes through life worried and distressed, as though he is rising high into the sky, or going up a rough, hard track carrying neither food nor drink, and expecting no comfort at the end.

The *sūrah* draws a sarcastic caricature of this person with grim features, frowning, thinking hard and trying to find fault with the Qur'ān. He is obsessed with trying to find an apt and negative description to label the Qur'ān with: "*He thought and he schemed. Damn him, how he schemed! Again, damn him, how he schemed! He looked around, then he frowned and glared, then he turned his back and gloried in his arrogance, and said, 'This is just sorcery handed down from olden times! This is nothing but the word of a mere mortal!'*" (Verses 18–25) The image we are given here takes us one glimpse at a time, step by step, and movement by movement. It is like watching a paint brush at work, rather than hearing words giving a meaning. More than that, it is like a scene in a film, consisting of many frames. One frame shows him thinking and scheming. This is coupled with an invocation, '*Damn him!*' and a derisive remark, '*how he schemed.*' Both invocation and derisive remark are repeated to heighten the effect. Another frame shows him looking here and there, in affected seriousness, again inviting ridicule. The next frame shows him frowning, and another shows his features grim. In both, the impression is that he is trying to concentrate, but in a laughable way. Yet, after all this labour, he comes up with nothing. He closes his eyes to the light and turns away from the truth. All he can say is: "*This is just sorcery handed down from olden times! This is nothing but the word of a mere mortal!*" (Verses 24–25)

These glimpses of such a sad individual are impressed on our minds more strongly than a painting or a film. Moreover, the man becomes the laughing stock for the rest of time. His miserable picture is raised there for all future generations to see.

Once the picture is hung in place and this miserable creature is seen by all there then comes a frightening warning: "*I will cast him into the scorching fire.*" (Verse 26) The warning is made even stronger by the

366

enigmatic air that surrounds the fire: "*Would that you knew what the scorching fire is like!*" (Verse 27) It is too great to be imagined! Yet another description is added to make it even more terrifying: "*It leaves nothing, and spares nothing.*" (Verse 28) It swallows everything, obliterating whoever or whatever is cast into it, leaving no trace. Moreover, it presents itself before people: "*It appears before mankind.*" (Verse 29) This echoes the verse in an earlier *sūrah*: "*It will claim all who turn their backs, and turn away from the truth.*" (70: 17) It thus shows itself, deliberately striking fear into those who are destined to suffer its torment. Guards stand there: "*Guarded by nineteen.*" (Verse 30) We do not know if the number refers to individual angels who are '*stern and mighty*', as described in *Sūrah* 66, or whether it refers to rows or types of angels. This is merely a piece of information to which more will be added in the *sūrah*.

A Test for Unbelievers

The believers received God's words with the sort of acceptance worthy of one who trusts his Lord and shows the sort of manners a servant should have. They neither doubted this piece of news nor questioned it. The unbelievers, on the other hand, received it all with hearts devoid of faith or seriousness. They had no reverence of God. Hence, they made sarcastic comments, making the number, i.e. the 19, the subject of endless jokes. One of them said: 'Will not each 10 of you be sufficient to overcome one of them?' Another said: 'You take care of two of these and I will take care of the rest. You will have nothing to worry about from them.'

It was then that the next verse was revealed, explaining God's purpose behind giving this piece of information on something that belongs to the realm beyond human perception and mentioning this particular figure. It makes clear that that realm and the knowledge of all that relates to it belongs to God alone. It also mentions the ultimate end that results from the mention of the scorching fire and its guard:

We have appointed none other than angels to guard the fire, and We have made their number a test for the unbelievers. Thus those who have been granted revelations in the past may be convinced and the believers may grow yet more firm in their faith; and so those who have been granted revelations and the believers will entertain no doubt; but the sick at heart and the unbelievers will ask, 'What could God mean by this image?' Thus God lets go astray whomever He wills, and guides whomever He wills. No one knows your Lord's forces except Him. This is all but a reminder for mankind. (Verse 31)

The verse begins by mentioning the nature of the 19 guards whose number the unbelievers joked about: "*We have appointed none other than angels to guard the fire.*" (Verse 31) They belong to that species of creature the nature and strength of which are known only to God Almighty. He mentions elsewhere in the Qur'ān that the angels "*never disobey God in whatever He commands them and always do what they are bidden to do.*" (66: 6) This statement makes it clear that they always obey God's orders and that they have the power to do whatever He bids them. Since He has assigned to them the task of guarding hell, then they have been given the power to undertake this task and fulfil it as it should be done. Thus, there is no way that human beings can fight with them or subdue them. Such talk only betrays the unbelievers' crude ignorance of the nature of God's creation and how He conducts affairs.

"*We have made their number a test for the unbelievers.*" (Verse 31) It is the unbelievers that start arguing when the number is mentioned, because they cannot distinguish when an argument is out of place. Since this question belongs to the realm beyond, and mankind have no knowledge of it, then whatever God says about it should be accepted without argument. It should also be understood that mentioning this fact only, without adding further details, is the appropriate and beneficial way. To argue about it is futile, because argument can only be based on knowledge that does not fit with the information to hand. Their exact number, whatever it signifies, is determined by the One who coordinates everything in the universe and creates everything according to a specific measure. This number is like any other, and a person who wants to argue will make the same objection to any other number. Why are the heavens seven? Why was man created from dried clay, like pottery while the *jinn* were created from raging flames of fire, as mentioned in *Sūrah* 55? Why does pregnancy last nine months? Why do tortoises live for centuries?

Why this, and why that! The answer is that because the Creator who holds sway over all things has willed it so, and His will is always done! This is the final answer in such matters.

"Thus those who have been granted revelations in the past may be convinced and the believers may grow yet more firm in their faith; and so those who have been granted revelations and the believers will entertain no doubt." (Verse 31) Both groups will find in the number of the guards of hell what will give some of them more certainty and give others firmer faith. The people given revelations in the past must have known something of this fact so that when they heard the Qur'ān confirming it, they were certain about it. As for the believers, whatever God says will add to their faith and make it firmer, because their hearts are open to receive facts directly, happy with every new piece of information from God. They realize that such a number serves a particular purpose in God's accurate and fine scheme of creation. Their faith thus grows firmer. This fact thus becomes more firmly established in the hearts of both groups and neither will then doubt anything that comes from God.

"But the sick at heart and the unbelievers will ask, 'What could God mean by this image?'" (Verse 31) The same fact leaves opposite effects on different hearts. While the people of the scriptures and the believers will have more faith as a result of mentioning the number of hell's guards, the very mention of this makes the unbelievers and hypocrites wonder about the reason for giving such an image. They neither appreciate the wisdom behind this strange matter, nor acknowledge God's absolute wisdom of creation. Besides, they are in doubt about the information given and the good purpose served by it.

"Thus God lets go astray whomever He wills, and guides whomever He wills." (Verse 31) God mentions facts and puts up signs and indicators. Different hearts receive it differently. A group will be guided to the truth by such facts, as God wills, while another will go astray, also as God wills. Everything is ultimately determined by God's will which is absolutely free. Human beings were created by God's will with a dual tendency to follow either His guidance or error. Thus, every person acts within God's will whether he follows guidance or goes astray.

When we fully appreciate the fact that God's will is absolutely free, without restriction or impediment, and that everything that occurs in the universe ultimately reverts to His will, and when we put this in the proper perspective, we spare our minds the narrow and endless argument on what people call 'predestination'. Such argument is futile, because it looks at this question, which relates to God the Infinite, from a narrow angle, limiting it to human logic and experience.

God clearly put before us two ways: one follows His guidance and the other leads to error. He has laid down for us a method of action which will, if we implement it, ensure that we have all the guidance we need, live happily and earn His reward. He has also pointed out to us other methods which lead us into error, misery and ruin. He has not required us to know anything beyond this, and has not given us the power to know more. He tells us that His will is absolutely free and inevitable. We should, therefore, deal with understanding this within our abilities and limitations, following the way of guidance and avoiding the different ways leading into error. We must not enter into any futile argument about something that we will never be able to fathom, because it pertains to the world beyond. When we do so, we arrive at the conclusion that all the efforts theologians and philosophers put into the question of predestination, in the way they argued it, were useless, because they were the wrong efforts put into the wrong field.

We do not know what God's hidden will is concerning us, but we do know what God wants of us: namely to deserve His grace which He has committed Himself to bestow upon us. Our proper course, then, is to devote our efforts to the fulfilment of what He has required us to do, leaving His hidden will to Him alone. What will happen to us is according to His will, and we will know it when it happens, and not before. What happens will fulfil His purpose and will be according to His wisdom.

"*No one knows your Lord's forces except Him.*" (Verse 31) The nature, function and effect of these forces are all matters beyond our perception. Of these, He reveals to us what He wishes. His decision is final. No one need argue about anything God has chosen not to inform us about. Such argument is futile.

"*This is all but a reminder for mankind.*" (Verse 31) 'This' may be a reference to God's forces, or to hell and those guarding it as these are also part of God's forces. Mentioning these is meant to alert and warn people, not to open a way for conjecture. Believing hearts will certainly benefit by such reminders, but erring ones will continue to argue endlessly.

A Look at the Universe

The *sūrah* now relates the truths of the life to come, the scorching fire of hell and God's forces to various aspects of His fine creation in the universe, which people often overlook because of long familiarity. Yet these are evident proofs of God's limitless power of creation and His perfect design of the universe:

> *No! By the moon! By the night when it departs, and the shining dawn! It is indeed one of the mighty things, a warning to all mankind.* (Verses 32–36)

The sight of the moon, the departing night and the shining dawn are certainly inspiring. They say much to the human heart, whispering secrets and arousing deep feelings. In its quick reference to these, the Qur'ān touches our innermost selves where feelings and secrets are settled. It is rarely the case that people contemplate the sight of the moon as it rises, travels or sets without the moon whispering some universal secret in their ears. It sometimes takes no more than to stand in the moonlight in order to feel your heart being washed, as if you were bathing in light. It is hardly possible for anyone to look carefully at the night as it starts to depart, at that time of complete serenity before sunrise, when the world starts to wake up and opens its eyes, without being profoundly affected by it. Likewise, it is hardly possible for anyone not to be alert to the scene of dawn as it breaks and begins to shine without experiencing a sense of opening up that makes us aware of a change of feeling. This change makes us ready to receive the light that shines within our hearts just as we receive the light shining over the world around us.

God, the Creator of the human heart, knows that these very sights can sometimes work wonders with this heart, as though they are recreating it. Beyond these shining feelings and openings up, the moon, the night and the dawn all refer to a great truth to which the Qur'ān alerts us.

They all point to God's power of creation, His limitless wisdom and His fine coordination of His creation.

God Almighty swears by these great universal truths in order to alert those who are oblivious to their greatness and the message they impart. He swears that the scorching fire, or its guards, or the hereafter and its events, is one of the great wonders that serve as a warning to mankind of the impending danger ahead: "*It is indeed one of the mighty things, a warning to all mankind.*" (Verses 35–36) The very oath, its contents and subject matter are all like hammers striking hard at people's hearts. This is in perfect harmony with the sounding of the trumpet mentioned earlier, and with the opening of the *sūrah* as it addresses the Prophet and bids him to arise and warn. The whole atmosphere is one of hard hitting, warning of an impending danger.

Individual Responsibility

The *sūrah* now declares that every soul bears responsibility for itself, leaving everyone to choose for themselves. It also states that each soul will have to account for its choices and be judged according to its deeds:

> *It is indeed one of the mighty things, a warning to all mankind, to those of you who choose to go ahead or to lag behind. Every soul is held in pledge for what it has wrought.* (Verses 35–38)

All people, every single one of them, are responsible for themselves, choosing their own positions, going ahead or lagging behind, achieving an honourable status or bringing humiliation upon themselves. Thus, every soul is tied to what it does and the action it takes. God has shown all people the way that leads to Him so that they can take that way with open eyes. As this declaration of individual responsibility is made against the backdrop of inspiring universal scenes, as well as the scene of the scorching fire that spares nothing, it has its profound effect.

It is further declared, however, that an exception is made in the case of the believers who are referred to here as the ones on the right hand. These are untied. They are also given the right to ask the guilty about what has perpetrated their fate:

Except for those on the right hand. They will be in gardens, and will ask about the guilty ones: 'What brought you into the scorching fire?' They will answer: 'We were not among those who prayed, neither did we feed the needy; but we indulged with others in vain talk, and we denied the Day of Judgement until there came upon us that which is certain.' (Verses 39–47)

That the believers are thus excepted is due to God's grace, for He blesses their good deeds and multiplies them. This declaration, at this particular point, touches all hearts. It first touches the hearts of the guilty who were bent on denying the truth. They see themselves in such a humiliating position, making long confessions, while the believers, whom they looked down upon in this world, stand in a position of dignity, asking them as if they are put in a position of authority: "*What brought you into the scorching fire?*" (Verse 42) It also touches the hearts of the believers who used to be at the receiving end of much hardship from those same guilty ones. Now they see themselves in a high position while their arrogant enemies of old are placed in such humiliation. The image is so powerful that it gives both sides a feeling that it is actually taking place now, as though the life of this world has come to an end and is now a thing of the past.

The long confession by the guilty gives details of the many wrongs they have perpetrated, and for which they are led to the scorching fire. They humbly admit to these in front of the believers. "*They will answer: We were not among those who prayed.*" (Verse 43) This is a reference to faith altogether, rather than to the act of prayer. It highlights the great importance of prayer in the Islamic faith, presenting it as a symbol and proof of faith. Denying it puts a person in the ranks of the unbelievers.

"*Neither did we feed the needy.*" (Verse 44) This comes next to denying the faith. It is an act of worship in respect of His creatures, following worship dedicated to Him only. The fact that this quality is expressed so strongly in several places in the Qur'ān gives us an impression of the social environment the Qur'ān addressed. It was a hard environment where kindness to the poor was rare, despite showing great generosity when that served social interests. Such generosity did not apply in situations of real need or pure kindness.

"But we indulged with others in vain talk." (Verse 45) This describes how they took faith lightly and treated it carelessly, in jest, when it was the most important matter in man's life. Indeed man should resolve this issue of faith within his own mind and heart, before he attends to any other matter in life, because it is the issue that gives him his concept of life, values and standards. It provides him with the light that shows him his way in life. How, then, can man take it other than seriously? How can he treat it as vain talk in which he indulges with similarly careless people?

"And we denied the Day of Judgement." (Verse 46) This is the core guilt. A person who denies the Day of Judgement will have no proper standard by which to evaluate things. All values are shaken in his mind. To him, the scope of life becomes too narrow as it dwindles into this limited space of his time on earth. He looks at the consequences of events as they are within this limited space of time and place, and he is unhappy. How can he be otherwise when he does not take the final outcome into account? Indeed, all his standards, and all matters of this life will be defective, before his evaluation of the life to come and his position there becomes faulty. Hence, he ends in utter ruin.

The guilty admit that they continued in that situation, unwilling to pray, being uncharitable to the needy, indulging in vain talk and denying the Day of Judgement, *"until there came upon us that which is certain."* (Verse 47) What came upon them is death, which ends all doubt, bringing the final say and leaving no room for regret, repentance or the mending of one's ways.

The *sūrah* comments on their abject humiliation by raising no hope of any change in their status: *"So, of no benefit to them could be the pleas of any intercessors."* (Verse 48) The whole thing is settled. The end of the guilty has been determined. There is no one to intercede on their behalf anyway. Assuming that such intercessors are there and willing, which is not the case, their pleas will be of no benefit to the guilty.

Who Heeds the Reminder?

The *sūrah* now puts them back in this life, where they have the chance to do something before facing such an abject outcome. Yet they turn away, fleeing from the guidance that would bring them only what is good. The means of salvation are shown to them, but they run away from them. Therefore, the *sūrah* draws a sarcastic image of their situation:

> *What is the matter with them that they turn away from all admonition like terrified asses fleeing from a lion?* (Verses 49–51)

The scene of asses or zebras in great agitation, running in all directions as they hear a lion roaring, was well known to the Arabs. It is a scene of fast movement in a state of panic. Hence, when it is applied to humans, it invites loud laughter. This is especially so if those humans were in real fear of some impending danger. What can be said about them if such is their state, like terrified asses, only because someone is reminding them of their Lord and their eventual destiny, showing them the way to avoid such misery and pain? The image drawn is profound and effective. Those who contemplate it will be too ashamed if they find themselves in it.

Such is their external condition. The *sūrah*, however, describes their inner feelings as well: "*Every one of them demands to be given revelations unfolded before him.*" (Verse 52) It is, then, a question of envy. They begrudge the Prophet for God having given him this exceptional favour. Each one of them is so keen to attain the same status and to be given scriptures to announce to mankind. This must be a reference to their elders who felt hurt that they were bypassed when divine revelations were granted to Muḥammad (peace be upon him). Hence, they said: "*Why was not this Qur'ān revealed to some great man of the two cities?*" (43: 31) God certainly knows to whom to entrust His final message. He chose for this task a great man with the noblest of hearts. This was enough to fill those unbelievers with rancour. Their unjustifiable grudges were also enough for the Qur'ān to expose.

The *sūrah* continues its presentation of their inner feelings. As it censures their envy, which lacks sound basis, the *sūrah* now gives another reason for the unbelievers' continued denial of the truth and their rejection of the message: "*No! They do not fear the life to come.*" (Verse 53) It is indeed their lack of fear of what may happen in the life to come that leads to their heedless attitude to reminders. It makes them react illogically to the divine message. Had they genuinely felt the truth of the hereafter they would have had a totally different reaction.

The *sūrah* repudiates their attitude once more, as it puts its final word to them, leaving them to choose for themselves what they may: *"No! This is indeed an admonition. Let him who will, take heed."* (Verses 54–55) This Qur'ān to which they refuse to listen, and from which they turn away like frightened asses, is a reminder highlighting the truth. Everyone adopts the attitude they want towards it. Whoever is willing to be reminded will have the reminder. Others choose their own way. The outcome is either heaven and the dignity it imparts or hell and the humiliation it involves. It all depends on one's own choice.

The *sūrah* concludes with a restatement of God's free will which ultimately determines all affairs. This is the truth the Qur'ān is keen to state whenever an occasion arises in order to give the believers the correct concept concerning His will, and its being absolutely free and universally applicable.

They, however, will not take heed unless God so wills. He is the Lord to be feared, the Lord of forgiveness. (Verse 56)

Whatever happens in the universe is tied to God's grand will and occurs within it. It is not possible for anyone or anything to will something that is in conflict with God's will. It is His will that controls everything in the universe. It is the will that brought the universe into existence and established its rules and forces. Therefore, the universe, with all living things in it, moves within the framework of God's will that is unbound by limit or restriction.

Taking heed is something that God facilitates for everyone He knows to deserve it. When a servant of His shows that he or she has sincerity of intention, He directs them to what brings them closer to Him. No servant knows what God's will is for him, but everyone knows what God wants of them. He has explained this to them. Therefore, He helps, according to His free will, everyone who is sincere in the attempt to fulfil the duties He has assigned to them.

The Qur'ān aims to impress on every Muslim mind the dual notion that divine will is absolutely free and that it incorporates every will; this so that we turn to it willingly and submit to it completely. This is the essential notion without which Islam cannot be firmly established in one's heart. When it is thus established, it initiates a comprehensive vision to which a Muslim resorts in all life events. This is why this principle is emphasized whenever the Qur'ān promises believers they will be in heaven, warns unbelievers against hell, and speaks of guidance and error. To take such a statement in a narrow way arguing about predestination is no more than taking a partial view of a universal truth, forcing it into a narrow vision that leads nowhere.

"*They, however, will not take heed unless God so wills.*" (Verse 56) Their will cannot be on a collision course with God's will. Indeed, they cannot move in any direction without the operation of God's will that so enables them to move. God is "*the Lord to be feared,*" by His servants. Hence, they are required to demonstrate this. He is also "*the Lord of forgiveness,*" who bestows this on His servants by His will. To fear God is to deserve forgiveness, and God is the Lord of both.

The *sūrah* concludes with this humbly felt glorification of God. It leaves us looking up to God. It leaves us hoping that He will guide us to His remembrance, so that we will always fear Him and that He will then grant us forgiveness.

SŪRAH 75

Al-Qiyāmah
(The Resurrection)

Prologue

This *sūrah* puts forward such a great number of truths, scenes, images, special effects, tones and touches that no attentive heart can easily handle or escape from them. Furthermore, its distinctive style and musical cadence also combine to enhance its effect and bring it to a level that is again difficult to resist or to shed. It starts with two short verses with distinctive notes about the Day of Resurrection and the self-reproaching soul: "*I need not swear by the Day of Resurrection and I need not swear by the self-reproaching soul!*" (Verses 1–2) The *sūrah* then continues with a discourse that from start to finish relates to both the human soul and the Day of Resurrection, often coupling them together. It is as if the opening two verses sum up the subject matter of the whole *sūrah*, or that they set the tone influencing its notes in a fine and beautiful way.

One of the great truths the *sūrah* speaks about is death. The reality of how death applies to every living creature, and from which none can escape or divert it from a loved one is a hard truth. It occurs at every moment, and is applicable to young and old, rich and poor, strong and weak alike. All stand in the same position: there is no escape, no evasion, no resistance, no intercession and no deferment. This suggests that death comes from a higher source, one mankind cannot influence in any way. When it occurs, man simply submits to this higher source.

379

This is the note with which the *sūrah* takes hold of our hearts: "*Yet when the departing soul comes up to the throat, when it is said, 'Can any charmer [do something now]?' When he knows it is the final parting, and one leg will be joined with another, to your Lord he will on that day be driven.*" (Verses 26–30)

Another great truth highlighted in the *sūrah* is how man comes into existence in the first place, and its significance in confirming the truth of resurrection. In this way we see how man's creation occurs according to careful planning. God informs people of the fine stages of their coming into existence, and how these stages succeed one another in such a marvellous procession that only He could have designed. Indeed, even those who deny the resurrection do not claim a different origin for this process. This, in itself, provides irrefutable evidence of the presence of the One God, who deals death and determines its timing. Moreover, death provides clear evidence that resurrection is easy, and also implies that it is necessary. It is, thus, seen as being consistent with the planning whereby man has a clear purpose, and that his life does not end without him accounting for his deeds. This is the note that touches hearts at the beginning of the *sūrah*: "*Does man think that We will not put his bones together again?*" (Verse 3) As it draws to its end, the *sūrah* says: "*Does man think that he will be left without purpose? Was he not a mere drop of emitted sperm? It then became a clinging cell mass, and then God created and shaped it, fashioning out of it the two sexes, male and female. Is He not, then, able to bring the dead back to life?*" (Verses 36–40)

One of the scenes the *sūrah* paints is that of the Day of Resurrection and the great celestial events that take place on that day. In this, we see the psychological upheaval that leaves man at a loss, unable to decide how to face these events. Thus, the great upheaval occurs in the centre of the universe, as well as in the very depths of the human soul, leaving man like a mouse in a trap. This comes in response to man as he wonders, with much doubt, about whether the Day of Resurrection will ever come. In so doing, he treats it with carelessness, persisting in his erring ways. God's response to all this is delivered with a quick rhythm, one that paints a fast succession of images and glimpses: "*Yet man wants to deny what lies ahead of him. He asks: 'When will this Day of Resurrection be?' When the sight is dazzled and the moon eclipsed, when the sun and the moon are brought together, on that day man will say: 'Where to flee?' But no! There is no refuge. On that day, to your Lord all shall return. Man will be told on that day all that he put forward and all that he put back. Man will be a witness against himself, even though he may put up his excuses.''* (Verses 5–15)

One of these images is that of the believers, with full trust in their Lord, looking up to His benevolent face in the midst of all this horror. Another image is of those on the other side, who have no bond with their Lord and no hope of His grace. These expect to receive what their earlier denials, disbelief and disobedience entail. This image is presented forcefully, as if it is taking place at the very moment the *sūrah* is being recited. It responds to people's love of this present world and their disregard of the life to come: *"Yet you love this fleeting life, and give no thought to the life to come. Some faces will on that day be radiant with happiness, looking towards their Lord; and some faces will on that day be overcast with despair, realizing that a great calamity is about to befall them."* (Verses 20–25)

Four verses interrupt this sequence of truths to deliver a special directive to the Prophet concerning the way he receives Qur'ānic revelations. It would also appear that this directive relates to something in particular about this *sūrah*. The Prophet had feared that he might forget something of what was being revealed to him, and in his eagerness to ensure that he did not forget, he used to repeat its verses, one by one, as they were recited to him. He would vocalize the words to make sure that he learnt them by heart. Therefore, he was given the following instruction: *"Do not move your tongue repeating its words in haste. We shall see to its collection and recitation. When We recite it, follow its recitation. Then it will be for Us to make its meaning clear."* (Verses 16–19) This instruction is given to the Prophet to reassure him that the revelation of the Qur'ān, its preservation, collection and explanation of its message are left to the Almighty, the Author of the Qur'ān. The Prophet's own role is to receive the message and deliver it as he receives it. Therefore, he need not worry. He should receive the revelation in full and then he will find it engraved in his heart without change. This was exactly what happened. This instruction, however, has been retained at the precise point where it occurred. Is it not given in God's own words? God's word is sure to stay in place, whatever purpose it addresses. These four verses, therefore, represent words He said, and therefore, they stay in His book like the rest of it. In fact, retaining these four verses in the middle of the *sūrah* points to an inspiring truth concerning all God's words, whatever their purpose happens to be. It tells us that every word God said to His Messenger, Muḥammad (peace be upon him), has been recorded; not a single letter has been lost.

As it listens to this *sūrah*, the human heart realizes that there is no escape. Man will have to account for his deeds, with no one to protect him from God. His existence, in both this life and the life to come, is determined by God, according to His knowledge and planning. Meanwhile, man plays around and thinks himself too important: "*He neither believed nor prayed, but denied the truth and turned away, then he went back to his people full of arrogance.*" (Verses 31–33) As he faces this large number of truths, images and special effects, man is given an implicit but highly effective warning: "*Your doom, man, comes nearer and nearer, and ever nearer and nearer.*" (Verses 34–35)

We see how the *sūrah* deals with man's obstinate rejection of the divine message, making him feel, in all clarity, the seriousness of its discourse about resurrection, the human soul and the accurate measure of life. It tells him that the Qur'ān is also a very serious matter: not a single letter of it will ever be lost because it is all God's own words.

We have thus outlined the truths and images presented in the *sūrah* individually, but when these are read in the *sūrah* itself and as a whole they give a totally different effect. The sequence of these images, the way they are intertwined, and their presentation of an aspect of the truth at one time and then giving another aspect of it a little later are all characteristics of the Qur'ān's inspiring style as it addresses the human heart. No other style or method could possibly achieve a similar effect.

Al-Qiyāmah
(The Resurrection)

In the Name of God, the Lord of
Grace, the Ever Merciful

لَآ أُقۡسِمُ بِيَوۡمِ ٱلۡقِيَـٰمَةِ ۝

I need not swear by the Day of
Resurrection (1)

وَلَآ أُقۡسِمُ بِٱلنَّفۡسِ ٱللَّوَّامَةِ ۝

and I need not swear by the self-
reproaching soul! (2)

أَيَحۡسَبُ ٱلۡإِنسَـٰنُ أَلَّن نَّجۡمَعَ عِظَامَهُۥ ۝

Does man think that We will not
put his bones together again? (3)

بَلَىٰ قَـٰدِرِينَ عَلَىٰٓ أَن نُّسَوِّىَ بَنَانَهُۥ ۝

Yes, indeed! We are able to put in
perfect order his very fingertips!
(4)

بَلۡ يُرِيدُ ٱلۡإِنسَـٰنُ لِيَفۡجُرَ أَمَامَهُۥ ۝

Yet man wants to deny what lies
ahead of him. (5)

يَسۡـَٔلُ أَيَّانَ يَوۡمُ ٱلۡقِيَـٰمَةِ ۝

He asks: 'When will this Day of
Resurrection be?' (6)

فَإِذَا بَرِقَ ٱلۡبَصَرُ ۝

When the sight is dazzled (7)

وَخَسَفَ ٱلۡقَمَرُ ۝

and the moon eclipsed, (8)

وَجُمِعَ ٱلشَّمۡسُ وَٱلۡقَمَرُ ۝

when the sun and the moon are
brought together, (9)

on that day man will say: 'Where to flee?' (10)

يَقُولُ ٱلْإِنسَٰنُ يَوْمَئِذٍ أَيْنَ ٱلْمَفَرُّ ﴿١٠﴾

But no! There is no refuge. (11)

كَلَّا لَا وَزَرَ ﴿١١﴾

On that day, to your Lord all shall return. (12)

إِلَىٰ رَبِّكَ يَوْمَئِذٍ ٱلْمُسْتَقَرُّ ﴿١٢﴾

Man will be told on that day all that he put forward and all that he put back. (13)

يُنَبَّؤُا ٱلْإِنسَٰنُ يَوْمَئِذٍ بِمَا قَدَّمَ وَأَخَّرَ ﴿١٣﴾

Man will be a witness against himself, (14)

بَلِ ٱلْإِنسَٰنُ عَلَىٰ نَفْسِهِۦ بَصِيرَةٌ ﴿١٤﴾

even though he may put up his excuses. (15)

وَلَوْ أَلْقَىٰ مَعَاذِيرَهُۥ ﴿١٥﴾

Do not move your tongue repeating its words in haste. (16)

لَا تُحَرِّكْ بِهِۦ لِسَانَكَ لِتَعْجَلَ بِهِۦٓ ﴿١٦﴾

We shall see to its collection and recitation. (17)

إِنَّ عَلَيْنَا جَمْعَهُۥ وَقُرْءَانَهُۥ ﴿١٧﴾

When We recite it, follow its recitation. (18)

فَإِذَا قَرَأْنَٰهُ فَٱتَّبِعْ قُرْءَانَهُۥ ﴿١٨﴾

Then it will be for Us to make its meaning clear. (19)

ثُمَّ إِنَّ عَلَيْنَا بَيَانَهُۥ ﴿١٩﴾

Yet you love this fleeting life, (20)

كَلَّا بَلْ تُحِبُّونَ ٱلْعَاجِلَةَ ﴿٢٠﴾

and give no thought to the life to come. (21)

وَتَذَرُونَ ٱلْأَخِرَةَ ﴿٢١﴾

Some faces will on that day be radiant with happiness, (22)

وُجُوهٌ يَوْمَئِذٍ نَّاضِرَةٌ ﴿٢٢﴾

looking towards their Lord; (23)

إِلَىٰ رَبِّهَا نَاظِرَةٌ ﴿٢٣﴾

and some faces will on that day be overcast with despair, (24)

وَوُجُوهٌ يَوْمَئِذٍ بَاسِرَةٌ ﴿٢٤﴾

realizing that a great calamity is about to befall them. (25)

تَظُنُّ أَن يُفْعَلَ بِهَا فَاقِرَةٌ ﴿٢٥﴾

Yet when the departing soul comes up to the throat, (26)

كَلَّا إِذَا بَلَغَتِ ٱلتَّرَاقِيَ ﴿٢٦﴾

when it is said, 'Can any charmer [do something now]?' (27)

وَقِيلَ مَنْ رَاقٍ ﴿٢٧﴾

When he knows it is the final parting, (28)

وَظَنَّ أَنَّهُ ٱلْفِرَاقُ ﴿٢٨﴾

and one leg will be joined with another, (29)

وَٱلْتَفَّتِ ٱلسَّاقُ بِٱلسَّاقِ ﴿٢٩﴾

to your Lord he will on that day be driven. (30)

إِلَىٰ رَبِّكَ يَوْمَئِذٍ ٱلْمَسَاقُ ﴿٣٠﴾

He neither believed nor prayed, (31)

فَلَا صَدَّقَ وَلَا صَلَّىٰ ﴿٣١﴾

but denied the truth and turned away, (32)

وَلَٰكِن كَذَّبَ وَتَوَلَّىٰ ﴿٣٢﴾

then he went back to his people full of arrogance. (33)

ثُمَّ ذَهَبَ إِلَىٰٓ أَهْلِهِۦ يَتَمَطَّىٰٓ ﴿٣٣﴾

Your doom, man, comes nearer and nearer, (34)

أَوْلَىٰ لَكَ فَأَوْلَىٰ ﴿٣٤﴾

and ever nearer and nearer. (35)

ثُمَّ أَوْلَىٰ لَكَ فَأَوْلَىٰٓ ﴿٣٥﴾

Does man think that he will be left without purpose? (36)

أَيَحْسَبُ ٱلْإِنسَٰنُ أَن يُتْرَكَ سُدًى ﴿٣٦﴾

Was he not a mere drop of emitted sperm? (37)

أَلَمْ يَكُ نُطْفَةً مِّن مَّنِىٍّ يُمْنَىٰ ﴿٣٧﴾

It then became a clinging cell mass, and then God created and shaped it, (38)

ثُمَّ كَانَ عَلَقَةً فَخَلَقَ فَسَوَّىٰ ﴿٣٨﴾

fashioning out of it the two sexes, male and female. (39)

فَجَعَلَ مِنْهُ ٱلزَّوْجَيْنِ ٱلذَّكَرَ وَٱلْأُنثَىٰٓ ﴿٣٩﴾

Is He not, then, able to bring the dead back to life? (40)

أَلَيْسَ ذَٰلِكَ بِقَٰدِرٍ عَلَىٰٓ أَن يُحْـِۧىَ ٱلْمَوْتَىٰ ﴿٤٠﴾

Self-Reproaching Soul

I need not swear by the Day of Resurrection and I need not swear by the self-reproaching soul! Does man think that We will not put his bones together again? Yes, indeed! We are able to put in perfect order his very fingertips! Yet man wants to deny what lies ahead of him. He asks: 'When will this Day of Resurrection be?' When the sight is dazzled and the moon eclipsed, when the sun and the moon are brought together, on that day man will say: 'Where to flee?' But no! There is no refuge. On that day, to your Lord all shall return. Man will be told on that day all that he put forward and all that he put back. Man will be a witness against himself, even though he may put up his excuses. (Verses 1–15)

The *sūrah* starts with a reference to making an oath, but then decides not to make it. This has a deeper effect than a straightforward oath, and this is what is intended. Indeed, a more literal rendering would be: 'I do not swear by…' When this has been stated, the truths of the resurrection and self-reproaching soul appear in view.

There is much discussion of resurrection in the *sūrah*. As for the self-reproaching soul, various reports explain this. Al-Ḥasan al-Baṣrī says: "You will always find a believer questioning himself: 'What did I mean by this word? What did I eat this food for? What do I mean by speaking to myself thus?' A transgressor will go on never blaming himself." Al-Ḥasan says: "Every single soul in the heavens and earth will be blaming himself on the Day of Judgement." 'Ikrimah says: "It is the soul that blames itself for good and bad things, saying: if only I did this or that." Saʿīd ibn Jubayr said the same. Ibn 'Abbās says: "It is always blaming." He also says: "It is often blaming, much criticized." Mujāhid says: "It regrets what has passed and blames for it." Qatādah says: "It is the one tending towards evil." Jarīr says: "All these definitions are in practically the same vein. However, what is closer to the apparent meaning of the Qur'ānic statement is to say that it is the soul that blames a person for whatever he does, good or bad, and regrets what has passed." For our self, we prefer the first definition stated by al-Ḥasan al-Baṣrī.

Such a pious, self-reproaching soul, one that fears God's punishment, and is always cautious, looking around, reviewing its actions, identifying what it desires, making sure not to cheat itself, is certainly so honoured by God as to warrant mention alongside the Day of Resurrection. It is the opposite of the soul of one who wants to indulge in sin undeterred; who lies, turns away from the truth and then returns to his people full of arrogance, never taking stock of his actions and paying no heed to the truth.

"*I need not swear by the Day of Resurrection and I need not swear by the self-reproaching soul!*" (Verses 1–2) What is at the centre of this opening is the arrival of the Day of Resurrection, but when the oath is left aside, the *sūrah* does not mention the subject of that oath further. Instead, it picks it up in another form, as if to start a discourse having alerted our minds to it with this clear opening: "*Does man think that We will not put his bones together again? Yes, indeed! We are able to put in perfect order his very fingertips!*" (Verses 3–4)

The essential difficulty for the unbelievers was that they could not imagine that bones becoming dust and being swallowed by the earth could then be gathered together again to bring a human being back to life. This is also most probably true of some people today! The *sūrah* responds to this sort of thinking, confirming that putting everyone's bones back together will assuredly take place: "*Yes, indeed! We are able to put in perfect order his very fingertips!*" (Verse 4) The *sūrah* reasserts this process of putting bones back together by stating something more complex, which is to put fingertips in their respective positions, just as they were in life. This implies that man will be brought back to life, with every little detail or small aspect of his physique put back in perfect order. Nothing is lost, however small!

This reconfirmation is enough here. Towards the end of the *sūrah*, we have another proof derived from the fact of man's first creation. Here, however, the *sūrah* exposes the mental flaw leading to this sort of thinking that cannot conceive of bones being put back together. Man simply wants to persist in his denial so that he goes on the loose, with nothing to check or restrain his march. He does not want to face any reckoning or requital. Therefore, he expects no resurrection and no answerability: "*Yet man wants to deny what lies ahead of him. He asks: 'When will this Day of Resurrection be?'*" (Verses 5–6) This question is stated in the Arabic with the interrogative pronoun *ayyāna*, which adds to the normal equivalent of 'when', which is *ayna*, the doubling of the '*y*' sound and a long '*a*'; a form that suggests the improbability of happening. This is in line with the desire of the questioner to run loose and continue with his sinful ways, undeterred by any thought of the hereafter. Indeed, the hereafter often acts as a restraint checking the desire to indulge in sin. Now this person tries to remove this restraint so that he can go ahead with sinful practices undeterred.

The answer that comes is swift, decisive, maintains a fast beat and uses hard-hitting words. It draws a scene of the Day of Resurrection in which human senses and feelings combine with celestial images to produce an awesome effect: "*When the sight is dazzled and the moon eclipsed, when the sun and the moon are brought together, on that day man will say: 'Where to flee?'*" (Verses 7–10) The sight is very swiftly distracted here and there, like lightning, and the moon is eclipsed and no longer reflects any light, while the sun and the moon are brought together after they have long been parted. Their familiar operation is disrupted since the entire celestial system, known for its accuracy of movement, is no longer operating. In the midst of all this upheaval, man stands terrified, asking, 'Where to flee?' The very question imparts a feeling of fear and utter panic. Man looks lost, wherever he turns his eyes he sees nothing but a blocked way.

There is no refuge or protection. No one can avert God's power and punishment, since all return to Him and there is no hiding place to seek other than the one He determines: "*But no! There is no refuge. On that day, to your Lord all shall return.*" (Verses 11–12) So what man has desired, hoping to be able to continue with his erring ways, fearing neither reckoning nor requital, is not what happens. On the contrary, everything will be reckoned, and he will be reminded of anything he may have forgotten. It will all be brought before him so that he faces his fair requital: "*Man will be told on that day all that he put forward and all that he put back.*" (Verse 13) He will be told of what he did before his death, as also what effects his actions produced after his death, whether good or evil. Some actions produce long-lasting effects, and these effects are added to the account of the person who performed them.

Whatever excuses man may try to put forward, none will be accepted. He is responsible for himself, and it is his duty to bring himself to divine guidance. When he let himself sink into evil, only he himself can be answerable for this: *"Man will be a witness against himself, even though he may put up his excuses."* (Verses 14–15)

It is worth noting here that every expression in the *sūrah* thus far is short and quick: the verses, the endings, the rhythm, the images and the reckoning process. This appears to be a response to man's attempt to disregard the whole idea of the Day of Reckoning and to think that it is too far off.

God's Guarantee

Then come the four verses giving the Prophet special instruction as regards the way he received Qur'ānic revelations:

> *Do not move your tongue repeating its words in haste. We shall see to its collection and recitation. When We recite it, follow its recitation. Then it will be for Us to make its meaning clear.* (Verses 16–19)

In addition to what we have already said about these four verses in the Prologue, we note that God takes all responsibility for the Qur'ān: its revelation, preservation, collection and explanation. All this is undertaken by none other than God Almighty. The Prophet's role is no more than to receive and deliver it. We also note here how the Prophet was so eager and keen to fully understand what was being revealed to him, taking it most seriously, fearing to forget a phrase or a word. Hence why he repeated the words after the Angel Gabriel recited them to him, to make sure that he had not omitted any of it. The fact that this is recorded in the Qur'ān itself further emphasizes what we have just said.

Opposite Positions

The *sūrah* now reminds the unbelievers of their love of this present world, which is their main concern, and their disregard of the hereafter. It shows them the state in which they will end up in the life to come in a highly inspiring image:

Yet you love this fleeting life, and give no thought to the life to come. Some faces will on that day be radiant with happiness, looking towards their Lord; and some faces will on that day be overcast with despair, realizing that a great calamity is about to befall them. (Verses 20–25)

The first thing we notice, which adds to the harmony of style, is that this life is described at this point as '*fleeting*'. This not only stresses the short duration of this present life, which is the intended meaning, but also provides an element of harmony between these connotations and those of the preceding verses speaking of the Prophet as he repeated the words of the Qur'ān. In both, haste is a common feature. It also appears to be a feature of mankind in this present world.

These last quoted verses paint two contrasting images: "*Some faces will on that day be radiant with happiness, looking towards their Lord.*" (Verses 22–23) This is a very quick reference to a situation no words can describe and no imagination can fully understand. Those people are promised a kind of happiness that is unlike any other. Indeed, heaven and all the happiness it includes appear too small by comparison. These beaming faces are so radiant with happiness because they are looking towards their Lord! They are looking towards God! How sublime! What pure, perfect and absolute happiness!

Sometimes man's soul looks briefly at an aspect of beauty God has placed in the universe or within man. It may see this in the full moon, the still night, the breaking dawn, the stretching shadow, the bustling sea, the endless desert, the blossoming garden, the happy face, the noble heart, the unshakable faith, the unwavering patience or many other manifestations of beauty in this world. Looking at such beauty, man feels ecstatic, flowing with happiness, flying into a world of light and purity. All adversity seems to shrink and disappear. So how will man's soul feel when he looks, not at the beauty of God's creation, but at God's own beauty? This is a position that needs both help and reassurance from God so that man can steady himself and begin to enjoy such indescribable happiness: "*Some faces will on that day be radiant with happiness, looking towards their Lord.*" (Verses 22–23) How could these faces be anything but radiant and beaming when they are looking towards their Lord and His beauty?

391

We experience a feeling of happiness that rises from our hearts and gives our faces a beaming look, simply because we see the beauty of something God has created: a bright face, a lovely flower, a spread-out wing, a noble soul or a kindly deed. What feelings, then, will overwhelm us when we look at the beauty of perfection, and when we are free of all life's concerns that may distract us from appreciating such beauty? When we speak of 'life's concerns' we do not mean only in the world around us but also in terms of our own shortcomings and needs.

How do those happy people look; with what organ and by what means? These are questions that do not even occur to a heart touched by the happiness that this Qur'ānic statement radiates into a believer's soul. Why, then, do some people deprive their souls from enjoying this light that overflows with happiness and joy? Why do they, instead, get involved in futile arguments about an abstract that human minds, restricted as they are by their familiar world, cannot fathom? Only man's release from the shackles of his worldly existence will give him the hope of facing the absolute truth on the Day of Resurrection. Without such release, man cannot even imagine what facing that truth will be like.

This means that the seemingly endless arguments the Mu'tazilah entered into with their Sunnī theological opponents and other philosophers were absolutely futile, leading nowhere. They argued about the nature of 'the look' and 'the sight' on that day. They used earthly standards, speaking about encumbered man, man restricted by what he knows when on earth, and so looked at the whole question with faculties that are essentially limited in scope.

The very import of the words is restricted by what our finite minds and imaginations understand. If our minds are freed from such restrictions, the very words may acquire different meanings. Words are only symbols, and what they symbolize differs in accordance with man's thoughts and concepts. When man's powers and faculties change, his concepts change and, consequently, the significance of words change. In our life on earth, we deal with these symbols according to our power. Why, then, should we argue about something when we are not even sure about the significance of the words expressing it? Let us, then, look up to this absolutely serene happiness and pure joy which we feel when we try, as we can, to imagine that position. Let our souls revel in that happiness, for the mere looking up to such happiness is a great blessing of far-reaching dimensions.

"And some faces will on that day be overcast with despair, realizing that a great calamity is about to befall them." (Verses 24–25) These are faces looking absolutely grim, with their sins and misdeeds casting a dark shadow over them. Their expectation of an impending calamity that crushes their very backbones weighs heavily on them and heightens their immense sorrow. How dreadful and ghastly they look!

Such is the life to come which they ignore, preferring to indulge in this life of fleeting pleasures. They love this life despite having ahead of them that day which brings widely different fates.

The Scene of Death

The scenes painted so far of the Day of Judgement and its great upheavals and divergent fates derive their effect from the truth they represent and the Qur'ān's own powerful style, bringing them alive before us. The *sūrah* now comes closer and closer so as to present a scene of something that occurs all the time. Indeed, people encounter this most clearly at every moment in their lives. It is the scene of death that overtakes every living soul. No one can evade or escape death, which separates a person from his loved ones. Death moves along its course, uninterrupted by anything. It does not respond to an impassioned appeal, an outcry of grief, a fervent desire or a seizure of panic. It takes the most powerful giants as easily as it takes the weakest dwarfs, and overcomes tyrants in the same way as it overcomes the oppressed. Mankind have no way to prevent death, yet they do not consider the great power that deals it:

Yet when the departing soul comes up to the throat, when it is said, 'Can any charmer [do something now]?' When he knows it is the final parting, and one leg will be joined with another, to your Lord he will on that day be driven. (Verses 26–30)

This is the scene of approaching death, presented to people by the Qur'ān as if it is happening now. It comes out from within the words, just like a picture comes out of a painter's brush.

"*Yet when the departing soul comes up to the throat.*" (Verse 26) At this point the dying person is in his last throes, with distress all around. Those present look everywhere, trying to think of something or some means to save the one suffering this distress: "*when it is said, 'Can any charmer [do something now]?'*" (Verse 27) Could a charm possibly be of any use? The suffering one is writhing with pain, "*and one leg will be joined with another.*" (Verse 29) All means are of no use. The road ahead becomes clear; it is the road every living being will eventually have to walk: "*To your Lord he will on that day be driven.*" (Verse 30) The scene almost moves in front of us and almost talks. Every verse draws a movement, and the image of approaching death is clearly visible spreading impassioned feelings of loss and panic, before facing the bitter, hard truth no one can escape from. The inevitable end then clearly appears: "*To your Lord he will on that day be driven.*" (Verse 30) The curtains are drawn over this distressing scene, leaving a distinct image in our eyes, prominent feelings in our hearts and a clear sense of grimness in the air.

Arrogant Rejection

By contrast, we have an image of those bent on denying the truth. They do not prepare for the inevitable end by doing something in obedience of God. Rather, they arrogantly indulge in disobedience and sin:

> *He neither believed nor prayed, but denied the truth and turned away, then he went back to his people full of arrogance.* (Verses 31–33)

It is reported that these verses refer to a particular person, Abū Jahl 'Amr ibn Hishām, who used to visit the Prophet sometimes and listen to the Qur'ān. He would then go away, refusing to believe. In fact, he was neither polite nor fearful of God. He would continue to hurt the Prophet by what he said, and would try to turn people away from Islam. He would also take pride in such actions, treating his evil deeds as something to be proud of. The Qur'ān derides his attitude. In its description of his arrogant movements, it invites the listeners' scorn.

Yet there are many like Abū Jahl whom the message of Islam faces. They listen but turn away. They are inventive in their opposition to the word of truth, pouring harm on its advocates, working out evil schemes and feeling proud of their evil deeds and of the corruption they spread on earth. Hence, the Qur'ān issues a clear threat to such people:

> *Your doom, man, comes nearer and nearer, and ever nearer and nearer.* (Verses 34–35)

The *sūrah* uses here an idiom, *awlā laka fa 'awlā*, which implies a strong threat and repeats it twice. Hence the translation expresses the implied meaning. On one occasion, the Prophet held Abū Jahl by the scruff of his neck and used this expression as it occurs in the *sūrah*. Abū Jahl said: "Are you threatening me, Muḥammad? By God, neither you nor your Lord can do anything to me. I am the most powerful man ever to walk in between these hills." When the Battle of Badr took place, God killed him by the hands of Muḥammad's followers. Before him, Pharaoh said to the chiefs of his people: "*Nobles! I know of no deity that you could have other than myself.*" (28: 38) He also said: "*My people, is the kingdom of Egypt not mine, with all these rivers flowing at my feet?*" (43: 51) Yet God smote him down, drowned him.

The history of the divine message is full of people who forgot God and His power, of those who feel their own power, relying on tribes, forces and authority, thinking that all these will give them protection. Then such people are taken away like a fly or a mosquito. Remember then, when the time of death comes it cannot be put forward or backward by even a fraction of a second.

Can it be Without Purpose?

As the *sūrah* draws to its conclusion, it presents another truth from this world that carries a clear pointer to God's design of human life as also to the life to come:

> *Does man think that he will be left without purpose? Was he not a mere drop of emitted sperm? It then became a clinging cell mass, and*

then God created and shaped it, fashioning out of it the two sexes, male and female. Is He not, then, able to bring the dead back to life? (Verses 36–40)

This last section strikes powerful notes and points to great truths, which those who were addressed by the Qur'ān at the time of its revelations could never imagine. The first of these refers to the deliberate design and planning in man's life: *"Does man think that he will be left without purpose?"* (Verse 36) Those people used to think that life was merely a process that takes place, having neither cause nor goal. Women get pregnant and give birth, and graves take the dead away! In between, there is nothing other than idle play, putting on some adornments, competing for good things, and enjoyment that is not much different from animals. To think that it all goes according to an elaborate law, serving a definite goal and purpose; that man's arrival in this life is according to a deliberate will and a set plan; that it all ends with accountability and requital, and that the journey of life is a test before the final requital was far beyond people's thoughts. Few could recognize in all this the wisdom of God, that He does everything for a clear purpose and towards a pre-willed end.

What distinguishes man from animals is man's recognition of the link between time, events and objectives and that human life has a definite purpose linked to that of the universe around him. The greater and broader this feeling is in man's consciousness and the more refined is his concept of the law that links things and events, the higher he rises in his humanity. Thus, he does not live his life one minute or one event after another. On the contrary, time, place, the past, present and future are all connected in his consciousness. They are all related to the existence of the great universe and its laws. These are the result of a higher will that creates, plans and designs. This higher will does not create people and leave them to a life without purpose.

The Qur'ān put this profound concept in people's minds so long ago. It was a great departure from the concepts that prevailed at the time. It remains greatly removed from all concepts about the universe that philosophers of olden and modern times have advanced.

"*Does man think that he will be left without purpose?*" (Verse 36)
This is a fine touch, which the Qur'ān uses to alert the human mind
to think and reflect, looking at bonds, goals, causes and effects that
link his existence to that of the universe and to the will that conducts
everything in that universe.

In a clear and simple manner, the *sūrah* cites clear evidence confirming
that man will not be left without purpose. These are taken from man's
first origins: "*Was he not a mere drop of emitted sperm? It then became a
clinging cell mass, and then God created and shaped it, fashioning out of
it the two sexes, male and female.*" (Verses 37–39) What is man? How
does he come into existence? What are his origins? How does he grow
into his present status? What journey did he make before arriving on
this planet? Was he not a mere drop of a certain emitted fluid? Did not
this one-celled drop transform into a cell mass that clung to the wall of
the uterus to survive and be nourished? Who guided it to do this, and
who gave it this ability?

Then again, who made out of it an embryo with perfectly shaped
organs, composed of millions and millions of cells, when it only
originated as a single cell that fertilized an egg? Its journey from one cell
to a fully-shaped embryo is far longer than man's journey from birth
to death. The changes and transformations it goes through during the
embryonic journey are much more varied and wider than all that a man
encounters through his life journey from the moment of birth to the
moment of death. Who guided his long eventful journey while he was
a helpless creature without an intellect, perception and experience?

Ultimately, who brought out of the single cell the two types, male
and female? What will did this cell have to develop into a male while
the other developed into a female? Or, who indeed can claim to have
intervened to guide their different routes to make this choice in the
dark depths of the uterus?

There is no escape! Everyone admits the presence of the gentle hand
that guided the emitted drop of fluid along its long way and brought it
to its final shape, according to an elaborate plan: "*Fashioning out of it
the two sexes, male and female.*" (Verse 39)

As this truth imposes itself on our human senses, the *sūrah* concludes
with a note that brings together the truths outlined through its verses:

"*Is He not, then, able to bring the dead back to life?*" (Verse 40) Yes, indeed! God Almighty is able to bring the dead back to life. Yes, indeed! Limitless is He in His glory, God is able to bring about the second life. Yes, without doubt. Man can say nothing to this, other than submit to its truth.

Thus the *sūrah* concludes, with such a powerful and decisive note that allows the truth of human existence and the elaborate planning behind it to fill our minds.

SŪRAH 76

Al-Insān
(Man)

Prologue

Some reports suggest that this *sūrah* was revealed in Madīnah, but it is a Makkan revelation. Its Makkan character is indeed very obvious considering its subject matter, its flow and other characteristics. Hence, we give more credence to those reports stating its revelation in Makkah. In fact, there are indications in the way it runs suggesting that it was among the earlier *sūrahs* to be revealed in Makkah. We may cite for example the detailed images of happiness and torment in the life to come, the directive given to the Prophet to remain patient, awaiting his Lord's judgement, and not to obey any sinner or unbeliever from among them. These are the things Makkan revelations always emphasized, particularly when the persecution of the advocates of the Islamic message was becoming fierce. Moreover, the Prophet is encouraged to hold firmly to the truth he has been given, allowing the unbelievers respite but not to incline to or listen to them. Such directives are found in *Sūrahs* 68, 73 and 74 in this volume. These directives are similar to the ones found in this *sūrah*. Therefore, the possibility that it was revealed in Madīnah is remote and better discounted.

In totality, the *sūrah* is a calm address encouraging people to turn to God, obey Him, seek His pleasure, remember His favours, work to avoid His punishment, maintain alertness to the test He puts His servants to and understand His wisdom in creation, bestowing favours, testing and giving the unbelievers respite.

The *sūrah* begins with an inspiring touch, asking the question: where was man before coming into this life? Who gave him his existence? Who gave him the position he occupies in this life after he had none: "*Was there not a period of time when man was not yet something to be thought of?*" (Verse 1) This is followed by a second touch speaking about man's origins and God's wisdom manifested in his creation and His giving him his energies and faculties: "*We have created man from a drop of mingled fluid, so that We might try him. Therefore, we have endowed him with hearing and sight.*" (Verse 2) The third touch speaks of guiding man to the right way, giving him help to go along this way before leaving him to choose the way he wants to go and the fate he wants to end up with: "*We have shown him the way, [giving him the choice] to be thankful or ungrateful.*" (Verse 3) These three touches set the human heart thinking deeply, glancing back and casting a look forward, and then reflecting before choosing which way to go. Then the *sūrah* gives clear advice to man as he stands at the crossroads, warning him against taking the way leading to hell and encouraging him in every way to take the way to heaven, pointing to the great variety of pleasure that awaits him there: "*For the unbelievers, we have prepared chains and shackles, and a blazing fire. The righteous shall drink from a cup mixed with* kāfūr, *a fountain where God's servants shall drink, making it flow in abundance.*" (Verses 4–6)

Before completing its description of what believers will enjoy, the *sūrah* now draws a sketch showing the features of those righteous people. In so doing, it uses some fine words and expressions that are in perfect harmony with the splendid bliss these people enjoy in heaven: "*They are the ones who fulfil their vows and stand in awe of a day of woes that fly far and wide, who give food – though they need it themselves – to the needy, the orphan and the captive, [saying within themselves,] 'We feed you for the sake of God alone. We desire neither recompense from you, nor thanks. We fear the day of our Lord: a bleak, distressful day.*'" (Verses 7–10)

The *sūrah* then presents the reward which will be given to these people who willingly attend to difficult duties, who fear the bleak, grim day, the generous who feed others despite themselves being in need, and who only seek God's pleasure, hoping for no reward from anyone else. As the *sūrah* presents this, we find that it is a reward of security, happiness and perfect enjoyment: "*God will save them from the woes of that day, and will grant them radiance and joy, and will reward them for their patience in adversity with a garden and [garments of] silk. They will recline there on soft couches, feeling neither burning sun nor severe cold. Its shades will come low over them, and its clusters of fruit will hang low, within easy reach. They will be served with silver plates and goblets that seem to be crystal, crystal-clear, but made of silver, the measure of which they are the ones to determine. They will be given to drink of a cup flavoured with ginger, from a spring there called* Salsabīl. *They will be waited upon by immortal youths. If you see them, you would think they were scattered pearls. If you were to look around, you would see only bliss and a vast kingdom. They shall be arrayed in garments of fine green silk and brocade; and adorned with bracelets of silver. And their Lord will give them a most pure drink. This is a reward for you. Your endeavours are well appreciated.* (Verses 11–22)

The *sūrah* then addresses the Prophet encouraging him to stand firm in the face of those who turn away, persist in disbelief and deny the truth. He is directed to remain patient in the face of all this adversity and to await God's judgement. He should maintain his tie with his Lord, deriving strength from Him whenever he feels that the road he has to travel is too long: "*It is We who have bestowed the Qur'ān upon you by gradual revelation. Await, then, your Lord's judgement in all patience, and pay no heed to any of these sinners and unbelievers. Remember your Lord's name morning and evening. At night prostrate yourself before Him, and extol His limitless glory throughout the long night.*" (Verses 23–26)

In conclusion, the *sūrah* reminds the unbelievers of the heavy day that they do not reckon with. This is the day feared by the righteous who are keen to guard against its punishment. It tells them that they represent no serious issue to God who gave them all the power they have and is able to replace them with others. He bestows His favours on them in fulfilment of His wish to put people to the test. The *sūrah* ends with a brief mention of the results of this test: "*These people love the fleeting life, and leave behind them a day that will be heavy. It is We who have created them and strengthened their constitution. If it be Our will, We can replace them entirely with others of their kind. This is but a reminder. Let him who will, take the way to his Lord. Yet you cannot will except by the will of God. God is indeed All-Knowing, Wise. He admits to His grace whoever He will, but for the wrongdoers He has prepared grievous suffering."* (Verses 27–31)

The *sūrah* begins with a reminder of how man comes into existence and God's design in so originating him to undergo a test, and it concludes with the outcome of this test, as determined by God at the point of origination. Thus, the beginning and the end point to the deliberate and elaborate planning of life. Man performs very badly if he remains heedless, unaware of the purpose of his life when he is being put to a test, and has been equipped with the faculties that help him pass this test.

Between the opening and close, the *sūrah* gives the longest, or perhaps one of the longest if we take *Sūrah* 56 into account, description of the blessings granted to the people of heaven. These are mostly material, but they are coupled with God's acceptance and the honour He grants. The fact that this description is so detailed points to its being a Makkan revelation, because the addressees were newcomers to Islam, having lived in *jāhiliyyah*, or ignorance. They were fond of material luxuries. They would be very impressed with its prospect. There will always be people who store much by such luxuries. God knows His creation best, and knows what suits them and what has a deep effect on their hearts and minds. There is definitely a higher and more refined type of happiness and joy, such as the one mentioned in the preceding *sūrah*, The Resurrection: *"Some faces will on that day be radiant with happiness, looking towards their Lord."* (75: 22–23)

Al-Insān (Man)

In the Name of God, the Lord of Grace, the Ever Merciful

بِسۡمِ ٱللَّهِ ٱلرَّحۡمَٰنِ ٱلرَّحِيمِ

Was there not a period of time when man was not yet something to be thought of? (1)

هَلۡ أَتَىٰ عَلَى ٱلۡإِنسَٰنِ حِينٞ مِّنَ ٱلدَّهۡرِ لَمۡ يَكُن شَيۡـٔٗا مَّذۡكُورًا ١

We have created man from a drop of mingled fluid, so that We might try him. Therefore, we have endowed him with hearing and sight. (2)

إِنَّا خَلَقۡنَا ٱلۡإِنسَٰنَ مِن نُّطۡفَةٍ أَمۡشَاجٖ نَّبۡتَلِيهِ فَجَعَلۡنَٰهُ سَمِيعَۢا بَصِيرًا ٢

We have shown him the way, [giving him the choice] to be thankful or ungrateful. (3)

إِنَّا هَدَيۡنَٰهُ ٱلسَّبِيلَ إِمَّا شَاكِرٗا وَإِمَّا كَفُورًا ٣

For the unbelievers, we have prepared chains and shackles, and a blazing fire. (4)

إِنَّآ أَعۡتَدۡنَا لِلۡكَٰفِرِينَ سَلَٰسِلَاْ وَأَغۡلَٰلٗا وَسَعِيرًا ٤

The righteous shall drink from a cup mixed with *kāfūr*, (5)

إِنَّ ٱلۡأَبۡرَارَ يَشۡرَبُونَ مِن كَأۡسٖ كَانَ مِزَاجُهَا كَافُورًا ٥

a fountain where God's servants shall drink, making it flow in abundance. (6)

عَيۡنٗا يَشۡرَبُ بِهَا عِبَادُ ٱللَّهِ يُفَجِّرُونَهَا تَفۡجِيرًا ٦

They are the ones who fulfil their vows and stand in awe of a day of woes that fly far and wide, (7)

يُوفُونَ بِٱلنَّذۡرِ وَيَخَافُونَ يَوۡمٗا كَانَ شَرُّهُۥ مُسۡتَطِيرًا ٧

403

who give food – though they need it themselves – to the needy, the orphan and the captive, (8)

وَيُطْعِمُونَ الطَّعَامَ عَلَىٰ حُبِّهِ مِسْكِينًا وَيَتِيمًا وَأَسِيرًا ۝

[saying within themselves,] 'We feed you for the sake of God alone. We desire neither recompense from you, nor thanks. (9)

إِنَّمَا نُطْعِمُكُمْ لِوَجْهِ اللَّهِ لَا نُرِيدُ مِنكُمْ جَزَاءً وَلَا شُكُورًا ۝

We fear the day of our Lord: a bleak, distressful day.' (10)

إِنَّا نَخَافُ مِن رَّبِّنَا يَوْمًا عَبُوسًا قَمْطَرِيرًا ۝

God will save them from the woes of that day, and will grant them radiance and joy, (11)

فَوَقَاهُمُ اللَّهُ شَرَّ ذَٰلِكَ الْيَوْمِ وَلَقَّاهُمْ نَضْرَةً وَسُرُورًا ۝

and will reward them for their patience in adversity with a garden and [garments of] silk. (12)

وَجَزَاهُم بِمَا صَبَرُوا جَنَّةً وَحَرِيرًا ۝

They will recline there on soft couches, feeling neither burning sun nor severe cold. (13)

مُّتَّكِئِينَ فِيهَا عَلَى الْأَرَائِكِ لَا يَرَوْنَ فِيهَا شَمْسًا وَلَا زَمْهَرِيرًا ۝

Its shades will come low over them, and its clusters of fruit will hang low, within easy reach. (14)

وَدَانِيَةً عَلَيْهِمْ ظِلَالُهَا وَذُلِّلَتْ قُطُوفُهَا تَذْلِيلًا ۝

They will be served with silver plates and goblets that seem to be crystal, (15)

وَيُطَافُ عَلَيْهِم بِآنِيَةٍ مِّن فِضَّةٍ وَأَكْوَابٍ كَانَتْ قَوَارِيرَا ۝

crystal-clear, but made of silver, the measure of which they are the ones to determine. (16)

قَوَارِيرَا۟ مِن فِضَّةٍ قَدَّرُوهَا تَقْدِيرًا ۝

They will be given to drink of a cup flavoured with ginger, (17)

وَيُسْقَوْنَ فِيهَا كَأْسًا كَانَ مِزَاجُهَا زَنجَبِيلًا ۝

from a spring there called *Salsabīl*. (18)

عَيْنًا فِيهَا تُسَمَّىٰ سَلْسَبِيلًا ۝

They will be waited upon by immortal youths. If you see them, you would think they were scattered pearls. (19)

وَيَطُوفُ عَلَيْهِمْ وِلْدَٰنٌ مُّخَلَّدُونَ إِذَا رَأَيْتَهُمْ حَسِبْتَهُمْ لُؤْلُؤًا مَّنثُورًا ۝

If you were to look around, you would see only bliss and a vast kingdom. (20)

وَإِذَا رَأَيْتَ ثَمَّ رَأَيْتَ نَعِيمًا وَمُلْكًا كَبِيرًا ۝

They shall be arrayed in garments of fine green silk and brocade; and adorned with bracelets of silver. And their Lord will give them a most pure drink. (21)

عَٰلِيَهُمْ ثِيَابُ سُندُسٍ خُضْرٌ وَإِسْتَبْرَقٌ وَحُلُّوٓا۟ أَسَاوِرَ مِن فِضَّةٍ وَسَقَىٰهُمْ رَبُّهُمْ شَرَابًا طَهُورًا ۝

This is a reward for you. Your endeavours are well appreciated. (22)

إِنَّ هَٰذَا كَانَ لَكُمْ جَزَآءً وَكَانَ سَعْيُكُم مَّشْكُورًا ۝

It is We who have bestowed the Qur'ān upon you by gradual revelation. (23)

إِنَّا نَحْنُ نَزَّلْنَا عَلَيْكَ ٱلْقُرْءَانَ تَنزِيلًا ۝

Await, then, your Lord's judgement in all patience, and pay no heed to any of these sinners and unbelievers. (24)

فَٱصۡبِرۡ لِحُكۡمِ رَبِّكَ وَلَا تُطِعۡ مِنۡهُمۡ ءَاثِمًا أَوۡ كَفُورًا ۝

Remember your Lord's name morning and evening. (25)

وَٱذۡكُرِ ٱسۡمَ رَبِّكَ بُكۡرَةً وَأَصِيلًا ۝

At night prostrate yourself before Him, and extol His limitless glory throughout the long night. (26)

وَمِنَ ٱلَّيۡلِ فَٱسۡجُدۡ لَهُۥ وَسَبِّحۡهُ لَيۡلًا طَوِيلًا ۝

These people love the fleeting life, and leave behind them a day that will be heavy. (27)

إِنَّ هَٰٓؤُلَآءِ يُحِبُّونَ ٱلۡعَاجِلَةَ وَيَذَرُونَ وَرَآءَهُمۡ يَوۡمًا ثَقِيلًا ۝

It is We who have created them and strengthened their constitution. If it be Our will, We can replace them entirely with others of their kind. (28)

نَّحۡنُ خَلَقۡنَٰهُمۡ وَشَدَدۡنَآ أَسۡرَهُمۡ وَإِذَا شِئۡنَا بَدَّلۡنَآ أَمۡثَٰلَهُمۡ تَبۡدِيلًا ۝

This is but a reminder. Let him who will, take the way to his Lord. (29)

إِنَّ هَٰذِهِۦ تَذۡكِرَةٌ فَمَن شَآءَ ٱتَّخَذَ إِلَىٰ رَبِّهِۦ سَبِيلًا ۝

Yet you cannot will except by the will of God. God is indeed All-Knowing, Wise. (30)

وَمَا تَشَآءُونَ إِلَّآ أَن يَشَآءَ ٱللَّهُ إِنَّ ٱللَّهَ كَانَ عَلِيمًا حَكِيمًا ۝

He admits to His grace whoever He will, but for the wrongdoers He has prepared grievous suffering. (31)

يُدۡخِلُ مَن يَشَآءُ فِي رَحۡمَتِهِۦ وَٱلظَّٰلِمِينَ أَعَدَّ لَهُمۡ عَذَابًا أَلِيمًۢا ۝

When Man Was Nothing

Was there not a period of time when man was not yet something to be thought of? We have created man from a drop of mingled fluid, so that We might try him. Therefore, we have endowed him with hearing and sight. We have shown him the way, [giving him the choice] to be thankful or ungrateful. (Verses 1–3)

This question with which the *sūrah* opens signifies a statement, but it is phrased in this way so that man should ask himself: 'Am I not aware that there was a period of time when I was nothing to be thought of?' This should lead to further questioning: should he not reflect on this fact? Should not such reflection guide him to how he was ushered in on life's stage where lights were focused on him to make of him a creature of note? The interrogative form in this instance facilitates some fine thoughts, encouraging us to reflect further.

One point of reflection takes us to the stage before man comes into existence. What was the universe like before man's advent? Man is so full of himself that he tends to forget that the universe was there long, long before he was. Perhaps the universe never expected that a new creature, man, would ever come into existence and certainly not until God willed it to so happen.

Another point takes us to the moment when human existence first began. Our imagination can paint different visions of that moment, known only to God, which added this new creature to the universe. Yet this was taken into account by God before it happened, with this new creature's role within the life of the universe well determined.

We should also reflect on how God's hand placed this new creature on life's stage, assigning a role to him and preparing him for it. Indeed, the same hand has linked his life to the life of the universe and provided the circumstances that ensure his survival and ability to fulfil his role easily. It monitors his progress, step by step.

Further reflections can be added, all coming from this short statement, culminating in the realization that the initiation, the life journey and the end are all determined according to an elaborate scheme.

Man's development and survival is also outlined in the *sūrah*: "*We have created man from a drop of mingled fluid, so that We might try him.*

Therefore, we have endowed him with hearing and sight." (Verse 2) The *'drop of mingled fluid*' perhaps refers to its formation when the man's sperm fertilizes the woman's egg. Alternatively, it may refer to the genes, or units of heredity, which distinguish the human species in the first place and transmit features from parent to offspring.

So, man is created from a drop of mingled fluid, neither by coincidence nor in idle play. He is created so that he can be tested. God certainly knows man, his test and the outcome of this test. What is meant here is that all this should come out on life's stage, producing its effects which cling to man so that he is requited in accordance with the outcome of his test. It is for this reason that God endowed man with the faculties of hearing and sight. He has been given these faculties of perception so that he can receive and respond, measure things and values, judging them and picking his choices. He will be rewarded in accordance with his choice.

In addition to knowledge and its acquisition, God gave man the ability to choose his way in life. He has shown him the way of guidance, i.e. the one that leads to Him, and left him to choose this way by himself or to stray from it, opting instead for one of the many other ways that do not lead to Him: "*We have shown him the way, [giving him the choice] to be thankful or ungrateful.*" (Verse 3) The verse refers to following divine guidance by being thankful, because the first thought that occurs to someone receiving guidance is to express gratitude for it. He is now aware that God has willed for him to be a creature of note after having being nothing to be thought of. God also granted him sight and hearing, as well as other faculties to be able to learn and acquire knowledge. He then provided him with guidance and left the choice to him. If such a person is a believer, then the first thought that occurs to him is to be thankful. If he does not give thanks, then he is certainly ungrateful.

With these three touches given at the opening of the *sūrah*, man realizes that there is a purpose behind his creation. He becomes aware that he is tied to a central point; that he is equipped with knowledge and is answerable for it; and that he is set a test and needs to pass it. In other words, his life on earth is a trial, not a period of idle play and neglect. These three short verses give him such a range to reflect upon. He acquires a very serious outlook on life and knows that the results of the test will be announced once it is all over. Hence, how these verses change his vision in life and his feelings towards it and towards life values in general.

When the Test is Over

Now that the test has been put, and man has chosen one way or the other, what happens next? What awaits the unbelievers is briefly stated in one verse, because the general ambience of the *surah* is one of luxury, comfort and blessing. The torment prepared for the unbelievers is summed up: "*For the unbelievers, we have prepared chains and shackles, and a blazing fire.*" (Verse 4) They will have chains for their feet and shackles for their wrists, and then they will be cast into the blazing fire. The *surah* then quickly moves on to speak about the happiness of the other group:

> *The righteous shall drink from a cup mixed with* kāfūr, *a fountain where God's servants shall drink, making it flow in abundance.* (Verses 5–6)

This statement implies that the drink given to the righteous who are in heaven will be mixed with *kāfūr*, i.e. the calyx of sweet-smelling flowers, and that they will receive this drink in a cup filled from a fountain which flows in abundance. The Arabs used to mix their wine with *kāfūr*, or ginger, to give it a fine taste. Now, they know that their drink in heaven will be mixed with this and that it is plentiful. As for the nature of this drink, we understand that it is much finer and purer than any type of drink in this world, and that its enjoyment will be that much more enhanced. In our limited world, we cannot define the level or kind of enjoyment in the life to come. These are merely descriptions that give us an impression of what there is, because God knows that mankind cannot imagine what is beyond their world.

The *surah* calls the dwellers of heaven '*the righteous*' in the first verse, and describes them as '*God's servants*' in the second, honouring them first by acknowledging their moral standing and then referring to them as close to God. It then describes the qualities that earned them such a prize:

They are the ones who fulfil their vows and stand in awe of a day of woes that fly far and wide, who give food – though they need it themselves – to the needy, the orphan and the captive, [saying within themselves,] 'We feed you for the sake of God alone. We desire neither recompense from you, nor thanks. We fear the day of our Lord: a bleak, distressful day.' (Verses 7–10)

This is a bright picture of people with sincere hearts, sincere in their determination to fulfil the duties required by their faith, compassionate to those who are less fortunate, putting them ahead of themselves, keen to earn God's pleasure and wary of incurring what may earn His punishment. Thus, they are God-fearing and serious in approaching their duties.

Sincere and Generous

"They are the ones who fulfil their vows." (Verse 7) They thus fulfil what they intend to do of acts of worship and the duties they commit themselves to perform, taking the question of faith very seriously. They neither shirk their duty nor evade their commitment. The Qur'ānic statement is wider in scope than the literal meaning of *nadhr*, the Arabic word used here meaning pledge, vow, etc. *"And stand in awe of a day of woes that fly far and wide."* (Verse 7) They realize what sort of day it will be. It is a day of woes and these woes can spread all over, affecting those who fall short of fulfilling their duties and those who are even worse, doing badly. Hence, they fear that some of these woes may apply to them. This fear is characteristic of people who are God-fearing, aware of the heavy duty placed on them, worried that they may not be up to its fulfilment however much they do of good deeds.

"Who give food – though they need it themselves – to the needy, the orphan and the captive." (Verse 8) This statement describes their compassionate feelings, symbolized in their offering of food, which they need for themselves, to people who are less fortunate than themselves. In other words, they put such needy people, orphans and captives ahead of themselves, feeding them despite their own need of the food they give them. This picture suggests that the social environment that prevailed

410

in Makkah upon the advent of Islam was hard, lacking in compassion. Yet these Arabs paid generously when it was a question of competing for social standing. The righteous servants of God were like an oasis in this hard and barren desert: they gave food out of genuine compassion, sincerely dedicating their action to God: "*We feed you for the sake of God alone. We desire neither recompense from you, nor thanks. We fear the day of our Lord: a bleak, distressful day.*" (Verses 9–10) We see compassion overflowing from such hearts that seek God's pleasure, looking for no reward or praise from any creature. They do not hold up their favours in an attitude of conceit. They simply want to avoid the woes of a bleak and grim day, which they genuinely fear. The Prophet showed them the way to spare themselves its woes, as he said: "Save yourself from the fire by as little as half a date."[1]

Giving food to the needy in such a direct manner was at the time the proper expression of these people's own compassion and the most needed type of help. Ways and forms of charity may be completely different in other circumstances and social environments. What is important is the need to maintain such compassion towards others and the desire to do good only for God's sake, looking for no earthly recognition or reward.

Taxes may be regulated in society, and a portion of such taxes may be allocated for social security, ensuring that the poor are helped. However, this meets only one part of the Islamic objective that these verses refer to. Islam imposes the *zakāt* duty to fulfil this part of meeting the needs of the poor and the deprived. Islam, however, considers an equally important part of this objective, the feelings of those who give; in other words their desire to give elevates them to a high, noble standard. We must not belittle the importance of this objective. Yet some people seek to turn such high standards upside down, describing the Islamic system of *zakāt* and voluntary charity as ugly and claiming that it humiliates those

---

1. This *ḥadīth* urges kindness to the poor, making it clear that even a small act of kindness can be greatly rewarded. A person who has only one date and gives half of it to someone who is in dire need may have done enough to ensure his salvation on the Day of Judgement. Needless to say, a wealthy person needs to make his charity commensurate with his means. – Editor's note.

who take and corrupts those who give. Islam is a faith that sets a system to cultivate people's better feelings and sentiments. Kindly feelings and generosity refine those who are charitable and benefit the ones in need. They, thus, meet both aspects of the Islamic social objective. Hence, the Qur'ānic praise of this noble feeling.

> *God will save them from the woes of that day, and will grant them radiance and joy.* (Verse 11)

The *sūrah* mentions straightaway that they will be saved from whatever they feared on that day, thus reassuring them of their outcome while they are still in this life, believing in the Qur'ānic revelations they received. It also mentions that they will be blessed with radiant faces and joy in recompense for their hearty feelings towards others and their God-fearing attitude. The *sūrah* moves on to describe the comforts they will receive in heaven:

> *And will reward them for their patience in adversity with a garden and [garments of] silk. They will recline there on soft couches, feeling neither burning sun nor severe cold. Its shades will come low over them, and its clusters of fruit will hang low, within easy reach.* (Verses 12–14)

They will thus have the garden of heaven to dwell in, and garments of silk to wear. "*They will recline there on soft couches, feeling neither burning sun nor severe cold.*" (Verse 13) They are comfortable as they sit on these soft couches, in a pleasant atmosphere with no extreme temperatures. We should add here that this is a different world, one that has neither the sun we know, nor similar suns. "*Its shades will come low over them, and its clusters of fruit will hang low, within easy reach.*" (Verse 14) When shades come low and fruits are near, a feeling of ease and happiness spreads.

Such is the overall picture of heaven where God rewards His righteous servants who are given such a fine description of their status in this world. The *sūrah* adds more details of the luxuries they will have and the services provided for them:

They will be served with silver plates and goblets that seem to be crystal, crystal-clear, but made of silver, the measure of which they are the ones to determine. They will be given to drink of a cup flavoured with ginger, from a spring there called Salsabīl." (Verses 15–18)

As they sit on their soft couches in the pleasant shade, enjoying the fine atmosphere and delicious fruits, they find themselves served such pleasantries on silver plates and in silver goblets, yet these are as transparent as crystal, and so are unknown in this world. Moreover, these are of the right measure to give them maximum pleasure. Their drink is mixed with ginger, while it was previously mixed with *kāfūr*. These goblets are filled from a running spring called *Salsabīl*, a name implying a sweetly tasting drink.

To increase their enjoyment, those who bring them their plates and serve them their drinks are handsome youths whose young looks are permanent, unaffected by the passage of time, always looking like pearls: "*They will be waited upon by immortal youths. If you see them, you would think they were scattered pearls.*" (Verse 19) The *sūrah* then casts a general look at the scene and sums it up as well as its effect: "*If you were to look around, you would see only bliss and a vast kingdom.*" (Verse 20) That is how those servants of God, the righteous, live, in utter bliss and a vast kingdom. One aspect of all this bliss is highlighted, as though to justify this general description and further explain it: "*They shall be arrayed in garments of fine green silk and brocade; and adorned with bracelets of silver. And their Lord will give them a most pure drink.*" (Verse 21) All these luxuries and all this bliss they receive directly from God, which adds greatly to its value. A more welcoming gesture is then added: "*This is a reward for you. Your endeavours are well appreciated.*" (Verse 22)

Thus the presentation ends, having given us an inspiring and detailed picture of the bliss and luxury enjoyed by the dwellers of heaven. All this is given in contrast with the chains, shackles and blazing fire the unbelievers suffer. We, thus, see the two widely different ends to the two widely divergent ways.

No Compromise

The *sūrah* now looks at the situation of the unbelievers who persist in their opposition to the divine faith. These did not understand the nature of what the Prophet advocated. Therefore, they tried to compromise with him, hoping that he would stop, or at least forgo the part of it that most offended them. The last section of the *sūrah* deals with this situation against the backdrop of their seeking a compromise with the Prophet, persecuting his followers, turning people away from God's message and rejecting the way of goodness that ensures reward in heaven:

> *It is We who have bestowed the Qur'ān upon you by gradual revelation. Await, then, your Lord's judgement in all patience, and pay no heed to any of these sinners and unbelievers. Remember your Lord's name morning and evening. At night prostrate yourself before Him, and extol His limitless glory throughout the long night.* (Verses 23–26)

These four verses sum up an important principle of the Islamic faith, one which its advocates should fully understand and appreciate. They should study its effects within the human soul and in practical life.

God's Messenger faced the unbelievers directly, calling on them to believe in God's oneness. In advocating his message, the Prophet was not merely facing different beliefs. Had it been so, the case would have been much easier. The unbelievers' polytheistic beliefs were too flimsy and groundless to give them any solid ground to reject the clear, simple and logical Islamic faith. Instead, what led to their fierce and determined opposition, reported in history and recorded in the Qur'ān, was a host of circumstances and considerations. Social position as well as pride in prevailing values and what they might entail of material interest constituted the first factor motivating such people to hold tight to their flimsy and false beliefs, resisting those that were evidently true. Similarly, life under a system of *jāhiliyyah* allowed indulgence in every type of pleasure and gratification of every desire. Hence, people who were keen to indulge in these were expected to resist a faith that adopted a serious approach to morality and high values, stamping out all immoral and carnal practices. All these factors stood up against the Islamic message when it was first advocated. They continue to stand up against it in every community and every generation. They represent the essential forces in the battle of faith, making it a hard-fought battle, requiring those fighting for faith to stand firm in the face of all such difficulties, willing to make great sacrifices. Therefore, advocates of Islam, regardless of place or time, must fully understand the truth summed up in these four verses and learn the circumstances leading to their revelations so that they apply to them too.

The Prophet received instructions from his Lord requiring him to warn his people. When he began carrying out his instructions, he was faced with those factors and circumstances that turned people away from his message and motivated them to persist with their own beliefs, knowing how flimsy and insupportable these were. They were very stubborn, and fought hard to preserve their beliefs, social order, personal interests and familiar practices and indulgences. They realized that the new faith threatened all these. Their defence of their system and old ways took several manifestations, starting with persecuting the few believers who responded to the new faith and trying to turn them back to the old way by force and physical torture. They also tried to give the new faith a bad image, making false accusations and spreading false rumours about it and the Messenger preaching it. They hoped that in this way they could prevent people from joining it. They thought that stopping people joining the new faith would be much easier than trying to turn them back from it after they had embraced and felt its truth.

At the same time, the unbelievers also tried different aspects of temptation, alongside the usual pressures and threats, to persuade the Prophet to meet them halfway. They wanted him to stop his onslaught against their beliefs, traditions and practices, and to work out some compromise, which would be acceptable to both parties. People normally try to work out a sort of *modus vivendi* when they have conflicting interests and claims. These same methods, or very similar ones, are often faced by the advocates of Islam.

It is true that, as a Messenger of God, the Prophet enjoyed God's protection and help, yet he was a human being facing difficult pressures and supported only by a small band of believers who were far weaker than their opponents. God was aware of all this. Therefore, He did not abandon him, leaving him to face all this without support, or without marking the road ahead for him to follow. These four verses thus provide the essence of this much-needed support.

"It is We who have bestowed the Qur'ān upon you by gradual revelation." (Verse 23) This is the first point, stating where this message comes from and who has assigned the duty of its advocacy. It comes from God, having no source other than Him. It is the message the Qur'ān outlines. It cannot be mixed up with anything that does not come from its pure source. It will incorporate nothing that comes from anywhere other than its own source. It will borrow nothing alien to its nature. Moreover, God, who revealed the Qur'ān and entrusted the message to its advocate, will not abandon him or leave him to his own devices when it is He who gave him the Qur'ān.

Yet falsehood behaves with insolence, and evil blows its own trumpet. Hardship is inflicted on the believers and they are subjected to persecution. The enemies of the divine faith possess the means to turn people away from it, and they use different tactics to achieve their purpose. They appear adamant about maintaining their beliefs, preserving their traditions and following their erring and corrupt ways. Then, suddenly, they offer the opportunity for reconciliation and hold out the prospect of compromise. In such circumstances, such an offer is hard to resist.

Here comes the second point, stating a clear directive: *"Await, then, your Lord's judgement in all patience, and pay no heed to any of these sinners and unbelievers."* (Verse 24) All matters are subject to God's will. He may allow evil and falsehood to have their day, and He may allow the believers' trial to last long. All this will be for a purpose that sees His will being done: *"Await, then, your Lord's judgement in all patience,"* until it comes at its appointed time. The instruction given to the Prophet requires him to persevere despite all the harm to which he may be exposed, and all the trials he may be put through. He is to remain patient even when he sees falsehood achieving victory, and evil taking airs. Moreover, he is to persevere in holding to the truth the Qur'ān lays down. He is not to listen to any offer of compromise or a meeting halfway if this is at the expense of the message he is advocating: *"Pay no heed to any of these sinners and unbelievers."* They do not offer anything good or beneficial.

416

How can they, when they are sinners and unbelievers? All that they offer you, when they try to compromise, is a share of sin and disbelief. They offer what they think will please and tempt you. They offered him what was indeed tempting: power, wealth and women. They were willing to make him their leader and to make him the richest among them. They also offered him pretty women. 'Utbah ibn Rabī'ah said to him: "Abandon this matter you are advocating and I will give you my daughter as your wife. I have the prettiest daughters among the Quraysh." Those advocating falsehood always make such tempting offers to advocates of the truth, seeking to silence their message.

"*Await, then, your Lord's judgement in all patience, and pay no heed to any of these sinners and unbelievers.*" (Verse 24) There is no meeting point between you and them. No bridge can be built over the wide gulf separating your method from theirs, your truth from their falsehood, your light from their darkness, your faith from their disbelief, your message of truth from their *jāhiliyyah*.

The Prophet is told to remain patient, even though the adversity may be continuous, the trial hard, and the temptation powerful. Yet patience does not come easy. Help and support are always needed. Hence: "*Remember your Lord's name morning and evening. At night prostrate yourself before Him, and extol His limitless glory throughout the long night.*" (Verses 25–26) This, in a nutshell, is all the help and support that is needed: remembering God's name at the beginning and end of the day, prostrating before Him at night, and glorifying Him at length. The Prophet is told that these are the means to maintain the bond with God who gave him the Qur'ān and who entrusted him with His message. He is the source of all power. The way ahead is long, the burden he carries is heavy, and he needs much support. Now, the support is identified as maintaining contact with God by glorifying Him through the long night. Thus, the servant meets his Master alone, speaking to Him directly, looking up to Him for favour and support, feeling His compassion that removes all trouble and relieves exhaustion. His power will transform His servants' weaknesses and lack of numbers. When they shed their earthly burdens and look at the great task entrusted to them, they will think little of all the hardships they are going through and their resolve to get on with the task ahead will be that much strengthened.

God is ever merciful. He entrusted His servant, the Prophet, with His message and revealed the Qur'ān to him. He is aware of the hardship he would meet along his way. Therefore, He did not leave him without support. On the contrary, He gave him the support and help He knew to be most useful and effective along his difficult journey. This remains the support needed by all advocates of the divine message, regardless of time, circumstance or place. It is the same message, with the same circumstances, facing the same intransigent opposition by falsehood, and for the same reasons. Falsehood employs the same tools and means against it. Let, then, the means the truth employs be the ones God knows to be the most effective.

The truth advocates of the divine message should always bear in mind is the one God impressed on the first advocate of this message, the Prophet Muḥammad (peace be upon him). The duty to advocate the message is assigned by God, and it remains His message. The truth it outlines can never be mixed with the falsehood advocated by sinners and unbelievers. Hence, there can be no meeting point or reconciliation between the truth and falsehood. Nor can there be any halfway meeting between those advocating the truth and those advocating falsehood. They follow two ways that never meet. Should falsehood at times be very powerful and able to subdue the believers, who may be weak and small in number, it will be so because God, in His infinite wisdom, allows this. In such a situation, the only way is to remain patient and await God's judgement. In the meantime, support should be sought through night worship and glorification of Him. This is the only help that is guaranteed to work. This is an essential truth that must be fully understood by those who want to follow the Prophet's footsteps and tread along his way.

Divergent Ways

The *sūrah* continues to emphasize the fact that the Prophet's way has no meeting point with that of the unbelievers. They are so oblivious to what serves their own good, completely preoccupied with trivialities: "*These people love the fleeting life, and leave behind them a day that will be heavy.*" (Verse 27) Their concerns are petty, their goals insignificant, they are fully immersed in the fleeting life of this world, caring little

418

for the heavy day ahead. It is heavy with accountability and outcome. Such people cannot be heeded, and their way cannot be followed. They share no goal with the believers. Hence, no thought should be paid to their life, wealth, power and comfort. They all belong to this fleeting life and are, therefore, of little value. Their preference for this fleeting life indicates their inability to see what is good for them. This verse, then, continues with strengthening the Prophet and his followers as they faced the unbelievers' opposition. It also implies a warning for the unbelievers of the difficulty that lies ahead for them on the Day of Judgement.

The *sūrah* makes it clear that God, who created them and gave them all the power they enjoy, can easily replace them by others. However, in His infinite wisdom, He gives them time to reconsider:

It is We who have created them and strengthened their constitution. If it be Our will, We can replace them entirely with others of their kind. (Verse 28)

This is a reminder to those unbelievers, who are proud of their strength, of the source of their power, and indeed the source of their very lives. It reassures the believers, few and weak as they were, that they actually advocate the message of the One who grants power to whom He will. It assures them that God's will operates according to His wisdom and to fulfil His purpose, until He makes His judgement. He is certainly the best of judges.

"If it be Our will, We can replace them entirely with others of their kind." (Verse 28) They cannot use their power to defy God; it is He who has created them and given them their power. He is able to replace them with other people. If he gives them respite, this is an aspect of His grace that He bestows on His creatures. It is all His judgement and a manifestation of His wisdom.

Again, this verse aims to give the Prophet and the believers further strength, stating the respective positions of believers and unbelievers. It alerts the unbelievers who are so preoccupied with their love of this world and its pleasures, and who think too highly of their strength, that they must express their gratitude for God's favours and treat these as a test.

The *sūrah* alerts them further to the chance they still have as the Qur'ān, including the present *sūrah*, is recited to them: "*This is but a reminder. Let him who will, take the way to his Lord.*" (Verse 29)

This is followed by re-emphasizing God's absolute will, to which everything refers. This is mentioned here so as to ensure that people submit to its judgement, and that they recognize it as the ultimate power: "*Yet you cannot will except by the will of God. God is indeed All-Knowing, Wise.*" (Verse 30)

People should know that God Almighty is the One who decides and acts, and that He conducts the universe and holds sway over all things. They will then learn how to turn to Him and submit to His will. This is how such texts should be understood, recognizing at the same time that God has willed to give human beings the ability to distinguish truth from falsehood and to choose their way to either one or the other. They, thus, make their choice in accordance with God's will who knows the nature of human hearts and who has helped His servants by giving them knowledge, showing them the right way, sending messengers and revelation of the Qur'ān. Yet all this ends up determined by God's will. It is He who will guide a person to the right path through obedience and glorification of Him. When a person does not recognize God's controlling power and does not appeal to Him for help, then he has no guidance to what is good and will not glorify God.

Hence, "*He admits to His grace whoever He will, but for the wrongdoers He has prepared grievous suffering.*" (Verse 31) As we have repeatedly said, His will is free and absolute, taking whatever action He wishes. It is part of His will that His grace is granted to whoever He chooses. These are the ones who turn to Him, seeking His help and following His guidance. As for the wrongdoers, He gave them respite and granted them time, but they chose wrongly, so as to end in grievous suffering.

There is perfect harmony between the end and the beginning of the *sūrah*. The end gives an outline of the completion of the test to which man, whom God created from a drop of mingled fluid, is subjected. This after giving him guidance and allowing him to choose the way he wants to follow.

SŪRAH 77

Al-Mursalāt
(Sent Forth)

Prologue

This *sūrah* bears sharp features, powerful images and strong notes. Indeed, it sounds like a spitting fire. It puts hearts to trial, presenting questions and threats that pierce like sharp arrows. We see a host of images from both this life and the life to come, the universe and the human soul, as well as scenes of the suffering that unbelievers will endure. After each main scene, the *sūrah* levels a fire-like strike at those hearts who deny the truth, saying: "*Woe on that day betide those who deny the truth.*" This comment is repeated ten times in this *sūrah* alone, as it is the final note deployed in each of its sections. It is an especially apt comment, given its sharp features and strong beat. In this respect, it reminds us of *Sūrah* 55, The Lord of Grace, where the same verse is repeated after the mention of every aspect of blessing: "*Which, then, of your Lord's blessings do you both deny?*" Likewise, in *Sūrah* 54, The Moon, the same comment is used after every image of punishment is drawn: "*How grievous was My punishment and how true were My warnings.*" The verse repeated in this *sūrah*, as in other *sūrahs*, serves to give its distinctively sharp tone.

The *sūrah* is composed of sections with short, quick verses. It changes its rhyme with each section, although some rhyming sounds are picked up again after they have been changed. All these sections, rhymes and

421

short verses are sharply felt, one after the other. One hardly recovers after one sharp note when a new one begins. Right from the outset, the general atmosphere is tempestuous, starting with a scene of strong winds, or angels: "*By those sent forth in swift succession; and those tempestuously storming on; and those scattering far and wide; and those separating [right and wrong] with all clarity; and those giving a reminder, with an excuse and a warning.*" (Verses 1–6) This opening is perfectly consistent with the ambience of the *sūrah*.

The Qur'ān is extraordinary in the way in which it uses particular frameworks to enhance the atmosphere of certain *sūrahs*. In *Sūrah* 93, The Morning Hours, which speaks about God's care and kindness, the framework is drawn from the bright morning hours and still nights. In *Sūrah* 100, The Coursers, which depicts the scattering of grave contents and the gathering of what is in people's breasts, we have a framework drawn from snorting horses striking sparks of fire. Further examples could be given in plenty.

Each of the ten sections that follow the opening of the *sūrah* represents a special round or a journey into a different world. This gives the *sūrah* great scope for reflection, feeling, ideas and responses. This scope is also much wider than the words and sentences imply.

The first round paints scenes from the day of distinction, showing the great upheaval that will take place in the universe. This is the appointment defined by God's messengers to mankind: "*When the stars are dimmed, and the sky is rent asunder, and the mountains are scattered like dust, and the messengers are given their appointed time... For what day has all this been set? For the day of distinction. Would that you knew what the day of distinction is! Woe on that day betide those who deny the truth.*" (Verses 8–15)

The second round refers to the fates suffered by communities of olden times, highlighting the divine law that applies to those who deny the divine message: "*Did We not destroy those people of old? We shall certainly cause later ones to follow them. Thus do We deal with the guilty. Woe on that day betide those who deny the truth.*" (Verses 16–19)

Round three takes us to the origins of man and the impression they give of God's overall planning: "*Have We not created you from a humble fluid, placing it in a safe lodging for a pre-determined term? Thus have We determined; excellent indeed is how We determine. Woe on that day betide those who deny the truth."* (Verses 20–24)

In the fourth round we see how the earth, which takes its children, living or dead, to its bosom, has been equipped with the facility of stable life and with water that is necessary for life: *"Have We not made the earth an abode for the living and the dead? We have placed on it firm, lofty mountains and provided you with fresh water to drink. Woe on that day betide those who deny the truth."* (Verses 25–28)

The fifth round speaks of those who reject the divine message and how they are received with strong rebuke, as well as their impending punishment, on the day of distinction: *"Go to that which you used to deny! Go to a shadow rising in three columns; giving no shade, nor relief from the flame. It throws up sparks as huge as forts, as bright as yellow camels. Woe on that day betide those who deny the truth."* (Verses 29–34)

The next two rounds continue with the unbelievers, adding further rebuke: *"On that day they will not utter a word, and they will not be allowed to offer any excuse. Woe on that day betide those who deny the truth. This is the day of distinction: We have gathered you with all those people of old. If you have a scheme left, then use it against Me now. Woe on that day betide those who deny the truth."* (Verses 35–40)

Round eight speaks of the God-fearing and the blessings prepared for them: *"The God-fearing shall dwell amid cool shades and springs, and fruits as they may desire. Eat and drink to your hearts' content in return for what you did. Thus do We reward those who do good. Woe on that day betide those who deny the truth."* (Verses 41–45)

The last two rounds provide quick glimpses of the people who are bent on denying God's message. The first reproaches them and the second shows them in obstinate rejection: *"Eat and enjoy your life for a little while, for you are certainly guilty. Woe on that day betide those who deny the truth. When they are told to bow down before God, they do not bow down. Woe on that day betide those who deny the truth."* (Verses 46–49)

These rounds, their images and sharp notes conclude with a single verse asking: *"In what message, after this, will they believe?"* (Verse 50)

The listener follows the quick rhythm of the *sūrah* feeling almost out of breath at its succession of images. The subject matter of the *sūrah* is covered in several other *sūrahs*, particularly Makkan ones. However, the

Qur'ān tackles the truth it presents from different angles, in different lights, and with different emphases according to the situations they face. Such approaches address hearts and souls as best suits them, according to their conditions known to the One who has revealed the Qur'ān to His Messenger. They thus appear new with every new situation, because they produce new responses.

We see that this *sūrah* draws new images of hell, and takes a new approach in showing these images to unbelievers; in other words, it employs a new style of address. Thus, the *sūrah* acquires a distinctive character with intense features, sharp images and a rapid rhythm.

Al-Mursalāt (Sent Forth)

In the Name of God, the Lord of Grace, the Ever Merciful

بِسْمِ اللَّهِ الرَّحْمَنِ الرَّحِيمِ

By those sent forth in swift succession; (1)

وَالْمُرْسَلَاتِ عُرْفًا ۝١

and those tempestuously storming on; (2)

فَالْعَاصِفَاتِ عَصْفًا ۝٢

and those scattering far and wide; (3)

وَالنَّاشِرَاتِ نَشْرًا ۝٣

and those separating [right and wrong] with all clarity; (4)

فَالْفَارِقَاتِ فَرْقًا ۝٤

and those giving a reminder, (5)

فَالْمُلْقِيَاتِ ذِكْرًا ۝٥

with an excuse and a warning, (6)

عُذْرًا أَوْ نُذْرًا ۝٦

what you have been promised shall be fulfilled. (7)

إِنَّمَا تُوعَدُونَ لَوَاقِعٌ ۝٧

When the stars are dimmed, (8)

فَإِذَا النُّجُومُ طُمِسَتْ ۝٨

and the sky is rent asunder, (9)

وَإِذَا السَّمَاءُ فُرِجَتْ ۝٩

425

and the mountains are scattered like dust, (10)

وَإِذَا ٱلْجِبَالُ نُسِفَتْ ﴿١٠﴾

and the messengers are given their appointed time… (11)

وَإِذَا ٱلرُّسُلُ أُقِّتَتْ ﴿١١﴾

For what day has all this been set? (12)

لِأَيِّ يَوْمٍ أُجِّلَتْ ﴿١٢﴾

For the day of distinction. (13)

لِيَوْمِ ٱلْفَصْلِ ﴿١٣﴾

Would that you knew what the day of distinction is! (14)

وَمَا أَدْرَىٰكَ مَا يَوْمُ ٱلْفَصْلِ ﴿١٤﴾

Woe on that day betide those who deny the truth. (15)

وَيْلٌ يَوْمَئِذٍ لِّلْمُكَذِّبِينَ ﴿١٥﴾

Did We not destroy those people of old? (16)

أَلَمْ نُهْلِكِ ٱلْأَوَّلِينَ ﴿١٦﴾

We shall certainly cause later ones to follow them. (17)

ثُمَّ نُتْبِعُهُمُ ٱلْآخِرِينَ ﴿١٧﴾

Thus do We deal with the guilty. (18)

كَذَٰلِكَ نَفْعَلُ بِٱلْمُجْرِمِينَ ﴿١٨﴾

Woe on that day betide those who deny the truth. (19)

وَيْلٌ يَوْمَئِذٍ لِّلْمُكَذِّبِينَ ﴿١٩﴾

Have We not created you from a humble fluid, (20)

أَلَمْ نَخْلُقكُّم مِّن مَّآءٍ مَّهِينٍ ﴿٢٠﴾

placing it in a safe lodging (21)

فَجَعَلْنَٰهُ فِى قَرَارٍ مَّكِينٍ ﴿٢١﴾

for a pre-determined term? (22)

إِلَىٰ قَدَرٍ مَّعْلُومٍ ﴿٢٢﴾

Thus have We determined; excellent indeed is how We determine. (23)

فَقَدَرْنَا فَنِعْمَ ٱلْقَٰدِرُونَ ﴿٢٣﴾

Woe on that day betide those who deny the truth. (24)

وَيْلٌ يَوْمَئِذٍ لِّلْمُكَذِّبِينَ ﴿٢٤﴾

Have We not made the earth an abode (25)

أَلَمْ نَجْعَلِ ٱلْأَرْضَ كِفَاتًا ﴿٢٥﴾

for the living and the dead? (26)

أَحْيَآءً وَأَمْوَٰتًا ﴿٢٦﴾

We have placed on it firm, lofty mountains and provided you with fresh water to drink. (27)

وَجَعَلْنَا فِيهَا رَوَٰسِىَ شَٰمِخَٰتٍ وَأَسْقَيْنَٰكُم مَّآءً فُرَاتًا ﴿٢٧﴾

Woe on that day betide those who deny the truth. (28)

وَيْلٌ يَوْمَئِذٍ لِّلْمُكَذِّبِينَ ﴿٢٨﴾

Go to that which you used to deny! (29)

ٱنطَلِقُوٓا۟ إِلَىٰ مَا كُنتُم بِهِۦ تُكَذِّبُونَ ﴿٢٩﴾

Go to a shadow rising in three columns; (30)

ٱنطَلِقُوٓا۟ إِلَىٰ ظِلٍّ ذِى ثَلَٰثِ شُعَبٍ ﴿٣٠﴾

giving no shade, nor relief from the flame. (31)

لَّا ظَلِيلٍ وَلَا يُغْنِى مِنَ ٱللَّهَبِ ﴿٣١﴾

It throws up sparks as huge as forts, (32)

إِنَّهَا تَرْمِى بِشَرَرٍ كَٱلْقَصْرِ ﴿٣٢﴾

as bright as yellow camels. (33)

كَأَنَّهُ جِمَٰلَتٌ صُفْرٌ ﴿٣٣﴾

Woe on that day betide those who deny the truth. (34)

وَيْلٌ يَوْمَئِذٍ لِّلْمُكَذِّبِينَ ﴿٣٤﴾

On that day they will not utter a word, (35)

هَٰذَا يَوْمُ لَا يَنطِقُونَ ﴿٣٥﴾

and they will not be allowed to offer any excuse. (36)

وَلَا يُؤْذَنُ لَهُمْ فَيَعْتَذِرُونَ ﴿٣٦﴾

Woe on that day betide those who deny the truth. (37)

وَيْلٌ يَوْمَئِذٍ لِّلْمُكَذِّبِينَ ﴿٣٧﴾

This is the day of distinction: We have gathered you with all those people of old. (38)

هَٰذَا يَوْمُ ٱلْفَصْلِ جَمَعْنَٰكُمْ وَٱلْأَوَّلِينَ ﴿٣٨﴾

If you have a scheme left, then use it against Me now. (39)

فَإِن كَانَ لَكُمْ كَيْدٌ فَكِيدُونِ ﴿٣٩﴾

Woe on that day betide those who deny the truth. (40)

وَيْلٌ يَوْمَئِذٍ لِّلْمُكَذِّبِينَ ﴿٤٠﴾

The God-fearing shall dwell amid cool shades and springs, (41)

إِنَّ ٱلْمُتَّقِينَ فِى ظِلَٰلٍ وَعُيُونٍ ﴿٤١﴾

and fruits as they may desire. (42)

وَفَوَٰكِهَ مِمَّا يَشْتَهُونَ ﴿٤٢﴾

Eat and drink to your hearts' content in return for what you did. (43)

كُلُوا۟ وَٱشْرَبُوا۟ هَنِيٓـًٔا بِمَا كُنتُمْ تَعْمَلُونَ ﴿٤٣﴾

Thus do We reward those who do good. (44)

إِنَّا كَذَٰلِكَ نَجْزِى ٱلْمُحْسِنِينَ ﴿٤٤﴾

Woe on that day betide those who deny the truth. (45)

وَيْلٌ يَوْمَئِذٍ لِّلْمُكَذِّبِينَ ﴿٤٥﴾

Eat and enjoy your life for a little while, for you are certainly guilty. (46)

كُلُوا۟ وَتَمَتَّعُوا۟ قَلِيلًا إِنَّكُم مُّجْرِمُونَ ﴿٤٦﴾

Woe on that day betide those who deny the truth. (47)

وَيْلٌ يَوْمَئِذٍ لِّلْمُكَذِّبِينَ ﴿٤٧﴾

When they are told to bow down before God, they do not bow down. (48)

وَإِذَا قِيلَ لَهُمُ ٱرْكَعُوا۟ لَا يَرْكَعُونَ ﴿٤٨﴾

Woe on that day betide those who deny the truth. (49)

وَيْلٌ يَوْمَئِذٍ لِّلْمُكَذِّبِينَ ﴿٤٩﴾

In what message, after this, will they believe? (50)

فَبِأَىِّ حَدِيثٍ بَعْدَهُۥ يُؤْمِنُونَ ﴿٥٠﴾

Enigmatic Beginning

By those sent forth in swift succession; and those tempestuously storming on; and those scattering far and wide; and those separating [right and wrong] with all clarity; and those giving a reminder, with an excuse and a warning, what you have been promised shall be fulfilled. (Verses 1–7)

429

The question here is that of the resurrection which the unbelievers found very hard to accept, yet the Qur'ān confirms it time after time, in many *sūrahs*, and in various ways. It was especially necessary that the Qur'ān take such care in establishing the truth of resurrection, this so that the faith can be properly established in people's minds and hearts and further that their standards and values could then be redefined. Belief in the Day of Judgement is the corner-stone of both the divine faith and human life. It is the pivot around which everything in life turns, and the criterion that judges all values and standards. Hence, establishing the truth of resurrection and subsequent reckoning and judgement needed such a sustained effort.

The *sūrah* begins with an oath by God that this promise of a life to come is certainly true. The way the oath is phrased suggests that that by which God swears belongs to the realm beyond our perception. It mentions some hidden forces that have a definite effect on the universe and on human life. Early scholars differed as to what these were: some said that they all refer to winds, and some said they refer to angels, while a third group said that some refer to winds and some to angels. It is clear, then, that these terms are ambiguous, which makes them best suited for an oath by God confirming an event which only He knows about. Just as these ambiguous things exist and have an effect on human life, this event belonging to the world beyond our perception will certainly take place.

"By those sent forth in swift succession." (Verse 1) Abū Hurayrah says that this is a reference to the angels. The same is reported to have been said by Masrūq, Abū al-Ḍuḥā, Mujāhid (in one report), al-Suddī, al-Rabī' ibn Anas and Abū Ṣāliḥ. Thus the verse means an oath by the angels that are sent forth in successive waves, like running horses. Abū Ṣāliḥ says that the next four verses also refer to the angels.

Ibn Mas'ūd is reported to have said that *'those sent forth'* refers to the wind, which means that winds are sent in succession like horses running. He is reported to have said that those *'storming on'* and *'scattering far and wide'* [mentioned in the next two verses] also refer to the wind. This view is shared by Ibn 'Abbās, Mujāhid (in a second report), Qatādah and in another report by Abū Ṣāliḥ.

Ibn Jarīr al-Ṭabarī is uncertain whether '*those sent forth*' mentioned in the first verse refers to the angels or to the wind, but he is certain that the stormers and scatterers are the winds. He explains that the winds scatter the clouds in the sky.

Ibn Masʿūd says that "*those separating [right and wrong] with all clarity; and those giving a reminder, with an excuse and a warning,*" refer to the angels. This is also stated by Ibn ʿAbbās, Masrūq, Mujāhid, Qatādah, al-Rabīʿ ibn Anas, al-Suddī and al-Thawrī. It is the angels that come down carrying God's orders to His messengers, separating right from wrong, and giving revelations to those messengers that contain justification and a warning to mankind.

We note that the ambiguity is intended to give these matters by which the oath is made a particularly awesome air. This is the same as in *Sūrahs* 51 and 79. The first of these begins with the oath: "*By the winds that scatter far and wide.*" *Sūrah* 79 also starts with an ambiguous oath: "*By those that pluck out vehemently.*" This ambiguity, evident in the differences of opinion about their meaning, is intended, because their very ambiguity combines with the quick rhythm employed in the opening of the *sūrah* to produce a jolt or a shake in the listener or reader. This fits perfectly with the subject matter of the *sūrah*. In fact, every subsequent section delivers such a jolt. Thus the *sūrah* may be compared to someone in authority taking a person by the collar as he questions him about a misdeed or about his negation of something very obvious, then releasing him with a strong warning: "*Woe on that day betide those who deny the truth.*"

Universal Upheaval

This enigmatic beginning is now followed by a strong jolt as we are shown images of great events that take place in the universe on the day appointed for God's messengers to present the results of their having delivered the divine message to all generations of mankind:

When the stars are dimmed, and the sky is rent asunder, and the mountains are scattered like dust, and the messengers are given their

431

appointed time... For what day has all this been set? For the day of distinction. Would that you knew what the day of distinction is! Woe on that day betide those who deny the truth. (Verses 8–15)

On that day, the stars lose their light, and the sky is split apart, while the mountains crash and scatter like dust. Similar images of this universal upheaval are given in several *sūrahs*, all suggesting that the system of the universe we see will collapse and its collapse will be accompanied by great crashes and explosions unlike any of the smaller events – volcanoes erupting, thunderbolts, earthquakes and the like – that nonetheless leave people absolutely terrified. To compare what will happen on that day to volcanoes and earthquakes is the same as comparing bonfires organized on festive occasions to nuclear explosions. This is merely to give an idea of what will happen. In fact, it is impossible to describe the great horror that will take place when the universe explodes and scatters. That horror is beyond all human imagination.

Alongside this horror, the *sūrah* mentions another important event that is delayed until that day. It is the time appointed for God's messengers to present the outcome of their efforts in advocating the divine message throughout all generations of human life. Presenting this final account is greater than what happens to the skies, the earth and the mountains. It will entail a judgement by God of all matters relating to life on earth. This is the final word concerning all human generations across the centuries. Its description is given an air of awe that suggests that its true nature is beyond human comprehension: *"For what day has all this been set? For the day of distinction. Would that you knew what the day of distinction is!"* (Verses 12–14) It is clear that these verses are speaking about something great and serious. When this sense of seriousness, which is greater than the stars losing their light and the rending of the skies and the crashing of the mountains, is clearly felt, a frightening warning is given: *"Woe on that day betide those who deny the truth."* (Verse 15)

This warning by the Almighty, against the backdrop of the great universal upheaval and the majestic scene when God's messengers submit their final account on the day of distinction, is very serious indeed.

432

Three Quick Rounds

The first round taking us to the expected universal upheaval on the Day of Judgement is followed by one going back to the fates suffered by earlier communities that rejected the divine faith. Later communities could follow on their heels:

Did We not destroy those people of old? We shall certainly cause later ones to follow them. Thus do We deal with the guilty. Woe on that day betide those who deny the truth. (Verses 16–18)

One strike to reveal the fates of past communities, numerous as they were and another to reveal what could happen to later ones, numerous as they may be. The scene of destruction stretches as far as anyone can see. Now the warning comes clear, stating the law God set in operation: "*Thus do We deal with the guilty.*" (Verse 18) It is His law that never fails. As those who are guilty expect a fate like earlier communities, the warning of impending doom is repeated: "*Woe on that day betide those who deny the truth.*" (Verse 19)

The next round turns to the living and how they are brought into life, in accordance with elaborate planning:

Have We not created you from a humble fluid, placing it in a safe lodging for a pre-determined term? Thus have We determined; excellent indeed is how We determine. Woe on that day betide those who deny the truth. (Verses 20–24)

The long and remarkable journey of an embryo, from the moment of conception, is included here, in a few fine touches, starting with a humble fluid being placed after conception in the uterus that gives it a safe lodging until an appointed time. The whole journey is planned with remarkable accuracy at every stage. A comment is added here to emphasize the infinite wisdom that assigns a fine, accurate measure to everything: "*Thus have We determined; excellent indeed is how We determine.*" (Verse 23) With this planned determination that applies

433

universally, the warning is repeated again: "*Woe on that day betide those who deny the truth.*" (Verse 24)

We then have a round on earth and the life God has determined on it for mankind, giving it the facilities that make such human life easy:

Have We not made the earth an abode for the living and the dead? We have placed on it firm, lofty mountains and provided you with fresh water to drink. Woe on that day betide those who deny the truth. (Verses 25–28)

These verses alert us to what we see on earth, which is made an abode embracing its children in life and death. Lofty mountains are placed on it, making it firm, and over their tops the clouds gather and then clear water runs down via them to the ground. Could all this have come about by anything other than elaborate and wise planning? How can those unbelievers continue to deny the truth they see with their own eyes: "*Woe on that day betide those who deny the truth.*" (Verse 28)

The Release

Having filled our senses with such effects as these images and rounds produce, the *sūrah* suddenly moves to the Day of Judgement when accounts are checked and requital determined. The dreaded command is given to the guilty to go on their way to suffer the punishment they were wont to deny. The command is coupled with a strong and painful rebuke:

Go to that which you used to deny! Go to a shadow rising in three columns; giving no shade, nor relief from the flame. It throws up sparks as huge as forts, as bright as yellow camels. Woe on that day betide those who deny the truth. (Verses 29–34)

Now that you have been long restrained on this day of distinction, you may go. But where can they go? To remain constrained is much better than this release, because they are told: "*Go to that which you used to deny.*" (Verse 29) It is present here before their very eyes. "*Go to a shadow rising in three columns.*" (Verse 30) The smoke of hell rises in three columns giving a shadow to which they are told to go. Yet the scorch of the flame is better than this shadow, because it is "*giving no shade, nor relief from the flame.*" (Verse 31) It is suffocating and burning. To call it a shadow or shade, the Arabic word *ẓill* carrying both meanings, is merely sarcastic.

They are told to go, and they know where they will have to go. Therefore, their destination is not mentioned by name: "*It throws up sparks as huge as forts, as bright as yellow camels.*" (Verses 32–33) Sparks are thrown in quick succession, but they are as big as large stone buildings, looking like yellow camels grazing. Such are the sparks thrown up by this fire. What is that fire like? At the moment we are absorbed in thought about this, the stern warning is repeated: "*Woe on that day betide those who deny the truth.*" (Verse 34)

The *sūrah* has described the physical horror, giving us an image of hell. Now it presents the psychological horror that leaves the guilty speechless:

> *On that day they will not utter a word, and they will not be allowed to offer any excuse. Woe on that day betide those who deny the truth.* (Verses 35–37)

The horror described here is that deafening silence, when everyone is utterly speechless. All look humble, without a word of excuse. The time for arguments and excuses is over. Woe is present now: "*Woe on that day betide those who deny the truth.*" (Verse 37) Elsewhere in the Qur'ān we have scenes describing their sorrow and grief, as well as the excuses they present and the oaths they swear. That day is very long, and both situations happen then, as Ibn 'Abbās explains. Here, the image given is that of absolute silence as it fits better with the general ambience of the *sūrah*.

> *This is the day of distinction: We have gathered you with all those people of old. If you have a scheme left, then use it against Me now. Woe on that day betide those who deny the truth.* (Verses 38–40)

This is, then, the day of distinction, not one for submitting excuses and justifications. You are gathered here together with all communities that lived before you so that if you can work out a plan or you are able to contrive something, you can go ahead and do it. None, however, can devise or contrive anything. The painful rebuke is met with deep silence. "*Woe on that day betide those who deny the truth.*" (Verse 40)

The Other Group

Now the *sūrah* gives us an image of the God-fearing and how they are honoured on that day:

> *The God-fearing shall dwell amid cool shades and springs, and fruits as they may desire. Eat and drink to your hearts' content in return for what you did. Thus do We reward those who do good. Woe on that day betide those who deny the truth.* (Verses 41–45)

These shades the God-fearing enjoy are real ones, unlike the shadow of three columns that gives no protection from the fire. They dwell among springs of water, not in the midst of choking smoke. They have "*fruits as they may desire.*" (Verse 42) What is more is that such material luxuries are given to them in front of all people gathered on that day. They all listen as the God-fearing are honoured: "*Eat and drink to your hearts' content in return for what you did. Thus do We reward those who do good.*" (Verses 43–44) How welcome is such friendly honour bestowed upon them by the Almighty. In contrast, the warning is repeated to the other group: "*Woe on that day betide those who deny the truth.*" (Verse 45)

The *sūrah* has so far shown nothing of this present life. Now it gives a very quick glimpse of it. We are now back on earth, where strong reproach is levelled at those who are guilty:

> *Eat and enjoy your life for a little while, for you are certainly guilty. Woe on that day betide those who deny the truth.* (Verses 46–47)

Thus the two lives, the present one and the other to come, are shown in quick succession, in two images that appear to be before us now, even though the gap between them stretches into the future, age upon age. The address was given first to the God-fearing in the life to come. It is then directed to the guilty here in this life. It is as if they are being told to consider the difference between the two moments. You may eat and enjoy yourselves a little here in this world, but you will then be deprived of it all in the next, where you will receive your due punishment: "*Woe on that day betide those who deny the truth.*" (Verse 47)

The *sūrah* wonders at their attitude as they are presented with divine guidance and called upon to follow it. Yet still they persistently refuse:

> *When they are told to bow down before God, they do not bow down. Woe on that day betide those who deny the truth.* (Verses 48–49)

Yet they are given every opportunity to see the guidance and consider the warning. Still, they continue with their erring ways. Hence, the question: "*In what message, after this, will they believe?*" (Verse 50) A person who listens to this discourse, which shakes firm mountains, who still does not believe will never come to believe, no matter how he is addressed. He is only fit for utter misery and a fate only the most miserable will suffer.

Thus the *sūrah* concludes. Its construction, musical beat, powerful images, sharp comments combine to make of it an attack that no heart can resist. Infinite in His glory is God who revealed this Qur'ān and gave it this powerful effect.

Index